THE
SILVER PALATE
GOOD TIMES
C·O·O·K·B·O·O·K

THE
SILVER PALATE
GOOD TIMES
C·O·O·K·B·O·O·K

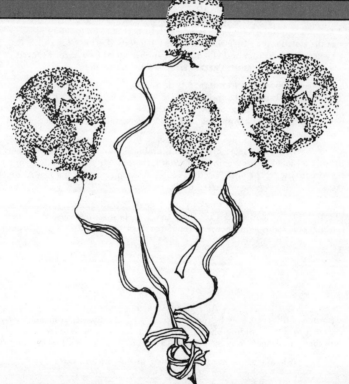

BY JULEE ROSSO & SHEILA LUKINS

WITH SARAH LEAH CHASE

ILLUSTRATED BY SHEILA LUKINS

WORKMAN PUBLISHING, NEW YORK

Library of Congress Cataloging in Publication Data
Rosso, Julee.
The Silver Palate good times cookbook.
Includes index.
1. Cookery. 2. Entertaining.   I. Lukins, Sheila.
II. Silver Palate (Shop)   III. Title.
TX715.R8415   1985   641.5   85-5368
ISBN 0-89480-832-X
ISBN 0-89480-831-1 (pbk.)

Book design by Wendy Palitz/Julienne McNeer
Cover photograph © Susan Wood

Workman Publishing Company, Inc.
1 West 39th Street
New York, NY 10018

Manufactured in the United States of America

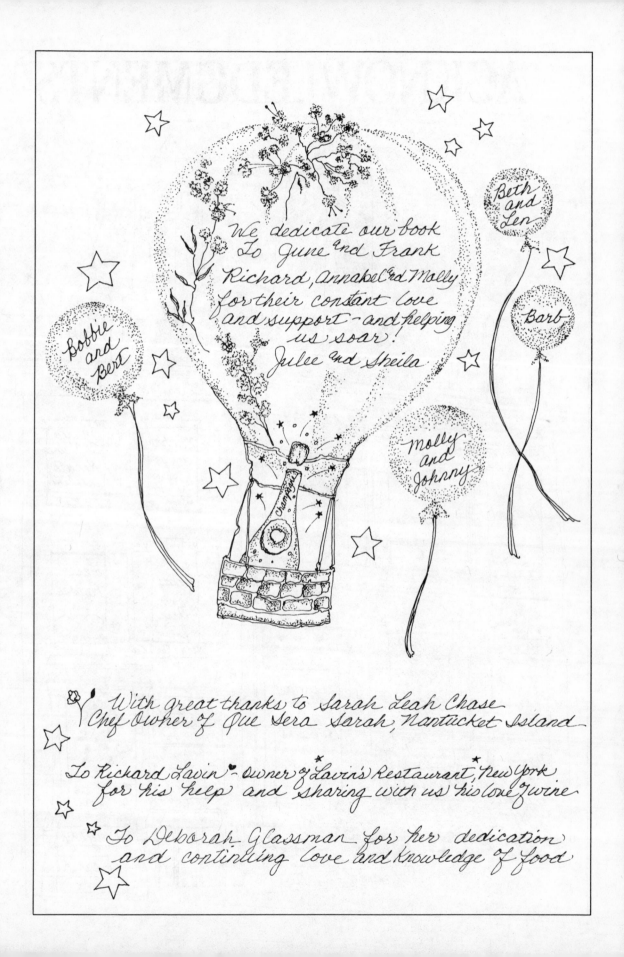

We dedicate our book
To June and Frank
Richard, Annabel and Molly
for their constant love
and support - and helping
us soar!
Julee and Sheila

Bobbie and Bert

Beth and Len

Barb

Molly and Johnny

With great thanks to Sarah Leah Chase
Chef Owner of Que Sera Sarah, Nantucket Island

To Richard Lavin - owner of Lavin's Restaurant, New York
for his help and sharing with us his love of wine

To Deborah Glassman for her dedication
and continuing love and knowledge of food

ACKNOWLEDGMENTS

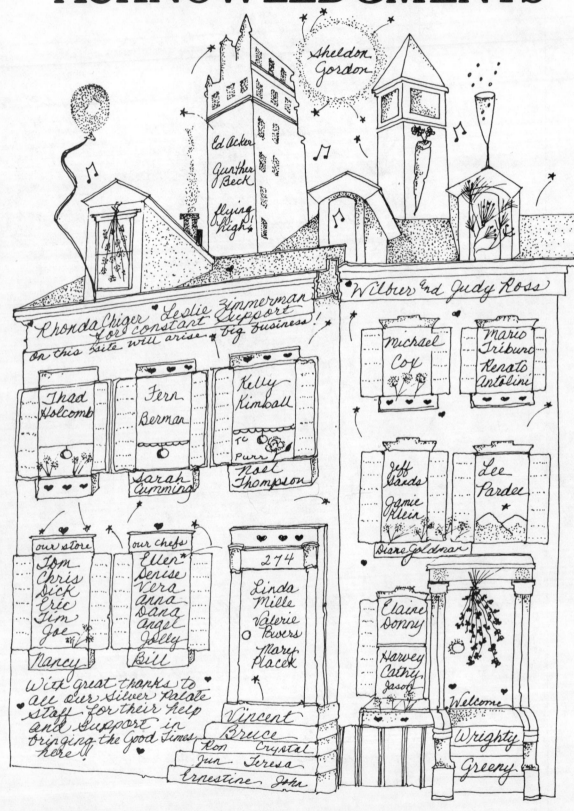

Jeff Weinberg

With thanks to all our dear customers!

Peter Workman

Rick Hinden

1 West 39th   Construction   complete

Mart
Gene

Alan
Klavins

Sid
Silver

Suzanne Rafer
Julienne McNeer
Paul Hanson
Barbara Ottenhoff
Margery Tippie
Kathie Ness

Jerri Thomas
Maureen Kelly
Bert Snyder
Carolan Workman

Jim McCaffrey
John Roberts
Hank Sieban

Andy Hinterman

Berta
and
Mike
Alderman

Ken Daley
Charles Barthel
Carmine Cocco
Don Sharp
Leo Lovero

Arthur Klebanoff

appreciation

Jim
McGilloway

Beatrice
Leikins

Café des Artistes

CONTENTS

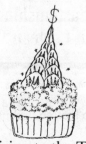

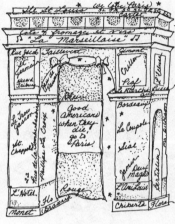

A TOAST TO THE GOOD TIMES

It was a good time
It was the best time
It was a party
Just to be near you

It was a good time
It was the best time
And we believed
That it would last
forever
—©Maurice Jarre

"It was the best time! Everyone wanted the party to last forever!" Rave reviews are what every host or hostess hopes for—and they're our goal at The Silver Palate.

When The Silver Palate first opened, women were scarce in the food business, and much to our chagrin we were often called "the girls." We hated it. However, as our business expanded and the gray hairs multiplied, we started to have second thoughts! Now, after eight years of cooking almost every day, we're happy to be known as "the girls," and with any luck, as "the good times girls."

Through it all we've had the best times. We've made many wonderful friends—cookbook writers, editors, critics, some of the greatest chefs in the world, our entrepreneurial colleagues in retailing and manufacturing, restaurateurs, educators, and many, many, good home cooks who share our passion for food. Our travels have taken us to Europe, the Orient, and seemingly every nook and cranny of America. Sheila has taught at most of the major cooking schools in America; Julee has spoken at numerous gastronomical symposiums and workshops.

Over those years we've planned almost every kind of party imaginable—cocktails aboard the *Intrepid,* black-tie garden dances, Broadway opening nights, Fourth of July fireworks dinners, silver anniversary square dances, Christmas balls, after-opera suppers, a luncheon for the Archbishop of Canterbury, picnics in the park, a wedding for a rock star, political fund-raisers, and Valentine dinners for two. Practice does make perfect, and we'd like to share with you our experience in creating those good times.

The emerging American cooking style has long been our passion, yet it is difficult to define. It's not the culinary tradition we inherited nor the regional dishes that have become coast-to-coast favorites, and it's most certainly not the cuisine of other cultures replicated with American ingredients.

"Elegance is the art of not astonishing." —Jean Cocteau

American cuisine is in the process of developing, as we learn to lighten up but retain taste, trim quantities without sacrificing pleasure, create simple, fresh, clear, and distinctive flavors, use our sense of humor, and allow enthusiasm and ingenuity to reign. The new cuisine is exciting—it is our own American style.

Our Silver Palate recipes are created in response to this excitement. They are inspired by our travels, or adapted from favorites lovingly shared with us by friends and professional colleagues, or are our contemporary versions of classic dishes. Our style is strongly influenced, also, by our living in one of the most culturally diverse, sophisticated, challenging, and intellectual cities in the world. All these recipes have been tested by our staff, tasted by our clients, and then added to The Silver Palate recipe box—which we're opening to share with you.

It has never been easier to plan a party—the best ingredients are widely available today—but the most important ingredient to being a successful host or hostess is to have a passion for people and a love of good food. Like staging a symphony or a

"When love and skill work together, expect a masterpiece." —John Ruskin

play, the final result is far more than the sum of its parts. Of course, each element should be as good as good can be, but that is not enough. An overall party plan needs to impart a sense of harmony and fluidity to an occasion. We love parties that are easy-going and comfortable, conveying the feeling of inclusiveness rather than exclusivity.

Sharing a meal with friends is one of the most enjoyable social encounters. There was a time not too long ago when entertaining was a "should do" or a "have to"—when it was a gesture, however gracious, designed to maintain a social position or to repay a debt. We like to think it's now done just for fun, that hosts make the extra effort not to

impress but to guarantee their guests a good time. That's the difference—entertaining has become fun, and food a playful part of life. There's a world of good eating in the difference.

When we begin to plan a party at The Silver Palate, we think of it as making magic. The inspiration might be a spur-of-the-moment celebration of the first daffodils or a grand formal holiday gathering. The guests are an interesting mix—people we like, not people we owe! The setting suits the mood—by a stream or in a candlelit dining

"One cannot think well, love well, sleep well, if one has not dined well." —Virginia Woolf

room—and so does the menu. It is a pleasure to indulge in the season's best—the first asparagus, the new fall Beaujolais—with a spirit of inventiveness. The wine, the flowers, the music, all help to create an atmosphere of wit and good talk. The *Good Times Cookbook* is filled with suggestions and ideas for making this all come together.

Every season of the year provides inspiration and an excuse for celebration. So go ahead and experiment. You are the ringmaster... get into the spirit, pull out all the stops, and have a good time!

Julee Rosso
and Sheila Lukins
New York City
April, 1985

THE SPLURGE OF SPRING

Spring surprises. It creeps up on us year after year, yet each year we are caught unawares—and are enchanted. So much happens in such a short time! Early crocuses and hyacinths appear almost before winter ends, shy ferns shoot forth their curled heads, daffodils dance in the blustery winds, stalks of rhubarb pop up pink, shad swim upstream, and fruit trees send down carpets of fragrant blossoms. The air is charged with energy and contagious enthusiasm. Everyone wants to celebrate.

Spring entertaining takes place in that wonderful time between the cozy, hearty fireside fare of winter and the casual outdoor style of summer. Our celebrations tend to be as mercurial as the season itself. At times we want to reward our hard efforts of spring cleaning and planting with luscious dinners, and at other times we want simply to indulge to our heart's content in fleeting seasonal delights.

Spring teases with mild days when we love waking up at dawn, flying kites, flirting, and letting the sunshine sparkle our souls. And then it torments with endless spells of rain, puddles, and mud. This is when we like to escape with dreams and lush visions of the Italian countryside. It seems that there is something in the effervescence of the Italian spirit and the whimsy of pasta dishes like *primavera* and *puttanesca* that blends perfectly with our notions of spring entertaining.

In all, the good times are many. No matter what the occasion, spring entertaining is about capturing a delicate and fleeting freshness. The inside of your home should burst with as much life as the season outside. Each course should say "spring" in color, flavor, and texture.

Spring is a new beginning, a fresh start, a perfect time to express and define your entertaining style and above all to merge with the splurge of spring!

FRESH STARTS

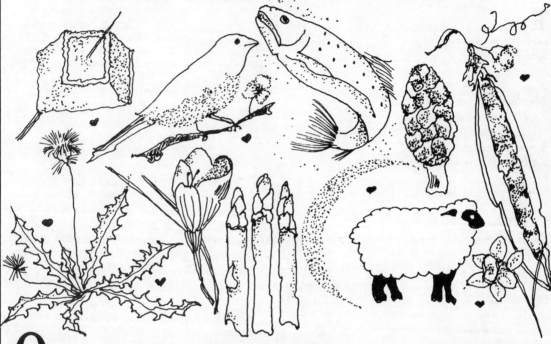

Our biggest craving at The Silver Palate is for new cocktail fare. Spring is the perfect time to gather friends after winter's hibernation and dazzle them with lots of fresh ideas that transform the ordinary cocktail party into the extraordinary.

"A good laugh is sunshine in the house."
—William Makepeace Thackeray

SMOKED SALMON SPREAD

This spread is perfect brunch fare on black bread or bagels. Or hollow out a thin loaf of French bread, fill it with the mixture, and slice it for an hors d'oeuvre.

8 ounces cream cheese, room temperature
¼ cup heavy or whipping cream
1 scallion (green onion, white part and 3 inches green), thinly sliced
1 teaspoon fresh lemon juice
Dash Tabasco sauce
4 ounces smoked salmon, gently shredded
2 tablespoons red salmon caviar

Gently mix the cream cheese and cream in a mixing bowl. Stir in the scallion, lemon juice, and Tabasco sauce. Gently fold in the smoked salmon and caviar until well combined, but do not overmix. The shreds of salmon and the caviar should remain whole.

2 cups

SALMON TARTARE WITH AQUAVIT

This is an unconventional sushi with the flair of steak tartare. Serve with rounds of pumpernickel and rye and icy glasses of aquavit or vodka.

2 pounds salmon fillets
1 medium-size red onion, finely minced
3 tablespoons capers, drained
½ cup chopped fresh mint
3 tablespoons aquavit
2 tablespoons best-quality olive oil
Fresh lemon juice, to taste
Salt and freshly ground black pepper, to taste

1. Remove any remaining bones from the salmon and cut the flesh into fairly small pieces, separating it from the skin as you cut.
2. Place the salmon in a food processor fitted with a steel blade and process, using repeated pulses, just until finely minced. Be careful not to purée the salmon by overprocessing it.
3. Combine the salmon, onion, capers, mint, aquavit, oil, and lemon juice, salt, and pepper to taste in a medium-size bowl.
4. Refrigerate covered until cold. Taste and adjust seasonings and remove to a serving bowl.

10 to 12 appetizer portions

FRESH SALMON BEIGNETS

A perfect little hot hors d'oeuvre. Serve beignets in a flat basket with a pretty pink flower for decoration.

3 cloves garlic, chopped
1 pound poached fresh salmon, skinned, boned, and flaked
¾ cup mashed cooked potato
1 to 1½ cups best-quality olive oil
¼ cup heavy or whipping cream
1½ tablespoons fresh lemon juice
Salt and freshly ground black pepper, to taste
2 tablespoons unsalted butter
⅓ cup water
½ cup unbleached all-purpose flour
2 eggs
Vegetable oil for frying

SUSHI SAVOIR-FAIRE

SUSHI: A combination of raw or cooked fish set on a mound of vinegared rice and sometimes wrapped in a seaweed called *nori*. The best Japanese sushi bars make elegant and striking platters of mixed sushi arrangements. Sushi is usually prepared in front of the customer by a skilled chef.

SASHIMI: Raw fish sliced in a way that makes it as tender and flavorful as possible.

GARI: A delicious condiment of pickled ginger root used to clear the palate between bites of sushi.

SU: Rice vinegar of very high quality used in preparing the rice for sushi.

WASABI: A nose-tinglingly sharp Japanese horseradish. It is usually sold powdered and is mixed with a small amount of water before serving. Wasabi paste in tubes is also available.

1. Mince the garlic and salmon together in a food processor fitted with a steel blade. Add the potato and process until puréed, about 1 minute.

2. With the machine running, pour in enough of the oil in a thin steady stream to give the mixture the consistency of smooth mashed potatoes.

3. Add the cream and lemon juice and process to blend. Season with salt and pepper to taste. Scrape into a bowl and wash the work bowl and blade of the food processor.

4. Heat the butter and water to boiling in a small saucepan over medium-high heat. When the mixture boils, add all the flour at once and stir until the flour is absorbed and the dough forms a ball. Continue stirring and cooking for about 1 minute more to dry out the dough. Remove from heat and let stand 5 minutes.

5. Process the dough in the food processor for about 10 seconds to break the dough into granules. Add the eggs and process until well blended and smooth. Add 1½ cups of the salmon brandade and process until thoroughly blended. Taste and adjust seasonings.

6. Heat 3 inches vegetable oil in a deep-fat fryer to 375°F.

7. Using two teaspoons, shape and drop small bite-size balls of the batter into the hot oil. Fry 6 to 8 beignets at one time until golden brown. (The beignets will roll over by themselves when one side is browned.) Remove them from the oil with a slotted spoon and drain on paper towels. Serve warm in a basket lined with a starched napkin.

35 to 40 beignets

Note: The remaining salmon brandade can be served as a spread on warm toast points or used to make another batch of beignets, for the recipe yields about 3 cups salmon brandade.

"Imagination is more important than knowledge."
—Albert Einstein

RILLETTES

Rillettes are made in France traditionally from a simmered blend of pork pieces and fat. They are often sold in crocks or cans and are good picnic fare, especially spread on crusty bread. We particularly like our version made with smoked trout, as we find it lighter and less fatty than the usual fare.

RILLETTES OF SMOKED TROUT

A lighter version of classic French rillettes.

3 smoked trout, skinned and boned
6 tablespoons (¾ stick) unsalted butter
4 ounces pork fat or bacon, diced
3 cloves garlic
1½ cups dry white wine
½ cup chopped fresh dill
2 tablespoons fresh lemon juice
Salt and freshly ground black pepper, to taste

1. One day before serving, place the trout, butter, pork fat, garlic, and wine in a large saucepan. Heat to boiling. Reduce heat and simmer until all the liquid evaporates. Let stand 20 minutes to cool.

2. Process the dill in a food processor fitted with a steel blade until minced. Add the trout mixture and process until well combined. Add the lemon juice and salt and pepper to taste and process until mixed. Spoon into a crock and refrigerate covered overnight to allow flavors to blend.

3. Before serving, let warm to room temperature. Serve with crackers or toasted bread rounds.

1 ½ cups

ROSY SEAFOOD SAUSAGE

A colorful twist on the classic *boudin blanc*. The sausages are a lovely shade of pink, flecked with orange and green from carrots and leeks, and plump with milky white bay scallops. Delicate, sensuous, and a delicious way to begin a very special occasion.

2 pounds salmon fillets
2 cups water
2 cups dry white wine
4 tablespoons (½ stick) unsalted butter
2 carrots, peeled and minced
2 leeks, well rinsed, dried, and minced
2 ripe tomatoes, seeded and chopped
½ cup chopped fresh dill
½ cup fresh bread crumbs
2 egg whites
2 tablespoons Pernod
2 tablespoons fresh lemon juice
1 cup heavy or whipping cream
1 teaspoon dried tarragon
Pinch ground nutmeg
Pinch cayenne pepper
Salt and freshly ground black pepper, to taste
8 ounces fresh bay scallops, halved

1. Poach the salmon fillets in the wine and water in a large skillet just until cooked through. Cool and flake the salmon meat, removing all the bones. Refrigerate covered until cold.

2. Melt the butter in the skillet over medium-high heat. Add the carrots and leeks and sauté for 7 minutes. Add the tomatoes and cook for 2 minutes more. Remove from heat and stir in the dill and bread crumbs.

3. Process the salmon in a food processor fitted with a steel blade until smooth. Add the egg whites and process until blended. Add the Pernod, lemon juice, and cream and process until very smooth. Season with the tarragon, nutmeg, cayenne, and salt and pepper to taste. Remove to a large mixing bowl.

4. Add the vegetable mixture and the halved bay scallops to the salmon mixture and stir to combine. Lay out a large sheet of strong plastic wrap. Shape a sixth of the seafood

CHAMPAGNE TIMES

Some of our favorite Champagne occasions are:

♥ The first day of spring
♥ The New Year
♥ Valentine's Day
♥ Launching the boat
♥ August stargazing
♥ Autumn's first fireplace fire
♥ A job promotion
♥ A tax rebate
♥ While reading a classic
♥ A new baby
♥ A special anniversary
♥ Thursday
♥ Falling in love
♥ A 40th birthday
♥ A caviar splurge
♥ Spotting a rainbow
♥ Absolutely no reason at all!

"The night they invented champagne, It's plain as it can be They thought of you and me."
—©Alan Jay Lerner & Frederick Loewe

✛ FROM THE SILVER PALATE NOTEBOOK

Shrimp is always a favorite at a dinner party or large buffet. We present shrimp in many ways, but if it's served plain with dipping sauces, remember always to serve it over crushed ice.

One thing we love to do, as it makes the shrimp look larger and fresher, is to leave the tail shells on while cleaning. Your guests can use them as little handles. Have large seashells available for guests to put the tails in. Tuck small pink lilies inside the shells.

mixture into a log, 6 inches long and 1½ inches wide, in the center of the plastic wrap. Wrap up very securely and twist each end of the plastic very tightly to make a mock sausage casing. Secure the ends with kitchen string if necessary. Repeat with the remaining seafood mixture to make 6 sausages. Refrigerate the sausages until firm, about 3 hours.

5. When ready to cook, fill a large Dutch oven or stock pot with water and heat to boiling. Add the sausages, still wrapped in plastic wrap, and simmer for 15 minutes, turning once halfway through the cooking time.

6. Remove the sausages from the water. Unwrap and cut into thin slices. Serve hot, napped with Tomato Beurre Blanc (page 215).

6 sausages, 12 appetizer portions

JUMBO SHRIMP IN HERBED OIL

This shrimp presentation is dazzling. Bathed in lemon juice and olive oil, the shrimp are enlivened with sliced red and yellow peppers and perfumed with fresh basil, dill, rosemary, and thyme.

1 cup dry white wine
1 teaspoon mustard seeds
½ teaspoon (or to taste) red pepper flakes
2 bay leaves
1 lemon half
2 pounds jumbo shrimp, shelled and deveined, tails left on
3 tablespoons chopped fresh basil
3 tablespoons chopped fresh dill
1 tablespoon chopped fresh rosemary
1 tablespoon chopped fresh tarragon
1 tablespoon chopped fresh thyme
3 cloves garlic, minced
1½ tablespoons herb mustard
5 tablespoons fresh lemon juice
1 cup best-quality olive oil
Salt and freshly ground black pepper, to taste
1 small sweet red pepper, cored, seeded, and diced
1 small sweet yellow pepper, cored, seeded, and diced

1. Combine the wine, mustard seeds, ½ teaspoon red pepper flakes, the bay leaves, and lemon half in a 4-quart pan. Add water to fill the pan three-fourths full. Heat to boiling. Add the shrimp and cook over high heat until opaque in the center, 3 to 4 minutes. Drain and cool.

2. Combine the basil, dill, rosemary, tarragon, thyme, garlic, mustard, and lemon juice in a large bowl. Whisk in the oil and season to taste with salt, pepper, and additional red pepper flakes if desired.

3. Stir in the red and yellow peppers and add the shrimp. Let the shrimp marinate in the oil at least 3 hours.

4. Serve at room temperature with crusty bread.

8 to 10 appetizer portions

Variation: The shrimp and marinade combined with cold cooked rice makes a refreshing summer salad.

CRABMEAT MOUSSE

A light variation on our favorite salmon mousse—fresh lump crabmeat is always the most luxurious. Serve as an hors d'oeuvre, appetizer, or light lunch. Fresh dill and chives sparkle the flavor.

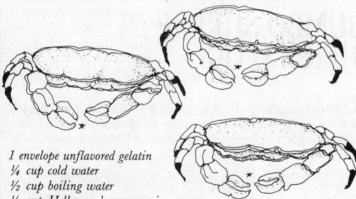

1 envelope unflavored gelatin
¼ cup cold water
½ cup boiling water
½ cup Hellmann's mayonnaise
2 tablespoons finely snipped fresh or freeze-dried chives
2 tablespoons finely chopped fresh dill
1 tablespoon grated onion
1 tablespoon fresh lemon juice
Dash Tabasco sauce
¼ teaspoon sweet paprika
1 teaspoon salt
2 cups flaked lump crabmeat, picked over for shells
1 cup heavy or whipping cream
Fresh dill sprigs (garnish)

1. Soften the gelatin in the cold water in a large mixing bowl for 3 minutes. Stir in the boiling water and slowly whisk until the gelatin dissolves. Cool to room temperature.

2. Add the mayonnaise, chives, chopped dill, onion, lemon juice, Tabasco, paprika, and salt and whisk until

SPRING HOUSEWARMING

Crabmeat Mousse

Smoked Chicken with Basil Parmesan Mayonnaise

Fresh Salmon Beignets

Bucheron Tart with Fresh Herbs

Asparagus with Oriental Mayonnaise

Best Vegetable Pâté

Cashew Sticks

Spring tonics

SPRING HOUSEWARMING

Give a spring housewarming dinner for your new neighbors—even if they moved in last February while you were away. Invite the neighborhood and make it festive by serving a menu of the freshest foods of the season. If there are no new neighbors, get together with friends to congratulate one another after spring cleaning!

INVITATIONS

The party invitation is the first clue to the nature of the party. It may be formal, filled with confetti, contained in a tiny present, a handwritten note, tied in a spring bouquet, or written in the sky. Or it may be a gracious telephone call, which allows an instant RSVP. With so many people on the go, most hosts telephone if the party is a fairly small one. If we do mail an invitation and receive no response, we always follow up with a phone call.

"If you haven't got anything nice to say about anybody, come sit next to me."
—Alice Roosevelt Longworth

completely blended. Refrigerate until slightly thickened, about 20 minutes.

3. Fold the crabmeat into the gelatin mixture. Whip the cream in a separate bowl until it forms soft peaks and fold gently into the crab mixture.

4. Remove the mixture into a medium-size bowl or decorative 6- to 8-cup mold. Refrigerate covered at least 4 hours.

5. Unmold the mousse onto a serving platter and garnish with dill sprigs. Serve with black bread or crackers, or spoon into ripe avocado halves and serve as a first course.

12 generous appetizer portions

BABY ARTICHOKE FRITTERS

Baby artichokes are perfect for bite-size fritters. Fry until golden and serve sprinkled with lots of freshly grated Parmesan in napkin-lined baskets.

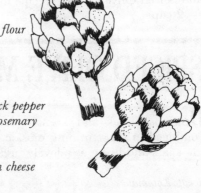

18 baby artichokes
1 lemon, sliced
1 cup unbleached all-purpose flour
2 cloves garlic, minced
2 teaspoons dried oregano
2 teaspoons dried basil
1 teaspoon salt
1 teaspoon freshly ground black pepper
½ teaspoon crumbled dried rosemary
6 large eggs
Vegetable oil for frying
1 cup freshly grated Parmesan cheese
2 lemons, cut into wedges

1. Remove the tough outer leaves of the artichokes and trim the bottoms and tops with scissors. Cut each artichoke in half. Fill a large bowl with cold water, add the artichokes and lemon slices, and let stand 30 minutes.

2. Mix the flour, garlic, oregano, basil, salt, pepper, and rosemary in a mixing bowl. Beat the eggs in another bowl.

3. Drain the artichoke halves and pat them dry with a kitchen towel.

4. Heat vegetable oil in a deep-fat fryer to 375°F.

5. Dip the artichokes first in the flour mixture and then into the beaten eggs. Fry 6 to 8 artichoke halves in the oil until golden on the outside and tender inside, 10 to 12 minutes. Drain on paper towels. Keep warm on a serving platter while frying the remaining artichokes.

6. When all the artichokes have been fried, sprinkle them with the Parmesan. Serve with lemon wedges and pass the peppermill.

36 fritters

HERBED CHÈVRE

Lemon juice and lemon zest make this herbed chèvre very refreshing. We've snipped lots and lots of chives into it and added freshly ground black pepper to complement the cheese.

1 log (12 ounces) Montrachet or other soft mild chèvre
¼ cup heavy or whipping cream
3 bunches (about 12 stems each) chives, finely snipped
1 teaspoon dried thyme
½ teaspoon freshly ground black pepper
½ teaspoon fresh lemon juice
1 teaspoon grated lemon zest

1. Break the log of Montrachet into 4 pieces and process in a food processor fitted with a steel blade while slowly adding the cream. Process until smooth. Scrape into a mixing bowl. Whisk in the chives, thyme, pepper, and lemon juice and zest. Refrigerate for several hours to allow flavors to blend.

2. Transfer to a serving bowl and serve with crusty bread and Spiced Olive Mosaic (recipe follows).

2 cups

SPICED OLIVE MOSAIC

Delicious Greek and French black and green olives are combined in this stunning mosaic. Pack in decorative clear glass jars and bring as a lovely bread-and-butter gift.

1 cup Kalamata olives
1 cup Niçoise olives
1 cup Picholine olives
1 cup best-quality olive oil
½ cup water
¼ cup dry white wine
2 large cloves garlic
2 large bay leaves
2 dried whole chiles (2 inches long)
½ teaspoon dried oregano
½ teaspoon coarsely ground
*   black pepper*
2 lemon slices (¼ inch thick)
1 full branch fresh or dried thyme
Chopped fresh thyme (garnish)

1. Combine the olives in a bowl; drain off all the liquid.
2. Combine the oil, water, and wine in a small heavy saucepan and heat just to boiling. Remove from heat. Add the garlic, bay leaves, chiles, oregano, and black pepper. Let

CHEVRES

No longer the precious secret of just a few, chèvres—cheeses made from goat's milk—seem to be taking over more and more of the cheese counter. Whether French, Italian, or American, we're crazy about their zingy fresh taste and versatility. Some of our favorites are:

BANON: a French cheese which is dipped in a brandy bath before being wrapped up in chestnut leaves and tied with straw.

BOULE DE PERIGORD: a creamy white cheese permeated with finely chopped walnuts; slightly sweet in taste and good to serve with fruit, port, or sherry.

BRIN D'AMOUR: a larger Corsican cheese coated all over with aromatic herbs. The name means ''morsel of love,'' and it is one of our favorites.

BUCHERON: a fat log-shaped French variety with a soft ivory rind and snowy white, chalky interior. One of the most popular goat cheeses.

BUCHETTE A L'AIL: a tiny cylindrical cheese flecked with garlic and herbs; good as an appetizer or crumbled over salads.

CAPRELLA: a round Italian cheese slightly larger than a small wheel of Brie, with a rind like a Brie and a very creamy, runny interior.

CHEVREESE: a fresh American log from New Jersey; great to roll in herbs or marinate in fruity olive oils.

CHEVRE A LA FEUILLE: a semi-spherical cheese from Périgord. It comes in three different flavors—truffle, herb, paprika—and has a very chalky interior.

COEUR: a heart-shaped romantic little cheese, available with or without ash; very much like Montrachet.

CROTTIN: a hard little disk-shaped cheese made on many French farms. It makes a zesty appetizer when marinated in oil, herbs, and peppercorns.

MONTRACHET: a soft fresh chèvre produced in the same region of France as the celebrated white wine of the same name. It is pure white, available with or without ash, and is one of the most popular varieties.

NEW YORK STATE GOAT: several different styles of cheese made on small farms in upstate New York. All are aged at least four months and have a mild but well-developed flavor.

PYRAMIDE: a particularly mild and typically goaty cheese when young; increasingly hard and pungent as it ages.

SAINT-CHRISTOPHE: a soft and flavorful log constructed around a small stick for structural support.

VALENCAY: pyramid in shape with a Brie-type rind, this cheese has a crumbly snow-white interior and a characteristic tang; it goes best with salads.

cool for 20 minutes.

3. Place 1 lemon slice in the bottom of a 1-quart glass jar. Add the mixed olives and, at the same time, arrange the chiles, garlic cloves, remaining lemon slice, bay leaves, and thyme branch in the jar so that they show on the outside.

4. Pour the oil mixture into the jar and cover with a lid. Marinate at least 12 hours before serving.

5. Serve the olives in a clear bowl or flat ceramic dish, garnished with fresh thyme.

1 quart

BUCHERON TART WITH FRESH HERBS

Our chèvre tart is a delicious variation on the usual quiche. A crisp herby bite is perfect for hors d'oeuvres or as a luncheon dish.

CRUST:

3 cups unbleached all-purpose flour
1 teaspoon salt
1 cup (2 sticks) unsalted butter, cold, cut into small pieces
⅓ cup ice water

FILLING:

11 ounces Bucheron or other soft mild chèvre
½ cup ricotta
¾ cup (1½ sticks) unsalted butter, room temperature
3 egg yolks
⅓ cup unbleached all-purpose flour
Salt and freshly ground black pepper, to taste
2 tablespoons chopped fresh rosemary or 1 teaspoon dried
2 tablespoons chopped fresh thyme or 1 teaspoon dried

1. To make the crust, process the flour and salt in a food processor fitted with a steel blade just to combine. Add the butter and process just until the mixture resembles coarse meal. With the machine running, pour in the water in a thin steady stream and process just until the dough gathers into a ball. Wrap in plastic wrap and refrigerate 30 minutes.

2. Roll out the dough on a lightly floured surface into a rectangle large enough to line a 13 x 9-inch baking pan. Line the pan with the dough and trim and crimp the edges. Freeze for 10 minutes.

3. Preheat oven to 400°F.

4. Line the pastry with aluminum foil and weight with dried beans or pie weights. Bake for 10 minutes. Remove from oven and remove the foil and pie weights from the tart shell. Let the tart shell cool. Reduce heat to 375°F.

5. To make the filling, process the Bucheron, ricotta, and butter in the food processor until smooth. Add the egg yolks, one at a time, processing to combine after each addition. Add the flour and salt and pepper to taste; process just until blended.

6. Pour the filling into the tart shell. Sprinkle the top with the rosemary and thyme. Bake until puffed and brown, 25 to 30 minutes.

7. Cut into small squares and serve immediately.

16 appetizer portions or 8 main-course portions

PALMIERS WITH HONEY MUSTARD AND PROSCIUTTO

You'll love these light puff-pastry palmiers and the variation. Or let your imagination play.

*1 sheet puff pastry (18 x 11 inches),
    homemade or packaged
3 tablespoons honey mustard
4 ounces thinly sliced prosciutto
1 cup freshly grated Parmesan cheese
1 egg
2 teaspoons water*

1. Place the puff pastry on a work surface and spread the mustard over the top. Arrange the prosciutto evenly over the mustard to cover all the pastry, and then sprinkle with the Parmesan. Lightly press the cheese into the prosciutto with a rolling pin.

2. Starting at one long edge, roll up the puff pastry like a

CAJUN CUISINE

Cajun is a Louisiana-born style of cooking with French roots. The Cajun people emigrated to Nova Scotia from the south of France in the early 1600s and settled a colony called Acadia. They were later driven out by the British and many settled in Louisiana, where they found a home in the existing French culture.

Thus, Cajun cooking has its roots in old French country cooking but has been adapted according to location. The dishes make great use of crawfish, chicken, pork, and seasonal game. Primary Cajun seasonings include filé powder (from the sassafras tree), parsley, bay leaves, cayenne, black pepper, and a variety of fresh hot peppers. Crawfish étouffée, gumbo, and jambalaya are typical Cajun dishes.

Cajun cooking is often confused with Creole cooking. Creole originated in New Orleans from a mixture of many ethnic traditions—including French, Spanish, Italian, American Indian, and African.

jelly roll just to the middle of the dough; then roll up the other side in the same fashion, making two rolls that meet in the center. Using a serrated knife, cut the rolls crosswise into ½-inch slices. Place the slices on cookie sheets lined with parchment paper and press lightly with your hands to flatten. Refrigerate for 15 minutes.

3. Preheat oven to 400°F.

4. Beat the egg and water together in a small bowl. Brush the top of each palmier with the egg wash. Bake until puffed and lightly golden, about 10 minutes. Serve warm or at room temperature.

20 palmiers

Variation: Spread the puff pastry with ⅓ cup Basic Pesto (page 398) and sprinkle with 1 cup grated Parmesan cheese. Press the cheese into the dough with a rolling pin and proceed as directed.

CAJUN CHICKEN MORSELS

These chicken pieces are perfect party food because they can be made in advance and reheated before serving. Serve with a variety of mustards for dipping and plenty of cold beer.

1 ½ cups unbleached all-purpose flour
1 cup chopped (medium fine) pecans
1 tablespoon dried oregano
2 teaspoons ground cumin
1 teaspoon dried thyme
½ teaspoon cayenne pepper
Salt, to taste
12 tablespoons (1 ½ sticks) unsalted butter
4 whole chicken breasts (8 halves), skinned, boned, and cut into
    1-inch pieces

1. Combine the flour, pecans, oregano, cumin, thyme, cayenne, and salt to taste in a shallow dish.

2. Melt 6 tablespoons of the butter in a small saucepan. Dip each chicken piece first in the butter, then in the flour mixture to coat well.

3. Melt 3 tablespoons of the remaining butter in a large skillet over medium heat. Add half the chicken pieces and sauté until browned on all sides and cooked through. Remove from the pan and keep warm. Repeat with the remaining 3 tablespoons butter and the chicken.*

4. Serve the chicken morsels with toothpicks and your favorite mustard for dipping.

8 appetizer portions

*The cooked chicken can be stored covered in the refrigerator. Before serving, heat the chicken, wrapped in aluminum foil, at 350°F for 10 minutes.

CURRIED PEANUT CHICKEN

A wonderfully simple hors d'oeuvre. All the elements can be prepared ahead of time and assembled shortly before serving. Keep a bowl of raisins nearby. This is a miniature curry.

2 whole chicken breasts (4 halves), skinned and boned
2 cups half-and-half
1½ cups Hellmann's mayonnaise
3 tablespoons mango chutney
2 tablespoons dry sherry
1 tablespoon sherry vinegar
2 tablespoons plus 1 teaspoon curry powder
1 teaspoon turmeric
2 cups salted roasted peanuts, finely chopped
Chopped fresh coriander (garnish)

1. Preheat oven to 350°F.
2. Place the chicken breasts in a shallow baking dish just large enough to hold them. Pour the half-and-half over them and bake for 30 minutes. Let cool and cut into 1-inch cubes.
3. Process the mayonnaise, chutney, sherry, vinegar, curry powder, and turmeric in a blender or food processor fitted with a steel blade until blended.
4. Dip the chicken pieces into the curry mayonnaise and then roll in the chopped peanuts. Refrigerate 30 minutes.
5. Serve each piece on a small skewer arranged on a serving plate. Garnish with coriander and accompany with small bowls of giant raisins.

About 40 hors d'oeuvres

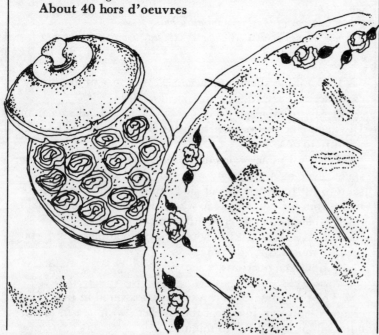

CURRY

In India cooks shop daily among lush and glorious-looking spices for the grinding of their private-formula curry powder. As this is not our tradition, we need to be aware that curry powders vary in composition, degree of hotness, and freshness. When trying a new blend, add it cautiously to a dish until the desired flavor and intensity is attained.

"By planting flowers one invites butterflies ... by planting pines one invites the wind ... by planting bananas one invites the rain, and by planting willow trees one invites cicadas."
—Chao Ch'ang

SPRING FEVER

Spring fever is one fever we love to feed. The symptoms are most agreeable—no sniffles, chills, or aches—just pure cravings for the seasonal splendors. The first pussy willows and early forsythia induce the fever and fill us with anticipation that grows and grows until we are forced to take the only cure we know—pure indulgence in feasts of asparagus, fiddleheads, rhubarb, and shad roe. The more we indulge, the more we wish that spring and its fevers could last all year long.

RICH ASPARAGUS SOUP

Made in the style of a puréed vegetable soup, the addition of the bright green floating tips gives a bit of crunch, and chopped tomato adds a colorful confetti effect.

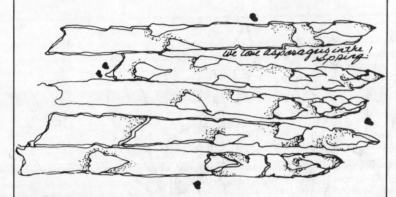

we love asparagus in the spring!

½ cup (1 stick) unsalted butter
2 large yellow onions, coarsely chopped
4 large cloves garlic, coarsely chopped
1 ½ quarts Berta's Chicken Stock (page 396)
3 pounds asparagus
1 bunch fresh parsley, stems removed, chopped (1 cup)
2 medium-size carrots, peeled and cut into 1-inch pieces
8 fresh large basil leaves
1 tablespoon dried tarragon
1 teaspoon salt
1 teaspoon freshly ground black pepper
Pinch cayenne pepper
1 cup sour cream
1 ripe large tomato, seeded and cut into small dice

1. Melt the butter in a heavy large saucepan over low heat. Add the onions and garlic and cook uncovered until wilted, about 25 minutes.

2. Add the stock and heat to boiling.

3. Trim the woody ends from the asparagus and cut the stalks into 1-inch pieces. Reserve the tips. Add the asparagus pieces, parsley, carrots, basil, tarragon, salt, pepper, and cayenne to the stock. Reduce heat to medium-low and simmer covered until the vegetables are tender, about 50 minutes.

4. Remove the soup from heat and let cool. Process in batches in a blender or a food processor fitted with a steel blade until smooth. Strain the soup through a medium-size sieve to remove woody fibers.

5. Return the strained soup to the pan, add the asparagus tips, and simmer over medium heat until the tips are tender, about 10 minutes.

6. Ladle the soup into soup bowls. Dollop each serving with sour cream and sprinkle with diced tomato.

8 portions

TARRAGON

The French call tarragon the king of herbs. Its mild anise flavor is both mysterious and seductive—think of the best béarnaise sauce you've ever tasted! Tarragon also combines well with poultry, veal, eggs, and in a salad dressing with mustard and lemon.

ASPARAGUS WITH FLAVORED SAUCES

WELCOME SPRING DINNER

Rich Asparagus Soup

Roast Veal with Lemon and Capers

Lemon Rice

Fiddleheads with browned butter

Semolina bread

Cappuccino Ice Cream and Espresso Cookies

California Sauvignon Blanc or Graves

Whether you're on the way to La Scala to listen to Verdi or to the Majestic to watch Sam Shepard's new play, our Welcome Spring Dinner has a finale with punch enough to keep you awake.

Asparagus is such an exquisite vegetable that it is worthwhile to peel the stalks, which makes the spears look as precious as they taste. Snap off the tough bottoms and peel the stalks two-thirds of the way up with a swivel-bladed vegetable peeler. This makes the entire stalk tender and creates a beautiful contrast of pale and dark greens in the cooked spears. To cook, place the spears in a skillet and add water just to cover. Heat the water to boiling and cook just a few minutes until tender but still firm. Drain at once and pat dry with a kitchen towel. Serve the asparagus accompanied by a special sauce. The following are four of our favorites.

PISTACHIO-ORANGE SAUCE

6 tablespoons (¾ stick) unsalted butter
3 tablespoons shelled pistachio nuts
3 tablespoons fresh orange juice
1 tablespoon grated orange zest
Freshly ground black pepper, to taste

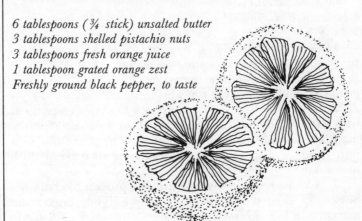

1. Melt the butter in a small skillet over medium heat. Add the pistachios and toast the nuts in the butter about 5 minutes.

2. Whisk in the orange juice and zest. Cook 1 minute more. Pour over 1½ pounds hot cooked asparagus and sprinkle with pepper to taste.

¾ cup

GREEN SAUCE

2 cups fresh parsley leaves
3 scallions (green onions, white and green parts), sliced
½ cup fresh dill sprigs
3 anchovy fillets, drained
3 cloves garlic, roughly chopped
1 tablespoon capers, drained
6 tablespoons fresh lemon juice
¾ cup olive oil
Salt and freshly ground black pepper, to taste
2 hard-cooked eggs, finely chopped

Mince the parsley, scallions, and dill in a food processor fitted with a steel blade. Add the anchovies, garlic, capers, and lemon juice. Process until smooth. With the machine running, add the oil in a thin, steady stream. Season to taste with salt and pepper. Remove to a serving bowl and stir in the eggs.

1 ½ cups

ORIENTAL MAYONNAISE

2 cloves garlic, minced
1 tablespoon finely chopped fresh ginger root
¼ cup soy sauce
2 tablespoons rice vinegar*
2 tablespoons brown sugar
3 whole star anise
1 egg
1 tablespoon sesame mustard*
¾ cup safflower oil
¼ cup sesame oil*
Several drops hot chili oil*
8 ounces enoki mushrooms*

1. Combine the garlic, ginger, soy sauce, vinegar, brown sugar, and star anise in a small saucepan. Heat to boiling. Reduce heat and simmer uncovered 10 minutes. Remove from heat and discard the star anise.

2. Process the egg and mustard in a food processor fitted with a steel blade until blended, about 20 seconds. With the machine running, pour the safflower and sesame oils in a thin steady stream through the feed tube to make a thick mayonnaise.

3. Add the reduced soy mixture and process to combine. Season to desired hotness with the chili oil. Spoon the mayonnaise into a bowl and refrigerate covered until ready to serve.

4. Place a small bowl of the mayonnaise to one side of a large oval or round serving platter. Arrange the asparagus spears in a spokelike pattern around the bowl on the larger side of the platter. Arrange small bundles of the mushrooms between the asparagus spokes and serve.

About 1 ½ cups

*available in some supermarkets, Oriental groceries, and other specialty food shops

SOY BUTTER

2 tablespoons unsalted butter
2 tablespoons soy sauce

Melt the butter in a small saucepan. Whisk in the soy sauce. Pour over 1 pound hot cooked asparagus.

¼ cup

BORAGE

Borage is a large plant that produces beautiful blue star-shaped flowers, nice as a garnish in salads or drinks. It has a slight cucumber flavor and will attract bees to your garden.

Borage was smuggled into the drinks of prospective husbands to give them the courage to propose.

CHIVES

This sweet and mild onion is easy to grow indoors and out. The flavor is the essence of spring, best when snipped into irregular pieces and scattered over a dish at the last moment. Keep a pot growing by a sunny window year round, and don't go forget to use the pretty lavender blossoms as a garnish for soups and salads.

"Asparagus, when picked, should be no thicker than a darning needle."
—Alice B. Toklas

STIR-FRY OF ASPARAGUS WITH CASHEWS

A simple preparation for one of our favorite vegetables.

1 ½ pounds asparagus
2 tablespoons olive oil
2 teaspoons sesame oil
1 tablespoon finely chopped fresh ginger root
½ cup coarsely chopped roasted cashews
1 tablespoon soy sauce

1. Cut off the tough lower stems of the asparagus and discard. Cut each stalk diagonally into 2 or 3 pieces.
2. Heat the oils together in a wok over high heat. Add the ginger and stir-fry for 1 minute.
3. Add the asparagus and stir-fry until tender but still crisp, 4 to 5 minutes.
4. Stir in the cashews and soy sauce. Serve immediately.
6 portions

WARM SWEETBREAD SALAD

To make this wonderful combination yet more special we've added the tartness of a sorrel vinaigrette. The dish is perfect for a formal spring luncheon.

2 pounds veal sweetbreads
1 pound fresh asparagus
2 packages (12 ounces each) baby carrots
1 Belgian endive, leaves separated, rinsed, and patted dry
4 cups watercress leaves (2 bunches)
8 ounces fresh wild mushrooms, well rinsed and patted dry
¼ cup fresh lemon juice
1 tablespoon Dijon-style mustard
2 tablespoons chopped shallots
3 tablespoons chopped fresh or bottled sorrel
¾ cup olive oil
⅓ cup walnut oil
Salt and freshly ground black pepper, to taste
3 tablespoons Crème Fraîche (page 399)
½ cup unbleached all-purpose flour
4 tablespoons (½ stick) unsalted butter

1. One day before serving, soak the sweetbreads for 1 hour in 3 changes of cold water and drain. Place the sweetbreads in a medium-size saucepan and add water to cover.

TIE A YELLOW RIBBON LUNCHEON

Crabmeat Mousse

Warm Sweetbread Salad

Goat-Cheese Popovers

Rhubarb Sorbet
Orange-Almond Snails

Sancerre or Sauvignon Blanc

Invite your guests to a bridge luncheon by sending an invitation tied with colorful ribbons. Decorate place cards with ribbons, use them as napkin rings, and echo their color in flowers, tablecloth and napkins, and menu. It creates a lovely, gracious touch for your guests. We know of one woman who tied her ribbons around her thank-you note.

Heat to boiling; reduce heat and simmer uncovered 3 minutes, turning the sweetbreads over once. Drain the sweetbreads and rinse under cold water to refresh.

2. When the sweetbreads are cool enough to handle, remove the fat and connecting tubes. Place the sweetbreads on a large plate and cover with a board or cookie sheet. Place several weights (bags of flour or sugar, or cans) on top of the board and refrigerate overnight.

3. The day you plan to serve the salad, prepare the vegetables. Peel the asparagus and cook just until tender but still firm. Drain and refrigerate until cold.

4. Peel the baby carrots, leaving them whole. Cook in boiling salted water until tender but still firm. Drain, slice lengthwise in half, and refrigerate until cold.

5. Arrange the endive leaves in a spoke pattern on each of 6 luncheon plates. Fill the center of each plate with a bed of watercress leaves. Alternate the spears of asparagus and baby carrot halves in a circle on each plate. Slice the wild mushrooms and sprinkle them over each salad.

6. Whisk the lemon juice, mustard, and shallots together in a mixing bowl. Stir in the sorrel. Gradually whisk in the oils and season to taste with salt and pepper. Stir in the crème fraîche.

7. Slice the sweetbreads into 1- to 1½-inch pieces. Season the flour with salt and pepper and dredge the sweetbreads lightly with the mixture.

8. Melt the butter in a sauté pan over medium-high heat, add the sweetbreads, and sauté until nicely browned, 2 to 3 minutes on each side.

9. Divide the sweetbreads evenly among the 6 plates, placing them in the center of each salad. Drizzle with the vinaigrette and serve immediately.

6 portions

YELLOWTAIL FILLETS WITH ASPARAGUS

A fresh and light fish preparation that uses wine and orange juice in place of rich butter and cream.

*6 yellowtail or other flat fillets, such as flounder or sole (about
    8 ounces each)*
Salt and freshly ground black pepper, to taste
1 cup fresh orange juice (2 large oranges)
1 cup dry white wine
2 tablespoons orange liqueur
12 ounces baby carrots, peeled
1½ pounds asparagus, stalks trimmed and peeled
1 carrot, peeled and cut into thin julienne
2 leeks, well rinsed, dried, and cut into thin julienne
2 tablespoons unsalted butter

THE HERB GARDEN

Cooking with fresh garden herbs has become such an essential part of our cooking style that we can't imagine many of our meals, or anyone else's for that matter, without them.

Herbs are fun to grow because they are so versatile. You needn't have a country estate, a greenhouse, a farm, or even a backyard. A one-room apartment in the middle of a city will do, for many herbs thrive just as well in flowerpots placed by a sunny window. The only secret is to make the most of the space available and plant as many varieties of herbs as you can, so that you can truly enjoy your efforts.

If you do have some yard space, you might enjoy planting a traditional knot herb garden like those so popular in the nineteenth century. Or you might want to make an herb garden the focal point of a brick patio. Herb gardens can be as beautiful as flower gardens and are certainly as fragrant. Herbs are also nice when integrated into the rows of a larger vegetable patch, and some even have the powers to ward off garden pests.

One of the best notions for an herb garden is to make it a secret garden as well. Tucked away by a favorite gnarled old tree or in the vale of a distant meadow, it is a wonderful place to retreat to in sunlight or moonlight for a fragrant moment of peace and meditation. Short of that, we like to place a window box full of herbs by a favorite reading spot. Summer breezes will fill the whole room with sweet and savory herb scents.

In addition to the culinary value and fragrance of herbs, we like their cool colors—silver-green sage, dusty purple basil, feathery blue-green dill. They soothe us in summer's worst heat waves. We always make a point of planting our herb garden in a contrasting patchwork pattern, alternating lavender with lemon thyme, sweet marjoram with rose geranium, purple sage with tarragon, opal basil with green basil, and so on.

The joy of harvesting herbs needn't end with the first threat of frost. At the end of the season, we pick our herbs in bunches, tie them with big bows, and hang them upside down to dry in the kitchen. The kitchen immediately takes on a harvest glow, is filled with good smells, and there are plenty of herbs to last us through the winter. Our favorite drying herbs are oregano, marjoram, rosemary, sage, and bay. Preserve greener herbs, like basil, parsley, tarragon, and dill by puréeing the leaves with a little oil and freezing in small containers for later use.

1. Sprinkle the fillets lightly with salt and pepper. Pour the orange juice and wine into a large skillet. Add the fillets and heat over medium-high heat until simmering. Reduce the heat to keep the liquid at a simmer and poach the fillets just until cooked through, 7 to 8 minutes. Remove the fillets to a platter, cover, and keep warm.

2. Pour the cooking liquid into a small saucepan and add the orange liqueur. Cook over high heat until reduced by half.

3. While the liquid is reducing, cook the baby carrots and asparagus separately in simmering water until tender but still crisp. Drain and keep warm. Cook the carrot and leek julienne in the butter in a skillet over medium heat until tender, 7 to 10 minutes.

4. Place 1 fish fillet on each of 6 serving plates. Spoon the carrots and asparagus on both sides of the fillets. Scatter the carrot and leek julienne over the fillets and spoon the reduced cooking liquid over the fillets and vegetables.

6 portions

BEST VEGETABLE PATE

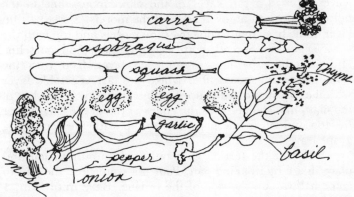

We created this pâté after being very disappointed with the pretty but tasteless vegetable terrines we'd sampled. We think the lemon zest in this recipe makes it the best and freshest vegetable pâté we've ever tasted.

1 pound boneless skinless chicken breasts, cut into chunks
Finely grated zest of 1 lemon
Pinch cayenne pepper
Pinch ground nutmeg
Salt and freshly ground black pepper, to taste
2 egg whites
2 cups heavy or whipping cream
½ cup chopped fresh basil
8 ounces thin asparagus spears, ends trimmed
2 carrots, peeled and cut into thin julienne
2 small yellow summer squash, cut lengthwise into quarters
2 sweet red peppers
½ ounce dried morels
12 to 14 grape leaves (packed in water), rinsed and patted dry
Tomato Vinaigrette (recipe follows)

1. One day before serving, place the chicken breasts, lemon zest, cayenne, nutmeg, and salt and pepper to taste in a food processor fitted with a steel blade; process to a purée. Add the egg whites and process 10 seconds. Remove to a bowl and place in a larger bowl of crushed ice. Chill, stirring occasionally, for 1 hour. Remove from the ice and stir in the cream, 1 tablespoon at a time. Process a third of the mousseline and all of the basil in the food processor until blended. Refrigerate both mousselines separately.

2. Blanch the asparagus, carrots, and summer squash separately in boiling water until tender but still crisp. Drain and refresh under cold running water. Pat dry and refrigerate covered until cold.

3. Preheat the broiler.

4. Roast the red peppers under the broiler until the skins are blistered and black all over. Let stand in a covered bowl for 10 minutes. Remove the blackened skins, the cores, and seeds from the peppers; cut into thin strips.

5. Soak the morels in hot water to cover for 30 minutes. Drain, pat dry, and cut lengthwise in half.

6. Preheat oven to 300°F.

7. To assemble the pâté, line the bottom and sides of an oiled 12 x 4-inch terrine with a single layer of the grape leaves. Spread a thin layer of the plain mousseline in the bottom. Top with an even layer of the morels. Spread a thin layer of the basil mousseline over the morels and top with the summer squash. Spread another layer of the plain mousseline and add the asparagus in an even layer. Top with the remaining basil mousseline. Make the last vegetable layer with the carrot and red pepper strips. Spread with the last of the plain mousseline. Fold the edges of the grape leaves over the top and fill in the gaps on the top with the remaining grape leaves.

8. Cover the terrine with buttered aluminum foil and place in a larger baking pan. Pour hot water into the pan to come halfway up the side of the terrine. Bake until firm, 1 hour to 1 hour 15 minutes. Cool to room temperature and refrigerate overnight.

9. Just before serving, make the tomato vinaigrette.

10. Cut the pâté into thin slices and serve cold on a pool of vinaigrette.

12 to 15 appetizer portions

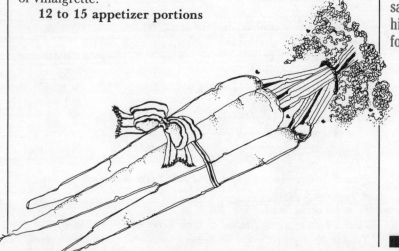

''What was paradise, but a garden full of vegetables and herbs and pleasure? Nothing there but delights.''
—William Lawson

Of the world's many traditions for welcoming spring, one of our favorites is Setsubun, the Japanese Bean-Throwing Festival. On February 3, each family member throws roasted soy beans inside and outside the house while chanting *Fuku-wa-uchi-ohi-wa-soto*. It is said to cleanse away the evil spirit of winter and invite spring in. Then one eats the same number of beans as his age to ensure good fortune for the next year.

TOMATO VINAIGRETTE

¾ cup best-quality olive oil
¼ cup red wine vinegar
Salt and freshly ground black pepper, to taste
1 ripe medium-size tomato, peeled, seeded, and puréed
1 tablespoon tomato paste
3 tablespoons heavy or whipping cream

Whisk the oil, vinegar, and salt and pepper to taste together in a small bowl. Add the tomato and tomato paste and mix well. Whisk in the cream and taste and adjust seasonings.
1½ cups

VEAL STEW WITH ARUGULA AND ASPARAGUS

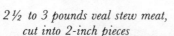

The rich, deep flavor of wild mushrooms balances beautifully with the gentle flavors of veal and asparagus. The green arugula adds just the right peppery flavor and green color to make this dish take on the colors of a spring forest.

2½ to 3 pounds veal stew meat,
    cut into 2-inch pieces
½ cup plus 2 tablespoons unbleached all-purpose flour
Salt and freshly ground black pepper, to taste
8 tablespoons (1 stick) unsalted butter, room temperature
3½ cups Berta's Chicken Stock (page 396)
1 cup dry white wine
3 or 4 veal bones
1 onion, quartered
2 carrots, broken in half
3 cloves garlic, quartered
Bouquet garni (2 bay leaves, 3 parsley sprigs, and 2 sprigs fresh
    thyme tied in cheesecloth)
1 pound white pearl onions
4 cups arugula leaves (2 bunches), cut into ¼-inch strips
½ cup heavy or whipping cream
Fresh thyme, to taste
8 ounces fresh wild mushrooms, well rinsed, patted dry, sliced
2 pounds asparagus, ends trimmed, cut diagonally into 1-inch pieces

ACADEMY AWARDS BUFFET

Fiddlehead Soup

---

*Veal Stew with Arugula and
Asparagus*

*Endive and watercress salad
with walnut vinaigrette and
fresh domestic chèvre*

---

*Ginger Soufflé with
Rhubarb Ginger Sauce*

---

*California Chardonnay or
Chablis*

On Academy Awards night, invite your guests to dress as their favorite movie star, and spend the cocktail hour guessing who all the stars are and which film roles the costumes represent. Whoever correctly guesses the most wins an "Oscar."
   To continue the excitement as the evening unfolds, have everyone cast their own votes for winners in the most important categories—and in some of the trickier ones. The star of the evening is the guest who correctly guesses the most award-winners. This will keep your party in suspense until the wee hours, as the results come in.

1. Toss the veal with ½ cup flour seasoned with salt and pepper to taste. Melt 4 tablespoons of the butter in a Dutch oven over medium-high heat. Brown the veal, a few pieces at a time, in the butter.

2. Pour the stock and wine over the veal. Add the bones, onion, carrots, garlic, and bouquet garni. Heat to boiling. Reduce heat and simmer covered until the meat is tender, about 1½ hours.

3. While the meat is simmering, cut a small X in the root of each pearl onion. Heat a pan of salted water to boiling, drop in the onions, and boil until tender, 10 to 15 minutes. Drain and plunge into cold water. When cool enough to handle, slip off the skins.

4. Remove the veal from the Dutch oven and combine with the onions. Strain the cooking liquid and return to the pan. Cook until reduced by half.

5. Make a *beurre manié* by mixing 2 tablespoons of the remaining butter and the 2 tablespoons flour in a small bowl until smooth. Stir in a few tablespoons of the reduced cooking liquid and then stir into the remaining liquid in the Dutch oven. Cook, stirring constantly, several minutes.

6. Stir in the arugula and cook gently for 5 minutes. Stir in the cream and season to taste with salt, pepper, and thyme. Return the veal and onions to the sauce.

7. Sauté the mushrooms in the remaining 2 tablespoons butter and add to the veal. Heat until warmed through.*

8. At the same time, cook the asparagus until tender but still crisp. Stir into the stew and serve immediately.

6 to 8 portions

*The stew can be prepared up to 1 day in advance. Refrigerate covered and add the asparagus just before serving.

SAUTEED SPRING MORELS

We think that spring morels are such a precious treat that we prepare them very simply in order not to detract from their wonderful earthy essence. If you are lucky enough to have a source for morels, indulge a few special friends with this appetizer on a blustery May day.

8 cups water
4 tablespoons fresh lemon juice
1 pound fresh morels
2 tablespoons unsalted butter
2 cloves garlic, finely minced
Salt and freshly ground black pepper, to taste
2 tablespoons chopped fresh Italian parsley

1. Pour the water into a large glass bowl and stir in half the lemon juice. Add the morels and soak for 30 minutes to remove all the dirt. Drain thoroughly and pat dry on paper towels.

BLUE SKY BRUNCH

Transform spring Sunday into a special occasion with a spring bird-watching brunch by a large sunny window. Celebrate the fruit tree blossoms by setting a table all in pink and white linen. Put your butter and jams in a variety of little ceramic pots. Make grapefruit mimosas with pink grapefruit juice and Champagne, and have field glasses and guides handy for bird watching.

WHERE TO FIND MORELS

Pick a sunny day just after a May rainstorm and look near:
- ♥ ash trees
- ♥ old stone walls
- ♥ shady orchards
- ♥ moist and grassy meadowlands

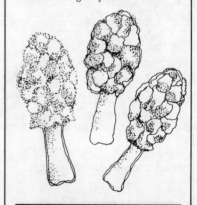

2. Heat the butter in a heavy large skillet over medium heat. Add the garlic and morels and quickly sauté just until the mushrooms are wilted. Remove from heat.

3. Sprinkle with salt and pepper to taste, the remaining 2 tablespoons lemon juice, and the parsley. Spoon in a neat little mound onto each of 4 small serving plates.

4 appetizer portions

FIDDLEHEAD SOUP

Once a year, in early spring, the fiddleheads come out. This soup is subtle, pale green, and delicious. Garnish with a few more fiddlehead ferns.

4 tablespoons (½ stick) unsalted butter
1 large yellow onion, chopped
5 cups Berta's Chicken Stock (page 396)
1 cup dry white wine
1 pound cleaned fiddleheads*
1 cup half-and-half
1 cup heavy or whipping cream
½ teaspoon ground nutmeg
3 tablespoons fresh lemon juice
Salt and freshly ground
*   black pepper, to taste*
Several lightly steamed
*   fiddleheads (garnish)*

1. Melt the butter in a large stock pot over low heat. Add the onion and sauté until soft and transparent, 15 to 20 minutes.

2. Pour in the stock and wine. Add the cleaned fiddleheads and simmer uncovered over medium heat for 45 minutes.

3. Let the soup cool slightly and then stir in the half-and-half, cream, nutmeg, and lemon juice.

4. Purée the soup in batches in a blender or food processor fitted with a steel blade until smooth. Season to taste with salt and pepper.

5. Gently heat the soup until hot and garnish with the lightly steamed fiddleheads.

6 to 8 portions

*available in specialty food shops

UP, UP, AND AWAY BRUNCH

Grapefruit Mimosas

Grapefruit halves with Lemon Sorbet

Shad Roe with Bacon

Asparagus with Orange-Pistachio Butter

Rhubarb Crisp

Sparkling Vouvray or Schramsberg Blanc de Noirs

Freshly brewed coffee

FIDDLEHEADS

Fiddleheads are the coiled tips of young fern fronds that have a wonderful, delicate flavor often described as a cross between asparagus and woodsy mushrooms. Three types of fiddleheads are gathered in the early spring: from the ostrich, cinnamon, and common bracken fern plants. As many other ferns are poisonous, we advise caution if you are tempted to gather your own from the woods. If you are not sure of your botany, it is best to purchase your fiddleheads from a specialty produce dealer.

For a great seasonal treat, try lightly steamed fiddleheads topped with bacon and melted Cheddar on a toasted English muffin.

SHAD ROE SAUTEED WITH BACON

Delicate shad roe is best simply prepared. A hint of smoky bacon and a squeeze of fresh lemon juice highlights this unique treat.

3 pairs shad roe
12 slices bacon, cooked crisp, fat reserved
Juice of 1 lemon
½ cup chopped fresh parsley
Salt and freshly ground black pepper, to taste
6 lemon wedges

1. Dip the roe in a bowl of cold water to rinse it and gently pat dry with paper towels. Carefully cut away the membrane that connects each pair, separating it into 2 lobes.

2. Heat the bacon fat in a skillet over low heat. Add the shad roe, cover the pan, and cook slowly, turning the roe every few minutes, until golden brown on the outside and a clamshell gray throughout the inside. It is important to cook the roe slowly to avoid breaking the fragile eggs.

3. Remove the roe to a serving platter and sprinkle with the lemon juice, parsley, and salt and pepper to taste. Top with the bacon slices. Serve immediately with lemon wedges.

6 portions

DUCK AND DANDELION GREEN SALAD

How we love dandelion greens—especially served with roasted duck breast and garnished with duck cracklings and radicchio.

6 duck breasts (3 whole breasts), boned
6 cups fresh tender dandelion leaves
1 small head radicchio
¼ cup fresh orange juice
3 tablespoons white wine vinegar
Finely grated zest of 1 orange
Salt and freshly ground black pepper, to taste

SHAD

American shad is a member of the herring family, and its Latin name, *sapidissima,* translates as "most delicious." Judging by the anticipation along the East Coast for the beginning of shad season, the name is well deserved.

Unfortunately, shad is no longer the plentiful fish it once was. Most market shad now comes from the Chesapeake Bay or Connecticut River. When the ocean water temperature begins to rise in the spring, the shad move into the rivers and start to swim upstream. The amount of time spent in fresh water after a long hard winter on a monotonous diet determines the flavor quality of the fish.

In the nineteenth century great disputes took place among chefs over which waters produced the best shad. Apparently the rivalry had a basis, as shad tends to be much more sensitive to pollution and water quality than other fish.

Female shad has always been considered the most desirable for its plump fillets and delicate roe. We like our shad and shad roe simply sautéed and served with the first asparagus of the season—truly a regional culinary triumph and a breath of spring air.

DANDELION GREENS

Dandelion greens are prized throughout Europe and are often grown commercially. The name comes from the French *dent de lion,* which means "lion's tooth," referring to the jagged-edged leaves. Slightly bitter, the leaves are used either raw in salads or cooked as a green. The youngest leaves are the sweetest and most tender. We love them, and encourage you to try them. Our guess is that after one taste you'll be less likely to curse those fluffy yellow pompoms all over your lawn.

1. Preheat oven to 350°F.

2. Place the duck breasts in a roasting pan and roast until the meat is medium-rare, 20 to 25 minutes. Let stand until they are cool enough to handle. Don't turn off the oven.

3. Meanwhile, measure ¾ cup of the duck fat from the roasting pan and pour it into a small saucepan.

4. Remove the skin from the duck meat and roast the skin in the roasting pan until very crisp, about 30 minutes.

5. While the duck skin is crisping, arrange the dandelion leaves in a circle on each of 6 salad plates. Garnish the edges with a few torn radicchio leaves.

6. Thinly slice the duck breasts at an angle. Arrange 1 sliced breast in a circle on the dandelion leaves on each plate.

7. Melt the duck fat in a small saucepan over medium heat. Stir in the orange juice, vinegar, and orange zest. Season to taste with salt and pepper.

8. Remove the crisp duck skin cracklings from the oven, cut into ¼-inch dice, and sprinkle over each salad.

9. Pour the warm vinaigrette over each salad and serve immediately.

6 portions

RHUBARB CRISP

A sweet and tart dessert of bright pink rhubarb with a delicious crumb topping. Serve with vanilla ice cream or lots of whipped cream.

8 cups diced rhubarb
1 cup granulated sugar
1 tablespoon grated orange zest
2 tablespoons cornstarch
⅓ cup Cointreau
¾ cup (1½ sticks) unsalted margarine, cold, cut into small pieces
2 cups unbleached all-purpose flour
1 cup old-fashioned rolled oats
¾ cup packed brown sugar
1 tablespoon ground cinnamon
¾ cup slivered almonds
Pinch salt
1 egg

1. Toss the rhubarb with the granulated sugar and orange zest in a 3-quart baking dish. Dissolve the cornstarch in the Cointreau, add to the rhubarb, and toss to coat.

2. Preheat oven to 350°F.

3. Place the margarine, flour, oats, brown sugar, and cinnamon in a mixing bowl. Mix together with your hands until crumbly. Stir in the almonds and salt and beat in the egg to bind the mixture loosely. Spread the topping evenly over the rhubarb.

4. Bake until the top is golden and the rhubarb is bubbling, 50 minutes. Serve warm.

6 portions

"The hostess must be like the duck—calm and unruffled on the surface, and paddling like hell underneath."
—Anonymous

FREEZING RHUBARB

Why not savor a touch of spring all year round? Rhubarb is easy to freeze as it requires no special preparation and keeps indefinitely. All you have to do is select stalks at their freshest, chop into ½-inch dice, place in airtight freezer bags, and freeze. You can drop the pieces still frozen into muffin and pancake batter or stew them with sugar and a little orange juice.

GINGER SOUFFLE WITH RHUBARB-GINGER SAUCE

A delicious and unusual soufflé further intensified by the pretty pink rhubarb-ginger sauce.

Rhubarb-Ginger Sauce (recipe follows)
6 tablespoons (3/4 stick) unsalted butter
6 tablespoons unbleached all-purpose flour
1 cup milk
½ cup heavy or whipping cream
5 egg yolks
½ cup sugar
½ cup finely chopped crystallized ginger
1 tablespoon orange-flower water
7 egg whites, room temperature
Pinch cream of tartar

1. Make the rhubarb sauce.

2. Melt the butter in a heavy small saucepan over medium heat until foamy. Stir in the flour and cook 1 minute. Gradually stir in the milk and cream. Cook, stirring constantly, until thick and smooth.

3. Remove from heat. Add the egg yolks, one at a time, whisking well after each addition. Stir in the sugar, then the ginger and orange-flower water.

4. Preheat oven to 450°F. Butter a 6-cup soufflé dish and coat with granulated sugar.

5. Beat the egg whites with the cream of tartar until stiff but not dry. Gently fold into the soufflé base. Pour the batter into the prepared dish.

6. Bake until puffed and golden, about 30 minutes. Serve immediately with rhubarb sauce spooned around each serving.

6 portions

SPRING FRUIT DESSERTS

The sun is setting on rich cakes for dessert. Those sumptuous layered confections have for the most part been relegated to birthday parties, festive holidays, and trips to Austria.

Fruit in all its guises is always a welcome way to finish a meal. Perfect ripe apricots, peaches, plums, and cherries, fresh or in a glazed tart, are the perfect combination—sweet and light.

♥ Sliced oranges with candied orange peel, sprinkled with fresh mint, drizzled with crème de cassis, and decorated with candied violets

♥ Grapefruit sections tossed with fresh orange juice and a bit of maple sugar, placed under the broiler for just a moment

♥ Raspberries and strawberries tossed with rosewater and framboise, and decorated with sprigs of fresh violets

♥ Honeydew, cantaloupe, and cucumber balls sprinkled with fresh lemon juice and chopped mint leaves

♥ Mango and pineapple chunks with chartreuse, lemon and lime zest, and garnished with yellow crocuses

♥ Bananas baked with thyme, honey, and a dash of Grand Marnier—served hot sprinkled with confectioners' sugar

♥ Pears poached in Sauternes and black pepper, topped with bittersweet fudge sauce and crème fraîche

♥ Dates, figs, lemons, and oranges in a fruity red wine flavored with lemon and orange zest, topped with a dollop of crème fraîche

♥ Fresh figs and a dollop of crème fraîche, sprinkled with walnuts and crystallized ginger

♥ Bananas, cherries, and fresh pineapple chunks, with fresh orange juice and topped with orange zest

RHUBARB-GINGER SAUCE

3 cups chopped rhubarb
⅓ cup sugar
⅓ cup orange liqueur
⅓ cup (or as needed) water
2 tablespoons finely chopped crystallized ginger

1. Combine the rhubarb, sugar, orange liqueur, and ⅓ cup water in a heavy large saucepan. Heat to boiling. Reduce heat and simmer uncovered, stirring occasionally, until as thick as applesauce, about 30 minutes.

2. Stir in the ginger and simmer another 15 minutes, adding more water if the sauce is too thick. Remove from heat and let cool to room temperature.

About 1½ to 2 cups

RHUBARB AND AMARETTI STRUDEL

Fresh spring rhubarb, brown sugar, orange zest, and walnuts combine with the unique flavor of Italian amaretti cookies to make this strudel a winner. Packaged phyllo dough takes the mystery and intensive labor out of strudel making.

1 pound fresh rhubarb stalks
9 sheets phyllo dough (about ½ package), thawed if frozen
1 cup (2 sticks) unsalted butter, melted
1 cup crushed amaretti
½ cup packed brown sugar
2 teaspoons ground cinnamon
Grated zest of 1 orange
½ cup chopped walnuts
Whipped cream or vanilla ice cream

1. Cut the rhubarb into ½-inch pieces. Blanch the pieces in boiling water for 1½ minutes. Drain and pat dry.

2. Place 1 sheet of the phyllo on a baking sheet the same size as the phyllo dough. Brush with the butter and sprinkle with a few tablespoons of the amaretti crumbs. Keep the remaining dough covered with a damp kitchen towel to prevent it from drying out. Layer 4 more sheets of phyllo on top of the first in the same manner, brushing each with butter and sprinkling with crumbs. Then layer 2 more sheets, brushing with butter but omitting the amaretti.

3. Preheat oven to 375°F.

4. Make a compact row of the rhubarb pieces 2 inches from one long edge of the dough. Sprinkle the rhubarb with the brown sugar, cinnamon, orange zest, walnuts, and any remaining amaretti crumbs.

5. Layer 2 more sheets of phyllo dough, brushing with

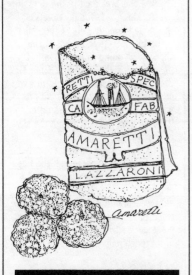

butter, over the rhubarb and last sheet of phyllo. Starting at the edge with the rhubarb, roll up the dough like a jelly roll. Turn seam side up and brush the top and sides of the dough with butter. Turn seam side down, fold both ends under to seal, and brush the top with butter.

6. Bake until golden brown, 40 to 50 minutes. Let stand several minutes, and then slice. Serve with whipped cream. The strudel can also be served cold or at room temperature.

8 portions

RHUBARB SORBET

A light pink, intensely flavored sorbet.

3 cups sliced fresh rhubarb
1 cup plus 2 tablespoons sugar
1½ cups water
3 tablespoons Cointreau
2 tablespoons framboise or cassis liqueur
1 tablespoon fresh lemon juice
3 tablespoons heavy or whipping cream

1. Place the rhubarb in a medium-size saucepan. Sprinkle with the sugar, and add ½ cup of the water, the Cointreau, and framboise. Simmer until the rhubarb is tender and almost puréed, 15 to 20 minutes.

2. Process the fruit with its syrup, the lemon juice, and cream in a food processor fitted with a steel blade until smooth. Taste for sweetness and adjust with more lemon juice or sugar if necessary. Remove from the food processor and stir in the remaining 1 cup water.

3. Freeze in an ice cream maker, following manufacturer's instructions.

1 quart

SPRING CRAVINGS

The sun on our faces on the first day of spring . . . the first red tulip . . . fresh woodsy morels . . . seeing the first crocus . . . hearing a flute outside the window . . . playing marbles . . . fresh ricotta cheese sprinkled with sugar . . . too much chervil in the garden . . . garnishing everything with cherry blossoms . . . wearing sandals for the first time . . . hickory-smoked scallops . . . sitting under a tree reading Wordsworth . . . fresh salmon . . . being awakened by a long-lost love . . . April in Paris . . . soft-shell crabs amandine . . . Italy . . .

. . . Bed and breakfast in the Berkshires . . . freckles . . . daffodils, violets, magnolia blossoms, lily of the valley, ginko trees . . . sweetbreads . . . lady slippers . . . being in love . . . a full moon . . . mischief on April Fool's Day . . . smoked salmon . . . flying to a different city for dinner . . . wit . . . watching a wedding procession in an Italian village . . . dusk when the sky is blue and the trees black . . . a roasted free-range chicken . . . driving down Fifth Avenue when all the flags are out . . . a preview screening of a hot new movie . . . fresh chives . . . only wearing pink . . . radishes . . . the smell of freshly mown grass . . . new potatoes . . . drinking Champagne out of a French jelly jar . . . fresh sorrel . . .

ON THE GRAPEVINE

The uncorking of a bottle of wine—whether a simple table wine or an elegant French Bordeaux—immediately introduces new flavors and a new feeling into a meal. But many of us feel intimidated when making a selection — and with the current wine boom it is little wonder, since even trained connoisseurs can hardly keep track of the dozens of new releases that arrive on the racks every month.

There needn't be any confusion, pretense, or snobbery surrounding a purchase. The ultimate test is always that you personally like the wine and that you feel comfortable serving it. We would like to equip you with the sort of knowledge that will enable you to purchase a decent bottle to share with friends or to splurge on a great vintage for a special evening with a lover. We want to help you untangle the current maze of vines and wines, rid it of its academic trappings, and restore it to its most simple and basic level of sensory enjoyment.

While there are many elements that go into the making of wine—climate, know-how, blending, the integrity of the winemaker, tradition—no factor is more important than the grape itself. In wine language, the type of grape is referred to as the "varietal." Names, labels, and methods may change, but knowing the characteristics of the grapes that produce wines provides a solid point of reference for further exploration. Our varietal description on the following pages is designed to polish your wine memory and knowledge.

WHITE VARIETALS

CHARDONNAY: A varietal with aromas of melons, figs, apples, and overtones of vanilla. The grapes can be vinified in either a rich, luscious style (without sweetness) or a more crisp and tart style. Complexity is often added by aging in small oak barrels.

SAUVIGNON BLANC: The principal white grape of Bordeaux, also grown throughout Pouilly and Sancerre. In California, the leading U.S. producer, it is vinified in styles producing aromas ranging from herbacious to smoky and is labeled Sauvignon Blanc or Fumé Blanc. The Sauvignon of Bordeaux is labeled Graves, Sauternes, or Barsac. In Barsac and Sauternes, the grape is blended with Semillon to produce the world's greatest dessert wines.

SEMILLON: The principal varietal of the great French dessert wines, Sauternes and Barsac. In Bordeaux the varietal is subject to a perverse trick of nature: at the end of a growing season, under the right conditions of humidity and warmth, the grapes are allowed to be attacked by a fungus, "noble rot." The disease causes a concentration of sugar and an intensification of flavor which creates extraordinarily luscious wines.

RIESLING: The great white grape of Germany, a late ripener that produces both dry and sweet wines. Riesling wines are straightforward, clean, and crisp—aromatic but not overpowering.

CHENIN BLANC: The primary grape for white Loire Valley wines such as Vouvray and Saumur. Its quite neutral flavor allows it to be vinified into widely different styles of wine; it can form the basis of dry, semisweet, and sparkling wines. In California, the Napa Valley wineries were the first to popularize Chenin Blanc and these are best drunk while young and fruity.

PINOT BLANC: Derived from the Pinot Noir grapes of Burgundy, though rarely grown there now. It is grown in Italy and California and produces wines that are secondary in quality to Chardonnays. The less defined character makes it a good grape for sparkling wines.

GEWURZTRAMINER: Originally a native of Germany, its popularity has spread to neighboring Alsace and abroad to the U.S. Alsatian Gewürztraminers are dry, with a musty, spicy flavor that stands up to hearty Alsatian foods. The majority of California producers bottle a Gewürztraminer that is sweeter than the French counterpart.

RED VARIETALS

PINOT NOIR: The grape responsible for French Champagne and France's velvet, noble, red Burgundies. Never blended in France, except in the making of Champagne, in California it is sometimes blended with Petite Syrah or Gamay grapes to produce lighter wines; otherwise California Pinot Noirs are dark and robust, with none of the elegance of their French counterparts.

CABERNET SAUVIGNON: The great grape of Bordeaux. Tiny and black, it has a distinctive flavor even when blended with other varietals. The wines have complex aromas ranging from fruity violets to harsher cedar. French wines blended from Cabernet grapes include Médoc, Graves, and St. Emilion. California vineyards make Cabernet Sauvignons in many different styles, using different aging and blending techniques.

GAMAY: The grape responsible for the fruity, light taste of Beaujolais. It is grown in both France and California, although California wines labeled Gamay or Gamay Beaujolais often refer to the wine-making technique and not the particular grape.

MERLOT: Widely grown in France, Italy, and California. The French use it as a blending grape in Bordeaux, the Italians produce both D.O.C. and table wines from it, while the Californians blend it with small amounts of Cabernet to produce a soft, mellow wine.

SYRAH: A small grape grown for over 1,000 years in the Rhône Valley where it is used mainly to enrich wines such as Hermitage—wines that are richly colored, high in alcohol, with a smoky aroma.

ZINFANDEL: This grape arrived in California in 1851 from an unknown origin in Europe and is now a California exclusive. The grapes make a heavy, dark, fruity wine with a strong bouquet, but are also very versatile in vinifying lighter white Zinfandels and Zinfandel Nouveau.

CABERNET FRANC: A slightly lesser cousin to Cabernet Sauvignon, grown in Bordeaux and the Loire, where it forms the base of Bourgueil, Chinon, and Saumur—gentle, clean red wines with floral bouquets.

NEBBIOLO: The most noble grape of Italy's Piedmont region and the base of Barolo, Barbaresco, and Grattinara. It is named after the fog (*nebbia*) which covers the vineyards of the Piedmont during the September harvest.

RAINY DAYS AND SUNDAYS

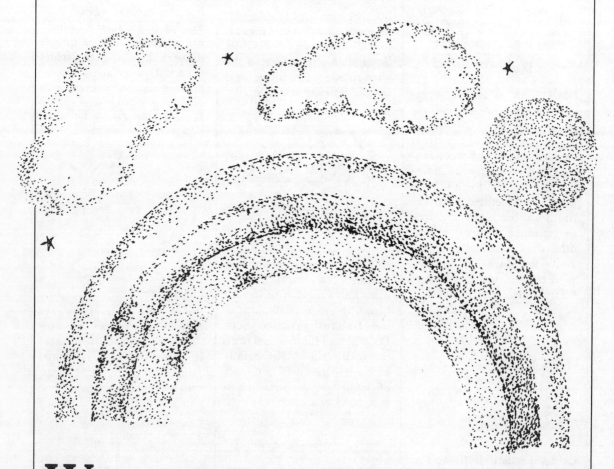

We all know that spring has more than its fair share of rainy days—and all too often they fall on the Sunday we had hoped to plant the garden, walk in the park, or go canoeing on the pond. No need for despair, however, as even the gloomiest of days can be made bright by a spontaneous and casual dinner with close friends. Many people like to reserve Sundays for spending time at home, but rain can bring on cabin fever and we think that some of the most successful and relaxed entertaining happens on Sunday evenings. Cheer up a friend or neighbor with an invitation for a supper of simple homey fare. Steaming bowls of soothing soup, toasty sandwiches, and plump roast chickens are all wonderful antidotes to the onset of Monday blues.

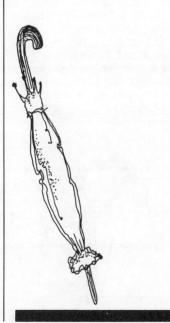

MINESTRONE WITH SWEET SAUSAGE AND TORTELLINI

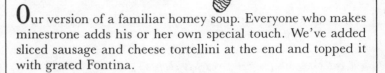

Our version of a familiar homey soup. Everyone who makes minestrone adds his or her own special touch. We've added sliced sausage and cheese tortellini at the end and topped it with grated Fontina.

⅓ cup best-quality olive oil
1 large yellow onion, cut into thin rings
4 large carrots, peeled and thickly sliced
1 fennel bulb, chopped
2 large potatoes, peeled and diced
1 green bell pepper, cored, seeded, and cut into ½-inch squares
3 medium-size zucchini, diced
1½ cups diagonally sliced green beans
1 medium-size green cabbage, shredded
5 cups Beef Stock (page 397)
5 cups water
1 can (35 ounces) Italian plum tomatoes
2 tablespoons dried oregano
1 tablespoon dried basil
Salt and freshly ground black pepper, to taste
Outer rind of a 2-inch chunk of Parmesan or Romano cheese
1½ cups canned cannellini (white kidney) beans, drained
1 pound cheese-stuffed tortellini
1½ pounds sweet Italian sausage, pan fried, drained, and sliced
Freshly grated Fontina cheese

1. Heat the oil in a large stock pot over medium heat. Add the onion and sauté for 10 to 15 minutes.

2. Stir in the carrots and sauté 2 to 3 minutes, tossing occasionally.

3. Add the fennel, potatoes, green pepper, zucchini, and green beans, sautéing each vegetable 2 to 3 minutes before adding the next. When all the vegetables have been added to the pot, stir in the cabbage and cook 5 minutes more.

4. Add the stock, water, tomatoes with their juices, oregano, basil, and salt and pepper to taste. Bury the Parmesan rind in the middle of the soup. Heat to boiling. Reduce heat and simmer covered over low heat for 2½ to 3 hours. The soup will be very thick.

5. Fifteen minutes before serving, stir in the cannellini beans and tortellini. Raise the heat to cook the tortellini, but stir the soup occasionally to keep it from sticking to the bottom of the pot. Just before serving, stir in the sausage.

6. Ladle the minestrone into shallow pasta bowls and garnish lavishly with Fontina.

10 to 12 portions

CHICKEN AND SAFFRON SOUP

An elegant soup for entertaining, with Italian overtones of Marsala and pine nuts. The saffron adds a beautiful golden glow.

1½ whole chicken breasts (3 halves), poached, skinned, boned, and
*   cut into fine julienne*
6 cups Berta's Chicken Stock (page 396)
¼ cup pine nuts (pignoli), coarsely chopped
½ cup Marsala
1 teaspoon saffron threads
3 egg yolks
¾ cup heavy or whipping cream
Salt, to taste

1. Combine the chicken, stock, and pine nuts in a medium-size saucepan. Heat to boiling. Reduce heat and simmer 5 minutes.

2. Add the Marsala and saffron. Simmer 2 more minutes. Remove from heat.

3. Whisk the egg yolks and cream together. Slowly pour the egg yolk mixture into the hot soup, whisking constantly. Season to taste with salt. Serve immediately.

6 portions

CARROT AND GINGER SOUP

The bright orange color and bright flavor distinguish this carrot soup from the ordinary. It is excellent hot or cold.

6 tablespoons (¾ stick) unsalted butter
1 large yellow onion, chopped
¼ cup finely chopped fresh ginger root
3 cloves garlic, minced
7 cups Berta's Chicken Stock (page 396)
1 cup dry white wine
1½ pounds carrots, peeled and cut into ½-inch pieces
2 tablespoons fresh lemon juice
Pinch curry powder
Salt and freshly ground black pepper, to taste
Snipped fresh chives or chopped fresh parsley (garnish)

SAFFRON

There is probably nothing in the kitchen so steeped in mystery as saffron.

Saffron is simply the dried stigma of the saffron crocus, which has been cultivated in the Old World since prehistoric times. The reason for the mystery is the expense. It takes almost 70,000 flowers to produce 1 pound of the spice—twelve days of backbreaking work for an experienced picker. By the time it reaches a retail shop in the U.S., saffron costs close to $5,000 a pound!

Saffron appears as a tangle of deep orange-red strands. It is best to obtain whole, or hay, saffron—now generally available in supermarkets. Try to avoid buying strands with pale ends; the fewer of these the better.

In Spain, one of the countries where saffron is grown, the men pick the flower in the fields and bring them home in baskets. Women and children—those with the nimblest fingers—split the crocus down the stem and pinch off the three stigmas where they join at the base. As the fresh saffron accumulates it is turned out into a fine-mesh sieve and dried over a gentle charcoal fire. After about half an hour it is reduced to a fifth of its fresh weight. It should be just dry enough to keep properly yet not so dry that it loses its flavor.

To add to the problems of making saffron, the bulbs must be dug up, sorted, and transplanted every three years. It isn't difficult to see why this ancient spice remains elusive and dear, but it should not be shrouded in mystery. It is too good. And after all, it takes only a pinch to make a dish special.

TOGA PARTY

We can think of no better cure for March blues than staging a toga party that re-creates the lavishness—bordering on decadence—of the Roman Empire. Togas are a quick costume theme, easily made from draped white sheets and a few deftly placed safety pins. Invite Caesar in the form of a salad or our wonderful lettuce purée. Your guests certainly need not beware of the Ides of March—only of having too good a time!

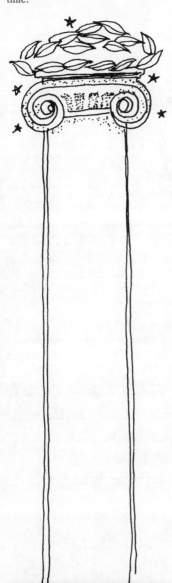

1. Melt the butter in a large stock pot over medium heat. Add the onion, ginger, and garlic and sauté for 15 to 20 minutes.

2. Add the stock, wine, and carrots. Heat to boiling. Reduce heat and simmer uncovered over medium heat until the carrots are very tender, about 45 minutes.

3. Purée the soup in a blender or food processor fitted with a steel blade. Season with lemon juice, curry powder, and salt and pepper to taste. Sprinkle with the chives or parsley. Serve the soup hot or chilled.

6 portions

IDES OF MARCH SANDWICH

Lettuce, Parmesan cheese, anchovies, garlic, lemon juice, and romaine lettuce have become famous in the form of a Caesar salad. We've puréed the ingredients and serve the resulting spread hot, as a vegetable or over French bread.

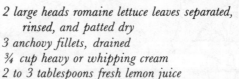

2 large heads romaine lettuce leaves separated, rinsed, and patted dry
3 anchovy fillets, drained
¾ cup heavy or whipping cream
2 to 3 tablespoons fresh lemon juice
Salt and freshly ground black pepper, to taste
5 tablespoons unsalted butter
½ cup Garlic Croutons (page 400), for vegetable variation
½ cup freshly grated Parmesan cheese

1. Cut away the thick central core of each romaine leaf in a deep V.

2. Heat a large stock pot of lightly salted water to boiling. Add the lettuce leaves, reduce heat, and simmer for 8 to 10 minutes.

3. Drain and cool the lettuce under cold water. Squeeze the lettuce, a handful at a time, to remove as much water as possible from the leaves.

4. Purée the lettuce and anchovies in a food processor fitted with a steel blade.

5. Add the cream, 2 tablespoons lemon juice, and salt and pepper to taste. Process until blended. Taste and adjust the lemon juice, salt, and pepper if necessary.

6. Melt the butter in a medium-size saucepan. Add the lettuce purée and simmer over low heat until heated through.

7. Place about ½ cup of the purée on each serving plate and sprinkle with croutons and cheese or make into a sandwich over split, toasted French bread.

6 portions

PARSLIED ROAST CHICKEN

Roasted or grilled, this simple chicken preparation is sure to become a favorite.

1 roasting chicken (3 to 4 pounds), ready to cook
4 cloves garlic, peeled
Salt and freshly ground black pepper, to taste
4 tablespoons (½ stick) unsalted butter
3 large bunches fresh Italian parsley, stems trimmed
½ cup rich Berta's Chicken Stock (page 396; see Note)
¼ cup fresh lemon juice

1. Preheat oven to 375°F. Prepare coals for grilling if desired.
2. Rub the cavity of the chicken with 1 garlic clove and sprinkle with salt and pepper. Rub 2 tablespoons of the butter inside the cavity and stuff the cavity with the remaining garlic and the parsley, reserving a bit for garnish.
3. Rub the skin of the chicken with the remaining butter and sprinkle with salt and pepper.
4. If you are using the oven, place the chicken, breast side up, in a roasting pan and pour the stock and lemon juice over. Bake for 20 minutes per pound, basting frequently and turning the bird twice. The chicken is done when the juices run clear when a thigh is pierced with a sharp skewer.
5. If you are going to grill the chicken, bake for 10 minutes per pound in the oven, turning the bird twice. Then, place the chicken on the grill, basting it with pan

"After a good dinner, one can forgive anybody, even one's own relations."
—Oscar Wilde

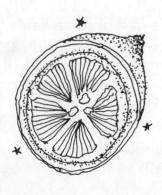

juices and turning it frequently. It should be done in about 30 minutes.

6. Carve the chicken and arrange on a large serving platter. Garnish with the remaining parsley and serve with seasonal vegetables.

2 to 4 portions

Note: For ½ cup rich stock, reduce 1 cup Berta's Chicken Stock over high heat.

BOBBIE'S CHICKEN

From one of our dearest friends, a chicken dish that brings back childhood memories. Julee and Bert would love to be served this every night, if only Bobbie would stop sculpting and keep basting. That is the magic . . . lots and lots of basting. It's terrific with warmed applesauce or chutney, rice, egg noodles or baked potatoes, and a simple green salad. We especially like to follow it with vanilla ice cream and Three-Ginger Cookies.

1 roasting chicken (about 4 ½ pounds), with giblets
1 lemon, cut in half
2 tablespoons dry mustard
2 tablespoons ground ginger
Salt and freshly ground black pepper, to taste
6 medium-size yellow onions, quartered
2 packages George Washington golden bouillon powder or 2 chicken
*   bouillon cubes*
2 ¾ cups water

1. Preheat oven to 425°F.

2. Rinse the chicken and pat dry. Squeeze the juice of the lemon all over the chicken and in the cavity.

3. Rub the chicken all over with the mustard, ginger, and salt and pepper to taste. Place in a roasting pan and scatter 4 of the onions in the pan. Roast undisturbed for 30 minutes.

4. Meanwhile, simmer the giblets, the remaining 2 onions, the bouillon powder, and 2 cups of the water in a small saucepan over medium heat for 25 to 30 minutes. Set aside.

5. Reduce the oven heat to 375°F and pour the remaining ¾ cup water into the pan. Roast the chicken 30 minutes more, basting occasionally with the pan juices.

6. Strain the giblet stock and pour ¾ cup of the stock into the roasting pan. Roast, basting occasionally, for 30 minutes more.

7. Remove the chicken from the oven and cut into serving pieces with a knife and fork (the chicken should be falling off the bone). Mix the chicken with the onions and juices in the pan and pour in the remaining giblet stock. Cover the pan with aluminum foil and bake for 15 minutes. Serve on a large platter surrounded by the juices.

4 portions

EASTER

Easter is the great spring rite of family and tradition. Even more than Christmas, it seems to bring out the child in all of us. After all, who can resist dyeing eggs in hues of robin's egg blue, lavender, rose, and sunny yellow? It is the one time we really feel we can get away with playful centerpieces. So we buy plenty of baskets and fill them with brightly colored cellophane grass, chocolate bunnies, marshmallow chickens, and lots and lots of jelly beans.

Our playfulness is tempered, however, with a bountiful dinner of traditional Easter food. After a day spent nibbling all our favorite candies, we can't wait to carve into a big pink ham or a rare roast leg of lamb. Creamy leek vichyssoise, fruity baked pineapple, tart sorrel flan, and golden Goat-Cheese Popovers round out our menus. A rich cheesecake sends all off to bed with sweet spring dreams.

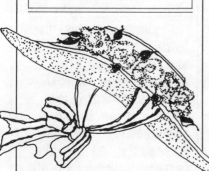

IN THE PINK

Pink peppercorns were once popular trademarks of nouvelle cuisine. Arriving in America via French importers, they became the most cherished little pink berries around. The American food industry, seeing a chance to jump on the bandwagon, began selling similar-looking Florida holly berries as pink peppercorns, and soon after the FDA received many complaints—these "peppercorns" were causing indigestion in humans. So, pink peppercorns, real and look-alikes, were recalled and banned in the U.S.

The whole botanical mess has been sorted out, and we can all enjoy real pink peppercorns once again without fear of bringing about unidentified illnesses. Just to be on the safe side, we recommend buying pink peppercorns imported from France and preferably picked on the Ile de Réunion.

POACHED LEEKS WITH PINK PEPPERCORN MAYONNAISE

A perfect appetizer salad. This dish is the very essence of delicate spring.

18 fat leeks, as unblemished as possible
1 egg
1 egg yolk
2 tablespoons fresh lemon juice
1 tablespoon tomato paste
2 teaspoons Dijon-style mustard
1 tablespoon pink peppercorns, plus additional for garnish*
¾ cup best-quality olive oil
½ cup vegetable oil
Salt, to taste

1. Trim the root end of each leek and cut 2 to 3 inches off the tops. Peel off any blemished outer leaves. Fringe the green top of each leek by making several lengthwise cuts, beginning where the white of the leek starts to turn green.

2. Soak the leeks in cold water and rinse, shaking to remove any sand that might be lodged in the inner leaves.

3. Using kitchen string, tie the leeks securely together from top to bottom in 3 bunches of 6 leeks each.

4. Heat a large pan of salted water to boiling and drop in the leeks. Simmer until tender but still firm, about 10 minutes. Slip a fork under the strings and remove the bundles to a colander to drain. Let cool and then refrigerate until cold.

5. Process the egg, egg yolk, lemon juice, tomato paste, mustard, and 1 tablespoon pink peppercorns in a food processor fitted with a steel blade until blended, about 10 seconds. With the machine running, add the oils in a thin steady stream through the feed tube to make a thick mayonnaise. Season to taste with salt.

6. To serve, arrange 3 leeks on each individual serving plate. Spoon a thick stripe of mayonnaise over the base of the leeks. Sprinkle the mayonnaise with several whole pink peppercorns. Serve with a knife and fork.

6 portions

*available at specialty food shops

VICHYSSOISE

Our version of this classic potato and leek soup is rich with milk and cream and flecked with fresh chives. It's been a favorite with our customers for years.

6 tablespoons (¾ stick) unsalted butter
8 large leeks (white part only), well rinsed, dried, and thinly sliced
1 large yellow onion, sliced
8 medium-size all-purpose potatoes, peeled and thinly sliced
6 cups rich Berta's Chicken Stock (page 396; see Note)
1½ tablespoons fresh lemon juice
3 cups milk
4½ cups heavy or whipping cream
Freshly ground black pepper, to taste
½ cup snipped fresh chives (garnish)

1. One day before serving, melt the butter in a stock pot over medium heat. Add the leeks and onion and sauté slowly until golden, about 15 minutes.

2. Stir in the potatoes, stock, and lemon juice. Boil gently for 45 minutes. Let cool slightly.

3. Process the soup in batches in a blender or food processor fitted with a steel blade to a slightly coarse purée.

4. Return the soup to the pot and stir in the milk and 3 cups of the cream. Season to taste with salt and pepper. Heat just until simmering. Cool and refrigerate covered overnight.

5. The following day, stir in the remaining cream. Refrigerate until ready to serve.

6. Sprinkle with the chives just before serving.

12 portions

Note: For 6 cups rich stock, reduce 8 to 10 cups Berta's Chicken Stock over high heat.

ROAST LEG OF LAMB

Many a great memory has been made with a roast leg of lamb dinner. Ours is roasted very simply with those flavors that have a wonderful affinity with lamb—garlic, rosemary, and lemon.

1 leg of lamb (about 6½ pounds)
3 cloves garlic, slivered
½ cup fresh lemon juice
1½ teaspoons dried rosemary
1½ teaspoons coarsely ground black pepper
Salt, to taste

At Easter time prepare a delightful surprise cheese basket to serve after the main course. Find tiny little chèvre balls, or shape your own small egg shapes using soft Montrachet logs. Roll the cheese in Easter-colored herbs and spices. Choose dry lavender, rich curry powder, crushed pink peppercorns, freeze-dried green peppercorns, crushed pecans, and almonds and paprika. Line a deep basket with purple and white lilacs, leaving the green leaves on, and arrange the cheeses so all the different colors show. Buy satin ribbons in the colors of the herbs and spices and tie mixed colored bows on the basket handle. Serve with slices of a fruity Easter bread.

SPRING LAMB

The enchantments of springtime are many—for poets, lovers, and gourmets. For the latter they include spring lamb, only a few months old, beautifully tender and at the height of its delicate flavor.

Lamb is one of those red meats we crave. Roast leg of lamb, flavored with lots of garlic and fresh rosemary sprigs and cooked only until pink, is one of our favorites. Rosemary is the first choice—but try mint, basil, sage, mustard, or lemon. Happily, lamb is becoming more and more popular with Americans—and you should be shepherded into the fold.

1. Preheat oven to 400°F.

2. Make small slits just large enough for the garlic slivers evenly in the leg of lamb and insert the garlic slivers. Rub all over with the lemon juice and then pat the rosemary and black pepper evenly over the surface. Sprinkle with salt to taste.

3. Place the leg of lamb in a roasting pan and put it in the oven. Immediately reduce heat to 350°F. Roast for 1½ hours for medium-rare. Let stand 10 minutes before carving.

6 to 8 portions

BAKED COUNTRY HAM

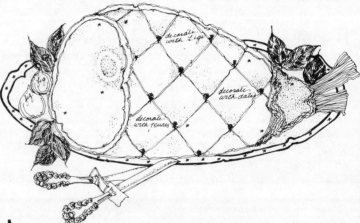

A spectacular presentation of a large country ham decorated with a mosaic of glistening dates, figs, and prunes.

1 precooked smoked ham with bone (about 16 pounds)
25 to 30 whole cloves
¼ cup Dijon-style mustard
1 cup (packed) dark brown sugar
2 cups apple juice
2 cups tawny port
2 cups pitted whole dates
2 cups dried figs
2 cups dried prunes
3 bunches watercress, rinsed, patted dry, stems trimmed

1. Preheat oven to 350°F.

2. Peel the skin from the ham and trim the fat to a ¼-inch layer. Using a sharp knife, score the fat in a diamond pattern.

3. Line a large shallow baking pan with aluminum foil and place the ham in the pan. Insert a whole clove in each intersection of the diamonds and pat the mustard evenly over the top and sides of the ham. Sprinkle the sugar over the top and pour the apple juice into the pan. Bake for 1½ hours,

A large fruit-studded ham always makes a spectacular presentation on a buffet table. We usually keep a backup ham in the kitchen. Thinly slice half of the display ham (always with the bone in) and lay the slices attractively over the bone so that people can help themselves or be served by waiters. When the sliced ham gets low, bring the platter back to the kitchen and replenish it with freshly sliced ham (the reserve). Your platters will always look lush and abundant.

"Carve a ham as if you were shaving the face of a friend."
—Henri Charpentier

basting frequently.

4. After putting the ham in the oven, combine the port, dates, figs, and prunes in a small bowl. Add the fruit and port to the pan after the ham has baked 1½ hours. Bake for 30 minutes, basting frequently.

5. Place the ham on a bed of watercress on a large serving platter.

6. Gently stir the fruit through the pan juices in the bottom of the pan. Arrange the figs, dates, and prunes in alternating rows across the ham, securing the fruit with small toothpicks. Drizzle a little of the pan juices over the top. Pour the remainder into a sauceboat and serve immediately.

20 to 25 portions

RABBIT WITH PINE NUTS AND CURRANTS

Don't let the strange list of ingredients in this recipe intimidate you. They all work together to create a truly fabulous dish.

1 rabbit (3 ½ pounds), cut into 8 pieces
¼ cup olive oil
8 tablespoons balsamic vinegar
¼ cup plus 2 tablespoons red wine
4 tablespoons (½ stick) unsalted butter
4 medium-size leeks, cut lengthwise in half, well rinsed, dried, and chopped
¼ cup finely chopped prosciutto
1 tablespoon sugar
1 teaspoon dried rosemary
Salt and freshly ground black pepper, to taste
1 ¼ cups rich Beef Stock (page 397; see Note)
3 tablespoons finely grated bittersweet chocolate
¼ cup dried currants
1 teaspoon grated lemon zest
¼ cup toasted pine nuts (pignoli; see Note)

A TRADITIONAL EASTER FEAST

Vichyssoise

Baked Country Ham

Pineapple Bake

Carrot and Peanut Purée

Biscuits

Easter Cheesecake

Sancerre

VIOLETS

Violets are a herald of spring. Pick them for nosegays, or eat them in tender green salads. Float violets in May wine, or crystallize them for fancy pastry decorations.

The violet is a symbol of humility and modesty, but according to Rachel Field, "Who bends a knee where violets grow / A hundred secret things shall know."

1. One day before serving, rinse the rabbit pieces and pat dry. Coat the rabbit with the oil, 2 tablespoons of the vinegar, and 2 tablespoons wine. Marinate overnight in the refrigerator.

2. Drain the rabbit and let warm to room temperature before cooking. Heat the butter in a medium-size Dutch oven over medium heat. Add the leeks, prosciutto, and rabbit and brown the rabbit on all sides, 5 to 10 minutes.

3. Heat the remaining 6 tablespoons vinegar, ¼ cup wine, and the sugar just to boiling in a small saucepan. Pour over the rabbit and add the rosemary and salt and pepper to taste. Pour in the stock. Cover and simmer until the rabbit is tender, 45 minutes to 1 hour.

4. Stir in the chocolate, currants, and lemon zest and simmer 10 more minutes.

5. Remove the rabbit to a serving platter and keep warm. Heat the sauce to boiling. Reduce heat and simmer until thickened. Taste the sauce and add more chocolate or more vinegar if needed for a pleasant balance of sweet and tart.

6. Pour the sauce over the rabbit, sprinkle with pine nuts, and serve immediately.

4 portions

Notes: For 1¼ cups rich stock, reduce 2 to 2½ cups Beef Stock over high heat.

Toast the pine nuts in a skillet over very low heat, shaking the pan frequently, until evenly golden, about 2 minutes.

CARROT AND PEANUT PUREE

A great lift to the carrot! Peanuts, ground ginger, butter, and a bit of sour cream make this a special vegetable purée.

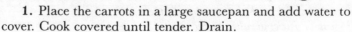

10 cups thinly sliced carrots
2 cups salted roasted peanuts
4 tablespoons (½ stick) unsalted butter
1 cup sour cream
1 teaspoon ground ginger
Salt and freshly ground black pepper, to taste

1. Place the carrots in a large saucepan and add water to cover. Cook covered until tender. Drain.

2. Process the peanuts and butter in a food processor fitted with a steel blade until smooth. Add the carrots and process until puréed (do this in batches if necessary). Add the sour cream, ginger, and salt and pepper to taste; process just to blend. Serve immediately.

12 portions

SORREL FLAN

An original accompaniment to spring entrées. The dish is also quite tasty when made with spinach, although the sorrel adds a special tartness.

4 tablespoons (½ stick) unsalted butter
¾ cup finely chopped shallots
8 cups sorrel leaves (about 8 ounces) or spinach leaves, well rinsed, dried, tough ribs or stems removed
12 eggs
4 cups heavy or whipping cream
½ cup chopped fresh parsley
½ teaspoon ground nutmeg
Salt and freshly ground black pepper, to taste
2 cups grated Gruyère cheese

1. Preheat oven to 350°F. Grease a 13 x 9-inch baking pan.
2. Melt the butter in a large skillet over medium heat. Add the shallots and sauté until translucent. Add the sorrel and cook covered until wilted, 10 to 12 minutes. Remove from heat.
3. Whisk the eggs and cream together in a large bowl. Add the parsley, nutmeg, and salt and pepper to taste and whisk to combine.
4. Spoon the sorrel mixture evenly over the bottom of the prepared pan.
5. Sprinkle the cheese over the sorrel mixture and pour the egg mixture over the cheese.
6. Bake on the middle rack of the oven until golden and the center is just firm to the touch, about 1 hour. Serve immediately.

8 hearty portions

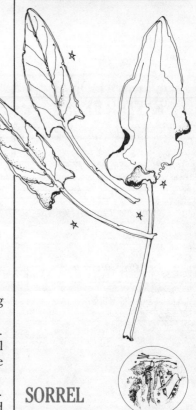

SORREL

Sorrel has long been a favorite of ours. We can remember picking it wild when we were kids. We called it sour grass then, and its pungent tartness used to make our mouths pucker instantly. Cultivated French sorrel is more refined in taste, and we enjoy its refreshing subtle tartness in soups, salads, and sauces. It is one green that should become a staple in your kitchen. If you can't find sorrel at your produce market, try growing this green.

PINEAPPLE BAKE

This is a very moist and delicious bread pudding—a lovely addition to an Easter menu.

8 thick slices day-old bread, cut into 1-inch cubes
2 cups drained crushed unsweetened pineapple
½ cup (1 stick) unsalted butter, melted
¾ cup packed brown sugar
4 eggs, beaten

1. Preheat oven to 350°F. Grease a 1½-quart baking dish.
2. Combine the bread and pineapple and place in the

BIRTHDAY DREAMS

Birthdays should be a special day of retreat from all obligations and a time to pamper yourself to the nines without feeling the need to make any explanations. Everybody deserves a dream day once a year, but all too often a birthday can turn into a day of accommodating the wishes of others who are helping to celebrate "your" day. We are firm believers in making it our own special day by celebrating it with an escape and thereby eliminating all expectations. Some of our favorite birthday indulgences are:

♥ Flying to another city for lunch
♥ Leaving on a vacation
♥ Taking the day off from work
♥ Preparing a romantic dinner of favorite foods to share with a close friend
♥ Lingering in a bubble bath
♥ Savoring a great bottle of Champagne, or buying a big bouquet of pink roses.

"Eggs of an hour, bread of a day, wine of a year, a friend of thirty years."
—Italian Proverb

prepared baking dish.

3. Mix the butter, sugar, and eggs and pour over the bread mixture.

4. Bake until puffed and golden, about 40 minutes. Serve immediately.

6 portions

LEMON RICE

A simple and refreshing way of preparing rice. This is so convenient when you need a contrasting color or delicate flavor with an important main course.

2½ cups canned chicken broth
½ teaspoon salt
1 clove garlic, slightly crushed
1 cup long-grain rice
1 tablespoon finely grated lemon zest
2 tablespoons chopped fresh dill
2 tablespoons unsalted butter
Freshly ground black pepper, to taste

1. Heat the broth, salt, and garlic in a heavy saucepan to boiling. Stir in the rice, cover, and simmer until the liquid is absorbed, about 20 minutes.

2. Remove from heat. Stir in the lemon zest and let stand covered for 5 minutes.

3. Remove the garlic. Gently stir in the dill and butter. Season to taste with pepper. Serve immediately.

4 to 6 portions

GOAT-CHEESE POPOVERS

These popovers can also be made in miniature muffin tins and served as an hors d'oeuvre.

Walnut oil
6 eggs
1½ cups unbleached all-purpose flour
1 teaspoon salt
½ teaspoon freshly ground black pepper
1 teaspoon dried thyme
Pinch ground nutmeg
2 cups milk
½ cup heavy or whipping cream
4 ounces herbed chèvre, cut into 18 to 20 pieces

1. Preheat oven to 400°F. Brush 18 to 20 muffin cups with walnut oil.

2. Place the eggs, flour, salt, pepper, thyme, and nutmeg in a blender container. Blend until well combined, about 10 seconds. Scrape down the sides of the container.

3. With the blender running, slowly pour in the milk and cream and blend until smooth.

4. Place the prepared muffin tins in the oven to warm slightly. Remove the warmed tins and fill each halfway with batter. Place a piece of the cheese in the center of each cup. Pour in the remaining batter to fill each cup two-thirds.

5. Bake the popovers until puffed and golden, 40 to 50 minutes. Serve immediately.

18 to 20 popovers

EASTER CHEESECAKE

An easy-to-make cheesecake, dense and creamy but refreshing with a zesty orange flavor throughout.

CRUST:

1 cup graham cracker crumbs
¼ cup coarsely chopped walnuts
2 tablespoons brown sugar
1 teaspoon ground cinnamon
½ cup (1 stick) unsalted butter, melted

FILLING:

2 cups sour cream
3 packages (8 ounces each) cream cheese, room temperature
3 eggs, lightly beaten
1 cup granulated sugar
½ teaspoon salt
2 teaspoons vanilla extract
Finely grated zest of 1 orange

1. Preheat oven to 375°F.

2. To make the crust, combine the crumbs, walnuts, brown sugar, and cinnamon. Add the butter and toss to combine. Reserve 3 tablespoons of the graham mixture for the top of the cheesecake and press the remaining evenly into the bottom and 1½ inches up the side of a 9-inch springform pan.

3. To make the filling, process the sour cream, cream cheese, eggs, sugar, and salt in a blender or food processor fitted with a steel blade until very smooth. Add the vanilla and orange zest and process just to blend.

4. Bake the cheesecake for 50 minutes. Sprinkle the reserved topping over the cake and bake until the filling is firm and the top is lightly golden, 10 to 15 minutes more.

5. Let cool completely. Remove the side of the pan and refrigerate until ready to serve.

10 to 12 portions

EASTER EGG HUNT

Let everyone enjoy the Easter Bunny's visit with an Easter egg hunt. Invite neighbors, relatives, young and old, to look for the eggs—brightly colored, monogrammed, "bejeweled," hand painted, and chocolate—all over the house and grounds. Then have a luncheon and use as the centerpiece special Easter baskets piled high with sweets for your guests.

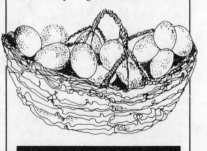

A TUSCANY RETREAT

Springtime in Italy is magical. Nowhere is the season greeted with more joy—and for good reason. Nature's rebirth heralds the pure and simple ingredients for which Italian cooking is famous.

For us, the *cucina* of the Italians is an inspiration, with its emphasis on the freshest, most perfect ingredients. There is a true genius in its simplicity of preparation that is cause for celebration. The clean, vibrant colors of the Italian flag—red, white, and green—are echoed repeatedly in dishes that are light yet full of flavor.

Italian cooks take the very best from nature and with great love harmonize it with a generous sense of hospitality. Every meal seems to be a party—you hear more hearty, contagious laughter at mealtime in Italy than anywhere else we know.

PASTA WITH THREE PESTOS

Once you understand the principles of pesto you can combine greens, nuts, oils, garlic, and other herbs to create your own. We've created three new ones here. Use your imagination and have a pesto party. The Olive and Pistachio and Mint Pestos make enough for 1 pound of pasta each, while the Arugula and Basil Pesto covers 2 pounds.

OLIVE AND PISTACHIO PESTO

¼ cup shelled pistachio nuts
4 cloves garlic
1 tablespoon green peppercorns (packed in brine), drained
1 cup pitted Picholine or other imported small green olives
    (about ½ pound; see Note)
1 cup olive oil
1 tablespoon fresh lemon juice
¾ cup freshly grated Parmesan cheese
Salt, to taste

1. Place the nuts, garlic, and peppercorns in a food processor fitted with a steel blade or a blender and process to a paste.
2. Add the olives and process until smooth.
3. With the machine running, pour in the oil in a thin steady stream. Add the lemon juice and Parmesan. Process until blended. Taste and add salt if needed.

   1½ cups

Note: Picholine olives are difficult to pit with a conventional pitter, hence you will have to do the job by hand. Allow for the extra time this will take—the resulting pesto is well worth the effort.

MINT PESTO

½ cup pine nuts (pignoli)
6 cloves garlic
3 cups fresh mint leaves
1 cup olive oil
Juice of 1 lemon
Salt and freshly ground black pepper, to taste
1 cup crumbled chèvre

1. Place the pine nuts and garlic in a food processor fitted with a steel blade or a blender and process to a paste.
2. Add the mint and process until finely chopped.
3. With the machine running, pour in the oil in a thin steady stream. Add the lemon juice and salt and pepper to taste. Process until blended.
4. Serve with the chèvre.

   1½ cups

"To an American writer seeing it for the first time, Italy was heaven."
—Alfred Kazin

PASTA PESTO MENU

Minestrone with Sweet Sausage and Tortellini

Spinach, tomato, and semolina pastas with Arugula and Basil Pesto Mint Pesto Olive and Pistachio Pesto

Parmesan cheese (on board with grater)

Warm Spinach and Basil Salad

Crusty Italian bread Sweet Gorgonzola cheese Fresh figs or cherries

Pear and Hazelnut Praline Soufflé

Chianti Classico

Cappuccino and Espresso Sambuca

ARUGULA AND BASIL PESTO

½ cup pine nuts (pignoli)
6 cloves garlic
5 cups arugula leaves (2 ½ bunches), well rinsed and dried
1 cup fresh basil leaves
¾ cup olive oil
Juice of 2 lemons
Salt and freshly ground black pepper, to taste
¾ cup freshly grated Parmesan cheese

1. Place the pine nuts and garlic in a food processor fitted with a steel blade or a blender and process to a paste.

2. Add the arugula and basil leaves, two handfuls at a time, and process to a thick green paste.

3. With the machine running, pour in the oil in a thin steady stream. Add the lemon juice and salt and pepper to taste and process until blended. Add the Parmesan and process until blended.

1 ½ pints

HOT PASTA PRIMAVERA

A pasta dish that celebrates spring.

7 tablespoons unsalted butter
4 shallots, minced
2 carrots, peeled and diced
½ cup Champagne or dry white wine
1 ½ cups Crème Fraîche (page 399)
3 tablespoons chopped fresh basil
1 tablespoon chopped fresh tarragon
2 cups diagonally cut 1-inch pieces fresh asparagus
2 leeks, well rinsed, dried, and cut into fine julienne
8 ounces fresh shiitake mushrooms, rinsed, dried, and sliced
1 ½ cups shelled fresh peas
Salt and freshly ground black pepper, to taste
¾ cup crumbled chèvre
1 pound hot cooked pasta, such as linguine or thin spaghetti

1. Melt 5 tablespoons of the butter in a large sauté pan over medium-high heat. Add the shallots and sauté for 5 minutes.

2. Stir in the carrots and cook for 3 minutes.

3. Add the Champagne, crème fraîche, basil, and tarragon. Cook until thickened to a good coating consistency, about 15 minutes.

4. Meanwhile, cook the asparagus in boiling salted water until tender but still firm. Drain. Blanch the leeks in boiling water 1 minute and drain. Sauté the mushrooms in the remaining 2 tablespoons butter.

5. When the sauce is thickened, stir in the asparagus, half the leeks, the mushrooms, and peas over low heat. Season to taste with salt and pepper and stir in the cheese. Spoon the sauce over the pasta. Garnish with the remaining leeks.

4 to 6 portions

FETTUCCINE WITH MUSSELS

Our version of an Italian clam sauce made with mussels and served over tomato fettuccine. The warm colors are enhanced with fresh basil and parsley. A little dice of tomatoes adds a garden fresh flavor.

1 cup dry white wine
36 mussels, scrubbed and bearded
⅓ cup best-quality olive oil
8 cloves garlic, minced
3 tablespoons chopped fresh basil
3 tablespoons chopped fresh parsley
2 teaspoons dried oregano
½ teaspoon red pepper flakes
1 tablespoon Pernod
1 ripe tomato, seeded and chopped
Salt and freshly ground black pepper, to taste
1 pound tomato fettuccine

1. Heat the wine in a large Dutch oven over medium-high heat to boiling. Add the mussels, cover the pan, and cook until the shells open, about 5 minutes. Remove the mussels from the shells and set aside. Discard the shells. Strain the cooking liquid and reserve.

2. Heat the oil in a large skillet. Add the garlic and sauté just until the garlic begins to turn golden. Add the basil, parsley, oregano, and red pepper flakes.

3. Stir in the reserved cooking liquid and the Pernod. Heat to boiling. Reduce heat and simmer for 7 to 10 minutes.

4. Stir in the mussels and the tomato. Season to taste with salt and pepper. Keep warm.

5. Cook the tomato fettuccine in boiling salted water until tender but still firm. Drain and toss with the mussel sauce. Serve immediately.

4 portions

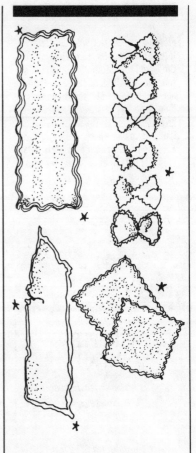

The Italians love to laugh, and their wit extends to the shapes of their pastas—*linguine* means tongues in Italian, *fettuccine* are narrow ribbons, and *cappelli d'angelo* means angel's hair. *Agnolatti* are priest's caps, *farfalle* are butterflies or bows, *fusilli* means little springs, *mostaccioli* are little moustaches, *penne* are quills, and *amorini pastina* are little cupids. *Orecchiatte* are little ears, and *ziti* means bridegrooms.

There is also a new shape, the first in many years, which was created by an Alfa Romeo designer—sleek but joyfully intricate, to help scoop up the sauce.

LESLIE RUSSO'S NEGRONI

¾ cup gin
¼ cup Campari
⅛ cup dry vermouth
½ teaspoon fresh lemon juice
2 lemon twists

Mix the gin, Campari, vermouth, and lemon juice. Pour over ice in two tall glasses and add the lemon twists.

2 drinks

MUSICAL NOTES

Infuse a spring cocktail party with lots of happy energy by playing a collection of Scott Joplin's sprightly piano rags.

Give a spring chicken dinner a real down-home feeling by playing square-dance and country music with lots of fiddling and banjo playing.

Make a fish dinner extra-special with background music of old Scottish sea shanties.

Add a dash of authenticity to an Italian dinner with background music—Verdi for opera lovers or Vivaldi for fans of the flute and oboe.

LINGUINE WITH PORCINI CREAM SAUCE

Cognac, Parmesan cheese, parsley, and pepper add an extra depth of flavor to this easily prepared pasta sauce. Dried porcini are available year round in specialty food stores.

1 ½ cups dried porcini
3 cups heavy or whipping cream
½ cup Cognac
Salt and freshly ground black pepper, to taste
1 pound linguine, preferably homemade
½ cup chopped fresh parsley
1 cup freshly grated Parmesan cheese

1. Soak the porcini in hot water to cover for 1 hour. Drain and cut into thin slivers.

2. Cook the cream in a medium-size saucepan over medium-high heat until reduced by about half, about 10 minutes.

3. Stir in the Cognac and simmer 5 minutes.

4. Add the porcini. Season to taste with salt and pepper. Simmer until thick and richly perfumed with the porcini, about 20 minutes.

5. Cook the pasta in boiling salted water until tender but still firm. Drain and toss with the porcini cream sauce immediately. Add the parsley and Parmesan and toss to combine. Serve immediately.

4 to 6 portions

PASTA PUTTANESCA

Serve over 12 ounces thin spaghetti.

½ cup olive oil
1 can (2 ounces) anchovy fillets, undrained
4 cloves garlic, crushed
1 can (35 ounces) plum tomatoes, drained
1 jar (2 ½ ounces) capers, drained
1 ½ cups pitted black olives, coarsely chopped
Freshly cracked black pepper, to taste

1. Place the oil, anchovies, and garlic in a heavy medium-size saucepan. Mash thoroughly to a paste.

2. Add the tomatoes, capers, and olives. Stir and heat to simmering over medium heat. Reduce heat to low and simmer uncovered for 1 hour, stirring occasionally. Season to taste with pepper.

4 appetizer portions

AMATRICIANA SAUCE

A bold, peasanty sauce loaded with the sweetness of coarsely chopped onion and the smokiness of Canadian bacon. We like to toss this sauce well with old-fashioned thick spaghetti before serving it family-style from a deep ceramic bowl. A splendid meal for the heartiest of appetites.

⅓ cup olive oil
4 medium-size yellow onions, coarsely chopped
8 ounces sliced Canadian bacon or smoked ham, cut into ¾-inch
    squares
4 cloves garlic, crushed
4 cups drained plum tomatoes
2 teaspoons sugar
¾ cup dry red wine
Salt and freshly ground black pepper, to taste

1. Heat the oil in a heavy medium-size saucepan over medium-high heat. Add the onions and sauté for 10 minutes.
2. Stir in the bacon and garlic and sauté for 5 minutes more.
3. Stir in the tomatoes, sugar, and wine. Season to taste with salt and pepper. Simmer uncovered for 45 minutes, stirring occasionally. Serve with 1 pound thick spaghetti or ziti and plenty of freshly grated Parmesan cheese.
Enough to sauce 1 pound pasta; 4 portions

PASTA WITH TOASTED BREAD CRUMBS

A unique combination that's simple to prepare and thrifty, too.

1 cup best-quality olive oil
4 cloves garlic, minced
1½ cups fine bread crumbs (day-old bread)
1 cup chopped fresh parsley
Salt and freshly ground black pepper, to taste
1 pound curly pasta

ITALIAN CHEESES

BEL PAESE: This is the registered trade name of a very popular cheese belonging to a range of semisoft, uncooked cheeses made from whole cow's milk. The name was inspired by Father Antonio Stoppani's book *Il Bel Paese (The Beautiful Country)*, originally published in 1873. The cheese was perfected for industrial production in 1906, and the author's portrait forms part of the label, superimposed on a map of Italy (in the U.S., the map shows the Western Hemisphere).

FONTINA: A mild, sliceable cheese which has been famous for centuries in the Val d'Aosta, under the protection of certification of origin. The most highly prized Fontina is the summer production, made high in the Alps. It has an extra-buttery consistency, from the higher fat content of the unpasteurized milk from which it is made. True Fontina should be very pale straw yellow, supple, and almost spreadable, with a few round holes evenly distributed throughout.

GORGONZOLA: For perhaps a thousand years the town of Gorgonzola has been the home of Italy's greatest blue cheese. Gorgonzola is injected with a different mold than most blue cheeses and is protected by official certification for authenticity. Firm in texture, it has a balance of rich, velvety flavor and sharp piquancy. Mountain Gorgonzola is considered the best, while Gorgonzola Dolce is a younger, sweeter version.

MASCARPONE: A fresh double-cream cheese that is most like a cross between sweet whipped butter and Devonshire cream. If you've ever tasted the cheese in Italy, you know that it has a richness of taste and texture that is unforgettable. Because it is highly perishable, we have never tasted imported Mascarpone that can compare with what we've had in Italy. Still, it is a wonderful dessert cheese to serve.

MOZZARELLA: Introduced in the U.S. as "pizza cheese," the real thing is nothing like the shrink-wrapped blocks sold in supermarkets. Italians like their mozzarella made from water-buffalo milk; it ripens very rapidly and is past its prime in a matter of days.

PECORINO ROMANO: The most ancient Italian cheese of all; its name is derived from the Italian word for sheep. Pecorino Romano is white or pale straw yellow, dense, and sharper than Parmesan. The rind is smooth and oiled with olive leaves. Pecorino Romano, Siciliano, and Sardo are all in the same family, varying in sharpness of taste, finishing oil, or flavorings, such as the addition of an herb or peppercorns.

PROVOLONE: This cheese comes in many versions—cured for only a short time, matured fully, or well aged. Shapes and sizes vary enormously too, since the plastic curd lends itself to improvization. When young, provolone has a delicate buttery taste which becomes sharp when aged for six months to two years. Aged provolone is an excellent grating cheese.

ROBIOLA: A soft, uncooked curd cheese, which takes its name from its reddish skin, Robiola relies heavily on surface ripening for correct consistency and flavor. It is produced throughout Lombardy and the Piedmont.

TALEGGIO: Taleggio is a star of that hazy galaxy of soft, full-fat Lombardian semisoft cheeses known as *stracchino*, whose styles vary as widely as Gorgonzola and Bel Paese. Mild and piquant to quite pungent, depending on age, it is made only in Milan, Como, Bergamo, Cremona, and Brescia.

TOMME: An uncooked, pressed, semihard cow's milk cheese made on both the Italian and French sides of the Alps. It is cured for one month in cold damp caves and has a lactic and pleasantly aromatic flavor.

TORTA: *Torta* means "cake" in Italian. These cheeses are composed of spectacular-looking layers of Robiola and Mascarpone alternating with a variety of herbs, nuts, fruits, and even smoked salmon. Our favorite is basil torta, which is studded with layers of fresh basil and pine nuts.

1. Heat 1 tablespoon of the oil in a medium-size skillet. Add the garlic and sauté until lightly golden. Remove from the pan and set aside.

2. Add the remaining oil to the skillet. Add the bread crumbs and stir to coat evenly with the oil. Toast the crumbs over medium heat, watching closely so that they do not burn and stirring frequently, until the crumbs are a deep golden brown. Remove from heat. Stir in the garlic and parsley. Season to taste with salt and pepper.

3. Cook the pasta in boiling salted water until tender but still firm. Drain and toss immediately with the bread crumb mixture.

4 to 5 portions

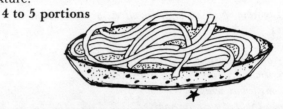

MACARONI WITH QUATTRO FORMAGGI

The standard American casserole of baked macaroni and cheese is transformed here with the rich Italian blend of *quattro formaggi*. Gorgonzola, Fontina, mozzarella, and Parmesan make this a cheese lover's dream.

5 tablespoons unsalted butter
¼ cup unbleached all-purpose flour
2½ cups milk
5 ounces Gorgonzola, crumbled
4 ounces Fontina, grated
Pinch ground nutmeg
Salt and freshly ground black pepper, to taste
1 pound ziti, cooked al dente and drained
4 ounces mozzarella, cut into ¼-inch cubes
4 ounces Parmesan cheese, grated
1 teaspoon paprika

1. Preheat oven to 350°F. Butter a 2-quart baking dish.

2. Melt the butter in a medium-size saucepan over medium heat. Stir in the flour and cook 1 minute. Gradually whisk in the milk. Cook, stirring constantly, until lightly thickened to the consistency of cream. Whisk in the Gorgonzola and Fontina. Cook, whisking constantly, until the cheeses are melted. Season with nutmeg and salt and pepper to taste. Remove from heat.

3. Combine the cheese sauce and cooked ziti. Stir in the mozzarella and spoon into the prepared baking dish. Sprinkle with the Parmesan and then the paprika.

4. Bake until bubbling and the top is browned, 30 to 40 minutes. Serve immediately.

4 portions

MARINATED OLIVES, SICILIAN STYLE

We all love to nibble olives—and these beautiful shiny black olives, combined with orange and lemon zests and fresh rosemary, are very attractive presented in a rustic ceramic bowl. Serve with breads, cheeses, and country pâtés.

1 pound Ligurian, Niçoise, or Greek olives, or a combination,
  drained
8 cloves garlic, cut lengthwise in half
Zest of ½ orange, cut into ¼-inch julienne
Zest of ½ lemon, cut into ¼-inch julienne
2 tablespoons fennel seeds
1 tablespoon chopped fresh rosemary
½ cup fresh lemon juice (2 lemons)
3 tablespoons best-quality olive oil

1. Combine the olives, garlic, citrus julienne, fennel seeds, and rosemary in a large bowl. Drizzle with lemon juice and oil. Marinate, stirring occasionally, at room temperature at least 24 hours.

2. Serve the olives as part of an hors d'oeuvre spread or simply as an accompaniment to aperitifs.

2 cups

WARM SPINACH AND BASIL SALAD

We've taken the flavors of pesto and combined them in a new treat for basil lovers.

6 cups fresh spinach leaves
2 cups fresh basil leaves (1 large bunch)
½ cup best-quality olive oil
3 cloves garlic, finely chopped
½ cup pine nuts (pignoli)
4 ounces prosciutto, diced
Salt and freshly ground black pepper, to taste
¾ cup freshly grated Parmesan cheese

1. Toss the spinach and basil together in a large salad bowl.

OLIVE OIL

For us, the silver green, twisted olive trees epitomize the serenity of the Italian landscape, and nothing evokes the Italian way of life as does the pungent taste of ripe black olives ready for pressing. Lawrence Durrell aptly described it as "a taste older than meat, older than wine. A taste as old as cold water." In fact, Italians are so proud of their olive oils that they find it unthinkable to add anything other than wine vinegar and salt when blending a dresssing for salad or simple boiled vegetables.

"It is easier to laugh in Italian than in French."
—Ungaro

ITALIAN DINING EXPERIENCES

CAFFE BAR—where most Italians breakfast on pastry and cappuccino, standing up at the *banco*, or counter.

TRATTORIA—similar to Parisian cafés or bistros, and to our luncheon restaurants. Can serve excellent fare, however simple.

OSTERIA—home-style restaurants serving a few very simple peasant-style dishes. In France these would be brasseries; in Italy they are often gathering places for political types.

RISTORANTE—the finer Italian restaurants, with a wide variety of specially prepared dishes.

PICNIC IN THE HILLS

Pizza Napoli

Baby Artichokes Provençal

Marinated Olives, Sicilian Style

Raspberry Tarts with Pine Nut Cream Filling

Chianti Classico

---

2. Heat the oil in a medium-size skillet over medium heat. Add the garlic and pine nuts and sauté until the nuts begin to brown slightly. Stir in the prosciutto and cook 1 minute more. Season to taste with salt and pepper.

3. Toss the spinach and basil with the warm dressing and sprinkle the salad with the Parmesan. Serve immediately and pass the peppermill.

6 portions

GRILLED CHEESE WITH QUATTRO FORMAGGI

Four delicious cheeses melted together make the best grilled cheese sandwich in the world.

2 tablespoons unsalted butter, room temperature
2 thick slices firm white bread, preferably homemade
½ teaspoon garlic powder
1 ounce sliced provolone
1 ounce sliced mozzarella
1 ounce sliced Fontina
½ ounce crumbled Gorgonzola

1. Spread half the butter on one side of each slice of bread. Sprinkle each buttered side with garlic powder. Layer the 4 cheeses between the unbuttered sides of the bread.

2. Grill the sandwich in a skillet over medium heat until both sides are golden brown. Serve immediately.

1 sandwich

PIZZA NAPOLI

One of our favorite open-face sandwiches inspired by our love for pizza. We layer sweet Gorgonzola, prosciutto, and plum tomatoes and season it with basil, thyme, pesto, and olives. Slice into 2-inch pieces for a hot hors d'oeuvre, or cut into sandwich-size pieces and serve with a crisp green salad and full-bodied red wine for lunch.

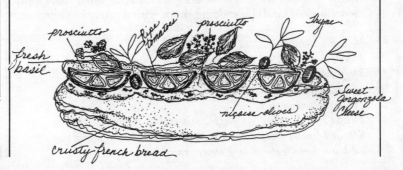

prosciutto · plum tomatoes · prosciutto · thyme · fresh basil · niçoise olives · sweet gorgonzola cheese · crusty french bread

1 baguette (about 15 inches long)
½ cup Fresh Tomato Sauce (page 397)
6 ounces sweet Gorgonzola or basil torta cheese, room temperature
¼ cup Basic Pesto (page 398)
4 thin slices prosciutto
4 ripe Italian plum tomatoes, cut lengthwise into ¼-inch slices
Freshly ground black pepper, to taste
1 tablespoon best-quality olive oil
2 tablespoons freshly grated Parmesan cheese
¼ cup chopped fresh Italian parsley
1 teaspoon dried basil or whole fresh leaves
1 teaspoon dried thyme
¼ cup pitted Niçoise olives
Fresh Italian parsley sprigs

1. Preheat oven to 350°F.

2. Cut the baguette lengthwise in half and scoop out most of the bread, leaving two ½-inch shells. Spread the tomato sauce evenly on both halves.

3. Divide the Gorgonzola in half and gently spread over the sauce. Spread the pesto over the cheese.

4. Place 2 slices of prosciutto on each bread half. Arrange the tomato slices decoratively on top of the prosciutto.

5. Grind pepper over the tomatoes and drizzle the oil over each bread half. Sprinkle with Parmesan, chopped parsley, basil, and thyme. Place the olives on top of the herbs and loosely wrap the pizzas separately in aluminum foil.

6. Bake on a cookie sheet for 10 minutes. Open the top of the foil and bake until the tomatoes are cooked and the Parmesan is melted, another 15 minutes. Cut into 2½-inch slices. Serve the slices on a tray, garnished with parsley sprigs.

12 slices, 6 portions

MEDALLIONS OF LAMB WITH HAZELNUT HOLLANDAISE

Hazelnuts

Red meat with a béarnaise or hollandaise sauce is always a favorite combination. We've added an extra touch to elegant medallions of lamb by saucing them with a nutty hollandaise.

½ cup hazelnuts, toasted and skinned
1 tablespoon unsalted butter, room temperature
3 egg yolks
1½ tablespoons fresh lemon juice
Pinch cayenne pepper
1 cup (2 sticks) plus 3 tablespoons unsalted butter
Salt and freshly ground black pepper, to taste
12 lamb medallions (3 to 4 ounces each)

VINO— THE WINES OF ITALY

The wines of Italy are much like its people—on the whole, hard to summarize. Wine is certainly an integral part of daily life—in fact, more is produced and drunk in Italy than in any other country.

Italy's wide range of geography and climate creates a myriad of different types of wine. Many are inexpensive yet surprisingly good, which makes Italian wines a smart choice when you're entertaining a crowd.

The first step in learning about Italian wines is understanding the labeling laws. D.O.C. (*Denominazione de Origine Controllata* or "Controlled Place Name") on a label insures the wine has been made according to time-honored traditions. Adding a G (*garantita* or "guaranteed") is a symbol for Italy's best.

THE REDS

AMARONE: A D.O.C. that can stand prolonged aging, Amarone is made from selected grapes which are set out to dry for three months to produce rich, dry wines with a high alcoholic content, at least 14 percent. A noble cousin to Valpolicella.

BARBARESCO: A D.O.C.G. wine from Piedmont, produced from the Nebbiolo grape, though soil conditions make for a wine gentler than its cousin, Barolo. Ready to drink after four years in the bottle.

BARBERA: Barbera wines are named after the varietal widely grown throughout Piedmont. Individual Barberas take on the names of the towns where they are produced, such as Barbera d'Alba. The wines are medium-bodied and fruity.

BARDOLINO: A light and fruity wine named after the town on the shore of Lake Garda. All Bardolinos are drunk while young; those labeled *Classico* are made from grapes in a limited growing area and are aged for a year.

BAROLO: A D.O.C.G. wine from southern Piedmont, produced from the Nebbiolo grape. The wine is rich in tannin and alcohol and has a wide range of aromas described variously as tar, truffles, faded roses, incense, or plums. Barolos benefit from aging ten to fifteen years.

BRUNELLO DI MONTALCINO: One of the four D.O.C.G. wines. Brunello is named for the grape, produced in Tuscany, and is a dry, concentrated wine. It is made on the same principle as the great Pétrus wine of Bordeaux and is aged in wood for four years before release. Brunello has a rich and brawny bouquet. Some top vintages take up to twenty-five years to reach their full potential.

CHIANTI: Certainly one of the most popular Italian wines, with the potential to be a great wine. Chianti comes from a region in central Tuscany and is made in two ways: one produces a young wine ready to drink in the March following the fall harvest; the better Chianti, Riserva, is aged in wood for three years and is often compared to a Bordeaux. *Classico* on the label indicates that the wine has been made from grapes grown in the heartland of the original Chianti area.

DOLCETTO D'ALBA: A pleasant soft wine from the land of the famed white truffles. Refreshing and best drunk while young.

GRATTINARA: Another Piedmont wine made from the Nebbiolo grape. Grattinara wines are not as exquisite as Barolos and tend to be lighter. They must be aged four years before release.

LAMBRUSCO: A fizzy sweet red or pink wine that sells well in the U.S. but really has no appeal for the discerning wine drinker.

RUBESCO: A noble red wine from Umbria. Some Rubescos are described as concentrated Chiantis.

VALPOLICELLA: When it is good it is one of Italy's best light red wines, with a fruity cherrylike bouquet. The wine should be drunk young. Look for Valpolicella Classico, made from the pick of the crop of the vineyards along the Adige River.

VINO NOBILE DI MONTEPULCIANO: One of the prized four D.O.C.G. wines. Quite similar to Chianti with perhaps a bit more finesse.

1. Process the hazelnuts and 1 tablespoon butter in a food processor fitted with a steel blade until ground.

2. Process the egg yolks, lemon juice, and cayenne in a blender for 30 seconds.

3. Melt 1 cup butter in a small saucepan until bubbly. With the blender running, pour in the hot butter in a thin steady stream to make a thick and creamy sauce. Season to taste with salt and pepper. Add the hazelnuts and process just until combined. Remove the sauce to a double boiler and keep warm while sautéing the lamb.

4. Sprinkle the lamb on both sides with salt and pepper.

5. Melt 3 tablespoons butter in a cast-iron skillet over medium-high heat. Add the lamb medallions and sauté 3 to 4 minutes on each side.

6. Place 2 medallions on each warmed individual serving plate and top each medallion with a tablespoon or so of the hazelnut hollandaise.

6 portions

VEAL RAGOUT WITH CEPES AND SAGE

A woodsy veal stew bursting with *cèpes* plumped in wine, plenty of garlic, and lots of fresh sage. The cassis and red currant jam make it a winner.

2 cups dry white wine
1 ounce dried cèpes, well rinsed, patted dry
¼ cup mild olive oil
4 tablespoons (½ stick) unsalted butter
2 pounds veal shoulder, cut into 1-inch cubes
1 head (12 large cloves) garlic, peeled
2 tablespoons potato starch
1 cup rich Berta's Chicken Stock (page 396; see Note)
½ cup loosely packed fresh sage leaves
¼ cup chopped fresh Italian parsley
¼ cup crème de cassis
Grated zest of 1 medium-size orange
Salt and freshly ground black pepper, to taste
1 tablespoon red currant jelly

1. Heat 1 cup of the wine in a small saucepan until hot. Pour over the *cèpes* in a small bowl and let stand 1 hour.

2. Preheat oven to 350°F.

3. Heat the oil and 1 tablespoon of the butter in a heavy

Dutch oven or casserole over high heat. Quickly brown the veal, a few pieces at a time, in the hot oil and butter and remove with a slotted spoon to a large bowl. Sauté the garlic in the Dutch oven for 2 minutes and add to the veal. Remove and discard the oil and butter from the pan.

4. Toss the veal and garlic with the potato starch.

5. Heat the remaining 1 cup wine to boiling in the Dutch oven over high heat, scraping loose the browned bits on the bottom of the pan. Reduce heat to low and whisk in the remaining 3 tablespoons butter. Add the veal and garlic, *cèpes* with wine, stock, sage, parsley, cassis, orange zest, and salt and pepper to taste. Stir to combine.

6. Place in the oven and bake covered for 40 minutes. Remove the cover and bake until the meat is tender, 35 to 40 minutes more. Stir in the jelly until melted. Serve immediately.

4 to 6 portions

Note: For 1 cup rich stock, reduce 2 cups Berta's Chicken Stock.

ROAST VEAL WITH LEMON AND CAPERS

This is a hot version of a veal *tonnato* without the tuna. The veal is baked in a lemon-caper mayonnaise that keeps it moist and also doubles as a serving sauce.

1 egg
1 egg yolk
2 teaspoons Dijon-style mustard
Grated zest of 3 lemons
Juice of 1 lemon
1 cup olive oil
1½ tablespoons capers, drained
1 teaspoon dried oregano
Salt and freshly ground black pepper, to taste
1 veal loin roast (3½ to 4 pounds), boned, rolled, and tied
4 slices bacon
4 cloves garlic
1 cup dry white wine
½ cup (1 stick) unsalted butter, room temperature

1. Preheat oven to 375°F.

2. Process the egg, egg yolk, mustard, and lemon zest and juice in a food processor fitted with a steel blade 10 seconds to combine.

3. With the machine running, pour the oil in a thin, steady stream through the feed tube to make a thick mayonnaise. Add the capers, oregano, and salt and pepper to taste and process 10 seconds more. You should have about 2 cups mayonnaise.

THE WHITES

ASTI: A true Italian invention, effervescent Asti Spumante is the world's most popular sparkling wine. Made from Muscat grapes, it ferments in tanks rather than in the bottle. Sweet and fruity and best served very cold, but not with entrées.

EST! EST!! EST!!!: A pleasant but undistinguished dry white wine produced near Rome. Thirst-quenching on a hot afternoon.

FRASCATI: One of Italy's most interesting whites, although it is said not to travel well. On the other hand it is certainly worth traveling *to* the vineyards just outside Rome, where the volcanic soil imbues the wine with a golden glow and a ripe, nutty flavor.

GAVI: Considered one of Italy's most promising whites, this Piedmont wine has even been compared to white Burgundies.

ORVIETO: A pale wine produced in two versions, dry and semisweet—but like Frascati, a poor traveler. A good Orvieto has a trace of honey and a velvety quality. Most, however, are undistinguished. Antinori is one of the better brands.

PINOT GRIGIO: A dry and fruity wine from the Fruili-Venezia region, which produces some of Italy's best white wines. It is meant to be drunk young and well chilled.

SOAVE: Probably Italy's best known white wine, named after a medieval fortified village surrounded by vineyards—which is far more enticing than the wine. Look for selections labeled *Superiore,* and serve well chilled.

TREBBIANO: A standard white wine from Emilia-Romagna, dry and lightly fizzy.

VERDICCHIO: A well-balanced dry wine with a clean finish. Look for its distinctive amphora-shaped bottle.

VERNACCIA DI SAN GIMIGNANO: The first Italian white wine to receive the D.O.C., reported to have been Michelangelo's favorite. If labeled *Riserva,* it has been aged in wood for one year.

VIN SANTO: A sweet farm wine of Tuscany, made from grapes that dry in the lofts until Christmas. It should be aged at least three years and has a pleasant sherrylike hue and sweetness.

4. Pour 1 cup of the mayonnaise over the veal roast in a shallow baking pan. Wrap the bacon slices around the roast over the sauce.

5. Purée the garlic with ⅓ cup of the wine in a food processor fitted with a steel blade. Sprinkle the garlic mixture evenly over the bacon. Place the butter on top of the roast to melt as it cooks.

6. Cook the roast for 2½ hours, basting occasionally with the remaining ⅔ cup wine and the pan juices. Slice the roast and serve with the bacon. Pass the remaining mayonnaise.

6 to 8 portions

TRATTORIA NUMERO UNO

Warm Spinach and Basil Salad

Chicken Legs Puttanesca

Saffron Risotto with Pistachios

Creamy Fennel Purée

Cappuccino Ice Cream Chocolate-Orange Cookies

Chianti

Sambuca with espresso beans

This robust menu is appropriate for spring or fall. The hearty colors of the food call for a red and white checkered tablecloth, candles in old raffia Chianti bottles, and *Tosca* on the stereo.

CHICKEN LEGS PUTTANESCA

A spicy tomato sauce to enhance chicken legs. Sun-dried tomatoes, balsamic vinegar, lots of garlic, olives, and anchovies add a new dimension to this classic peasant sauce. Add lots of pepper and serve it with a hearty Italian red wine!

3 tablespoons olive oil
8 chicken legs (drumstick and thigh)
1 medium-size onion, cut into thin rings
12 large cloves garlic, halved
1 can (35 ounces) plum tomatoes
1 can (2 ounces) anchovies, drained and chopped
½ cup pitted Niçoise olives
⅓ cup capers, drained
3 tablespoons coarsely chopped sun-dried tomatoes (packed in oil)
1 tablespoon mixed Italian herbs
1 tablespoon balsamic vinegar
Pinch red pepper flakes
Salt and freshly ground black pepper, to taste

1. Heat the oil in a large skillet. Add the chicken and brown on both sides. Remove from the pan and set aside.

2. Add the onion and garlic to the same pan and sauté until the onion is soft and translucent, 5 to 7 minutes.

3. Stir in the plum tomatoes with their liquid and then the remaining ingredients, one at a time. Return the chicken to the pan and coat well with the sauce.

4. Cover the pan and simmer until the chicken is tender, about 45 minutes. Serve immediately.

6 to 8 portions

SAFFRON RISOTTO WITH PISTACHIOS

An excellent dish to serve with roast lamb or a chicken and olive dish. Arborio rice is available in specialty food shops or Italian markets. The rice makes all the difference!

4 tablespoons (½ stick) unsalted butter
1 medium-size yellow onion, chopped
1 teaspoon saffron threads
2 cups Italian Arborio rice
1 cup dry white wine
4 to 5 cups Berta's Chicken Stock (page 396) or canned chicken
*   broth*
3 tablespoons shelled pistachio nuts
1 cup freshly grated Parmesan cheese

1. Melt the butter in a 10-inch skillet over medium heat. Add the onion and sauté for 5 minutes. Stir in the saffron and cook 1 minute more.

2. Add the rice and stir to coat with the butter and onions. Pour in the wine and 2 cups of the broth. Simmer covered until most of the liquid has been absorbed. Continue to simmer covered, adding the broth ½ cup at a time, until the rice is tender. The entire cooking time is usually about 30 minutes. The rice should be bound lightly together with a little of the cooking liquid.

3. Stir in the pistachio nuts and Parmesan. Serve immediately.

6 to 8 portions

ITALIAN CARROTS

In Italy carrots are boiled like beets and potatoes and peeled afterwards. Fresh dill and salty capers are a unique addition.

8 large carrots, unpeeled
2 teaspoons coarse (kosher) salt
3 tablespoons unsalted butter
½ cup Crème Fraîche (page 399)
3 tablespoons chopped fresh dill
1 tablespoon capers, drained
Salt and freshly ground black pepper, to taste

CARPACCIO

We are crazy about *carpaccio*, the transparently thin raw beef that is the specialty at Harry's Bar in Venice. The addictive melt-in-your-mouth taste has inspired us to conjure up many new serving variations. Always drizzle the slices with extra virgin olive oil, a squeeze of fresh lemon, a healthy grinding of black pepper—and serve:

♥ On a bed of arugula, garnished with shavings of aged Parmesan and a sprinkling of capers.

♥ On a bed of radicchio, topped with shavings of Romano cheese.

♥ On a bed of thinly sliced tomatoes and red onions, sprinkled with chopped fresh basil leaves.

♥ On a bed of watercress with a layer of julienned carrots, shredded prosciutto, and grated Parmesan.

♥ On a bed of arugula, with a layer of tomato and red onions, sprinkled generously with Niçoise olives and fresh oregano.

♥ On a bed of endive and fennel greens, with a layer of roasted red peppers and a sprinkling of Kalamata olives.

♥ On a bed of chicory, with a layer of sliced mushrooms, topped with crumbled Gorgonzola.

♥ On your very best plate with precious shavings of Italian white truffles.

Throw a party for watching vintage Italian movies with classics on the menu as well. Whether your tastes run to *Nights of Cabiria* or *The Godfather,* it's easy to rent a film and show a movie during cocktails. Just keep the fritters coming, and during intermission serve the pasta.

1. Soak the carrots in ice water for 30 minutes. Drain.

2. Heat a large pan of water to boiling. Add the coarse salt and the carrots. Cook until tender but still crisp, about 20 minutes. Drain and cool under cold running water.

3. When the carrots are cool enough to handle, gently remove the outer skins by rubbing the carrots with your hands. The skins will slip off easily. Cut the carrots diagonally into ¼-inch slices.

4. Melt the butter in a skillet over medium heat. Add the carrots and sauté for 5 minutes.

5. Stir in the crème fraîche, 1 tablespoon at a time, over medium heat, waiting for each addition to be absorbed before adding the next. Stir in the dill, capers, and salt and pepper to taste. Serve immediately.

6 to 8 portions

CHOCOLATE HAZELNUT CAKE

The ultimate cake for any chocolate lover's occasion.

CAKE:

1 cup granulated sugar
¼ cup water
1 tablespoon instant coffee powder
6 ounces semisweet chocolate, broken into pieces
1 teaspoon almond extract
½ cup (1 stick) unsalted butter, room temperature
8 eggs, separated, room temperature
1 cup skinned toasted hazelnuts, ground semifine
2 tablespoons graham cracker crumbs

FROSTING:

6 ounces semisweet chocolate, broken into small pieces
¼ cup water
1 tablespoon instant coffee powder
1 cup (2 sticks) unsalted butter, room temperature
3 egg yolks
1 cup sifted confectioners' sugar
¼ cup ground skinned toasted hazelnuts

1. Preheat oven to 350°F. Butter and flour two 9-inch cake pans.

2. To make the cake, simmer the sugar, water, and coffee powder in a small saucepan over medium-high heat for 3 to 4 minutes, stirring constantly. Remove from the heat and stir in the chocolate and almond extract. Stir until the chocolate is melted and the mixture is smooth. Set aside to cool.

3. Beat the butter in a mixer bowl until light and fluffy.

Add the egg yolks, one at a time, beating well after each addition. Stir in the cooled chocolate mixture. Then stir in the hazelnuts and graham cracker crumbs.

4. Beat the egg whites in a separate bowl with clean beaters until stiff but not dry. Fold a quarter of the egg whites into the chocolate mixture, and then gently fold in the remaining. Pour the batter into the prepared pans, dividing evenly.

5. Bake until the cake separates from the edge of the pan and springs back when lightly touched in the center, 25 to 30 minutes. Cool in the pans 5 minutes; then invert onto wire racks to cool completely.

6. To make the frosting, heat the chocolate, water, and coffee powder in a small saucepan over low heat until smooth. Set aside to cool.

7. Cream the butter in a mixer bowl until light and fluffy. Beat in the egg yolks, one at a time. Beat in the cooled chocolate mixture; then beat in the confectioners' sugar. Refrigerate the frosting until thick enough to spread.

8. Place 1 cake layer on a serving plate and frost the top. Place the second cake layer on the first and spread the top and side of the cake with the frosting, smoothing the frosting as you spread it. Press the ground hazelnuts all around the side of the cake. Pipe any remaining frosting through a pastry tube decoratively on the top of the cake.

10 to 12 portions

WHITE CHOCOLATE AND HAZELNUT CHEESECAKE

A dark chocolate crust encloses a creamy blend of melted white chocolate and cream cheese. This rich filling is further embellished with speckles of hazelnut praline and a good jigger of Frangelico.

1 cup Hazelnut Praline (page 242)
1 package (8 ½ ounces) chocolate wafers
¼ cup skinned toasted hazelnuts
2 tablespoons sugar
1 teaspoon ground cinnamon
14 tablespoons (1 ¾ sticks) unsalted butter, room temperature
2 pounds cream cheese, room temperature
4 eggs
1 egg yolk
1 pound best-quality white chocolate, melted
3 tablespoons Frangelico
1 tablespoon vanilla extract
Pinch ground nutmeg

1. Make the hazelnut praline. Process the praline in a food processor fitted with a steel blade until finely ground. Measure ¾ cup.

"The definitive recipe for any Italian dish has not yet appeared. We're still creating."
—Luigi Barzini

SPRING CELEBRATION

Spinach and Bacon Salad

Herb-roasted Rack of Lamb

Arugula Soufflé

Curried Carrots

White Chocolate and Hazelnut Cheesecake

Saint-Estèphe or Merlot

ITALIAN GELATI

Once you've tasted Italian *gelati*, you'll forever wonder why Americans can't make ice cream like the Italians. The flavors are unbelievably intense and the texture so smooth. The custard base differentiates it from a sorbet.

GELATI FLAVORS

Nocciola—hazelnut
Amaretto—macaroon
Crema—vanilla
Zabaione—marsala custard
Limone—lemon
Mandarino—tangerine
Arancia—orange
Albicocca—Apricot
Mirtillo—blueberry
Mellone—melon
Pesche—peach
Pera—pear
Ananas—pineapple
Fragola—strawberry
Menta—mint
Caffe—coffee
Gianduia—chocolate
Torrone—almond
Amarena—cherry
Noce—walnut
Malaga—rum raisin
Stracciatella—chocolate chip

2. Process the wafers, whole nuts, sugar, and cinnamon in a food processor fitted with a steel blade until finely crushed.

3. Butter a 9½-inch springform pan with 1 tablespoon of the butter.

4. Heat 5 tablespoons of the butter until melted and stir into the crumb mixture. Set aside 3 tablespoons of the crumb mixture to sprinkle over the cheesecake. Press the remaining crumbs into the bottom and up the side of the prepared pan. Refrigerate while you make the filling.

5. Preheat oven to 300°F.

6. Beat the cream cheese in a large mixer bowl until light and fluffy. Beat in the eggs, one at a time, and then the egg yolk. Beat in the remaining 8 tablespoons butter and the white chocolate. Add the Frangelico and vanilla and beat until smooth. Stir in the hazelnut praline and nutmeg. Carefully pour the filling into the crumb crust.

7. Bake the cheesecake for 1½ hours, sprinkling the top with the reserved crumbs 15 minutes before the cheesecake is done.

8. Let cool completely; then refrigerate covered until cold.

10 to 12 portions

KUMQUAT GELATO

The result of blending Italian tradition with American inspiration. The kumquats not only add tart flavor but also a wonderful texture that is similar to marmalade. A must for ice cream fanatics.

2 cups sliced kumquats
½ cup Grand Marnier
½ cup water
3 eggs
½ cup sugar
1½ cups milk, scalded
Juice of 1 lemon

1. Place the kumquats in a heavy saucepan and pour in the Grand Marnier and water. Simmer uncovered 15 minutes. Remove from heat and process the fruit with its syrup in a food processor fitted with a steel blade until nearly smooth. Some small pieces of skin are fine for texture.

2. Heat water in the bottom of a double boiler over medium heat. Beat the eggs and sugar together in the top and whisk in the scalded milk. Cook over the water, whisking constantly, until thickened to the consistency of a light custard, 7 to 10 minutes. Cool the custard.

3. Add the custard and lemon juice to the kumquats in the food processor; process until smooth.

4. Freeze in an ice cream maker, following manufacturer's instructions.

1 quart

CANTALOUPE GELATO

1 ripe cantaloupe, peeled, seeded, and cut into chunks
3 eggs
½ cup sugar
1½ cups milk, scalded
Juice of 1 lime or lemon

1. Process the cantaloupe in a food processor fitted with a steel blade or a blender until smooth.

2. Heat water in the bottom of a double boiler over medium heat. Beat the eggs and sugar together in the top part and whisk in the milk. Cook over the water, whisking constantly, until thickened to the consistency of a light custard, 7 to 10 minutes. Cool the custard.

3. Add the custard and lime juice to the cantaloupe in the food processor; process until smooth.

4. Freeze in an ice cream maker, following manufacturer's instructions.

1 quart

FRESH ORANGE AND SAMBUCA SORBET

The delightful result of going wild with a new ice cream maker one hot summer day.

4 cups fresh orange juice (about 1 dozen juice oranges)
1 cup Sambuca liqueur

Mix the orange juice and Sambuca. Freeze in an ice cream maker, following manufacturer's instructions. Serve with amaretti cookies.

1 quart

ESPRESSO COOKIES

½ cup (1 stick) unsalted butter, room temperature
3 tablespoons granulated sugar
1 cup ground toasted hazelnuts
1 cup unbleached all-purpose flour
1 ounce bittersweet chocolate, finely grated
1 tablespoon instant coffee powder
2 teaspoons hot water
36 skinned toasted whole hazelnuts
½ cup confectioners' sugar
1 tablespoon unsweetened cocoa powder

RASPBERRIES AND BALSAMIC VINEGAR

We recently learned from our Italian friends about sprinkling balsamic vinegar over fresh raspberries or strawberries and letting them steep for 2 to 3 hours with sugar to taste. Try it—you'll discover a flavor you didn't know possible. In fact, the Italians so love balsamic vinegar that they often drink a shot of it as a digestive.

A CELEBRATION OF SPRING

Arugula Soufflé

Grilled Jumbo Shrimp with Prosciutto and Basil

Saffron Risotto with Pistachios

Asparagus with Green Sauce

Orange and Sambuca Sorbet Espresso Cookies

Orvieto

The Italians greet the revival of life in spring with processions and feasts in every village. The springtime flavors in this menu are worth celebrating, too.

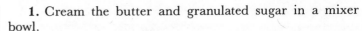

WHERE TO TASTE WINE WHEN IN ITALY

THE CANTINA belongs to a specific wine producer and serves only the wines of that vineyard. The Italian countryside is dotted with numerous informal *cantine* and a friendly visit and wine tasting often extends into a personal tour of the whole wine-making facility. The Italians are proud of their wines.

THE ENOTECA serves a variety of wines from a given region. It is set up to allow the visitor to taste, buy, and ship wines. Some *enotece* in major cities will carry the best wines from all over Italy.

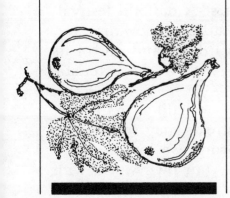

1. Cream the butter and granulated sugar in a mixer bowl.

2. Combine the ground hazelnuts, flour, and chocolate and stir into the butter mixture. Dissolve the coffee in the water and stir into the butter mixture.

3. Preheat oven to 325°F.

4. Shape the dough into balls, using about 2 teaspoons of the dough for each cookie. Place on ungreased cookie sheets and press a whole hazelnut into the center of each ball.

5. Bake the cookies until lightly colored, about 15 minutes. Let cool. Combine the confectioners' sugar and cocoa and sift over the cookies.

3 dozen cookies

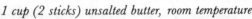

MARSALA AND FRUIT BISCUIT BREAD

put in a date

This very pleasant Italian-style biscuitlike cake goes well with coffee in the morning or espresso in the evening. It is also a good not-too-sweet bread to serve with cheese after an Italian meal. Try it toasted, too.

1 cup (2 sticks) unsalted butter, room temperature
1 cup sugar
4 eggs
3 tablespoons sweet Marsala
1 ½ teaspoons vanilla extract
Pinch salt
⅓ cup diced dried apricots
⅓ cup diced dates
⅓ cup diced dried figs
1 ¾ cups unbleached all-purpose flour
½ cup coarsely chopped toasted hazelnuts

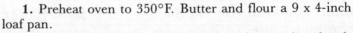

1. Preheat oven to 350°F. Butter and flour a 9 x 4-inch loaf pan.

2. Cream the butter and sugar in a large mixer bowl. Add the eggs, one at a time, beating well after each addition. Beat in the Marsala, vanilla, and salt.

3. Toss the dried fruits with the flour and stir into the batter with a wooden spoon until well combined. Stir in the hazelnuts.

4. Pour the batter into the prepared pan. Bake until golden, about 1 hour.

5. Remove from the oven and let stand for 10 minutes. Invert onto a wire rack to cool completely.

1 loaf

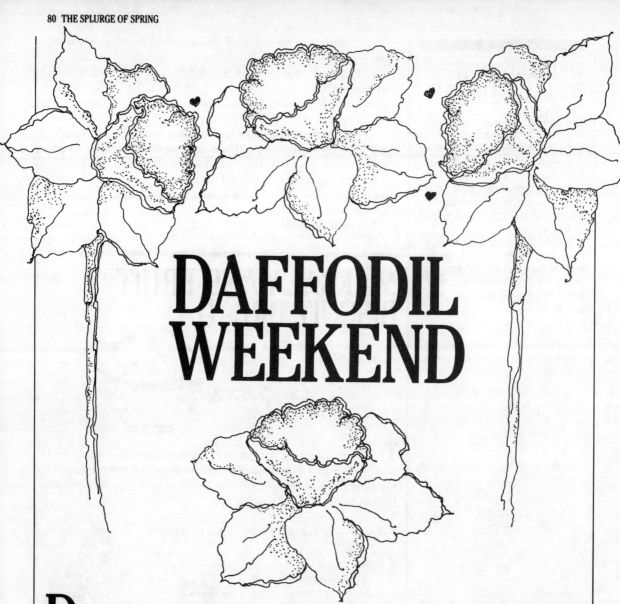

DAFFODIL WEEKEND

Daffodils, with their affinity for cool, moist climates, flourish more dramatically on Nantucket Island than any other place we know. Nantucketers take a great deal of pride in the appearance of their historic home, and members of the local garden club, along with other volunteers, have planted more than a million daffodil bulbs along the main roads of the island over the past ten years. A daffodil festival, complete with antique-car parade, extravagant store window displays, and a jovial tailgate picnic competition, brings the island out of its frozen winter isolation and welcomes spring with a characteristic Nantucket flair.

While the purity of design in the island's whaling mansions, shingled cottages, and rambling cobblestone streets may seem to be the perfect backdrop for this celebration of spring, we invite you to become inspired by the islanders and beautify your own world with daffodil plantings and pretty April picnics.

EGG SALAD WITH BACON AND HORSERADISH

A great breakfast classic translates into a glorious salad.

12 hard-cooked eggs, peeled and chopped
6 ribs celery, chopped
5 scallions (green onions, white part and 2 inches green), sliced
12 ounces bacon, cut into 1-inch squares, cooked crisp, and drained
2 tablespoons caraway seeds
3 to 4 tablespoons prepared white horseradish, drained
1 cup Hellmann's mayonnaise
Salt and freshly ground black pepper, to taste
½ cup chopped fresh parsley

1. Gently toss the eggs, celery, scallions, bacon, and caraway seeds together in a medium-size bowl to combine.
2. Mix the horseradish and mayonnaise and fold into the salad. Season to taste with salt and pepper. Garnish with the parsley.
8 to 10 portions

PICNIC PARADE

Iced vodka with lemon twists

Golden caviar with sweet butter and toast points

Mexican Egg Salad

Egg Salad with Bacon and Horseradish

Egg Salad with Poppy Seeds

Honey-Curry Bread

Asparagus vinaigrette

Pineapple Upsidedown Cake

EGG SALAD WITH POPPY SEEDS

Wonderful on black bread.

12 hard-cooked eggs, peeled and chopped
6 ribs celery, chopped
1 small red onion, chopped
1 sweet red pepper, cored, seeded, and diced
2 tablespoons capers, drained
3 tablespoons poppy seeds
1 tablespoon Hungarian sweet paprika
½ cup sour cream
½ cup (or as needed) Hellmann's mayonnaise
Salt and freshly ground black pepper, to taste

1. Combine the eggs, celery, onion, red pepper, and capers in a medium-size bowl.
2. Toast the poppy seeds in a small skillet over medium-high heat for 2 to 3 minutes.
3. Mix the poppy seeds, paprika, and sour cream in a small bowl and stir into the egg mixture.
4. Add enough of the mayonnaise to bind the salad and season to taste with salt and pepper.
5. Refrigerate several hours to allow flavors to blend.
8 portions

MEXICAN EGG SALAD

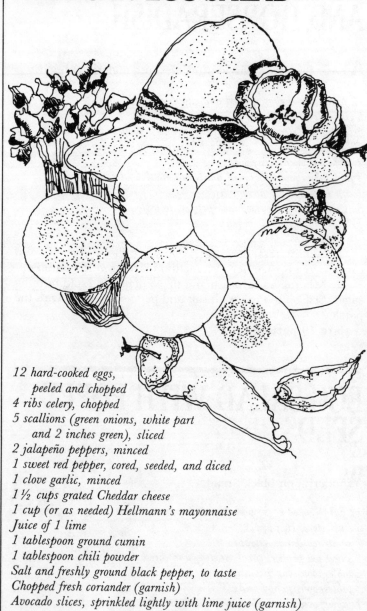

12 hard-cooked eggs,
    peeled and chopped
4 ribs celery, chopped
5 scallions (green onions, white part
    and 2 inches green), sliced
2 jalapeño peppers, minced
1 sweet red pepper, cored, seeded, and diced
1 clove garlic, minced
1½ cups grated Cheddar cheese
1 cup (or as needed) Hellmann's mayonnaise
Juice of 1 lime
1 tablespoon ground cumin
1 tablespoon chili powder
Salt and freshly ground black pepper, to taste
Chopped fresh coriander (garnish)
Avocado slices, sprinkled lightly with lime juice (garnish)

1. Place the eggs, celery, scallions, jalapeño peppers, red pepper, garlic, and cheese in a mixing bowl and toss to combine.

2. Mix 1 cup mayonnaise, the lime juice, cumin, and chili powder in a small bowl.

3. Gently fold the mayonnaise mixture into the egg mixture, adding more mayonnaise if needed to bind the salad well. Season to taste with salt and pepper. Transfer to a serving bowl.

4. Refrigerate several hours to allow flavors to blend. Garnish with fresh coriander and avocado slices.

10 to 12 portions

THE BEST PICNICS

At the summit of the mountain
While reading Proust at high noon
After a bicycling race
While studying for exams
During lunch hour from work
After a housecleaning spree
Watching the autumn foliage turn
After shooting the rapids
When you're doing your taxes
After cross-country skiing
At a rock concert
On the Fourth of July
To spiff up moving day
While building the wine cellar
As a birthday surprise
While watching time trials for the
    Olympics
After a tennis match
During half time of the big game
After planting an herb garden
While driving cross-country
While antique hunting
In celebration of your first year in
    business
After cleaning out closets with a
    friend
Organizing photo albums
During a day at the zoo
After washing the family car
During a backgammon tournament
While working on a Saturday
In a hot-air balloon
While doing inventory
After watching or running the
    marathon
While watching the rodeo
After a flying lesson
During the Boston Pops at Tanglewood
When you're writing a cookbook

ICED COFFEE

There are numerous ways of making iced coffee, but one rule always prevails: to make good iced coffee, you must first make good hot coffee. Be sure to make it strong, since the ice will dilute its flavor, and do not make it too far in advance. Sweeten it, if you wish, while it is still hot, then simply allow it to cool in the refrigerator in a glass or a china jug, covered to preserve as much of the aroma as possible.

For a final touch, add a strip of lemon peel, a sprig of fresh mint, or a dash of bitters or rum or chocolate or honey. And, of course, indulge now and again with a scoop of ice cream, vanilla or coffee.

DUCK CURRY

A perfect dish for a picnic—nice and moist with a great yellow glow. Accompany with peanuts, raisins, chopped scallions, and coconut served in little bowls. Put a daffodil in a tiny vase, too.

2 ducks (4 to 5 pounds each), cut into 6 pieces each
2 large yellow onions, coarsely chopped
6 ribs celery, coarsely chopped
6 cloves garlic, minced
2 Granny Smith apples, coarsely chopped
3 tablespoons mild curry powder
2 tablespoons hot curry powder
1 teaspoon ground ginger
1 teaspoon ground cardamom
½ teaspoon fennel seeds
Pinch cayenne pepper
⅓ cup unbleached all-purpose flour
4 cups Berta's Chicken Stock (page 396)
1 cup mango chutney
¾ cup grated coconut
¾ cup heavy or whipping cream
1 cup chopped dried figs
1 cup toasted cashew nuts
½ cup minced crystallized ginger

1. Place the duck pieces, skin side down, on a cutting board. Carefully trim the excess fat to the edge of the skin. Reserve the fat to make cracklings (page 249), if you wish.

2. Preheat oven to 375°F.

3. Brown the duck in a large oven-proof skillet over medium-high heat. Remove and discard all but ¼ cup of the fat from the skillet. Place the duck in the skillet and roast, uncovered, 15 minutes.

4. Remove the duck from the skillet and set aside. Add the onions, celery, and garlic to the pan and sauté over medium heat until softened, about 10 minutes.

5. Add the apples and stir in the curry powders, ginger, cardamom, fennel, and cayenne. Cook 2 minutes.

6. Stir in the flour and cook 2 minutes more. Gradually stir in the stock and cook, stirring constantly, until blended. Stir in the chutney and coconut.

7. Combine the duck and sauce in a large casserole or Dutch oven. Cook covered over medium heat for 1½ hours.

8. Remove the duck from the sauce. Stir the cream into the sauce and purée in a blender. Taste and adjust seasonings.

9. Return the duck and sauce to the casserole. Stir in the figs, cashews, and crystallized ginger. Bake uncovered for 15 minutes.

10. Serve immediately with hot cooked rice, curry accompaniments, and duck cracklings, if you made them.

8 portions

LAYERED CHEF'S SALAD WITH TUNA MAYONNAISE DRESSING

A chef's salad is so often the expected. Not ours, made with fresh basil, sun-dried tomatoes, smoked mozzarella, salami, smoked turkey, and arugula, then served with a delicate tuna mayonnaise—reminiscent of *vitello tonnato*. This salad must be made 6 to 24 hours before serving and should be arranged in a large glass bowl with straight sides to show off all the layers.

3 cups mixed torn greens (romaine, red leaf lettuce, radicchio, and
  arugula)
4 scallions (green onions, white part and 2 inches green), sliced
3 ripe tomatoes, seeded and sliced
4 sun-dried tomatoes (packed in oil), drained and chopped
1 cup fresh basil leaves
12 ounces smoked mozzarella cheese
Freshly ground black pepper, to taste
1 cup alfalfa sprouts
1 medium-size red onion, sliced
½ cup Niçoise olives, pitted
4 ounces hard salami, cut into julienne
4 hard-cooked eggs, peeled
Salt, to taste
8 ounces smoked turkey breast, cut into julienne
1 sweet red pepper, cored, seeded, and cut into rings
½ cup torn arugula leaves
1 jar (6 ounces) marinated artichoke hearts, drained and sliced
5 ounces prosciutto, cut into julienne
1 pound asparagus spears or broccoli florets, blanched
Tuna Mayonnaise (recipe follows)

1. Toss the greens with 2 of the sliced scallions in a large glass bowl. Top with the fresh tomatoes and then with the sun-dried tomatoes. Sprinkle half of the basil over the tomatoes.

2. Thinly slice 8 ounces of the mozzarella and arrange on the basil layer. Sprinkle with freshly ground black pepper to taste. Grate the remaining 4 ounces mozzarella and set aside.

3. Top the sliced cheese with separate layers of alfalfa sprouts, onion, half the olives, and all the salami.

4. Process the eggs, the remaining 2 scallions, and salt and pepper to taste in a food processor fitted with a steel blade just until the eggs are chopped. Spoon on top of the salami layer.

5. Place the turkey julienne over the eggs. Then add the red pepper and scatter with the ½ cup arugula. Layer artichoke hearts on top of the arugula and cover with the prosciutto julienne.

THE GARDEN CLUB PICNIC

Fiddlehead Soup

Layered Chef's Salad with Tuna Mayonnaise Dressing

Crusty rolls

Pineapple Upside-down Cake

Vouvray or California Chenin Blanc

6. Top with the remaining basil leaves, sprinkle with more pepper, and add the reserved grated mozzarella. Make a final layer of the asparagus, arranged in a spoke pattern, or the broccoli florets.

7. Make the tuna mayonnaise.

8. Spread a thick layer of the tuna mayonnaise on top of the salad. Garnish with the remaining olives.

9. Cover with plastic wrap and refrigerate 6 to 24 hours.

10. Use 2 large salad spoons to get down through all the layers to serve the salad.

6 portions

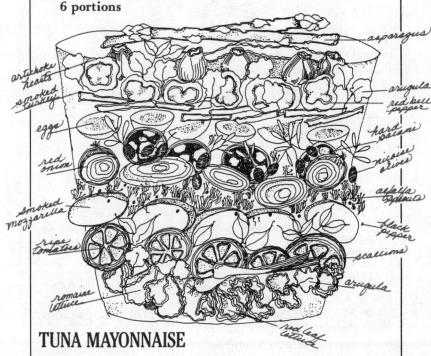

THE OLD-FASHIONED PICNIC

The word "picnic" originally meant a composite meal, each course or dish contributed by a different guest. By the late eighteenth century, however, picnics had a new sense—a party of refined persons eating an elaborate series of cold and fresh-cooked dishes out-of-doors. In the nineteenth century, the picnic offered respectable Victorians an acceptable opportunity for "the promiscuous intermingling of the sexes." Seating arrangements could be left to the landscape, conversation could be general, and laughter could be wholehearted once out of the drawing room.

TUNA MAYONNAISE

4 egg yolks
3 anchovy fillets, chopped
1 tablespoon capers, drained
3 tablespoons fresh lemon juice
1 tablespoon Dijon-style mustard
⅓ cup chopped fresh Italian parsley
1 cup olive oil
½ cup vegetable oil
Salt and freshly ground black pepper, to taste
1 can (6½ ounces) tuna (packed in oil)
½ cup sour cream

1. Process the egg yolks, anchovies, capers, lemon juice, mustard, and parsley in a food processor fitted with a steel blade for 15 seconds. With the machine running, pour the oils in a thin steady stream through the feed tube to make a thick mayonnaise. Season to taste with salt and pepper.

2. Flake the tuna and add it with its oil to the mayonnaise. Process until thoroughly blended.

3. Scrape into a small bowl, fold in the sour cream, and taste and adjust seasonings. Refrigerate covered until ready to use.

About 3 cups

HONEY-CURRY BREAD

This bread has a wonderful flavor and bright yellow color. It is great for sandwiches, such as roast beef and chutney. Try it toasted with lime marmalade.

½ cup warm water (105° to 115°F)
3 packages active dry yeast
3 tablespoons unsalted butter
2 tablespoons curry powder
⅔ cup honey
2 cups buttermilk
2 teaspoons salt
6 to 7 cups unbleached all-purpose flour
1 egg
2 teaspoons water
3 tablespoons slivered almonds

1. Pour ½ cup water into a large bowl. Stir in the yeast and let stand 5 to 10 minutes.

2. Meanwhile, melt the butter in a small saucepan and stir in the curry powder. Cook over low heat 1 minute. Stir in the honey and remove from heat.

3. Add the honey mixture, buttermilk, salt, and 3 cups of the flour to the yeast mixture. Stir with a wooden spoon to mix well. Gradually stir in enough of the remaining flour to make a soft dough.

4. Knead on a floured surface until smooth and elastic, about 5 minutes.

5. Place the dough in a well-buttered large bowl and turn to coat the dough with butter. Cover with a damp towel and let rise in a warm place until doubled in bulk, about 1 hour.

6. Punch the dough down and divide it in half. Divide 1 piece of the dough into thirds. Using your hands, roll the 3 pieces into 1-inch thick ropes and braid. Curl the braid around itself in a spiral to make a braided crown. Repeat with the remaining dough. Place each braided loaf on a buttered baking sheet, cover, and let rise for about 45 minutes.

7. Preheat oven to 375°F.

8. Beat the egg and 2 teaspoons water in a small bowl. Brush the tops of the breads with the egg wash. Sprinkle each loaf with almonds.

9. Bake until loaves are brown and sound hollow when the bottoms are lightly thumped, 40 to 45 minutes. Cool on wire racks to room temperature.

2 loaves

MILESTONE ROAD TAILGATE PICNIC

Pineapple spears with fresh mint sprigs

Duck Curry with condiments

Honey-Curry Bread

Rhubarb Crisp
Orange-Almond Snails

Gewürztraminer

"The pedigree of honey
Does not concern the bee;
A clover, any time, to him
Is aristocracy."
—Emily Dickinson

THE PINEAPPLE

The pineapple has long been a symbol of hospitality. It appears often as a door knocker design, stenciled on walls, and carved on antique bedposts. In the olden days, pineapples were rented by English growers to their friends to grace the centerpiece of a festive table.

Choose the ripest pineapple you can find in the market. Smell for sweetness, touch for tenderness, and watch carefully for color. Choose the one with the golden hue. Once they are picked, they no longer increase in sweetness, although they will become softer. Try not to refrigerate—just store at room temperature. They're so pretty around the kitchen.

PINEAPPLE UPSIDE-DOWN CAKE

A traditional American favorite spiked with rum and a bit of ground ginger is absolutely luscious served warm with whipped cream

6 tablespoons (¾ stick) unsalted butter
½ cup packed dark brown sugar
3 tablespoons dark rum
1 can (20 ounces) pineapple slices (packed in natural juice), drained but ½ cup juice reserved
12 to 15 pecan halves
½ cup (1 stick) unsalted margarine, room temperature
¾ cup granulated sugar
2 eggs
1 teaspoon vanilla extract
2 cups unbleached all-purpose flour
1 teaspoon ground ginger
1½ teaspoons baking soda
½ teaspoon salt
Whipped cream (garnish)

1. Preheat oven to 350°F.

2. Melt the butter and pour into the bottom of a 9½-inch springform pan. (Place the pan on a piece of aluminum foil to catch any butter that leaks through.) Press the brown sugar evenly over the butter and sprinkle with 2 tablespoons of the rum. Arrange 7 of the pineapple slices over the brown sugar. Fill in the spaces with the pecan halves. Set aside.

3. Cream the margarine and granulated sugar in a mixer bowl. Beat in the eggs, one at a time. Beat in the vanilla.

4. Purée the remaining 3 pineapple slices with the remaining 1 tablespoon rum in a blender or food processor fitted with a steel blade and beat into the butter mixture.

5. Sift the flour, ginger, baking soda, and salt together. Beat into the butter mixture alternately with the reserved pineapple juice.

6. Pour the cake batter over the pineapple slices in the springform pan. Bake until the center of the cake springs back when gently touched, 30 to 35 minutes.

7. While the cake is still hot, remove the side of the pan. Invert the cake onto a platter and remove the pan bottom. Serve the cake warm or at room temperature. Top with dollops of whipped cream.

8 portions

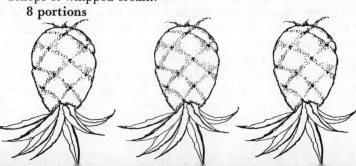

SPRING CHICKENS

Brillat-Savarin, the great culinary expert and writer, said, "Poultry is to the cook what canvas is to the painter." We couldn't agree more: spring chickens properly prepared can express the essence of the season. We paint our canvas with arugula and herb infusions, mild leek stuffings, and colorful sautés. Plump and succulent chickens are perfect for translating spring's wonders into flavors and using such flavors as paint for the palate.

CHICKEN CUTLETS WITH RASPBERRIES

Chicken breasts pounded very thin are quickly sautéed and served in a glistening sauce of red raspberries. A very fast entrée to prepare for a special intimate dinner.

6 whole chicken breasts (12 halves), skinned, boned, and pounded
   thin (¼ inch)
Salt and freshly ground black pepper, to taste
4 tablespoons (½ stick) unsalted butter
3 tablespoons raspberry vinegar
⅓ cup dry white wine
1 ½ cups fresh or frozen raspberries, thawed if frozen

   1. Sprinkle both sides of the chicken breasts with salt and pepper. Melt the butter in a large sauté pan over medium-high heat. Sauté the chicken, a few pieces at a time, in the butter just until browned on each side. Remove to a warmed serving platter.
   2. Pour the vinegar and wine into the pan to deglaze it. Stir in the raspberries and cook over high heat, stirring constantly, until slightly thickened. Pour the sauce over the chicken breasts and serve immediately.
   6 portions

we like our chickens not cooped up but.... out walking in the sunshine!

CHICKEN BREASTS STUFFED WITH ORANGE AND LEEKS

A light-tasting preparation of chicken breasts with one of our favorites from the onion family—leeks—is freshened with mint and orange juice and delicately coated with a lush cream sauce.

12 leeks, ½ to ¾ inch wide
8 tablespoons (1 stick) unsalted butter
2 oranges
Salt and freshly ground black pepper, to taste
6 whole chicken breasts (12 halves), skinned, boned, and each half pounded thin (¼ inch)
2 tablespoons melted unsalted butter
1 cup fresh mint leaves
1 cup heavy or whipping cream

1. Trim the root ends of the leeks. Cut the lower part of each leek into a piece that is roughly the same length as the width of the chicken breasts. Rinse all the leek pieces and remaining stems thoroughly and pat dry. Cut the tender stems into ½-inch slices.

2. Boil the 12 leek pieces in boiling salted water until tender, about 10 minutes.

3. Melt 6 tablespoons of the butter in a medium-size skillet over medium heat. Add the ½-inch leek slices and sauté until soft.

4. Grate the zest of the oranges and then squeeze the juice from the pulp. Stir the juice from the oranges and half the zest into the sautéed leeks and simmer covered over low heat for 15 minutes. Season to taste with salt and pepper.

5. Place the chicken breasts, boned side up, on a work surface. Brush each breast with a little of the melted butter. Sprinkle lightly with pepper and the remaining orange zest. Place 3 mint leaves down the center of each breast. Place 1 leek piece crosswise on each breast near the bottom and roll up tightly to form a neat package. Wrap and tie each breast in 2 or 3 places with kitchen string.

6. Sauté the rolls in the remaining 2 tablespoons butter in a large skillet until browned on all sides and cooked through, 15 to 20 minutes. Keep warm in the oven while you finish the sauce.

7. Pour the cream into the leek sauce, increase heat to high, and cook, stirring constantly, until thickened, about 7 minutes.

8. Chop any remaining mint and stir into the sauce. Cook 1 minute more.

9. Spoon a pool of the leek sauce on each plate, place 2 chicken breasts on each plate, and serve immediately.

6 portions

"Simple pleasures . . . are the last refuge of the complex."
—Oscar Wilde

CHICKEN WITH RED AND YELLOW PEPPERS

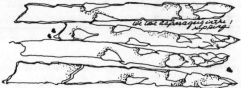

This dish is fun to prepare in front of friends. All the vegetables sparkle like jewels when quickly stir-fried in a wok. Sprinkle with fresh chives before serving and serve with Lemon Rice (page 59).

2 sweet red peppers
2 sweet yellow peppers
5 whole chicken breasts (10 halves), skinned, boned, and cut into
    1½- to 2-inch cubes
2 tablespoons unsalted butter
2 tablespoons best-quality olive oil
1½ pounds asparagus, trimmed and cut diagonally into 2-inch
    pieces
½ cup Madeira
1 tablespoon chopped fresh thyme or 1 teaspoon dried
1 tablespoon chopped fresh rosemary or 1 teaspoon dried
1 large tomato, seeded and chopped
2 tablespoons fresh lemon juice
¾ cup heavy or whipping cream
Salt and freshly ground black pepper, to taste
¾ cup snipped fresh chives

1. Core and seed the peppers and cut them into squares roughly the same size as the chicken pieces.

2. Heat 1 tablespoon of the butter and 1 tablespoon of the oil in a wok over medium-high heat. Add the red and yellow peppers and stir-fry until crisp-tender, about 4 minutes. Remove from the wok and set aside in a bowl.

3. Add the asparagus to the wok and stir-fry until crisp-tender, 5 to 8 minutes. Remove from the wok and add to the peppers.

4. Add the remaining butter and oil to the wok and heat. Add the chicken, in batches if necessary, and stir-fry just until cooked, about 8 minutes. Remove from the wok with a slotted spoon, leaving the juices in the pan, and add to the vegetables.

5. Add the Madeira, thyme, rosemary, and tomato to the wok. Heat to boiling and cook until syrupy.

6. Pour in the lemon juice. When boiling, stir in the cream and cook until thickened. Season to taste with salt and pepper.

7. Return the chicken and vegetables to the wok and coat with the sauce. Heat until the chicken is heated through. Remove to a serving bowl and sprinkle lavishly with chives. Serve immediately.

6 portions

KEYS TO SUCCESS

When you're expecting friends for the weekend, be sure you know when they expect to arrive so that you are home in plenty of time to greet them. Nothing gets a visit off to a shakier start than having your guests show up at your door to find no one home. If you can't be there, be sure a neighbor is around to let them in and have plenty of noshes and nibbles conveniently placed, plus a pitcher of something refreshing in the refrigerator, to keep your friends relaxed and happy until you get there. Cute notes describing where everything is are helpful placed near the front door, and, if anything is off limits, note that too.

The same holds true of departure times. To avoid any embarrassing situations, be sure you know exactly when your guests are leaving. We've all heard stories of the guest who forgot to leave, as well as the host who made plans that excluded the guest, thinking he or she would be gone by then. Don't let these simple details spoil what should be a terrific visit.

HOW TO PAMPER HOUSEGUESTS

♥ Leave a selection of the latest magazines and some favorite books in the guest room.
♥ Place bunches of lily of the valley, violets, roses, or another in-season flower near the guest bed to make the room bright and fragrant. Don't forget the bath, too.
♥ Turn down the guest bed and place a special sweet on the pillow.
♥ Make sure there is a clock radio in the guest room.
♥ Keep extra slippers, robe, and toothbrush around, in case they've forgotten to pack their own.
♥ Have coffee brewing before your guests awake, and have the newspaper waiting nearby.
♥ Don't force your guests into activities they may not want to do. Make yourself available, but flexible.
♥ Invite other friends over for cocktails or for one weekend meal. New people spark new conversation.

AUNT TANDY'S CHICKEN CROQUETTES

Sheila's favorite aunt made these very simple chicken croquettes, which were perfect as a light Sunday supper. Top with a bit of fresh tomato sauce.

4 slices (½ inch thick) challah or egg bread
¼ to ½ cup water
2 whole chicken breasts (4 halves), skinned, boned, and cut into 3-inch pieces
4 eggs
1 medium-size yellow onion, coarsely chopped
Salt and freshly ground black pepper, to taste
3 cups fresh bread crumbs
3 tablespoons paprika
3 tablespoons chicken fat or unsalted butter
3 tablespoons chopped fresh Italian parsley
4 cups corn oil

1. Soak the challah in ¼ cup water (add more if needed), squeeze dry, and coarsely shred.
2. Process the chicken in a food processor fitted with a steel blade until coarsely chopped. Add the bread, eggs, onion, and salt and pepper to taste and process until thoroughly blended. Refrigerate covered 30 minutes. The mixture will be loose at this point.
3. Combine the bread crumbs, paprika, chicken fat, and parsley in a bowl and pour onto a large plate.
4. Shape the chicken mixture into 10 patties and coat evenly with the bread crumb mixture. Place the patties on a sheet of waxed paper and refrigerate covered at least 2 hours.
5. Heat the oil in a deep-fat fryer over medium-high heat. Fry 2 croquettes at a time in the oil until golden brown, 7 to 8 minutes. Serve immediately.
10 croquettes

MANGO CHUTNEY CHICKEN

Make this chicken dish when you have a craving for the exotic flavors of India. It is guaranteed to provide quick passage out of the kitchen, if not to anywhere else.

6 tablespoons (¾ stick) unsalted butter
2 tablespoons curry powder
¼ cup dry white wine
2 frying chickens, cut into quarters
1½ cups mango chutney, chopped with syrup
2 tablespoons shredded coconut
1 tablespoon snipped fresh chives

1. Preheat oven to 350°F.

2. Melt the butter in a small saucepan over low heat. Add the curry powder and cook for 2 to 3 minutes. Add the wine and stir until blended. Remove from heat.

3. Place the chicken pieces in a baking pan and baste with the butter mixture.

4. Bake for 30 minutes. Remove from the oven and spread the chutney over the chicken. Bake for 30 minutes more, basting frequently.

5. Remove the chicken to a serving platter. Pour the pan juices into a small saucepan and boil for 3 to 4 minutes to reduce the sauce slightly. Pour the sauce over the chicken and sprinkle with coconut and chives. Serve immediately.

6 to 8 portions

CHICKEN STUFFED WITH ARUGULA

A wonderful peppery flavor is imparted to the chickens by the arugula mixture stuffed under the skin. A very succulent way to roast a chicken.

2 roasting chickens (2 ½ to 3 pounds each), ready to cook
10 tablespoons (1 ¼ sticks) unsalted butter, softened
5 shallots, minced
3 bunches fresh arugula, rinsed, dried, stems removed (6 cups leaves)
6 ounces cream cheese, softened
1 egg
1 cup shredded Swiss cheese
Salt and freshly ground black pepper, to taste
2 tablespoons olive oil
1 teaspoon dried thyme

1. Starting at the neck cavity of each chicken, use your fingers to separate the skin from the breast and leg meat, being careful not to tear the skin.

2. Melt 2 tablespoons of the butter in a sauté pan over medium-low heat. Add the shallots and sauté 10 minutes.

3. Chop the arugula coarsely and add it to the pan. Cook just until wilted, about 2 minutes. Cool completely.

4. Process the remaining 8 tablespoons butter and the cream cheese in a food processor fitted with a steel blade until smooth. Add the cooled arugula mixture and process until combined. Add the egg, Swiss cheese, and salt and

MEMORIAL DAY

The Memorial Day weekend is usually an active one—not warm enough for sunbathing on the beach, but a great time for friendly competition among friends. Before a lavish afternoon picnic structure a morning of individual or team events, with some guests acting as umpires, judges, and referees. The more the merrier as you strive for the gold with tennis, three-legged races, softball, touch football, soccer, croquet, volleyball, badminton, miniature golf, Frisbee tossing, and broad jumping. Keep score, provide lots of cold chicken and hot dogs, and stage an awards celebration.

SAGE

Sage grows well outdoors or on a sunny window sill. There are over 100 different varieties; we like to plant the common silvery green sage along with purple and pineapple varieties. The latter two are decorative garnishes for cheese boards and crudités. The Italians, who use sage in so many delicious ways, fry the leaves whole and eat them with gnocchi or veal scaloppine. Sage is also wonderful with duck, veal, or pork.

Sage symbolizes wisdom and immortality. Sage tea is supposed to be good for fevers and colds.

pepper to taste. Process just until combined.

5. Preheat oven to 450°F.

6. Spoon the arugula mixture evenly between the skin and the flesh of both chickens, pushing the mixture back into the corners and pockets. Tie the legs of each chicken firmly together to help seal the skin openings.

7. Rub each chicken with 1 tablespoon olive oil and sprinkle generously with salt, pepper, and thyme.

8. Place the chickens in a roasting pan and roast 15 minutes. Reduce heat to 350°F and roast, basting occasionally with the pan juices, until the juices run clear (not pink) when the thigh is pierced with a sharp skewer, about 1¼ hours.

9. Remove from the oven and let stand 5 to 10 minutes before carving.

6 to 8 portions

CORNISH HENS WITH HERB BUTTER

Fresh parsley, sage, rosemary, and thyme add the sweet fragrant taste just perfect for little hens. Butter and oil make them beautifully moist. Place on a bed of fresh herbs to serve.

6 Rock Cornish hens (¾ to 1 pound each)
Salt and freshly ground black pepper, to taste
¾ cup (1½ sticks) unsalted butter, room temperature
1 cup chopped fresh parsley
½ cup snipped fresh chives
2 tablespoons chopped fresh rosemary
2 tablespoons chopped fresh thyme
2 tablespoons chopped fresh sage
3 tablespoons olive oil
1½ tablespoons crumbled dried sage

1. Rinse the birds and pat dry. Sprinkle the cavity of each bird with salt and pepper.

2. Process to a paste the butter, parsley, chives, rosemary, thyme, and fresh sage in a food processor fitted with a steel blade. Carefully separate the skin from the breast of each bird. Spread about 2 tablespoons of the herb butter between the skin and breast of each bird. Smooth the skin into place and truss.

3. Preheat oven to 450°F.

4. Rub the oil over the birds and sprinkle with salt and pepper. Finally, rub the dried sage evenly over each bird and place in a roasting pan.

5. Roast for 20 minutes. Reduce the heat to 350°F. Continue roasting until juices run clear when the thickest part of a thigh is pierced, about 40 more minutes. Baste frequently with the pan juices. Serve immediately.

6 portions

DERBY WEEKEND

In spring any event is cause for celebration, and spring horse races are one of our favorite excuses for getting friends together for luscious brunches and special dinners. Which horse wins or loses is really of little consequence as the mixing of mint juleps, the timing of crown roasts of lamb, and the enjoyment of extravagant centerpieces of fresh flowers take center stage. We think our menus are a sure bet for winning top entertainment garlands.

PALE GREENS WITH WATERCRESS DRESSING

A simple and pretty salad of buttery Boston lettuce and graceful endive leaves. The peppery watercress dressing adds a dark green accent and just the right tang.

2 Belgian endives
1 large head Boston or other tender green lettuce
1 egg yolk
2 tablespoons fresh lemon juice
2 tablespoons tarragon vinegar
1 tablespoon Dijon-style mustard
1 teaspoon dried tarragon
¾ cup olive oil
1 cup minced watercress leaves
Salt and freshly ground black pepper, to taste

1. Separate the endive and Boston lettuce leaves. Rinse well and pat dry. Tear the Boston lettuce into large bite-size pieces. Toss the lettuce and endives together in a salad bowl.

2. Whisk the egg yolk, lemon juice, vinegar, mustard, and tarragon together in a mixing bowl. Gradually whisk in the oil. Whisk in the watercress and season to taste with salt and pepper.

3. Toss the salad with just enough of the dressing to coat the leaves. Serve immediately.

6 to 8 portions

DERBY WEEKEND BRUNCH

Honeydew wedges with fresh mint sprigs

Smoked Salmon and Cream Cheese Soup

Shad Roe with Bacon

Rich Rum Sticky Buns

Freshly brewed coffee with Vandermint liqueur

AVOCADO WITH RASPBERRY VINAIGRETTE

Raspberries, sherry vinegar, and a touch of lemon juice make one of the most luscious vinaigrettes. Use the vinaigrette in summertime to dress a fruit salad composed of thin melon and banana slices. You'll want it never to end.

1 package (10 ounces) frozen raspberries, thawed and drained
2 tablespoons sherry vinegar
2 tablespoons fresh lemon juice
½ cup best-quality olive oil
½ cup Crème Fraîche (page 399)
Pinch freshly grated nutmeg
Salt and freshly ground black pepper, to taste
3 ripe avocados

1. Process the raspberries in a food processor fitted with a steel blade until puréed. Strain through a sieve to remove

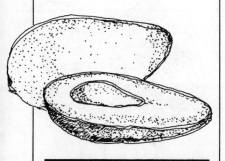

the seeds and return the purée to the food processor. Add the vinegar and lemon juice and process to blend. With the machine running, pour the oil through the feed tube in a thin steady stream. Add the crème fraîche and process until smooth. The sauce should be bright pink. Season with nutmeg and salt and pepper to taste.

2. Cut the avocados in half, remove the pits, and then peel. Cut each avocado half into thin slices and fan the slices of each half on a salad plate. Pour the vinaigrette over the middle of each avocado half and serve immediately.

6 portions

SWEETBREAD RAGOUT

A pale port-colored sauce coats these sweetbreads simmered ever so slowly with whole shallots and figs. Sprinkle in pink peppercorns just at the end.

1 ½ pounds veal sweetbreads
6 dried figs, quartered
1 cup ruby port
6 tablespoons (¾ stick) unsalted butter
24 shallots, peeled
3 tablespoons crème de cassis
½ cup dry red wine
¾ cup Beef Stock (page 397) or canned beef broth
Salt and freshly ground black pepper, to taste
¼ cup heavy or whipping cream
1 tablespoon pink peppercorns*

1. Soak the sweetbreads in 3 changes of ice water for 1 hour. Drain, place in a medium-size saucepan, and add water to cover. Slowly heat to boiling. Reduce the heat and simmer for 3 minutes, turning once. Drain and plunge into cold water to refresh.

2. When the sweetbreads are cool enough to handle, remove fat and connecting tubes. Place the sweetbreads on a large plate and cover with a board or cookie sheet. Place several weights (bags of flour or sugar or cans) on top of the board and refrigerate 2 to 3 hours or overnight.

3. Soak the figs in ½ cup of the port for 3 hours.

4. Melt 3 tablespoons of the butter in a medium-size saucepan. Add the shallots and sauté until coated and glistening with the butter, 5 to 7 minutes. Add the cassis and cook 2 to 3 minutes more to glaze the shallots. Remove from heat and set aside.

5. Melt the remaining 3 tablespoons butter in a sauté pan. Add the sweetbreads and brown about 3 minutes on each side. Pour in the wine and stock. Add the figs with the soaking liquid and the shallots and season to taste with salt and pepper. Quickly heat to boiling and cover the pan. Reduce heat and simmer about 40 minutes.

6. Using a slotted spoon, remove the sweetbreads, figs,

WINNER DINNER

Mint Juleps

Cashew Sticks

Avocado with Raspberry Vinaigrette

Sweetbread Ragout

Pale Greens with Watercress Dressing

Crusty French bread

Banana Bourbon Cake with Bourbon Crème Anglaise

Meursault

and shallots from the pan. Add the remaining ½ cup port to the pan and cook, stirring occasionally, until the liquid is reduced to about ¾ cup.

7. Stir in the cream and peppercorns and cook 3 minutes more. Taste and adjust seasonings. Return the sweetbreads, figs, and shallots to the pan and heat until warmed through. Serve immediately.

6 portions

*available in specialty food shops.

TRIPLE CROWN ROAST OF LAMB

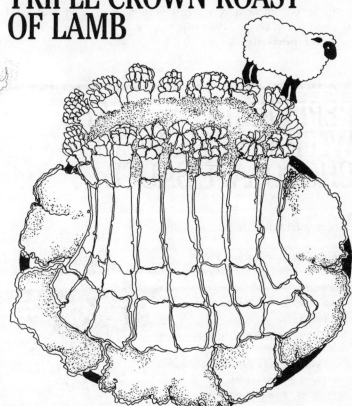

TRIPLE CROWN DINNER

Mint Juleps

Avocado with Raspberry Vinaigrette

Triple Crown Roast of Lamb

Lemon Rice

Sorrel Flan

Goat-Cheese Popovers

Orange-Almond Snails
Mint Chocolate Meringues

Saint-Julien

A crown roast is always a spectacular presentation for a special dinner party. What better way to celebrate the festivities of Kentucky Derby day? If your horse has won, a crown roast dinner could be in anticipation of the Triple Crown.

12 ounces ground lamb
6 cloves garlic, minced
½ cup heavy or whipping cream
2 tablespoons brandy
¼ cup minced fresh Italian parsley
¼ cup dried currants
1½ teaspoons ground cinnamon
Salt and freshly ground black pepper, to taste
1 crown roast of lamb (3½ to 4 pounds)
1 or 2 preserved grape leaves, rinsed
Coarse (kosher) salt

1. Preheat oven to 425°F.

2. Purée the ground lamb, garlic, and cream in a food processor fitted with a steel blade until quite smooth. Add the brandy, parsley, currants, cinnamon, and salt and pepper to taste. Process just until combined.

3. Place the crown roast in a shallow roasting pan. Spoon the stuffing mixture into the center and cover the top of the stuffing with 1 or 2 grape leaves. Rub the outside of the roast with coarse salt and freshly ground pepper.

4. Roast the meat 15 minutes. Reduce the heat to 375°F and roast 55 minutes more for rare to medium-rare meat.

5. Remove the grape leaves and scoop out the stuffing into a serving bowl. Top the lamb bones with paper frills and cut the roast into chops.

6. Serve immediately with lemon rice and buttered steamed green beans. Pass mint sauce.

4 to 6 portions

PEPPERMINT SOUFFLE WITH BITTERSWEET CHOCOLATE SAUCE

A very refreshing dessert soufflé.

2 tablespoons unsalted butter
3 tablespoons unbleached all-purpose flour
1 cup milk
¼ cup heavy or whipping cream
4 egg yolks
2 tablespoons peppermint schnapps
3 tablespoons sugar
¾ cup crushed pink peppermint candies
½ teaspoon ground cloves
7 egg whites, room temperature
Pinch cream of tartar
Bittersweet Chocolate Sauce (recipe follows)
Whole candied roses or chopped peppermint candies

1. Melt the butter in a heavy small saucepan over low heat until foamy. Whisk in the flour and cook 1 minute. Gradually whisk in milk and then the cream. Cook, stirring constantly, until thick and smooth.

2. Remove from heat. Whisk in the egg yolks, one at a time. Stir in the schnapps and sugar. Then stir in the crushed candies and ground cloves. (The candies can be crushed in a food processor fitted with a steel blade.)

3. Preheat oven to 375°F. Butter a 6-cup soufflé dish and coat with sugar.

4. Beat the egg whites with the cream of tartar until stiff but not dry. Gently fold into the soufflé base. Pour into the prepared dish.

DERBY DAY MINT JULEP

The perfect recipe may be a subject of controversy, but all agree that it is de rigueur to serve mint juleps in icy cold silver mugs or glasses that have been filled to the brim with crushed ice or ice cubes until an alluring frost congeals on the outside. The classic mint julep is made with Kentucky bourbon, but nonpurists may substitute any spirits desired—rye, brandy, applejack, vodka, gin, rum—just don't tell anyone!

For each chilled mug or glass, crush 4 sprigs of fresh mint leaves with 1 teaspoon of superfine sugar and 1 ounce of club soda in a small bowl. Add 2 jiggers (3 ounces) of bourbon or other spirits and let the mixture stand for 5 minutes.

Strain into ice-filled, chilled mugs, and stir well. Garnish each with a sprig of fresh mint and serve with a straw.

5. Bake for 30 minutes.

6. While the soufflé is baking, make the chocolate sauce.

7. Serve the soufflé immediately with warm chocolate sauce and garnish each serving with a candied whole rose or additional chopped peppermint candies.

4 to 6 portions

BITTERSWEET CHOCOLATE SAUCE

A thin dark sauce for lovers of bittersweet chocolate.

4 ounces semisweet chocolate, broken into small pieces
¼ cup unsweetened cocoa powder
½ cup water

Heat the chocolate, cocoa, and water in a heavy small saucepan over medium-low heat, stirring constantly, until smooth. Serve warm.

1 cup

BOURBON

Truly an original in the spirit of American independence, the first bourbons were distilled from corn in Bourbon County, Kentucky. We like to add a native American flair by substituting bourbon in recipes that call for Cognac or rum. For a change of pace, try flambéing dishes and dousing cakes with a splash of Kentucky's finest.

BANANA BOURBON CAKE WITH BOURBON CREME ANGLAISE

A rich fruit-filled cake that is incredibly moist and keeps well. Serve with the delectable bourbon sauce.

1½ cups coarsely chopped pecans
1½ cups golden raisins
3 cups unbleached all-purpose flour
3 teaspoons baking powder
1 teaspoon ground cinnamon
1 teaspoon ground ginger
½ teaspoon ground nutmeg
1 cup (2 sticks) unsalted butter, room temperature
2 cups sugar
3 ripe bananas
4 eggs
¾ cup bourbon
Bourbon Crème Anglaise (recipe follows)

1. Preheat oven to 350°F.

2. Toss the pecans and raisins with ½ cup of the flour and set aside.

3. Sift the remaining flour, the baking powder, cinnamon, ginger, and nutmeg together and set aside.

4. Beat the butter and sugar in a mixer bowl until light and fluffy. Mash the bananas and beat into the butter mixture. Add the eggs, one at a time, beating well after each addition.

5. Fold in the sifted flour mixture and bourbon alternately, beginning and ending with the dry ingredients. Fold in the pecan mixture. Pour the batter into an ungreased 10-inch tube pan.

6. Bake 1 hour 15 minutes. Cool and remove from the pan.

7. Make the bourbon sauce.

8. Cut the cake into slices and serve each slice with bourbon sauce spooned over it.

12 portions

BOURBON CREME ANGLAISE

1½ cups light cream
1 tablespoon brown sugar
6 egg yolks
6 tablespoons pure maple syrup
6 tablespoons bourbon

1. Heat the cream and sugar in a small saucepan just until the sugar dissolves. Remove from the heat.

2. Whisk the egg yolks together in a mixing bowl. Slowly beat in a third of the cream mixture; then whisk the egg yolks back into the cream mixture. Cook over low heat, stirring constantly, just until thickened. Be careful not to let the mixture boil.

3. Remove to a clean bowl. Stir in the syrup and bourbon. Cool completely.

About 2½ cups

ORANGE-ALMOND SNAILS

Anyone with memories of making butter and cinnamon tarts with their mother's leftover pie dough will enjoy these. This is a sophisticated version with plenty of ground almonds and zesty orange. Perfect to serve with afternoon tea or evening coffee.

1½ cups unbleached all-purpose flour
⅓ cup confectioners' sugar
9 tablespoons (1 stick plus 1 tablespoon) unsalted butter, cold, cut
*   into pieces*
1 egg
1 tablespoon (or as needed) water
2 cups ground almonds
⅔ cup granulated sugar, plus additional for coating
2 tablespoons finely grated orange zest
½ teaspoon almond extract

MORE SPRING CRAVINGS

...Sending a man balloons...shad roe ...watching Baryshnikov dance... listening to the Amadeus Quartet... carpaccio and panzotti at Mezzaluna ...sitting on the steps of the Metropolitan Museum of Art, watching the mimes...spring onions ...coming home from a black-tie party and going to the corner coffee shop...brook trout...bicycling to Wall Street on Sunday...unexpected flowers with no card...lime sorbet ...listening to Bobbie Short sing Cole Porter...sunsets, kites, and clouds ...more muffins...sitting in the Algonquin on Sunday night listening to Steve Ross...

1. Process the flour, confectioners' sugar, and butter in a food processor fitted with a steel blade until the mixture resembles coarse meal.

2. Add the egg and, with the machine running, add 1 tablespoon water by drops just until the dough starts to gather into a ball. Do not overprocess.

3. Wrap the dough in plastic wrap and refrigerate 2 hours.

4. Place the almonds, ⅔ cup granulated sugar, the orange zest and almond extract in the food processor. Process to a coarse paste.

5. Divide the dough in half and roll out each half on a floured surface into a rectangle about ⅛ inch thick. Sprinkle the almond filling evenly over the dough rectangles. Using a rolling pin, press the filling firmly into the dough. Roll up the dough like a jelly roll, starting from a long edge and rolling as tightly as possible.

6. Freeze the rolls on trays for 15 minutes so that they will be easier to slice.

7. Preheat oven to 350°F. Lightly grease cookie sheets.

8. Cut the rolls with a sharp knife into ¼-inch slices and place on the cookie sheets. Bake for 8 to 10 minutes.

9. Immediately remove the cookies to wire racks to cool. When cooled to room temperature, roll each cookie in a shallow bowl of granulated sugar to coat evenly.

4 dozen cookies

MINT CHOCOLATE MERINGUES

A crunchy and feathery light cookie with a surprise burst of mint chocolate.

3 egg whites, room temperature
½ cup superfine sugar
¾ cup coarsely chopped Andes Mints or other chocolate-covered mint patties

1. Preheat oven to 275°F. Line cookie sheets with parchment paper.

2. Beat the egg whites in a mixer bowl until foamy. Gradually beat in the sugar, 1 tablespoon at a time, and continue beating until the peaks are very stiff and glossy. Gently fold in the chopped candies.

3. Drop the meringue, in mounds of about 2 teaspoons, about 1 inch apart on the paper-lined cookie sheets. Bake until the meringues are quite dry but still slightly chewy inside, 1 to 1½ hours. Let cool completely.

3 dozen meringues

MINT

Its very name is synonymous with refreshment, and it is one of the easiest herbs to grow—in fact, it can be a garden pest. Peppermint and spearmint are the best-known varieties, and pineapple mint is becoming popular as a decorative herb. Be sure to have plenty on hand for garnishing iced tea and lemonade, mixing with cucumbers and melons, or chopping into tabouleh. Try crystallizing the leaves for an elegant pastry garnish.

In medieval times mint was thought to symbolize wisdom and virtue.

Pogo: "Winning isn't everything, but losing isn't anything."
—Walt Kelly

MOTHER'S DAY

Mother's Day is one of the year's busiest in restaurants across the country, but we feel that Mother's Day should be more personal—we like to treat Mom to a very special meal, cooked by her own offspring.

PEANUT NOSHES

18 slices Pepperidge Farm sandwich or other firm white bread
1 ½ cups chunky peanut butter
⅓ cup vegetable oil

1. Preheat oven to 350°F.

2. Trim the crusts from 12 slices of the bread and cut the trimmed bread into ½-inch squares. Place the squares flat on a baking sheet and bake just until lightly browned.

3. Place the trimmed crusts and the remaining 6 slices of bread on another baking sheet and bake until golden. Process in a blender or food processor fitted with a steel blade to fine crumbs. Remove to a shallow bowl.

4. Heat the peanut butter and oil in a small saucepan until blended and warm. Dip the toasted bread squares completely into the peanut mixture and then coat with the bread crumbs. Let the bread dry flat on a baking sheet. Store in an airtight container.

About 8 dozen

Show Mom there are more ways to serve peanut butter than as a favorite childhood spread. These noshes are so good, be sure to make plenty for nibbling with a cocktail before dinner.

CHILLED GREENS SOUP

many kinds of salad greens

The tangy tart greens, sweetened with fresh tarragon and cream, make a wonderfully refreshing starter. Serve the pale green soup in cut-glass bowls and garnish with shredded dark pink radicchio.

4 tablespoons (½ stick) unsalted butter
1 large yellow onion, chopped
2 tablespoons chopped fresh tarragon
2 tablespoons unbleached all-purpose flour
6 cups Berta's Chicken Stock (page 396) or canned chicken broth
1 cup dry white wine
2 cups diced celeriac
2 cups diced jicama
5 cups shredded lettuce (romaine, Boston, butter, red leaf, or a combination)
1 bunch watercress, rinsed, patted dry, and stems removed
1 bunch arugula, rinsed, patted dry, and stems removed
2 cups half-and-half
1 cup heavy or whipping cream
Salt and freshly ground black pepper, to taste
Finely shredded radicchio (garnish)

1. Melt the butter in a large stock pot over medium heat. Add the onion and fresh tarragon and sauté over medium-high heat until the onion is soft, about 10 minutes.

2. Stir in the flour and cook 1 minute. Add the stock and wine and stir until well blended. Stir in the celeriac and jicama. Reduce heat and simmer uncovered until the vegetables are tender, about 30 minutes.

3. Add the shredded lettuce and the watercress and arugula leaves. Simmer uncovered 15 minutes more.

4. Remove from heat and stir in the half-and-half, cream, and salt and pepper to taste.

5. Purée the soup in batches in a food processor fitted with a steel blade. (It is better to use the food processor than the blender with this soup, for the processor will retain more of the slightly crunchy texture of the soup.) Pour into a bowl and refrigerate at least 3 hours or overnight. Taste and adjust seasonings.

6. Ladle the soup into clear glass bowls and garnish with shredded radicchio.

6 to 8 portions

APRICOT AND CURRANT CHICKEN

This easy-to-prepare dish was a Silver Palate staple when our store first opened. The orange marmalade and ginger form a golden glaze over the chicken while the apricots and currants impart their fruity flavors to the juices and look wonderful sprinkled among the chicken pieces when presented on a large serving platter.

2 chickens (2½ to 3 pounds each), quartered
Salt and freshly ground black pepper, to taste
1 teaspoon ground ginger
1½ cups bitter orange marmalade
⅓ cup apple juice
⅓ cup fresh orange juice
8 ounces dried apricots
8 ounces dried currants
¼ cup brown sugar

1. Preheat oven to 375°F.
2. Place the chicken pieces, skin side up, in a shallow roasting pan and sprinkle generously with salt and pepper and then the ginger. Spread the marmalade over the chicken and pour the apple and orange juices into the pan. Bake 20 minutes.
3. Remove from the oven and add the apricots and currants to the pan, mixing the fruit evenly. Sprinkle the fruit with the brown sugar and return to the oven. Bake, basting the chicken frequently, until the chicken is golden brown and shiny on top, 40 to 45 minutes.
4. Remove the chicken, apricots, and currants to a warmed serving platter. Pour some of the pan juices over the top and pour the remaining juices into a sauceboat. Serve immediately.

6 to 8 portions

LEMON CHICKEN

Ideal for entertaining, this dish is easy to prepare and can be doubled for larger quantities. The fresh lemon flavor bursts forth after marinating.

MOTHER'S DAY DINNER

Peanut Noshes

Chilled Greens Soup

Apricot and Currant Chicken
or
Lemon Chicken

Lemon Rice

Baked Lima Beans with Gingersnaps

Williamsburg Orange-Sherry Cake

California Chardonnay

2 whole chickens (2½ to 3 pounds each), quartered
2½ cups fresh lemon juice (about 10 lemons)
1 cup unbleached all-purpose flour
1 tablespoon Hungarian sweet paprika
Salt and freshly ground black pepper, to taste
1 cup Berta's Chicken Stock (page 396) or canned chicken broth
2½ tablespoons brown sugar
1 lemon, thinly sliced
1 tablespoon herbes de Provence

1. One day before serving, place the chicken pieces in a shallow dish. Pour the lemon juice over the chicken and marinate in the refrigerator overnight, turning the pieces occasionally.

2. Preheat oven to 375°F.

3. Remove the chicken from the lemon juice; reserve the lemon juice. Combine the flour, paprika, and salt and pepper to taste. Dredge the chicken with the seasoned flour and place skin side up in a shallow baking pan.

4. Bake the chicken for 40 minutes.

5. While the chicken is baking, whisk the reserved lemon juice, the stock, brown sugar, and lemon slices together.

6. Pour the lemon mixture over the chicken and sprinkle with the *herbes de Provence.* Bake 20 to 25 minutes more, basting occasionally with the pan juices. Serve hot, at room temperature, or cold.

6 to 8 portions

BAKED LIMA BEANS WITH GINGERSNAPS

A lima bean preparation, spiked with the extra goodness of grainy mustard, brown sugar, and crumbled gingersnaps.

2 packages (10 ounces each) frozen lima beans, thawed
1 cup sour cream
2 tablespoons brown sugar
1 tablespoon grainy mustard
Dash Worcestershire sauce
1¼ cups crushed gingersnaps
4 tablespoons (½ stick) unsalted butter, melted

1. Preheat oven to 350°F.

2. Place the lima beans in a 1-quart baking dish. Mix the sour cream, brown sugar, mustard, and Worcestershire sauce and stir into the lima beans. Combine the gingersnaps and butter and sprinkle evenly over the beans.

3. Bake uncovered for 45 minutes. Serve hot.

6 to 8 portions

WILLIAMSBURG ORANGE-SHERRY CAKE

CAKE:

1 cup golden raisins
½ cup dry sherry
2 ½ cups sifted unbleached all-purpose flour
1 ½ teaspoons baking soda
½ teaspoon salt
¾ cup (1 ½ sticks) unsalted butter, room temperature
½ cup dark brown sugar
1 cup granulated sugar
3 eggs
1 ½ teaspoons vanilla extract
Finely grated zest of 1 orange
1 ½ cups buttermilk
½ cup chopped pecans

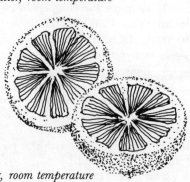

FROSTING:

½ cup (1 stick) unsalted butter, room temperature
1 pound confectioners' sugar
4 to 5 tablespoons Cointreau or other orange liqueur
2 tablespoons finely grated orange zest
Orange slices and pecan halves (garnish)

1. The night before you plan to make the cake, soak the raisins in the sherry and continue soaking overnight.

2. The following day, preheat oven to 350°F. Butter and flour two 9-inch cake pans.

3. To make the cake, sift the flour, baking soda, and salt together and set aside.

4. Cream the butter and sugars in a large mixer bowl. Add the eggs, one at a time, beating well after each addition. Beat in the vanilla and grated orange zest.

5. Add the flour alternately with the buttermilk, beating well after each addition. Stir in the pecans and raisins with sherry.

6. Pour the batter into the prepared pans. Bake until the cake begins to pull away from the edge of the pan and springs back when lightly touched in the center, 35 to 40 minutes.

7. Let cool 10 minutes. Invert onto wire racks to cool completely.

8. To make the frosting, cream the butter, sugar, and enough of the Cointreau to make the frosting spreadable but not runny. Beat in the orange zest.

9. Place 1 cake layer on a serving plate and spread evenly with some of the frosting. Top with the second layer and frost the top and side of the cake. Decorate the top of the cake with orange slices and pecan halves.

12 portions

Our version of an early American cake from colonial Williamsburg. The layers of cake are studded with sherry-soaked golden raisins, crunchy chopped pecans, and zesty orange rind. An old-fashioned confectioners' sugar icing bursting with orange zest makes this a great cake for family occasions.

"The most remarkable thing about my mother is that for thirty years she served the family nothing but leftovers. The original meal has never been found."
—Calvin Trillin

TEA FOR TWO

We love the British custom of afternoon tea—it is a most respectable excuse for a daytime rendezvous. Stealing away early from a day of hard work can spice this formal ceremony with a dash of intrigue. The setting should be intimate, centered around a Victorian windowseat, antique pastry wagon, or intricate wrought-iron garden bench. The tea should be steeped in a delicate china pot and accompanied by tea sandwiches and lacy cookies. Place a bouquet of daisies nearby and pluck the petals of one to see if he or she loves you.

SAUTERNES SABAYON

6 egg yolks
1 cup superfine sugar
1 ½ cups Sauternes
Several thin strips of lemon zest

1. Whisk the egg yolks and sugar together in a heavy medium-size saucepan. Cook, whisking constantly, over medium-low heat until thick and creamy, 5 to 8 minutes.

2. Place the pan in a larger pan filled with simmering water. Whisking constantly, pour in the Sauternes in a thin steady stream. Add the lemon zest and continue to whisk until the mixture froths to almost triple in volume.

3. Remove the pan from the water and let stand, whisking occasionally, until cooled to room temperature.

8 portions

ALMOND TUILES

Crisp and delicately flavored with orange, these tuiles are a lovely accompaniment to tea. Serve with fresh fruit or use them as shells for ice cream.

3 tablespoons unsalted butter, room temperature
⅓ cup granulated sugar
2 teaspoons orange liqueur
Pinch salt
3 egg whites, room temperature
3 tablespoons unbleached all-purpose flour
2 tablespoons cake flour
½ cup sliced almonds

1. Preheat oven to 425°F. Generously butter 2 cookie sheets.

2. Cream 3 tablespoons butter and the sugar in a mixer bowl. Add the liqueur, salt, and egg whites; beat until the mixture is light and fluffy, about 3 minutes. Stir in the flours thoroughly.

3. Drop large teaspoons of the batter onto the prepared cookie sheets. Using the back of the spoon, spread the batter into thin 2-inch circles. Sprinkle several almond slices on the top of each circle.

4. Bake until the outer edges of the cookies are browned, about 5 minutes. Remove from the oven and turn the cookies with a spatula. Bake for another 2 minutes.

5. Remove from the oven. Immediately place the warm cookies, almond side down, on a narrow rolling pin to get the correct shape. Let cool completely. Carefully stack together and store in an airtight container until ready to serve.

About 3 ½ dozen cookies

Tea is wonderful as an occasion in itself and is increasing in popularity as we find ourselves eating lighter foods. It's great for a business meeting, less caloric than a late dinner, and not limited to ladies' events. Afternoon tea can be the ideal setting for a small wedding reception, a baby shower, an engagement party, a graduation celebration, or a lazy afternoon of croquet.

HOW TO MAKE A PROPER CUP OF TEA

The best tea is brewed in a pot with loose tea rather than tea bags. Begin by filling a kettle with fresh cold tap water, and set it on the stove to boil. As the water nears the boil, pour a little into the teapot and swirl it around to warm the pot, then discard the water. Add the tea leaves to the pot, allowing one heaping teaspoon per cup plus one extra for the pot. Immediately pour boiling water over the tea, stir, and cover. Let it steep for 5 to 7 minutes. Pour the tea through a fine strainer into the teacups, and offer cold milk, lemon slices, and sugar or honey. Sip thoughtfully and enjoy a brief Mad Hatter respite in Wonderland.

SCENTED MADELEINES

Dip these dainty scallop-shaped sponge cookies in steaming tea on a quiet afternoon.

7 ounces almond paste, cut into small pieces
1 cup granulated sugar
5 eggs, room temperature
1 teaspoon almond extract
2 teaspoons orange-flower water
1 cup sifted unbleached all-purpose flour
1 teaspoon baking powder
10 tablespoons (1 ¼ sticks) unsalted butter, melted and cooled
Confectioners' sugar for dusting

1. Cream the almond paste and granulated sugar in a food processor fitted with a steel blade or with a heavy-duty mixer fitted with a paddle. Transfer to a large mixer bowl and add the eggs, one at a time, beating well after each addition. Add the almond extract and the orange-flower water and beat until light and fluffy, 1 to 2 minutes.

2. Sift the flour and baking powder together and gently fold into the almond mixture. Gently fold in the melted butter just until combined. Refrigerate the batter for 1 hour.

3. Preheat oven to 400°F. Brush madeleine molds with melted butter and dust lightly with flour.

4. Spoon the batter into the molds, filling them three-fourths full. Bake until lightly colored, 8 to 10 minutes.

5. Let cool for 5 minutes, and then gently remove to wire racks to cool completely. Allow the molds to cool before re-brushing with melted butter and repeating the process with the remaining batter. Dust with confectioners' sugar before serving.

36 to 40 madeleines

JUNE'S MERINGUES

These light cookies are embedded deep in our childhood memories.

6 egg whites, room temperature
⅛ teaspoon cream of tartar
2 cups sugar
1 teaspoon vanilla extract
1 tablespoon white vinegar

1. Preheat oven to 275°F. Grease 2 cookie sheets.

2. Beat the egg whites in a large mixer bowl until foamy. Add the cream of tartar and beat until somewhat stiff.

3. Gradually beat in the sugar. Then add the vanilla and

"She sent out for one of those plump little cakes called petites madeleines, which look as though they had been molded in the fluted scallop of a pilgrim's shell."
—Marcel Proust

MERINGUES

The story is that when Napoleon visited the Swiss town of Meringen, a local chef created a cookie made with sugar, cinnamon, nuts, and egg yolks—and in order not to waste the leftover egg whites, he whipped them together with sugar, then slow-baked puffy mounds of the new concoction until they were dry and crispy. He served them in saucers brimming with sweet cream, and Napoleon is said to have preferred the second creation, naming it after the town.

The secret to making most meringues is the timing—you must work quickly, so that the meringue doesn't wilt. And the added secret to ours is vinegar. We particularly like meringues filled with fresh strawberries and topped with whipped cream.

vinegar. Beat until very stiff and shiny, about 10 minutes more.

4. Place about ½ cup of the meringue on a cookie sheet. Using your hands, pull the meringue into a peak to resemble a large chocolate kiss. Smooth the sides. Repeat with the remaining meringue.

5. Bake until the meringues are lightly colored, about 45 minutes. Cool completely on wire racks.

8 large meringues

CHOCOLATE MINT SANDWICH COOKIES

A very elegant chocolate sandwich cookie.

½ cup (1 stick) unsalted butter, room temperature
½ cup sugar
1 egg
1 teaspoon mint extract
¼ cup unsweetened cocoa powder
1 cup sifted unbleached all-purpose flour
¼ cup heavy or whipping cream
4 ounces white chocolate
4 ounces semisweet chocolate

1. Cream the butter and ¼ cup of the sugar in a mixer bowl until light and fluffy, about 5 minutes. Add the egg and beat for 5 minutes. Add ¾ teaspoon of the mint extract and the cocoa and beat on low speed just until blended. Add the flour and stir with a wooden spoon just until combined. Flatten the dough into a thick circle, wrap in plastic wrap, and refrigerate at least 1 hour.

2. Heat the cream to boiling in a small saucepan over medium heat. Add the white chocolate, reduce heat to low, and heat, stirring constantly, just until the chocolate melts. Stir in the remaining ¼ teaspoon mint extract and remove from heat. Let cool slightly; beat with an electric mixer until light and fluffy.

3. Preheat oven to 350°F. Grease and flour 2 cookie sheets.

4. Divide the dough in half. Roll out each half ⅛ inch thick on a lightly floured surface and cut out with a 2-inch round cookie cutter. Gather the scraps, roll, and cut out as many additional circles as possible. Place the dough circles on the prepared cookie sheets and sprinkle lightly with the remaining ¼ cup sugar. Bake until lightly browned, 8 to 10 minutes. Remove to wire racks to cool completely.

5. Melt the semisweet chocolate in the top of a double boiler over simmering water and keep warm.

6. Spread each cookie with a thin layer of the melted chocolate. Sandwich a teaspoon of the white chocolate filling between 2 cookies, chocolate sides in. Refrigerate until firm.

36 cookies

TEA SANDWICHES

Tea sandwiches should be made on very thinly sliced, very fresh white or wheat bread, cut into 1-inch triangles, rounds, hearts, or flowers. They must be made as close to serving time as possible to avoid sogginess. All ingredients must be either thinly sliced or finely chopped for these dainty, bite-size morsels. Some of our favorite combinations are:

- ♥ Sweet butter, a thin slice of cucumber, a whole mint leaf, served open-face on white bread rounds.
- ♥ Sweet butter, watercress leaves, a thin slice of cucumber, sprinkling of salt and pepper, served as a closed sandwich on white bread rounds.
- ♥ Sweet butter, thin radish slices, a spoonful of caviar, served open-face on wheat rounds.
- ♥ Whipped cream cheese, smoked salmon, a sprig of dill, served open-face on white bread rounds.
- ♥ Basil-Parmesan mayonnaise, a thin slice of seeded tomato, served as a closed sandwich on white bread rounds.
- ♥ Chicken liver pâté, a thin slice of Bermuda onion, sandwiched between two wheat bread rounds.
- ♥ Finely shredded chicken meat, minced carrots, golden raisins mixed with mayonnaise and curry powder, sandwiched between two white bread diamonds.
- ♥ Whipped cream cheese mixed with finely crumbled crisp bacon, topped with an arugula leaf and served as a closed sandwich on white bread rounds.
- ♥ Softened chèvre and orange marmalade sandwiched between cut-out hearts of wheat bread.

PRIMAVERA WEDDING

We can think of no more symbolic time for a wedding than the springtime, when the earth itself is celebrating a new beginning. Our spring wedding is planned to be held outdoors in a meadow budding with wild flowers or in a woodland laced with delicate ferns. Our inspiration comes from Botticelli's two famous paintings, the *Primavera* and the *Birth of Venus*. Instead of carefully arranged florist's bouquets, we choose to have a *Primavera*-like carpet of spring flowers strewn among the clusters of moss and patches of ferns.

We also carry out the Botticelli theme in an hors d'oeuvre menu of earthly delights. The focal point is a large seafood buffet, much of it arranged Venus-style on large half shells. All is dipped in a fresh and herby cocktail sauce. Other offerings include stuffed grape leaves, salmon caviar hearts, and puff pastry palmiers shaped to resemble unfurling fiddleheads. To complete this rosy occasion, pink Champagne is poured to toast the happy couple.

GARDEN COCKTAIL SAUCE

Bright red colors and fresh tastes with sparks of green herbs make this sauce most dazzling with the clean pink, white, and silver seafood of the season. Serve in a pearly seashell surrounded by mounds of the freshest catch.

4 sweet red peppers
2 small fresh red chiles, cored, seeded
2 cloves garlic
2 cups tomato juice
1 tablespoon red wine vinegar
2 hefty dashes Worcestershire sauce
2 hefty dashes Tabasco sauce
1 tablespoon chopped fresh oregano
1 tablespoon snipped fresh chives
1 tablespoon chopped fresh tarragon
1 tablespoon chopped fresh thyme
2 teaspoons salt
2 teaspoons sugar

1. Preheat broiler.
2. Broil the sweet red peppers on all sides until the skin is black and blistered. Then place in a covered bowl and let steam for 5 minutes. Peel off the black skins and cut away the seeds and cores and discard. Coarsely chop the peppers.
3. Finely chop the chiles and garlic in a food processor fitted with a steel blade. Add the remaining ingredients and process, using repeated pulses, until blended but still a bit chunky.
4. Spoon into a seashell and serve with several varieties of seafood.

2 cups

SALMON CAVIAR HEARTS

A pretty and romantic little hors d'oeuvre that combines the jeweled luxury of caviar with the creamy pink of radish cream cheese. Perfect for a wedding celebration.

12 ounces cream cheese, room temperature
1 ½ cups finely minced radishes
2 tablespoons snipped fresh chives
1 tablespoon prepared horseradish
Salt and freshly ground black pepper, to taste
1 loaf very thinly sliced white bread
6 ounces red salmon caviar
Fresh parsley sprigs

1. Beat the cream cheese with an electric mixer until light and fluffy. Beat in the radishes, chives, horseradish, and salt

SEAFOOD BUFFET FOR A SPRING WEDDING

♥ Dozens of freshly opened raw oysters on the half shell, arranged in overlapping rows and sprinkled with freshly cracked pepper.

♥ Dozens of freshly opened cherrystone and littleneck clams arranged in alternating rows, drizzled with lemon juice.

♥ Lightly poached scallops arranged in clusters on scallop shells and sprinkled with lime juice and a dash of hot sauce.

♥ Mounds of shelled cooked shrimp in abalone or other giant seashells.

♥ Chunks of cooked lobster meat nestled back into cleaned lobster shell halves. Pretty toothpicks piled nearby.

♥ Poached mussels displayed on their reserved shells and garnished with curly parsley sprigs.

♥ A smoked seafood assortment laid out in contrasting colors on open giant seashells. Plenty of lemon, lime, and Bermuda onion slices all around.

♥ Fresh seaweed, arugula, or other leafy greens decoratively interspersed among the seashells.

"An archaeologist is the best husband a woman can have; the older she gets, the more interested he is in her."
—Agatha Christie

✦ FLOWERS FROM THE SILVER PALATE

The bride's bouquet—
fragrant white lilacs tied
with white satin streamers.
The bridesmaids—lavender
and purple lilacs tied with
rose satin streamers.

GARDEN WRAPS

Leafy garden greens—Bibb, arugula,
leaf lettuce, sorrel, chicory, radicchio,
Boston lettuce—are good wrappers
around tasty tidbits. They're fresh
and lighter than pastry or toasts. For
a tea party, spread the leaf as you
would a thin slice of bread, roll it up,
and place it on a serving dish seam
side down. Or tie each packet with a
fresh chive, with the blossom still
attached if possible.

and pepper to taste until blended. Refrigerate until firm.

2. Preheat oven to 325°F.

3. Cut sixty 1-inch hearts with a cookie cutter from the bread slices. Place in a single layer on baking sheets and bake until lightly toasted. Turn and toast the second side.

4. Spread each toast heart with a thin layer of the radish cream cheese. Place ½ teaspoon of the salmon caviar on the top center of each heart. Garnish each heart with a little parsley sprig.

60 hors d'oeuvres

SMOKED CHICKEN SALAD WITH BASIL-PARMESAN MAYONNAISE

One of our richest salads, perfect as a spring hors d'oeuvre as well as a main course. Serve in small amounts on the tips of Belgian endive leaves.

2 smoked chicken breasts (4 halves), cut into julienne
8 ounces prosciutto, cut into julienne
5 ounces Gruyère cheese, cut into julienne
8 sun-dried tomatoes (packed in oil), drained and cut into julienne
6 scallions (green onions, white part and 2 inches green), cut into julienne
8 ounces mushrooms, wiped clean, sliced
½ cup plus 2 tablespoons olive oil
5 tablespoons fresh lemon juice
2 egg yolks
⅓ cup grated Parmesan cheese
3 tablespoons chopped fresh basil
2 teaspoons grainy Dijon-style mustard
1 cup vegetable oil
Salt and freshly ground black pepper, to taste

1. Combine the chicken, prosciutto, Gruyère, tomatoes, scallions, and mushrooms in a large mixing bowl. Toss with the 2 tablespoons olive oil and 2 tablespoons of the lemon juice.

2. Process the egg yolks, Parmesan, basil, mustard, and remaining 3 tablespoons lemon juice in a food processor fitted with a steel blade for 30 seconds. With the machine running, pour the ½ cup olive oil and then the vegetable oil in a thin steady stream through the feed tube to make a thick mayonnaise. Season to taste with salt and pepper.

3. Add the mayonnaise to the salad and toss to combine.

6 to 8 main-course portions

STUFFED GRAPE LEAVES

This is a new version of the Greek classic. We have cinnamon, nutmeg, and oregano, but we've combined these spices with ground lamb, chèvre, and chopped walnuts for extra texture. Squeeze lots of lemon juice on top.

8 tablespoons olive oil
1 small onion, finely chopped
2 cloves garlic, minced
8 ounces ground lamb
1 tablespoon ground cinnamon
2 teaspoons dried oregano
1 teaspoon ground nutmeg
Salt and freshly ground black pepper, to taste
4 ounces chèvre, crumbled
¾ cup cooked rice
½ cup chopped fresh Italian parsley
½ cup chopped walnuts
1 jar (16 ounces) preserved grape leaves
¼ cup fresh lemon juice
½ cup water
Lemon slices (garnish)

1. Heat 2 tablespoons of the oil in a medium-size skillet over medium heat. Add the onion and garlic and sauté for 5 minutes.

2. Add the lamb and crumble with a fork. Cook until the lamb is no longer pink, about 15 minutes.

3. Season with cinnamon, oregano, nutmeg, and salt and pepper to taste. Stir in the chèvre and cook until the cheese melts. Remove from heat and stir in the rice, parsley, and walnuts.

4. Rinse the grape leaves under cold running water and pat dry. Place one leaf, vein side up, on a clean flat surface. Shape about 1 teaspoon of filling with your hands into a compact log, about 1 inch long, and center over the stem end of the leaf. Roll up the leaf to enclose the filling, folding the sides into the center. Repeat with the remaining grape leaves and filling.

5. Line the bottom of a medium-size saucepan with any torn grape leaves to prevent burning and sticking during cooking. Pack the stuffed grape leaves in the pan in concentric circles, making as many layers as necessary.

6. Pour the remaining 6 tablespoons oil, the lemon juice, and water over the grape leaves.

7. Place a small heat-proof plate on top of the stuffed leaves and place a large can, such as of tomatoes, on top of the plate to weigh down the grape leaves and to keep them from unrolling. Simmer over low heat for about 1 hour.

8. Serve warm, garnished with lemon slices, or, with Hollandaise Sauce (page 398) flavored with chopped fresh mint.

About 48 stuffed grape leaves

PRIMAVERA WEDDING

Seafood Buffet with Garden Cocktail Sauce

Smoked Chicken Salad with Basil Parmesan Mayonnaise

Stuffed Grape Leaves

Salmon Caviar Hearts

Cashew Sticks

Chèvre and Phyllo Kisses

Puff Pastry Palmiers

Asparagus Roll-ups

Apricot and Almond Wedding Cake

Pink Champagne

"By all means marry; if you get a good wife, you'll become happy; if you get a bad one, you'll become a philosopher."
—Socrates

WHICH RICE TO THROW AT THE BRIDE AND GROOM

WHITE RICE—the rice most often tossed is also the one eaten by the most people. The grains may be long or short, and the hull and bran have been milled away from each kernel. In the U.S., white rice is frequently enriched with iron, niacin, and thiamine.

CONVERTED RICE—the rice preferred at mixed marriages, it has had the surface starch removed through a steam-pressure process. It takes longer to cook than white rice, but it is richer in vitamins and mineral salts.

BROWN RICE—for couples who are exponents of health foods or who are vegetarians. It is rice in its most natural form, with only the outer hull removed. Bran gives it its characteristic brown color and keeps it crunchy even after being cooked.

WILD RICE—is a misnomer, as it is not rice at all but a wild grass grown mostly in Minnesota, Canada, and recently in California. It is expensive, and therefore is thrown at only the most exclusive weddings. Its hearty nutty flavor and tweedy look make it a favorite.

BASMATI—an aromatic long-grain rice from India with a special nutty flavor that makes it a perfect accompaniment to curries and other exotic foods. Search for it in Indian and Asian groceries. With the release of the well-received film *A Passage to India* and the popularity of TV's *Jewel in the Crown*, it has become important to throw basmati rice at trendy, upwardly mobile weddings.

ARBORIO—what all Italian brides get sprinkled with, the big round grains of this rice are essential for making the classic creamy risottos of Italian cooking. We love it cooked with lots of rich chicken stock, saffron, and a sprinkling of pistachio nuts.

CASHEW STICKS

A crunchy addition to any cocktail party.

16 slices Pepperidge Farm sandwich or other firm white bread
1 cup cashew butter
¼ cup vegetable oil

1. Preheat oven to 350°F.
2. Trim the crusts from 12 slices of the bread. Cut the trimmed bread into ½-inch-wide strips. Place the strips flat on a baking sheet and bake just until lightly toasted.
3. Place the trimmed crusts and the remaining 4 slices of bread on another baking sheet and bake until golden. Process to fine crumbs in a food processor fitted with a steel blade or a blender. Transfer to a shallow bowl.
4. Heat the cashew butter and oil in a small saucepan until blended and warm. Dip the toasted bread sticks completely into the cashew mixture and then coat with the bread crumbs. Let the breadsticks dry flat on a baking sheet. Store in an airtight container.
About 4 dozen

ASPARAGUS ROLL-UPS

An irresistible party hors d'oeuvre.

14 thin slices white bread, crusts trimmed
8 slices bacon, cooked crisp, drained, and crumbled
8 ounces cream cheese, room temperature
Finely grated zest of 1 lemon
28 asparagus spears, cooked crisp-tender
Melted unsalted butter

1. Flatten the bread slices by rolling over them with a rolling pin. Combine the bacon, cream cheese, and lemon zest. Spread an even layer of the cream cheese mixture on each flattened bread slice.
2. Place 2 asparagus spears, with the tips facing in opposite directions, on one edge of each bread slice. Roll up each slice like a jelly roll. Cut each roll in half and place seam side down on a lightly greased cookie sheet.*
3. Preheat broiler.
4. Brush the tops and sides of the roll-ups with melted butter. Broil 6 inches from the heat until lightly browned and toasted. Serve immediately.
28 hors d'oeuvres

*The roll-ups can be prepared up to this point 3 hours in advance. Store covered in the refrigerator.

CHEVRE AND PHYLLO KISSES

A wonderful bite-size hors d'oeuvre fresh from the oven, with the tangy flavor of chèvre and aromatic *herbes de Provence*. Crisp and delicious.

4 sheets phyllo dough
8 tablespoons (1 stick) unsalted butter, melted
4 ounces Montrachet or other soft mild chèvre
2 teaspoons herbes de Provence

1. Preheat oven to 350°F.
2. Working quickly, place 1 phyllo sheet on a flat surface and brush the entire surface with butter. Place the second sheet directly over the first and brush it with butter. Using a small sharp knife, cut the phyllo into 30 squares (5 rows of 6 squares).
3. Place a tiny bit of the chèvre in the center of each square and sprinkle the herbs over the cheese.
4. Gather the corners of each square and twist over the cheese to form a tiny kiss. Place on a cookie sheet. Brush the tops of the kisses with butter. Repeat the process with the remaining ingredients.
5. Bake until crispy and golden, about 10 minutes. Serve immediately.

60 pieces

beat yolk
egg yolk mixture
sugar
egg yolk

6" cake pan

10" cake pan

12" cake pan

APRICOT AND ALMOND WEDDING CAKE

CAKE:

1½ cups slivered dried apricots
1 cup Cognac
1½ cups milk
¾ cup (1½ sticks) unsalted butter
18 egg yolks, room temperature
3 cups sugar
2 teaspoons vanilla extract
4½ cups sifted cake flour
1 tablespoon baking powder
1 cup slivered almonds, lightly toasted

GLAZE:

1 cup apricot jam
3 tablespoons Cognac

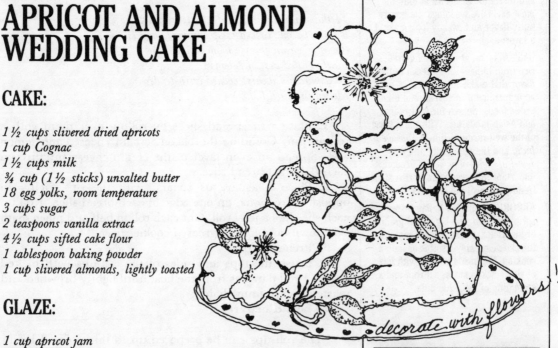

decorate with flowers!

THE BRIDE CUTS THE CAKE

We love the tradition of cutting the wedding cake with a silver knife that is a family heirloom—one that has survived the generations of happy marriages. Make your cake cutter festive by tying the handle with white satin ribbon and a floral sprig from the wedding bouquet.

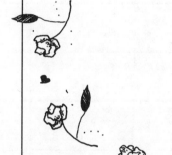

WEDDING CAKE

The first types of wedding cakes made in America were known as "great cakes" and were variations on fruit, nut, and spice cakes from old British recipes. Sometimes women would bake wedding cakes before finding a bridegroom as a demonstration of their culinary abilities. Until the nineteenth century, pieces of wedding cake were crumbled over the bride and groom. Now we just toss rice with our good wishes, thank goodness! As finely ground flour, baking powder, and baking soda became available just prior to the Civil War, the white wedding cake became popular. Today your favorite cake—properly dignified—will do just fine.

BUTTERCREAM:

2 ¼ cups sugar
¾ cup water
6 egg whites, room temperature
2 cups (4 sticks) unsalted butter, room temperature
6 tablespoons light corn syrup
1 teaspoon almond extract

1. To make the cake, heat the apricots and Cognac in a small saucepan to boiling, remove from the heat, and let stand 1 hour.

2. Preheat oven to 350°F. Butter and flour 3 cake pans, 12, 10, and 6 inches. Set aside.

3. Heat the milk in a small saucepan until hot to the touch. Remove from the heat and let stand to cool slightly. Melt the butter in another small pan and set aside to cool.

4. Beat the egg yolks and sugar in a large mixer bowl until very light and thick, about 10 minutes. Gradually beat in the milk and vanilla.

5. Sift the flour and baking powder together. Gradually beat into the egg yolk mixture at low speed; beat until thoroughly blended. Fold in the melted butter, and then the apricots with the Cognac and almonds.

6. Pour the batter into the prepared pans. Bake until the cake has pulled away from the side of the pan and springs back when lightly touched in the center, 30 to 50 minutes, depending on the size of the layer. Cool each 10 minutes and invert onto wire racks to cool completely.

7. To make the glaze, heat the apricot jam and Cognac in a small saucepan until the jam melts. Strain, and brush each cake layer all over with the glaze.

8. Cut 3 cardboard circles the same size as the cake layers. Place each cake layer on its cardboard and assemble in a tier.

9. To make the buttercream, heat 2 cups of the sugar and the water to boiling in a heavy saucepan, stirring constantly. Continue to heat, without stirring, to 240°F on a candy thermometer.

10. Beat the egg whites in a large mixer bowl until frothy. Gradually beat in the remaining ¼ cup sugar and continue beating until the peaks are stiff. Pour in the boiling syrup in a thin, steady stream, while beating at high speed. Beat until the heat from the syrup has dissipated and the bowl feels cool, 5 to 7 minutes.

11. Beat in the butter, 1 tablespoon at a time, then the corn syrup and almond extract until blended.

12. Spread the buttercream smoothly over the cake. Pipe the remaining buttercream decoratively on the cake, using a pastry bag and several different tips. The cake can be assembled and decorated up to 2 days before serving. Surround the base of the cake with fresh and feathery ferns. Arrange lots of fresh spring flowers on the ferns. We suggest lilacs, tiny rosebuds, freesia, and lilies of the valley.

40 to 50 portions

EASY LIVING ...

Summer is the easiest time of the year to entertain. Gentle breezes whisk away all the tensions of the advance preparations required for the cocktail bashes and formal dinner parties of other seasons. Clear sunny days and brilliant blue skies linger on into the evening and make us feel as if we're on vacation all of the time— whether in the city, the country, or at the seaside, we become carefree.

Summer has the magic that makes the shade of a big old tree in a city park as idyllic as the hollow of a shoreline dune. We want to be outdoors all the time—from sunrise to sunset and through the night to catch distant shooting stars. We surrender to the pleasures of summer and make our good times casual and spontaneous. We love all things alfresco—picnics in the park and movable feasts, grilling and red-hot barbecues, clambakes and cool-down cocktails, beach parties and big band concerts, croquet tournaments and Champagne stargazing, morning glory porch brunches and midnight swims.

Simplicity is the keynote in summer's lazy days—no one wants to sacrifice sun-filled hours of outdoor activity to be indoors cooking. Fortunately, there is little need to search for elusive ingredients—our own backyards, windowboxes, nearby farm stands, or corner markets are overflowing with native taste delights. The catch of the day, the discovery of a berry patch, or the picking of home-grown vine-ripened vegetables is cause enough for celebration. The world is filled with a salad of glorious food sensations just waiting to be tossed.

PORCH BRUNCHES

I t seems to us that people with porches have more friends than most. We envy them, as porches are an ideal spot for a summer morning brunch. They permit guests to sit out in the fresh air while sheltering them from the world at large before high noon.

We like porches that are made cozy with hanging baskets, pots of ferns and geraniums, old wicker furniture, and swinging hammocks. They make an ideal setting for welcoming pitchers of icy wake-up drinks, flaky croissant French toast, spicy sausages, and berry-filled muffins. And if your porch is to be the setting for a lazy day of solitude, don't forget to pick up the great American novel before settling in.

SUNNY BAKED EGGS

An easy way to fix eggs for a crowd on a sunny summer morning. The Brie makes these extra rich and creamy.

1 tablespoon chopped fresh parsley
1½ tablespoons minced ham
1½ tablespoons cubed Brie
2 eggs
1 tablespoon heavy or whipping cream
Salt and freshly ground black pepper, to taste

1. Preheat oven to 400°F.

2. For each serving, toss the parsley, ham, and Brie together in a 3-inch-wide ramekin. Break the eggs over the ham mixture and drizzle the cream over the eggs. Sprinkle with salt and pepper to taste.

3. Place the ramekins in a baking pan and pour hot water into the pan to come 1 inch up the ramekins. Bake 15 to 20 minutes, depending on how set you want the eggs. Serve immediately.

1 portion

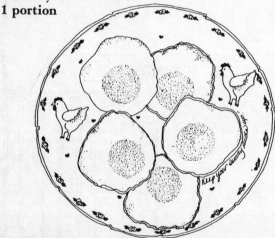

FABULOUS FRENCH TOAST

Terrific for a special breakfast or brunch, day-old croissants make the most sinful French toast we've tasted.

5 eggs
⅔ cup heavy or whipping cream
⅓ cup Triple Sec
2 tablespoons granulated sugar
Finely grated zest of 1 orange
2 teaspoons ground cinnamon
6 stale plain croissants, cut lengthwise in half
6 tablespoons (¾ stick) unsalted butter
Confectioners' sugar

DOZENS OF EGGS

SCRAMBLED WITH

1. Cottage cheese and chives
2. Smoked salmon and dill
3. Fresh garden herbs
4. Parmesan and fresh white truffle shavings
5. Grated Gruyère and fresh asparagus tips
6. Finely minced black truffle
7. Shredded prosciutto
8. Herbed Boursin
9. Lots of pepper and thin slices of sautéed fresh foie gras
10. Sautéed onions
11. Minced sun-dried tomatoes, jalapeño peppers, scallions, and grated Cheddar, garnished with a dollop of sour cream
12. Crumbled chèvre and sliced black olives

POACHED WITH

1. English muffins, Canadian bacon, hollandaise (a standard Benedict)
2. English muffins, tomato slices, pesto
3. English muffins, lettuce purée, anchovy strips
4. English muffins, arugula leaves, smoked salmon, hollandaise
5. English muffins, blanched asparagus, hollandaise
6. Toasted cornbread, avocado slices, salsa
7. English muffins, sautéed wild mushrooms, hollandaise
8. English muffins, steamed spinach, hollandaise
9. English muffins, fried ham, Cheddar sauce
10. French bread rounds sautéed in garlic butter, melted Swiss
11. Pumpernickel toast, corned beef hash
12. English muffins, tunafish salad, melted Swiss

1. Beat the eggs and cream together. Add the Triple Sec, granulated sugar, orange zest, and cinnamon and whisk until well blended. Pour into a shallow bowl or pie plate.

2. Dip each croissant half in the egg mixture, turning once. Melt a few tablespoons of the butter in a skillet over medium heat. Add as many croissants as will fit and fry until golden on both sides. Repeat with the remaining croissants, adding butter to the skillet as needed.

3. Sift confectioners' sugar over the croissants. Serve immediately.

6 portions

BASIL BREAKFAST STRATA

A jazzed up version of the classic egg and cheese strata makes for a great way to begin a summer day.

1 cup milk
½ cup dry white wine
1 day-old loaf Swiss peasant bread or French bread, cut into ½-inch slices (see Note)
8 ounces prosciutto, thinly sliced
2 cups arugula leaves (1 bunch)
3 tablespoons olive oil
1 pound basil torta cheese, thinly sliced
3 ripe tomatoes, sliced
½ cup Basic Pesto (page 398)
4 eggs, beaten
Salt and freshly ground black pepper, to taste
½ cup heavy or whipping cream

1. One day before serving, mix the milk and wine in a shallow bowl. Dip 1 or 2 slices of bread in the milk mixture. Gently squeeze as much liquid as possible from the bread without tearing it.

2. Place the bread in a 12-inch round or oval au gratin dish and cover with a slice of prosciutto, several arugula leaves dipped in olive oil, some slices of basil torta, and a few tomato slices. Drizzle sparingly with pesto. Repeat the layering, overlapping the bread slices slightly, until the dish is filled.

3. Beat the eggs with salt and pepper to taste and pour evenly over the layers in the dish. Cover with plastic wrap and refrigerate overnight.

4. The following day, remove the dish from the refrigerator and let warm to room temperature.

5. Preheat oven to 350°F.

6. Drizzle the top with the cream and bake until puffy and browned, 45 minutes to 1 hour. Serve immediately.

6 portions

Note: If you use a long, narrow baguette-type loaf, cut the slices on a 45° angle to allow for slightly bigger slices.

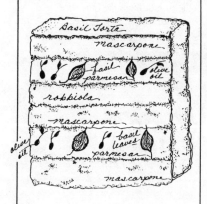

OH, WHAT A BEAUTIFUL MORNING BRUNCH

Sconset Sunrises

Basil Breakfast Strata

Crisp bacon rashers

Raspberry Streusel Muffins

Italian roast coffee

SPICY BREAKFAST SAUSAGE

Just the thing to wake up to on a country morning. Be sure your meat is not too lean because a bit of fat adds great flavor to these patties.

1 pound ground pork
1 pound ground beef
1 pound ground veal
4 cloves garlic, minced
1 bunch scallions (green onions, white
    part and 2 inches green), minced
1 large green bell pepper, cored,
    seeded, and minced
2 teaspoons ground cumin
1 teaspoon dried thyme
1 teaspoon fennel seeds
Pinch ground nutmeg
Red pepper flakes, to taste
Salt, to taste
Unsalted butter for frying

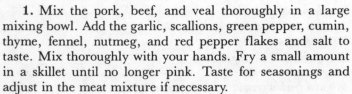

1. Mix the pork, beef, and veal thoroughly in a large mixing bowl. Add the garlic, scallions, green pepper, cumin, thyme, fennel, nutmeg, and red pepper flakes and salt to taste. Mix thoroughly with your hands. Fry a small amount in a skillet until no longer pink. Taste for seasonings and adjust in the meat mixture if necessary.

2. Divide the meat mixture in half. Roll each half into a log 7 inches long and about 2 inches in diameter. Wrap the logs separately in plastic wrap and refrigerate at least 3 hours or up to 2 days.

3. Cut the sausage logs into ½-inch slices. Fry the patties in a little bit of butter until well browned on each side. Serve with eggs, pancakes, or French toast.

8 to 10 portions

SCONSET SUNRISE

2 ounces vodka
½ cup cranberry juice
½ cup fresh orange juice
1 lime slice (garnish)
1 wild rose (garnish)

Fill a tall glass with ice. Pour in the vodka and juices. Stir to blend. Cut a slit halfway through the lime slice and place on the edge of the glass. Poke the rose through the lime slice.

1 drink

MORNING GLORY BRUNCH

Morning Glory Margaritas

---

*Fresh watermelon balls and
strawberries*

Fabulous French Toast
Spicy Breakfast Sausage

Espresso with lemon twists

Have clay pots of pink
geraniums clustered on the
table and around the porch.
Hang lots of fuschia plants
from the rafters.

RASPBERRY STREUSEL MUFFINS

These are beautiful for a lazy summer brunch or holiday
buffet table with the pink tint of fresh raspberries and the
yellow hue of lemons.

BATTER:

1 ½ cups unbleached all-purpose flour
¼ cup granulated sugar
¼ cup packed dark brown sugar
2 teaspoons baking powder
¼ teaspoon salt
1 teaspoon ground cinnamon
1 egg, lightly beaten
½ cup (1 stick) unsalted butter, melted
½ cup milk
1 ¼ cups fresh raspberries
1 teaspoon grated lemon zest

STREUSEL TOPPING:

½ cup chopped pecans
½ cup packed dark brown sugar
¼ cup unbleached all-purpose flour
1 teaspoon ground cinnamon
1 teaspoon grated lemon zest
2 tablespoons unsalted butter, melted

GLAZE:

½ cup confectioners' sugar
1 tablespoon fresh lemon juice

BERRY SPARKLER

3 tablespoons strained puréed
    strawberries
Chilled Champagne or sparkling
    wine
1 whole strawberry (garnish)
1 fresh mint sprig (garnish)

Spoon the strawberry purée into the
bottom of a tulip Champagne glass.
Fill with Champagne. Float a
strawberry and mint sprig on top.
    1 drink

1. Preheat oven to 350°F. Line 12 muffin cups with
paper liners.
2. To make the muffin batter, sift the flour, granulated
sugar, brown sugar, baking powder, salt, and cinnamon
together into a medium-size mixing bowl and make a well in
the center.
3. Place the egg, melted butter, and milk in the well. Stir
with a wooden spoon just until ingredients are combined.
Quickly stir in the raspberries and lemon zest. Fill each
muffin cup three-fourths full with the batter.

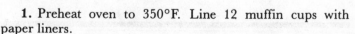

4. To make the streusel topping, combine the pecans, brown sugar, flour, cinnamon, and lemon zest in a small bowl. Pour in the melted butter and stir to combine. Sprinkle this mixture evenly over the top of each muffin.

5. Bake until nicely browned and firm, 20 to 25 minutes.

6. To make the glaze, mix the sugar and lemon juice. Drizzle over the warm muffins with a spoon. Serve the muffins warm.

1 dozen muffins

BLUEBERRY CORN MUFFINS

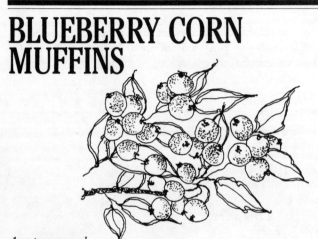

1 cup cornmeal
1 cup unbleached all-purpose flour
⅓ cup sugar
2 ½ teaspoons baking powder
¼ teaspoon salt
1 cup buttermilk
6 tablespoons (¾ stick) unsalted butter, melted
1 egg, slightly beaten
1 ⅔ cups blueberries

1. Preheat oven to 400°F. Line 12 muffin cups with paper liners.

2. Sift the cornmeal, flour, sugar, baking powder, and salt into a mixing bowl. Make a well in the center and pour the buttermilk, butter, and egg into the well. Stir just until combined.

3. Fold in the blueberries just until combined.

4. Fill each lined cup two-thirds full with batter. Bake until firm and golden, 20 to 25 minutes.

1 dozen muffins

RICH RUM STICKY BUNS

No one can resist sticky buns. We've made ours richer than ever with a raisin-pecan filling swirled through each bun plus plenty of pecans, brown sugar, and rum on top. A lot of work but definitely a labor well rewarded.

BREAKFAST COLADA

4 ounces pineapple juice
2 ounces white rum
2 ounces coconut cream
½ ripe banana, cut into chunks
5 ice cubes
1 lime slice (garnish)

Process the pineapple juice, rum, coconut cream, banana, and ice cubes in a blender until smooth. Pour into a tall glass and garnish with the lime slice.

1 drink

MORNING GLORY MARGARITA

⅓ cup fresh lime juice
⅓ cup tequila
2 tablespoons Sambuca liqueur
5 ice cubes
Coarse salt (optional)
Morning glory (garnish)

Process the lime juice, tequila, liqueur, and ice cubes in a blender until smooth. Pour into a wineglass, with a salted rim if desired, and garnish with a morning glory.

1 drink

PECANS

This is truly an American original. The pecan was introduced to early colonists by the Indians and is an important ingredient in American cuisine. The nut meat is very flavorful, making it versatile in cooking and baking because it blends in with other foods. We like to lightly toast pecans first to intensify their delectable flavor.

1 cup warm milk (105° to 115°F)
1 package active dry yeast
½ cup packed light brown sugar
5 to 5½ cups unbleached all-purpose flour
½ cup (1 stick) unsalted butter, room temperature
2 eggs
1 tablespoon grated orange zest
2 tablespoons ground cinnamon
1 teaspoon salt
1 cup plus 3 tablespoons packed light brown sugar
3 tablespoons granulated sugar
2 teaspoons ground cinnamon
1 cup chopped pecans
½ cup golden raisins
½ cup honey
1 cup (2 sticks) unsalted butter, melted
⅓ cup rum
1½ cups pecan halves

1. One day before serving, pour the milk into a large bowl. Stir in the yeast and ½ cup brown sugar and let stand 5 minutes.

2. Beat in 2 cups of the flour, all the softened butter, the eggs, orange zest, 2 tablespoons cinnamon, and the salt until blended. Gradually stir in enough of the remaining flour to make a soft dough.

3. Knead on a lightly floured surface until smooth and elastic, about 10 minutes.

4. Place the dough in a buttered large bowl and turn to coat the dough with butter. Cover with plastic wrap and let rise in the refrigerator overnight.

5. The following day, make the filling. Process 3 tablespoons brown sugar, the granulated sugar, 2 teaspoons cinnamon, and 1 cup chopped pecans in a food processor fitted with a steel blade until combined but still coarse and crumbly. Add the raisins and process very briefly to distribute the raisins evenly through the mixture. Set the filling aside.

6. Mix the remaining 1 cup brown sugar, the honey, and melted butter in a small bowl. Stir in the rum and pecan halves. Set the topping aside.

7. Remove the dough from the refrigerator and punch down. Roll the dough on a lightly floured surface into a large rectangle, about ⅓ inch thick. Sprinkle the filling evenly over the dough and press it into the dough with a rolling pin. Starting at one long edge, roll up the dough as tightly as possible like a jelly roll.

8. Lightly butter the sides of a 13 x 9-inch baking pan. Spread the topping evenly on the bottom.

9. Cut the dough crosswise into ¾-inch slices and arrange in rows of three over the topping, leaving room for the buns to rise. You should be able to fit 12 to 14 slices in the pan. Cover and let rise until doubled, 45 minutes to 1 hour.

10. Preheat oven to 350°F.

11. Bake the buns 25 to 30 minutes. Remove from the oven and let cool 10 minutes. Invert the buns onto a large platter and serve immediately.

12 to 14 large buns

"A simple porch that stands alone, plain and shy-looking but full of romance, hiding from every eye some imperishable secret of happiness and disenchantment...."
—Marcel Proust

COFFEE DOUGHNUT HOLES

We've doubled the pleasure of dunking doughnuts in coffee by flavoring the doughnuts themselves with coffee and adding a cappuccino sprinkling of cinnamon and sugar.

1 cup raw sugar
4 tablespoons (½ stick) unsalted butter
2 eggs
4 cups sifted unbleached all-purpose flour
1 tablespoon baking powder
1 tablespoon ground cinnamon
1 teaspoon salt
2½ tablespoons instant coffee powder
2 tablespoons hot water
¾ cup milk
Vegetable oil for deep frying
Cinnamon sugar for coating

1. Cream the sugar and butter in a large mixer bowl. Add the eggs, one at a time, beating well after each addition.

2. Sift the flour, baking powder, cinnamon, and salt together. Dissolve the instant coffee in the hot water. Add the flour mixture alternately with the milk and coffee to the butter mixture, beating well after each addition. The dough should be fairly stiff but smooth. Cover and refrigerate the dough at least 2 hours or overnight.

3. Divide the dough into 5 parts. Roll out 1 part dough ½ inch thick on a lightly floured surface. Keep the remaining dough refrigerated. Cut the dough into holes with a small round cookie cutter. Gather the scraps, roll, and cut out as many additional holes as possible.

4. Heat vegetable oil to 375°F in a deep-fat fryer.

5. Fry the doughnut holes, 8 to 10 at a time, turning once with tongs, until the holes are a deep golden brown. Drain on paper towels and then roll in a shallow bowl of cinnamon sugar. Repeat with the remaining dough.

100 doughnut holes

Note: Cooked doughnut holes can be stored in the freezer.

"Anyhow, the hole in the doughnut is at least digestible."
—H.L. Mencken

SUMMER CRAVINGS

Being the first on the beach . . . being the last on the beach . . . *fraises des bois* . . . skinny dipping . . . an all over tan . . . being buried in the sand . . . canoeing . . . steamed clams . . . a message in the sky . . . the sky just before a thunderstorm . . . a summer shower . . . the first shooting star . . . arugula from the garden . . . summer breezes . . . everybody outdoors until all hours . . . Mostly Mozart at Lincoln Center . . . the 1812 Overture . . . tomatoes . . . fireworks . . . falling asleep in a hammock . . . breakfast in a rose garden . . . milking a cow . . . chasing geese at the Goose Chase Farm . . . grilled lobsters . . . beachcombing for the perfect shell . . . rubbing linseed oil on driftwood . . . digging for clams with your toes . . . minty iced tea . . . fruit daiquiris . . .

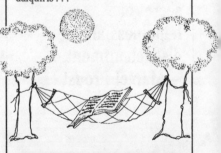

POMP AND CIRCUMSTANCE

A graduation is a celebratory event that brings the family together for one last important gathering before everyone scatters off in different directions to travel, begin a summer job, attend camp, relax. The ceremonies are filled with the pomp and circumstance of academic regalia, honorary degrees, achievement awards, and eloquent speeches that often address the philosophical questions of life's direction. They are occasions that are serious and joyous at once, as much about ending a phase in one's life as about commencing a new one. We feel a special dinner is in order to reward the efforts and accomplishments of the past and to say *bon voyage* for the journeys of the future.

"All a parent can give a child is roots and wings."
—Chinese Proverb

CREAM OF TOMATO SOUP WITH MINT

5 tablespoons mild olive oil
⅓ cup chopped shallots
1 large yellow onion, chopped
3 cloves garlic, minced
4 cups Berta's Chicken Stock (page 396) or canned broth
1 cup dry white wine
1 can (35 ounces) Italian plum tomatoes
Bouquet garni (½ teaspoon dried thyme, ½ teaspoon dried tarragon, 1 teaspoon celery seeds, 2 bay leaves, 8 black peppercorns tied in a cheesecloth bag)
3 ripe medium-size tomatoes, seeded and chopped
1 teaspoon sugar
2 tablespoons fresh lemon juice
2 cups heavy or whipping cream
Salt and freshly ground black pepper, to taste
5 tablespoons chopped fresh mint
3 tablespoons snipped fresh chives
1 large cucumber, peeled, seeded, and diced (if serving soup cold)

1. Heat 4 tablespoons of the oil in a large saucepan or Dutch oven over medium-high heat. Add the shallots, onion, and garlic, and sauté 10 minutes.

2. Add the stock, wine, canned tomatoes with their juices, and the bouquet garni to the pan. Simmer uncovered for 45 minutes.

3. While the soup is cooking, sauté the fresh tomatoes in the remaining 1 tablespoon oil for 2 minutes and set aside.

4. Remove and discard the bouquet garni and purée the soup in a blender. Stir the sugar, lemon juice, cream, and salt and pepper to taste into the soup. Return it to the saucepan and stir in the sautéed tomatoes, the mint, and chives.

5. Gently warm the soup over medium heat and serve immediately. The soup can also be served cold; add the cucumber just before serving.

8 to 10 portions

CHORUS LINE SEAFOOD SALAD

The idea of a Cobb salad translates beautifully into a spectacular seafood celebration. Use your imagination and substitute other varieties of shellfish and vegetables.

Horseradish Sauce (page 132)
1 head romaine, thick cores trimmed, leaves rinsed and patted dry
1 large bunch watercress, stems removed, leaves rinsed and patted dry
8 ounces snow peas, trimmed, stringed, and blanched for 1 minute
1 pound bay or sea scallops, poached 1 to 2 minutes in court bouillon
2 ounces salmon caviar or golden caviar
1 pound deveined peeled (tails left on) medium-size shrimp, cooked
1 small cucumber, cut lengthwise in half, seeded, cut into ⅛-inch slices
1 red onion, finely chopped
3 hard-cooked eggs, chopped
8 ounces Roquefort cheese, crumbled
1 pound lump crabmeat or lobster meat
2 ripe avocados, pitted, peeled, and sliced
10 radishes, sliced
2 dozen steamed littleneck clams or mussels on the half shell

1. Make the horseradish sauce.

2. Line a large serving platter with the outer leaves of the romaine. Shred the inner leaves, combine with the watercress leaves, and place in a flat bed on the center of the platter. Arrange the snow peas along the edge of the platter.

3. The remaining ingredients are arranged in rows to resemble the rows of corn on a cob (hence the name). Make a

A buffet is a wonderful medium to showcase your artistic and creative talents. Think of new and exciting ways to arrange your napkins; for instance, if you're short on space, decoratively fold the napkins around the utensils and group them in a pretty bowl with flowers, or perhaps in rustic baskets lined with lace doilies. This is your opportunity to dazzle your guests with your ingenuity and resourcefulness.

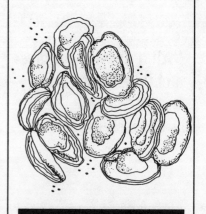

GRADUATION DINNER BUFFET

Cream of Tomato Soup with Mint

Herb Wrapped Filet of Beef

Horseradish Sauce

Chorus Line Seafood Salad

Warm Potato Salad with Fried Potato Skins

Squash Sauté

Peanut Ice Cream with Old-Fashioned Fudge Sauce

Zinfandel and Chardonnay

"Two criteria for success are to rise early and to have a good tan."
—Aristotle Onassis

center lengthwise row of the scallops on the platter. Place a narrow row of the caviar on both sides of the scallops. Arrange the shrimp, chorus-line fashion, in a row next to each row of the caviar. Proceed with scalloped rows of cucumber slices, then thin rows of onion, eggs, and Roquefort. Make rows of the crab or lobster and follow with the avocados and then the radishes. Finally, make rows of the clams or mussels on the half shell.

4. Serve the salad with the horseradish sauce.

6 portions

HERB-WRAPPED FILET OF BEEF

1 beef filet (about 4 pounds), ready to cook, wrapped in fat, and tied very loosely
1 bunch fresh rosemary
1 bunch fresh thyme
1 bunch fresh oregano
2 cloves garlic, cut into thin slivers
Salt and freshly ground black pepper, to taste
2 teaspoons chopped fresh Italian parsley

1. Preheat oven to 425°F.

2. Untie the string and carefully insert the rosemary, thyme, and oregano lengthwise under the fat, all around the filet. Retie the string, snugly this time.

3. With the tip of a sharp knife, cut slits through the fat and into the meat just large enough for the garlic slivers. Insert a sliver in each slit. Sprinkle the meat generously with salt and pepper to taste.

4. Place the filet, fat side up, in a shallow roasting pan just large enough to hold it comfortably.

5. Bake 10 minutes. Reduce the heat to 350°F and bake 20 to 25 minutes longer for rare meat (120°F on a meat thermometer) or 35 minutes longer for medium (130°F on a meat thermometer).

6. Remove the roast from the oven and let it stand 10 minutes before slicing. Remove and discard the fat, string, and herbs, and cut into thin slices. Garnish with parsley. Serve hot or at room temperature.

8 to 10 portions

HORSERADISH SAUCE

horseradish

granny Smith

This sauce is just as at home served with cocktail sandwiches, smoked fish, or a standing rib roast.

3 tablespoons plus 2 teaspoons prepared horseradish, rinsed, drained, and squeezed dry
3 tablespoons Hellmann's mayonnaise
1 tablespoon tarragon cider vinegar
2 teaspoons whole-grain mustard
1 teaspoon Dijon-style mustard
1 ¼ teaspoons sugar
½ teaspoon salt
Dash cayenne pepper
2 ounces Granny Smith apple with peel (about ¼ apple), grated
2 tablespoons finely chopped red onion

Whisk all ingredients except for the apple and onion in a large bowl until well blended. Add the apple and onion and fold in gently. Refrigerate several hours to allow flavors to blend. Serve in a small bowl or crock.

1 cup

SQUASH SAUTE

This is a quick and festive summer vegetable dish that can be served hot or at room temperature.

3 tablespoons olive oil
1 medium-size yellow onion, cut into thin wedges
2 medium-size yellow summer squash, unpeeled, cut into thin strips (1x¼ inch)
2 medium-size zucchini, unpeeled, cut into thin strips (1x¼ inch)
1 large sweet red pepper, cored, seeded, and cut into thin strips
1 large green bell pepper, cored, seeded, and cut into thin strips
1 teaspoon dried oregano
Salt and freshly ground black pepper, to taste
½ cup pitted Niçoise olives
½ cup finely crumbled soft mild chèvre
1 tablespoon fresh lemon juice

1. Heat the oil in a large sauté pan over medium-high heat. Add the onion and sauté for 5 minutes. Add the yellow squash, zucchini, and red and green peppers. Stir-fry until

HORSERADISH

The name "horseradish" refers to the coarse, very strong radish that is a hardy perennial plant of the mustard family.

Horseradish has always kept good company. It is the first of the "five bitter herbs" said to have been eaten by the ancient Jews during the eight days of Passover. Horseradish was brought to America by early settlers, and by 1806 it was included in lists of common edible American plants.

Horseradish spices up salads, juices, soups, and mayonnaises. It's great with raw oysters, broiled fish, roast meats, and smoked foods and can be used in pickling, to make sauces, or to perk up mustards.

FATHER'S DAY

Dads love quiet attention, or so they say. *Wrong.* Consider these joys we've brought to our Dads:

♥ A six-foot collage of his life in pictures.
♥ A poem run as an ad in the family section of the Sunday paper.
♥ Dragging a life-size cellophane-wrapped chocolate log home on a plane, knowing he was meeting the plane.
♥ Joining forces with other neighborhood kids in serenading our dads at dawn.
♥ Waxing the car for him—the old-fashioned way with a chamois.
♥ Helping him clean all the fish and doing the fileting properly.
♥ Not forcing him to go to father/daughter banquets.

the vegetables are tender but still crisp, 5 to 7 minutes.

2. Season the vegetables with the oregano and salt and pepper to taste. Quickly stir in the olives and cheese and sprinkle with the lemon juice. Serve immediately or let cool to room temperature.

6 to 8 portions

GOOD TIMES CHEERS!

Toasts are traditionally reserved for weddings, graduations, and commemorative dinners. We like them to be a part of every day. They may be prosaic, sentimental, your compliment to the host or hostess, but often one word will do. It's the feeling that counts—remember Rick's "Here's looking at you, kid."

Yum sen—Chinese
Skål—Danish
Proost—Dutch
A votre santé—French
Prosit—German
Eis Igian—Greek
L'Chaim—Hebrew
Cin cin—Italian
Kampai—Japanese
Skål—Norwegian
Na zdrowie—Polish
A sua saúde—Portuguese
Na zdorovia—Russian
Salud—Spanish
Skål—Swedish

WARM POTATO SALAD WITH FRIED POTATO SKINS

There have been many versions of warm French potato salads, but we have added a new twist for the many Americans who love potato skins.

8 medium-size boiling potatoes
12 slices bacon
1 medium-size red onion, chopped
¼ cup wine vinegar
¼ cup olive oil
1 heaping tablespoon Dijon-style mustard
Salt and freshly ground black pepper, to taste
1 cup chopped fresh Italian parsley
2 tablespoons chopped fresh tarragon
1 egg, beaten
Vegetable oil for deep frying

1. Scrub 3 of the potatoes under running water to remove any dirt. Peel the 3 potatoes with a paring knife in wide strips, taking about ⅛ inch of the potato flesh along with the peel. Cover the potato peels with water and set aside. Peel the remaining potatoes in the regular manner with a vegetable peeler and discard the peels.

2. Drop all of the potatoes in cold salted water to cover in a large pan and cook until tender but still firm, about 30 minutes.

3. Meanwhile, chop the bacon and fry in a medium-size skillet until crisp. Drain on paper towels.

4. Add the onion to the hot bacon fat and sauté until limp. Remove from heat and whisk in the vinegar, olive oil, mustard, and salt and pepper to taste.

5. When the potatoes are done, drain them, let cool slightly, and slice. Place the potatoes in a large bowl and pour the bacon fat dressing over the top. Add the parsley and tarragon and gently toss to combine. Taste and adjust seasonings. Fold in the bacon.

6. Cut the reserved potato skins into 1-inch squares and toss with the beaten egg. Heat oil in a deep-fat fryer to 375°F. Add the potato skins, shaking the basket to separate the peels, and fry until crisp and browned, 5 to 7 minutes.

7. Transfer the warm potato salad to a serving bowl and sprinkle the top with the fried potato skins. Serve warm.

8 portions

PEANUT ICE CREAM

A smooth ice cream loaded with peanut flavor. We love to serve this with hot fudge sauce and whipped cream. You'll think you're a kid again.

1 ½ cups milk
1 ½ cups heavy or whipping cream
½ cup packed brown sugar
6 egg yolks, room temperature
1 cup unsalted peanuts, puréed until smooth
⅓ cup smooth peanut butter
Old-Fashioned Fudge Sauce (recipe follows)

1. Heat the milk and cream in a medium-size saucepan until hot but not boiling.

2. Beat the sugar and egg yolks in a large mixer bowl until the mixture forms a slowly dissolving ribbon when the beaters are lifted. Slowly pour the hot milk and cream into the yolk mixture, beating constantly.

3. Return the mixture to the saucepan and cook over low heat, stirring constantly, until thick enough to coat the back of a wooden spoon. Remove from heat and cool.

4. Stir the puréed peanuts and peanut butter into the cooled mixture. Process in a blender until smooth.

5. Freeze the mixture in an ice cream maker, following manufacturer's instructions.

6. Serve generous portions of the ice cream with a pitcher of fudge sauce on the side.

1 quart

OLD-FASHIONED FUDGE SAUCE

6 tablespoons (¾ stick) unsalted butter
3 ounces unsweetened chocolate, chopped
4 ounces German's sweet chocolate, chopped
½ cup sugar
1 tablespoon instant coffee powder
5 ounces evaporated milk
⅓ cup heavy or whipping cream
1 teaspoon vanilla extract

1. Melt the butter in a medium-size saucepan. Remove from heat and stir in both chocolates, the sugar, coffee, evaporated milk, and cream. Heat to boiling over medium-high heat, stirring constantly. Reduce heat to low and simmer for 10 minutes, stirring constantly. Remove from heat and stir in the vanilla.

2. Serve the sauce immediately or refrigerate covered up to 2 weeks. Warm the sauce in the top of a double boiler over simmering water.

About 1 ½ cups

WE'RE NUTS ABOUT

- ♥ Toasted pecan halves sprinkled on fresh fruit salad
- ♥ Peanuts added to ice cream sundaes
- ♥ Chopped walnuts and Gorgonzola stuffed into fresh figs
- ♥ Pine nuts as a garnish for minestrone soup
- ♥ Macadamia nuts in curried chicken salad, and toasted almonds in chicken salad with crisp bacon
- ♥ Finely chopped toasted hazelnuts in a creamy salad dressing over bitter greens
- ♥ Walnut halves and fluffy cream cheese spread on old-fashioned date-nut bread
- ♥ Chopped pecans as a coating for chicken and fish filets
- ♥ Assorted nuts folded into plain yogurt mixed with honey, sliced strawberries, and grapes
- ♥ Jumbo cashews and a secret hiding place so we don't have to share
- ♥ Chopped pistachios sprinkled over bittersweet chocolate mousse
- ♥ Glacéed pecans as a decoration for carrot cake with cream-cheese frosting

peanut
fudge sauce
Tin Roof Sundae

FIREWORKS ON THE FOURTH

There is no doubt about it—spicy is hot in America right now. From exotic Thailand to neighboring Mexico, we crave the fiery flavors of these influential cuisines. Celebrate this Fourth of July with the snap of a Sousa march and fireworks that taste as hot as those in the sky. We thank the cuisines of the world for their inspiration and rejoice in the new spirit of American food!

In this sophisticated cousin to the corn tortilla nacho, a creamy blend of chopped chicken and cream cheese is spiced with jalapeño peppers, red onion, garlic, cumin, and chili powder. Lots of grated Jack cheese is folded in, then all is baked on pita bread until melted and puffed.

CREAMY CHICKEN AND JALAPENO NACHOS

1 whole chicken breast, poached, skinned, boned, and diced
12 ounces cream cheese, room temperature
2 jalapeño peppers, seeded and minced
3 tablespoons chopped red onion
2 cloves garlic, minced
1 teaspoon ground cumin
1 teaspoon chili powder
1 ½ cups grated Monterey Jack cheese
Salt and freshly ground black pepper, to taste
6 medium-size pita, each cut and separated into 2 rounds

1. Preheat oven to 375°F.

2. Combine the chicken, cream cheese, jalapeño peppers, onion, garlic, cumin, chili powder, and grated cheese in a large mixer bowl. Beat with an electric mixer until blended. Season to taste with salt and pepper.

3. Spread each pita round with a generous amount of the filling. Place on cookie sheets and bake until puffed and bubbling, 5 to 7 minutes. Immediately cut into wedges and serve in a napkin-lined basket.

About 100 nachos

MEAN, MEANER, MEANEST BARBECUE SAUCE

An adjustable sauce that lets you be as sweet or mean as you like.

⅔ cup olive oil
1 large yellow onion, chopped
1 bunch scallions (green onions), sliced
4 cloves garlic, minced
4 fresh ripe large tomatoes, seeded and chopped
1 large sweet red pepper, seeded, cored, and diced
1 large sweet yellow pepper, seeded, cored, and diced
3 jalapeño peppers, seeded and minced (meaner)
2 fresh cayenne peppers or small hot red chiles, seeded and minced (meanest)
1 can (35 ounces) tomatoes
3 tablespoons brown sugar
2 teaspoons chili powder
1 teaspoon dried oregano
¼ teaspoon ground cloves
6 tablespoons fresh lime juice
¼ cup Worcestershire sauce
3 tablespoons red wine vinegar
Salt and freshly ground black pepper, to taste

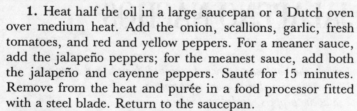

1. Heat half the oil in a large saucepan or a Dutch oven over medium heat. Add the onion, scallions, garlic, fresh tomatoes, and red and yellow peppers. For a meaner sauce, add the jalapeño peppers; for the meanest sauce, add both the jalapeño and cayenne peppers. Sauté for 15 minutes. Remove from the heat and purée in a food processor fitted with a steel blade. Return to the saucepan.

2. Process the canned tomatoes with their liquid, the sugar, and remaining oil in the food processor until smooth. Add to the saucepan. Stir in the chili powder, oregano, cloves, lime juice, Worcestershire sauce, red wine vinegar, and salt and pepper to taste. Simmer uncovered over low heat for 45 minutes.

2½ quarts

MEAN, MEANER, MEANEST BARBECUE BASTERS

Our barbecue sauce and its spicier variations are more of an accompaniment than a typical marinade. We like to brush it on meats or poultry just in the last few minutes of grilling and then place a bowl on the table for ladling to each person's liking. The degree of hotness you choose will depend purely on the spiciness of the crowd you're entertaining.

A PREPONDERANCE OF PEPPERS

Peppers come in a glorious array of colors and a fiery range of flavors these days. Sweet bell peppers are now available in four irresistible shades—red, yellow, green, and deep eggplant purple. When stuffing or roasting whole peppers, we like to mix and match the colors. Red and yellow peppers make bright and sweet vegetable purées, while purple peppers add a nice Mediterranean accent sliced raw into salads, and green peppers remain our favorite frying pepper.

There are a staggering number of types of hot peppers. The most widely available tend to be jalapeño, serrano, cayenne, and poblano, so popular in Tex-Mex style dishes. Cajun cooks are particularly fond of the banana and bird's-eye peppers native to Louisiana. Which pepper you choose will depend mostly on personal preference and local availability, as differences in flavor are often too slight to detect. A good rule of thumb when attempting to judge a pepper is to remember that usually the smaller the pepper, the hotter the taste. A dish can always be made milder or hotter by varying the amount of pepper added.

There is no better time to serve Fireworks Relish than at sunset on a Fourth of July picnic. Whether you've spent a cloudless day on the beach, at a tennis tournament, hot-air ballooning, or peacefully reading poetry, it's the moment of waiting for the fireworks to begin that epitomizes the Fourth.

GRILLED STEAK WITH RED PEPPER COULIS

A fiery way to serve a grilled sirloin or flank steak.

Red Pepper Coulis (recipe follows)
3 pounds sirloin, top round, or flank steak
Salt and freshly ground black pepper, to taste

1. Make the coulis.
2. Prepare hot coals with some mesquite for grilling the steak. Sprinkle the steak with salt and pepper.
3. Grill the steak to desired doneness, slice, and serve with the coulis spooned over the slices.
6 portions

RED PEPPER COULIS

½ cup olive oil
6 sweet red peppers, cored, seeded, and cut into ½-inch dice
12 large cloves garlic, cut lengthwise in half
2 tablespoons balsamic vinegar
1 tablespoon sugar
Pinch (or to taste) red pepper flakes
Salt and freshly ground black pepper, to taste
3 tablespoons finely chopped sun-dried tomatoes (packed in oil)
16 whole basil leaves

1. Heat the oil in a large skillet over medium heat. Add the sweet red peppers and garlic and sauté for 15 minutes.
2. Stir in the vinegar and sugar. Add the red pepper flakes, salt, and pepper to taste. Cook uncovered, stirring occasionally, over medium heat for 15 minutes more.
3. Stir in the tomatoes and basil. Simmer 10 minutes. Serve hot.
2 cups

FIREWORKS RELISH

10 large sweet red peppers (about 4 pounds)
4 lemons
2 medium-size yellow onions
8 cloves garlic, finely minced
2 cups red wine vinegar
2 cups (packed) light brown sugar
¼ cup ground ginger
1 teaspoon ground chiles
Pinch cayenne pepper

1. Core and seed the peppers and cut into julienne strips.

2. Remove the zest from the lemons with a citrus zester or a small sharp knife; cut into julienne strips. Squeeze the lemons and measure ½ cup juice.

3. Cut the onions into thin slices.

4. Combine all the ingredients in a heavy large saucepan. Cook uncovered over low heat for 2 hours, stirring frequently.

3 ½ cups

SOUTH-OF-THE-BORDER BREADSTICKS

Everybody loves a breadstick to crunch on. Ours are spicy and will make you well aware of what you're nibbling, for they are chock-full of jalapeño peppers, sun-dried tomatoes, and melted Jack cheese.

¼ cup warm water (105° to 115°F.)
1 package active dry yeast
Pinch sugar
1 tablespoon olive oil
6 scallions (green onions), sliced
2 jalapeño peppers, seeded and finely chopped
1 tablespoon finely chopped sun-dried tomatoes (packed in oil)
2 teaspoons ground cumin
2 teaspoons chili powder, plus additional for sprinkling
1 cup milk
½ cup (1 stick) unsalted margarine
1 cup yellow cornmeal
3 eggs
1 ½ teaspoons salt
3 ½ to 4 cups unbleached all-purpose flour
1 ½ cups grated Monterey Jack cheese
2 teaspoons water

1. Pour ¼ cup water into a small bowl. Stir in the yeast and sugar and let stand for 15 minutes.

2. Meanwhile, heat the oil in a skillet over medium heat. Add the scallions, jalapeño peppers, and sun-dried tomatoes and sauté for 10 to 15 minutes. Stir in the cumin and 2 teaspoons chili powder. Remove to a large bowl.

3. Heat the milk and margarine in a small saucepan over medium heat, stirring occasionally, until the margarine melts. Stir into the scallion mixture.

4. Using a wooden spoon, stir in the cornmeal, 2 of the eggs, the salt, yeast mixture, and 2 cups of the flour. Stir in the cheese and enough of the remaining flour to make a soft dough. Knead the dough on a floured surface for 10 minutes, adding more flour if necessary.

5. Coat a large bowl with olive oil. Place the dough in the bowl and turn to coat with oil. Cover with a damp towel and let the dough rise in a warm place until doubled in bulk,

HANDLING HOT PEPPERS

If Peter Piper picked a peck of hot peppers, you can be sure he handled them with care. The seeds contain the fire, and whenever you handle peppers, make sure you wash your hands before touching your mouth, rubbing your eyes, or hugging a friend.

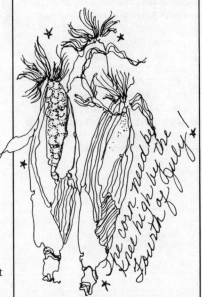

The corn need be knee high by the fourth of July!

"Where the corn is full of kernels and the colonels full of corn."
—William James Lompton

Use little individual cactus
plants as place-card
holders—put your guest's
name between the arm and
the main stem.

For a hot, glorious Fourth
of July bouquet, combine
orange day lilies (don't use
them at night—they close),
yellow lilies, and red
oriental poppies.

FOURTH OF JULY
FIREWORKS

*Creamy Chicken and
Jalapeño Nachos*

*Grilled Steak with Red
Pepper Coulis*

Hot Pepper Ratatouille

*Roasted Corn on the Cob
with Jalapeño Butter*

*South-of-the-Border
Breadsticks*

Fireworks Relish

Summer sorbet sampler

Beaujolais and Beer

about 1 hour.

6. Punch the dough down and let rest 5 minutes.

7. Break off small pieces of the dough and roll the pieces between your fingers into sticks, ½ inch wide and 8 to 10 inches long. Place on greased cookie sheets.

8. Cover the breadsticks with a towel and let rise for 45 minutes to 1 hour.

9. Preheat oven to 400°F.

10. Beat the remaining egg and 2 teaspoons water in a small bowl. Brush the breadsticks with the egg wash and sprinkle with chili powder. Bake until lightly browned, 12 to 15 minutes. Let cool to room temperature.

5 to 6 dozen breadsticks

CORN ON THE COB WITH FLAVORED BUTTERS

8 ears freshly picked corn in husks
8 tablespoons flavored butter (recipes follow)

1. Prepare hot coals for grilling the corn.

2. Peel back, but do not remove, the husks from the ears of corn. Remove the silk. Spread each ear with 1 tablespoon of the flavored butter. Rewrap each ear of corn in its husk and then wrap in aluminum foil.

3. Grill the corn about 4 inches from the hot coals, turning frequently, for about 30 minutes.

8 portions

ANCHOVY BUTTER

½ cup (1 stick) unsalted butter, room temperature
1 tablespoon fresh lemon juice
4 anchovy fillets, drained and finely chopped
1 tablespoon finely snipped fresh chives

Beat the butter and lemon juice with an electric mixer until blended. Beat in the anchovies and chives. Refrigerate covered until ready to use.

About ¾ cup

JALAPENO PEPPER BUTTER

½ cup (1 stick) unsalted butter, room temperature
2 jalapeño peppers, seeded and finely minced
½ teaspoon ground cumin

Beat the butter with an electric mixer until light. Beat in the jalapeño peppers, then the cumin. Refrigerate covered until ready to use.

About ½ cup

CURRY BUTTER

½ cup (1 stick) unsalted butter, room temperature
2 tablespoons good-quality curry powder

Beat the butter and curry powder with an electric mixer until blended. Refrigerate covered until ready to use.
About ½ cup

HOT PEPPER RATATOUILLE

A colorful blend of purple eggplant, yellow summer squash, mixed peppers, and red cherry tomatoes. Cumin and oregano give hints of Mexico to this ratatouille innovation. Add more jalapeño peppers if you like it fiery hot.

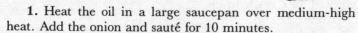

½ cup mild olive oil
1 large yellow onion,
thinly sliced
6 large cloves garlic, cut
into thin slivers
1 large eggplant, unpeeled, cut
into 1-inch cubes
1 sweet red pepper, cored,
seeded, and cut into
½-inch squares
1 green bell pepper, cored,
seeded, and cut into
½-inch squares
4 jalapeño peppers, seeded and
minced
2 yellow summer squash, cut into
1-inch cubes
1 tablespoon dried oregano
2 teaspoons ground cumin
Salt, to taste
24 ripe cherry tomatoes, halved
3 tablespoons chopped fresh coriander (garnish)

1. Heat the oil in a large saucepan over medium-high heat. Add the onion and sauté for 10 minutes.
2. Stir in the garlic and sauté for 5 minutes more. Add the eggplant and cook, stirring occasionally, over medium heat 15 minutes.
3. Add the red, green, and jalapeño peppers and summer squash. Sprinkle with the oregano, cumin, and salt to taste. Simmer covered, stirring occasionally, over medium-low heat for 25 minutes.
4. Stir in the cherry tomatoes and simmer 10 minutes more. Serve hot or at room temperature, garnished with the coriander.
6 portions

FIREWORKS

While the Fourth of July in America is incomplete without fireworks, we like to see them on other occasions as well. They've been used to celebrate:

- ♥ The Prince of Wales's birthday
- ♥ Russia's Vostok cosmonauts, August 1962—exploding over the Kremlin
- ♥ The Festa del Redentore in Venice, held on the third Sunday in July
- ♥ The 100th anniversary of the Brooklyn Bridge, May 24, 1983
- ♥ Ronald Reagan's inauguration in 1981
- ♥ The Monte Carlo International Fireworks Festival
- ♥ The closing ceremony at the Los Angeles Winter Olympics, 1984

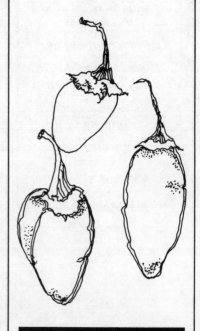

MUSICAL NOTES

Play lots of patriotic music and marches on the Fourth of July—Grofé's *Grand Canyon Suite*, Sousa marches, *Yankee Doodle*, the *Colonel Bogie March*, and the Marine Hymn.

For a summer get-together at the beach with old girlfriends, bring along tapes of the Ronettes, the Shangri-Las, the Crystals . . . or Cyndi Lauper—and remember, girls just wanna have fun!

Make a summer tapas party all the more authentic with Spanish guitar music in the background.

The island of Malta is so fireworks-happy that it is said that a man who successfully completes his morning shave there without a nick shoots a rocket out of his window to mark the occasion.

COFFEE BLOND BROWNIES

Everyone has a definite preference for one type of brownie. These are for those who love coffee more than chocolate, but find it hard to forgo chocolate altogether. A chewy addition to a brownie lover's repertoire.

1 pound dark brown sugar
¾ cup (1½ sticks) unsalted butter
2 tablespoons strong instant coffee powder
1 tablespoon hot water
2 eggs
2 tablespoons vanilla extract
2 cups unbleached all-purpose flour
2 teaspoons baking powder
½ teaspoon salt
1 cup chopped pecans
1 cup semisweet chocolate bits

1. Heat the brown sugar and butter in a medium-size saucepan over medium-low heat until the butter melts. Dissolve the coffee in the hot water and stir into the butter mixture. Let cool to room temperature.

2. Preheat oven to 350°F. Butter an 11 x 8-inch baking pan.

3. When the butter mixture is cool, beat in the eggs and vanilla with a hand-held mixer.

4. Sift the flour, baking powder, and salt together and stir into the butter mixture with a wooden spoon. Stir in the pecans and chocolate.

5. Spread the mixture evenly in the prepared pan with a rubber spatula. Bake until lightly browned, 25 to 30 minutes. Do not overbake.

6. Cool completely and cut into 2-inch squares.

20 brownies

LEMON SORBET

2 cups fresh lemon juice (8 lemons)
2 cups sugar
Grated zest of 3 lemons
1 cup heavy or whipping cream
½ cup water

Process all ingredients in a blender or a food processor fitted with a steel blade. Freeze in an ice cream maker, following manufacturer's instructions.

1 quart

SUMMER WHEN IT SIZZLES

The hot, hot, humid days of summer make us yearn for cool liquid refreshment. Strength for tennis matches, sailing, and sunbathing needs to be kept up with more than the odd cocktail and tonic. We've solved the problem by creating a host of chilled gazpachos and garden-fresh bisques.

As with soups, salad making and inventing is one thing we never grow tired of. Much of The Silver Palate's reputation began with praise for our fresh-tasting, unique combinations. Chicken salad is always the most popular, and we have conjured up endless varieties. Four new favorites are included in this chapter. Pasta salads continue to be popular with the summer crowd, so we've added some new twists. We also haven't forgotten elegant shrimp and lobster, substantial steak and lamb, and the always appealing garden-fresh vegetables.

Salad meals are perfect for summer's sizzling spells of unbearable heat. All of these convert nicely into luncheons and dinners, for they are bursting with fruity vinaigrettes and special homemade mayonnaises that impart flavors and nourishment far less elusive than a summer evening's fireflies.

SUMMER BY THE SEA

Sarah's Summer Soup

Soft-Shell Crabs Sterling

Lemon Rice

Ratatouille with Lemon and Basil

Crusty French bread

Chocolate Raspberry Torte

Chablis or Chardonnay

SARAH'S SUMMER SOUP

Raspberry vinegar heightens the flavors in this delicious pink soup. Crème fraîche adds another little bite to the sweet beets, and the dollop of the white cream makes a stunning presentation.

8 beets, peeled and cut into ½-inch dice
⅓ cup chopped shallots
2 cups Berta's Chicken Stock (page 396)
2 cups water
1½ cups fresh orange juice (3 large oranges)
Grated zest of 2 oranges
2 tablespoons sugar
2 tablespoons raspberry vinegar
1 cup Crème Fraîche (page 399) or heavy or whipping cream
Salt and freshly ground black pepper, to taste
Crème Fraîche (garnish)

1. Place the beets, shallots, stock, and water in a medium-size saucepan. Heat to boiling. Reduce heat and simmer uncovered until the beets are very tender, about 30 minutes.

2. Remove from the heat and stir in the orange juice and zest. Let cool to room temperature.

3. Stir in the sugar. Purée the soup in a blender or food processor fitted with a steel blade until smooth and pour into a bowl. Stir in the vinegar, 1 cup crème fraîche, and salt and pepper to taste. Refrigerate the soup until cold.

4. Ladle the soup into bowls and garnish each serving with a dollop of crème fraîche.

6 to 8 portions

POTATO, WATERCRESS, AND BASIL SOUP

This rustic soup is a perfect opener for an Italian or Mediterranean menu.

3 cups Berta's Chicken Stock (page 396) or canned chicken broth
3 Maine or other thin-skinned potatoes, unpeeled, diced
1 small yellow onion, diced
¼ cup tightly packed fresh basil leaves
2 leeks, well rinsed and dried
4 tablespoons (½ stick) unsalted butter
½ cup tightly packed watercress leaves
¼ teaspoon ground allspice
Salt and freshly ground black pepper, to taste
1 cup milk

1. Combine the stock, potatoes, and onion in a large saucepan. Cook, partially covered, over medium heat until the potatoes are almost tender, 15 to 20 minutes.

2. Meanwhile, dice the leeks, including the *light* green tops. Melt the butter in a skillet over medium heat. Add the leeks and sauté until almost tender, 5 to 10 minutes. Add the watercress leaves and sauté 5 more minutes.

3. Add the basil to the potato soup and cook another 5 minutes.

4. Add the leek mixture, allspice, and salt and pepper to taste to the soup.

5. Process the soup in batches in a food processor fitted with a steel blade to a purée. If a finer purée is desired, force the soup through a food mill.

6. Return the soup to the saucepan, stir in the milk, and reheat over low heat. Serve immediately.

6 portions

MUSSEL BISQUE

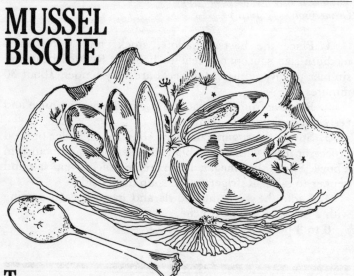

The essence of summer abundance is captured in this soup, which celebrates two harvests—from the seashore and from the garden.

2 cups water
About 3 cups dry white wine
3 pounds mussels, scrubbed and bearded
½ cup (1 stick) unsalted butter
1 large yellow onion, chopped
1 large leek (white part and two-thirds green), well rinsed, dried, and minced
2 carrots, peeled and minced
4 cloves garlic, minced
3 ripe medium-size tomatoes, seeded and chopped
2 tablespoons chopped fresh dill
3 tablespoons chopped fresh basil
2 cups light cream
1 cup heavy or whipping cream
Salt and freshly ground black pepper, to taste

✤ FLOWERS FROM THE SILVER PALATE

For a summer alfresco dinner, combine yellow, pink, and white snapdragons in a clear glass pitcher.

DINING ALFRESCO

Mussel Bisque

Butterflied Leg of Lamb
Patriotic Potato Salad
Sliced beefsteak tomatoes

Strawberry Sorbet with Strawberry Purée

Merlot

"Soup and fish explain half the emotions of human life."
—Sydney Smith

1. Pour the water and 1 cup of the wine into a large pan. Add the mussels, cover the pan, and cook over high heat until the mussels open. (Discard any that do not open.) When cool enough to handle, remove the mussel meats from the shells and set aside. Strain the cooking liquid through a sieve lined with a double thickness of cheesecloth and reserve.

2. Melt the butter in a large stock pot over high heat. Add the onion, leek, carrots, and garlic and sauté over high heat for 5 minutes. Reduce heat to low, cover the pot, and cook, stirring occasionally, for 25 minutes.

3. Add the tomatoes and cook uncovered 5 minutes.

4. Add enough of the remaining wine to the mussel cooking liquid to measure 5 cups. Add to the stock pot and heat to boiling. Reduce heat and simmer uncovered 15 minutes.

5. Stir in the dill and basil, then the light and heavy creams, and finally the mussel meats. Season to taste with salt and pepper. Heat just until the soup is warmed through. Serve immediately with lots of crusty bread.

10 portions

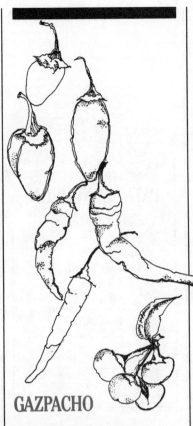

GAZPACHO

This pretty summer soup was originally a native of southern Spain, but it has now gained worldwide popularity. Everyone in Spain has a slightly different version of this "liquid salad," depending on family traditions and local produce. We've followed in their footsteps and have invented several of our own variations to keep us delightfully refreshed all summer long.

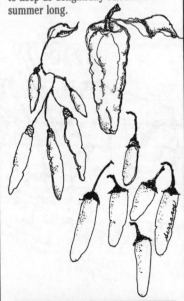

GREEN GAZPACHO

A refreshing summer soup loaded with all things green.

2 medium-size leeks (white part and 1 inch green), well rinsed and
    dried.
6 pale green Italian frying peppers, cored and seeded
3 large hothouse cucumbers, peeled and seeded (see Note, page 176)
4 cups arugula leaves (2 bunches)
2 cups watercress leaves (1 large bunch)
1 large shallot, peeled
3 eggs, lightly beaten
3 cups plain low-fat yogurt
1½ cups best-quality olive oil
¾ cup tarragon vinegar
1 teaspoon salt
½ teaspoon freshly ground black pepper
Pinch cayenne pepper
Dash Tabasco sauce
½ cup chopped fresh dill

1. Coarsely chop the leeks, peppers, cucumbers, arugula, watercress, and shallot. Combine in a large bowl.

2. Whisk the eggs, yogurt, oil, vinegar, salt, pepper, cayenne, and Tabasco together in a small bowl. Add to the vegetables and mix well.

3. Process the vegetable mixture to small chunks in a food processor fitted with a steel blade or a blender. Do not overprocess. Stir in the dill.

4. Refrigerate at least 4 hours before serving.

8 portions

FRUIT GAZPACHO

A combination that will dazzle your eyes and your palate.

2 cups tomato purée
3 cups freshly squeezed orange juice
2 teaspoons sugar
Grated zest of 1 orange
Grated zest of 1 lime
2 cups diced cantaloupe
2 cups diced honeydew melon
1 mango, peeled and diced
1 apple, peeled and diced
1 cup fresh blueberries
1 cup halved green or red seedless grapes
Fresh strawberries, hulled and cut in half (garnish)
1 or 2 kiwis, peeled and sliced (garnish)

1. Combine the tomato purée, orange juice, sugar, orange and lime zests, cantaloupe, honeydew, and mango in a large bowl. Process half of the mixture in a food processor fitted with a steel blade or a blender until smooth. Stir the purée into the remaining fruit mixture.

2. Stir in the apple, blueberries, and grapes. Refrigerate covered for several hours.

3. Ladle the soup into bowls. Garnish each serving with several strawberry halves and a couple of kiwi slices.

8 first-course portions

PALE ALMOND GAZPACHO

A light, refreshing soup with Middle Eastern accents of almonds, yogurt, cardamom, and mint. This soup travels well, so don't forget it for your next picnic.

1 cup blanched almonds
2 cups water
3 slices firm white bread, crusts trimmed torn into pieces
½ cup milk
2 cups unflavored yogurt
2 tablespoons raspberry vinegar
Juice of 2 lemons
Grated zest of 1 lemon
Grated zest of 1 lime
1 teaspoon ground cardamom
1 cucumber, peeled, seeded, and finely diced
½ honeydew melon, peeled and finely diced
1½ cups halved seedless green grapes
Salt, to taste
Fresh mint sprigs (garnish)

PATIO LUNCHEON

Fruit Gazpacho

*Peppers Stuffed with
Tomatoes, Basil, and
Chèvre*

*South-of-the-Border
Breadsticks*

Lime Daiquiri Sorbet

Beer

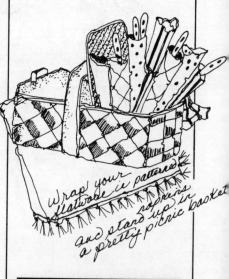

Wrap your
flatware in patterns
and stand napkers
a pretty picnic basket

1. Process the almonds and 1 cup of the water in a food processor fitted with a steel blade until almost smooth. Transfer to a large bowl.

2. Soak the bread in the milk, squeeze dry, and stir the bread into the almonds.

3. Stir in the yogurt, remaining 1 cup water, the vinegar, and lemon juice. Add the lemon and lime zests and cardamom and stir until blended. Stir in the cucumber, melon, and grapes. Season to taste with salt.

4. Refrigerate covered for several hours to allow flavors to blend. Serve in soup bowls. Garnish each serving with mint sprigs.

6 portions

ART SHOW LUNCHEON

Melon with lime wedges

Seafood Gazpacho

Crusty bread with assorted sheep's milk cheeses

Olives Sicilian Style

Peach Ice Cream

Gavi

We like a summertime luncheon to be calm, cool, and collected. It should be energizing and consist of food that looks fresh and attractive in daylight—clear, clean colors that can hold up to sun and shadow.

Make a centerpiece of a fragrant bouquet of herbs and garnish plates with the blossoms of an herb you have cooked with.

SEAFOOD GAZPACHO

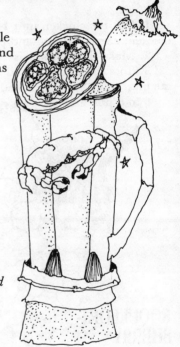

A luscious soup that needs little enhancement, although crab and avocado are delightful additions and make this gazpacho a perfect warm-weather meal. The colors are dazzling.

2 cups fresh bread crumbs
3 cloves garlic, minced
1 cucumber, peeled, seeded, and
  cut into ¼-inch dice
2 sweet red peppers, cored, seeded,
  and diced
3 jalapeño peppers, cored, seeded,
  and chopped
1 medium-size red onion, chopped
5 ripe tomatoes, seeded and chopped
5 cups tomato juice
½ cup fresh lime juice (4 limes)
½ cup olive oil
1 tablespoon ground cumin
Salt and freshly ground black pepper, to taste
1 pound lump crabmeat, picked over for shells
1 ripe avocado, pitted, peeled, and diced

1. Combine the bread crumbs and garlic and set aside.

2. Combine the cucumber, red peppers, jalapeño peppers, onion, and tomatoes in a large bowl. Pour in the tomato juice and lime juice and stir to combine. Add the bread crumb mixture and stir in the oil.

3. Purée half the soup in a food processor fitted with a steel blade or a blender and stir back into the half that is not puréed.

4. Season with cumin and salt and pepper to taste. Refrigerate until cold.

5. Just before serving, stir in the crabmeat and avocado.

10 portions

CHICKEN SALAD WITH RED GRAPES AND PECANS

A rich combination of jewel-colored red grapes, crunchy pecans, and gently poached chicken flavored with a pungent Roquefort-sherry mayonnaise and served on a bed of radicchio leaves.

4 whole boneless chicken breasts (8 halves), poached and skinned
1 cup diced celery
1 ½ cups seedless red grapes, halved
¾ cup pecan halves
Roquefort-Sherry Mayonnaise (recipe follows)
Radicchio leaves

1. Cut the chicken into 1-inch chunks, and combine the chicken, celery, grapes, and pecans in a large bowl.
2. Make the mayonnaise.
3. Toss the chicken salad with the mayonnaise. Refrigerate until cold. Serve on a bed of radicchio leaves.

6 to 8 portions

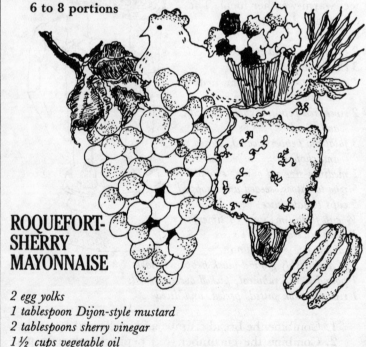

ROQUEFORT-SHERRY MAYONNAISE

2 egg yolks
1 tablespoon Dijon-style mustard
2 tablespoons sherry vinegar
1 ½ cups vegetable oil
1 cup crumbled Roquefort cheese
Salt and freshly ground black pepper, to taste

Process the egg yolks, mustard, and vinegar in a food processor fitted with a steel blade just to combine, about 30 seconds. With the machine running, pour the oil in a thin steady stream through the feed tube to make a thick mayonnaise. Add the Roquefort and process until combined but not smooth. Season to taste with salt and pepper.

About 3 cups

SUMMER FRUIT AND CHEESE COMBINATIONS

♥ Raspberries, strawberries, blueberries, and Montrachet
♥ Strawberries, green grapes, and L'Explorateur
♥ Bing cherries, Stilton, and wheatmeal biscuits
♥ Purple plums, Gorgonzola torta, and crusty French bread
♥ Peaches, nectarines, Mascarpone, and amaretti
♥ Peaches, Parmesan, and Italian peasant bread drizzled with extra virgin olive oil
♥ Fresh pineapple and blueberries with Saga
♥ Cantaloupe, prosciutto, and basil torta
♥ Granny Smith apples and Bing cherries with Morbier
♥ Raspberries, strawberries, Doux de Montagne, and rosé
♥ Assorted melons with smoked mozzarella

MORE SUMMER CRAVINGS

... Softball for grownups ... croquet
and cocktails ... peaches ... Trivial
Pursuit-Genus Edition ... supper at
Mashimic ... eating a tomato like an
apple ... ripe purple figs ... no
lizards ... beach rhythms ... sweet
baby silver corn ... living by the sun
... hydrangeas ... the smell of a
cottage breakfast ... an island of
one's own ... fresh mint ... riding
horseback around a lake before
breakfast ... looking toward
Portugal ... lemonade ...

CHICKEN AND PINEAPPLE SALAD

An interesting variation on the usual chicken and grape combination. The pale yellow of the pineapple is pretty, and its juicy sweetness is a pleasant surprise. All are bound together with mayonnaise lightened with whipped cream.

2½ pounds boneless chicken breasts, poached and skinned
2 cups diced celery
2 cups diced (½ inch) fresh pineapple
½ cup heavy or whipping cream, whipped
1 cup Hellmann's mayonnaise
Salt and freshly ground black pepper, to taste
Lettuce leaves

1. Cut the chicken into 1-inch chunks. Combine the chicken, celery, and pineapple in a mixing bowl.
2. Whisk the whipped cream and mayonnaise together until blended and pour over the chicken. Toss to coat thoroughly. Season to taste with salt and pepper.
3. Line 6 salad plates with lettuce leaves. Mound the salad on each plate and serve immediately.
6 portions

ORIENTAL CHICKEN SALAD

4 whole boneless chicken breasts (8 halves), poached, skinned, and
*   cut into ¼-inch-wide strips*
1 sweet red pepper, cored, seeded, and cut into julienne
1 small jicama, peeled and cut into julienne
1 can (5 ounces) water chestnuts, drained and halved
5 scallions (green onions, white part and 2 inches green), cut into
*   julienne*
4 dozen snow peas, trimmed, stringed, and blanched briefly in
*   boiling water*
¾ cup toasted cashews
2 tablespoons minced fresh parsley
2 cloves garlic, minced
½ cup bottled teriyaki sauce*
¼ cup sesame oil*
¼ cup safflower oil
¼ cup sesame paste (tahini)*
2 tablespoons rice vinegar*
2 tablespoons dry sherry
1 tablespoon brown sugar
2 teaspoons ground coriander
Few drops hot chili oil (optional)*
3 tablespoons toasted sesame seeds

1. Combine the chicken, red pepper, jicama, water chestnuts, and scallions in a large mixing bowl. Add the snow peas and cashews.

2. Process the parsley and garlic in a food processor fitted with a steel blade. Add the teriyaki sauce, sesame oil, safflower oil, sesame paste, vinegar, sherry, brown sugar, coriander, and chili oil, if desired. Process until smooth. Pour the dressing onto the salad and toss thoroughly.

3. Sprinkle with the sesame seeds. Refrigerate several hours before serving.

6 to 8 portions

*available in Oriental groceries and other specialty food shops

CHICKEN SALAD WITH PALE GREEN FRUIT

A light chicken salad to refresh on a hot summer day. Melon, cucumber, and green grapes perform a cooling magic.

3 pounds boneless skinless chicken breasts (about 3 whole)
1 cup heavy or whipping cream
2 cups honeydew melon balls
2 cups cucumber balls with skin (avoid the seeds)
2 cups green seedless grapes
1 cup blanched sliced almonds
1½ teaspoons freshly ground black pepper
1 teaspoon salt
Grated zest of 1 lemon
½ cup chopped fresh dill
1 cup Lemon Mayonnaise (recipe follows)

1. Preheat oven to 350°F.

2. Arrange chicken breasts in a single layer in a large baking pan. Spread evenly with the cream and bake until done to your taste, 20 to 25 minutes. Cool completely in the cream. Remove the chicken and save accumulated juices to enrich soups or sauces.

3. Shred the chicken into bite-size pieces and place in a large bowl. Add the melon and cucumber balls, grapes, and almonds, and toss to combine.

4. Sprinkle with the pepper, salt, lemon zest, and all but 2 tablespoons of the dill, and toss again until thoroughly mixed.

5. Fold in the mayonnaise. Spoon onto a serving platter and garnish with the remaining dill.

6 to 8 portions

A LAZY HAZY MENU

When it is just too hot to cook, buy a wide assortment of salads, cold hors d'oeuvres, and special taste treats from your favorite take-out food shop. Spread out a tapas-style buffet with everything placed on individual Italian or Portuguese glazed pottery plates. Set up a small open bar with an assortment of Spanish sherries and a huge pitcher of Sangría. End the evening under the moon with chilled buckets of Spanish champagne, sugared almonds, and bowls of fresh fruit and berries.

DILL

Both the leaves and the seeds of dill are used in cooking. The feathery, fernlike leaves add extra refreshment to soups, salads, eggs, fish, vegetables, and stews. Dill has a particularly wonderful affinity with salmon, fresh or smoked.

The seeds add flavor to breads and dips, and are used extensively in pickling cucumbers. The yellow flowers make a pretty summer garnish.

"Dill" comes from the Saxon *dilla*, meaning "to lull"—its seeds were first used to soothe babies to sleep.

"I like a cook who smiles out loud when he tastes his own work. Let God worry about your modesty; I want to see your enthusiasm."
—Robert Farrar Capon

TWO PEAS IN A POD

Peas must be picked when young and tender, just when it is most tempting to pop them straight into your mouth instead of into the pot—summer memories are made of this! Ripe pods will open with just a little pressure if they are fresh. Make sure you pick enough for the pot and try to go easy on the nibbling!

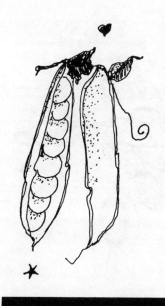

LEMON MAYONNAISE

2 eggs
2 tablespoons tarragon vinegar
2½ tablespoons fresh lemon juice
2 tablespoons Dijon-style mustard
1½ cups mild olive oil
1 cup corn oil
1 bunch fresh tarragon, leaves chopped, or 2 teaspoons dried tarragon
1 teaspoon coarse (kosher) salt
Pinch ground white pepper
Grated zest of 1 large lemon

1. Place the eggs, vinegar, lemon juice, and mustard in a food processor fitted with a steel blade and process 15 seconds.
2. Remove the feed tube, and with the machine running, add the oils in a thin, steady stream. Remove to a bowl.
3. Gently fold in the tarragon, salt, pepper, and lemon zest.

3 cups

MINTY PEA SALAD

A wonderful combination of fresh shelled peas and crispy snow peas. Sprinkle with bacon for great taste and texture.

1½ cups shelled fresh peas
8 ounces snow peas, trimmed and stringed
1 large bunch or 2 medium bunches fresh mint, stems removed (1 cup leaves)
⅓ cup sour cream
⅓ cup Hellmann's mayonnaise
Salt and freshly ground black pepper, to taste
8 slices crisp cooked bacon, crumbled

1. Heat 2 medium-size pans of water to boiling. Add shelled peas to one pan and cook just until tender, about 2 minutes. Add snow peas to the second pan and cook just until bright green and crisp, 30 to 60 seconds. Drain and rinse both pans of peas with cold water. Set aside to dry.
2. Reserve a few mint leaves for garnish and finely chop the rest.
3. Cut snow peas into julienne strips, reserving a few whole for garnish. Combine shelled peas with julienned snow peas in a medium-size bowl. Gently toss with the chopped mint.
4. Mix sour cream and mayonnaise and fold into peas. Season to taste with salt and pepper. Refrigerate covered until cold.
5. Sprinkle with the bacon and garnish with the reserved snow peas and mint leaves.

6 portions

MARINATED TOMATO AND CHEESE SALAD

4 ripe large tomatoes, seeded and cut into ½-inch cubes
1 pound Brie, rind removed, cheese cut into irregular pieces
1 cup fresh basil leaves (1 small bunch), cut into strips
3 cloves garlic, finely minced
⅔ cup best-quality olive oil
1 teaspoon salt
½ teaspoon freshly ground black pepper

1. Combine the tomatoes, Brie, basil, garlic, oil, salt, and pepper in a large serving bowl. Let stand covered at room temperature at least 2 hours.

2. Serve with crusty Italian bread and assorted charcuterie or as a filling for sandwiches.

6 to 8 portions

GREEK SALAD WITH FLAMED KASSERI

Familiar Greek salads have feta cheese, tomatoes, red onions, and olives. We've added new sparks and mix hot and cold—green beans for texture, anchovies to heighten the flavor of the dressing, and flaming Kasseri cheese. Quite a spectacular presentation.

1 pound Kasseri cheese, cut into twelve 2 x 1-inch rectangles
2 eggs, beaten
1 cup fresh bread crumbs
6 cups spinach leaves
½ cup Greek black olives
1 pound tender green beans, trimmed and blanched
3 ripe tomatoes, seeded and sliced
1 red onion, thinly sliced
1 can (2 ounces) anchovy fillets, drained
2 cloves garlic, minced
¾ cup olive oil
3 tablespoons balsamic vinegar
1 tablespoon fresh lemon juice
1½ tablespoons Dijon-style mustard
1 tablespoon capers, drained
1 tablespoon dried oregano
3 tablespoons heavy or whipping cream
Freshly cracked black pepper, to taste
¼ cup brandy

1. Dip each cheese rectangle into the beaten eggs and then coat with the bread crumbs. Place in a single layer on a

MEDITERRANEAN MAGIC

Greek Salad with Flamed Kasseri

Grilled Chicken with Lemon and Olives

Yellow Tomato Sauté

Garlic bread

Figs with Crème Fraîche and Raspberry and Sherry-Vinegar Purée

Verdicchio or Tavel Rosé

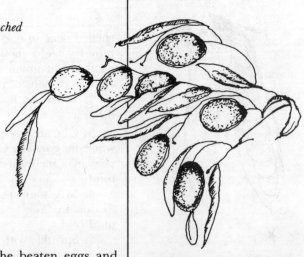

BASIL

This vivid green herb radiates an intoxicating fragrance redolent of all things Italian. The fresh leaves should be handled with care, as even the slightest bruise will blacken them. Basil grows well in a window box—with the added bonus that it is supposed to repel flies!

In medieval Europe, a basil leaf was thought to be a passport to heaven. Pesto lovers will certainly agree.

plate and refrigerate at least 1 hour.

2. Divide the spinach leaves among 6 shallow salad bowls. Then divide the olives, green beans, tomatoes, and onion among the 6 salads.

3. Heat the anchovies, garlic, and ½ cup of the oil in a small saucepan over medium heat until the anchovies dissolve. Reduce the heat to low and stir in the vinegar, lemon juice, mustard, capers, and oregano. Simmer 3 minutes. Stir in the cream and season to taste with black pepper. Keep warm over low heat or reheat for a minute before serving.

4. Heat the remaining ¼ cup oil in a large skillet over medium heat. Add the breaded Kasseri and sauté 2 to 3 minutes on each side. Pour in the brandy and, standing back, flame it. The brandy will flame quite high.

5. Place 2 pieces of the cheese in the center of each salad and drizzle the salads with warm anchovy dressing. Serve immediately.

6 portions

GARDEN FRESH TORTELLINI SALAD

A wonderful fresh host of vegetables play beautifully with spinach and egg tortellini. Coat it all with a vinaigrette made with balsamic vinegar, orange zest, and thyme. What a way to celebrate summer.

1 pound good-quality fresh or frozen spinach tortellini
1 pound good-quality fresh or frozen egg tortellini
1 head broccoli (1 pound), broken into florets and tender stems sliced
1 pound carrots, peeled and cut diagonally into ¼-inch slices
3 leeks (white part and 2 inches green), well rinsed, dried, and cut into thin julienne
1 large sweet red pepper, cored, seeded, and cut into julienne
1 large sweet yellow pepper, cored, seeded, and cut into julienne
½ cup chopped fresh basil
1 egg yolk
2 tablespoons fresh lemon juice
1 tablespoon Dijon-style mustard
1 tablespoon balsamic vinegar
1 cup vegetable oil
½ cup olive oil
1 teaspoon dried thyme
Finely grated zest of 1 orange
Salt and freshly ground black pepper, to taste

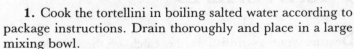

1. Cook the tortellini in boiling salted water according to package instructions. Drain thoroughly and place in a large mixing bowl.

2. Cook the broccoli florets, stems, and carrots separately in boiling salted water just until tender. Drain and combine with the tortellini.

3. Blanch the julienned leeks 1 minute in boiling water; drain. Add the leeks, red and yellow peppers, and fresh basil to the salad and toss to combine.

4. Process the egg yolk, lemon juice, mustard, and vinegar in a food processor fitted with a steel blade for 30 seconds. With the machine running, pour the oils in a thin steady stream through the feed tube to make a light mayonnaise. Add the thyme, orange zest, and salt and pepper to taste. Process to combine.

5. Pour the dressing over the salad and toss to coat thoroughly. Serve at room temperature or slightly chilled.

8 to 10 portions

CAESAR SALAD

Our version of this well-loved American salad classic. The pumpernickel croutons add an unusual touch. Don't forget to pass the peppermill.

1 head romaine lettuce, leaves separated
1 egg, lightly beaten
2 garlic cloves, crushed
3 tablespoons fresh lemon juice
½ cup olive oil
4 anchovy fillets, drained and chopped
2 hard-cooked eggs, peeled and quartered
½ cup freshly grated Parmesan cheese
¾ cup Pumpernickel Croutons (page 400; a variation of Garlic Croutons)

1. Rinse the lettuce and dry. Refrigerate wrapped in paper towels for several hours to crisp the leaves.

2. Whisk the raw egg, garlic, lemon juice, and oil together and pour into the bottom of a large salad bowl.

3. Add the lettuce, anchovies, and hard-cooked eggs and toss thoroughly with the dressing.

4. Add the cheese and toss again.

5. Sprinkle with the croutons and serve immediately. Pass the peppermill.

4 portions

SWORDFISH, PASTA, AND PECAN SALAD

Be sure your swordfish is the catch of the day for this surprising salad with pasta and pecans. The sweetness of the tarragon Béarnaise Mayonnaise ties it all together for a rich sublime taste.

PRIVET PORCH MENU

Bucheron Tart with Fresh Herbs

Swordfish, Pasta, and Pecan Salad

Stuffed Baby Zucchini

Crusty French bread

Vanilla Ice Cream with Bittersweet Chocolate Sauce

California Chardonnay

A summer home is a private place to escape from pressures and the public. Perfectly trimmed towering hedges guard innermost secrets and provide a protected setting for entertaining famous movie stars or harried friends. You won't even have to whisper the latest local scandals!

THE WINES OF SUMMER

It doesn't take intense chemical analysis to tell us which wines we should drink throughout the hot, sunny days of summer. Heat makes us crave foods that are light and often chilled; likewise we tend to drink crisp, fruity, and light white wines whose flavors are not so pronounced that they are destroyed by being served icy cold. We also tend to drink more liquids and thus like to choose wines that have lighter alcoholic content. Besides California Chardonnays, Cabernet rosés, white Zinfandels, Rieslings, Gewürztraminers, and sparkling wines, our favorite "cool-down" wines are:

MACON-VILLAGES AND MACON BLANC: Uncomplicated and pleasant Chardonnay wines. While they have the appeal of being produced in the Burgundy region, they have the advantage of being considerably less expensive than white Burgundies.

MUSCADET: An uncomplicated fresh fruity wine made to be consumed young.

POUILLY-FUISSE: Another Chardonnay wine of southern Burgundy that is a bit more complicated in flavor, and more expensive, than the Mâcon wines.

ROSE D'ANJOU: A slightly sweet, light pink wine that makes for festive summer sipping.

SAINT-VERAN: A Chardonnay from the Mâcon area known to have a little more richness of flavor than the Mâcon-Villages.

SANCERRE: An attractive fresh wine with some body and the flavor of black currants.

SPARKLING SAUMUR: Made from Chenin Blanc grapes using the Champagne method. Pleasantly dry, fruity, and effervescent . . . and half the price of Champagne.

VOUVRAY OR VOUVRAY MOUSSEUX: Light or sparkling wine from the Loire which ranges from dry to semisweet.

1 ½ pounds swordfish steaks (¾ to 1 inch thick)
4 tablespoons fresh lemon juice
¼ cup Hellmann's mayonnaise
1 pound thick spaghetti, cooked al dente and drained
¼ cup olive oil
1 cup pitted and sliced black olives
1 ½ cups pecan halves, toasted in 350°F oven for 10 minutes
Béarnaise Mayonnaise (recipe follows)
Fresh dill and tarragon sprigs (garnish)

1. Preheat broiler.

2. Sprinkle the swordfish steaks on both sides with 1 tablespoon of the lemon juice. Spread one side of the steaks with half the Hellmann's mayonnaise.

3. Broil the steaks, mayonnaise side up, 6 inches from the heat for about 5 minutes. Turn the steaks over, spread with the remaining Hellmann's mayonnaise, and broil until done, another 3 to 4 minutes.

4. Let the fish cool and then cut into ½-inch cubes.

5. Toss the pasta with the remaining 3 tablespoons lemon juice and the oil. Add the olives, pecans, and swordfish and toss together.

6. Make the mayonnaise.

7. Toss the mayonnaise with the pasta mixture, garnish with the fresh dill and tarragon, and refrigerate several hours to allow flavors to blend. Serve cold or let warm to room temperature.

6 portions

BEARNAISE MAYONNAISE

A classic sauce becomes a delectable mayonnaise.

2 shallots, minced
½ cup dry white wine
¼ cup white wine vinegar
2 tablespoons dried tarragon
2 tablespoons dried dill
2 egg yolks
2 tablespoons fresh lemon juice
2 teaspoons tarragon mustard
1 cup vegetable oil
½ cup olive oil
Salt and freshly ground black pepper, to taste

1. Heat the shallots, wine, vinegar, tarragon, and dill to boiling in a small saucepan. Cook until almost all of the liquid has evaporated. Remove from the heat.

2. Process the egg yolks, lemon juice, and mustard in a food processor fitted with a steel blade for 10 seconds. With the machine running, add the oils in a thin steady stream through the feed tube to make a thick mayonnaise. Turn off the processor and add the reduced shallot mixture. Process just until blended. Season to taste with salt and pepper.

2 cups

LOBSTER FIESTA SALAD

Wonderful shades of pinks, reds, and yellows give this salad its name. The cantaloupes and papayas should be just ripe and very flavorful. The ginger and chives accent the sweet fruit and lobster meat. Serve on a bright-colored ceramic platter and garnish with watercress.

2 pounds cooked fresh lobster meat
1 ripe papaya, peeled and cut into julienne
1 ripe small cantaloupe
2 ripe large plum tomatoes, seeded and diced
2 tablespoons chopped fresh dill
2 tablespoons chopped fresh chives
1 tablespoon finely chopped fresh ginger root
Orange Vinaigrette (recipe follows)
2 bunches watercress

    1. Remove any cartilage from the lobster meat, leaving the pieces as large as possible. Place the lobster and papaya in a large bowl.
    2. Cut the cantaloupe in half, remove the seeds, and, using a melon baller, cut the cantaloupe into balls over the bowl of lobster so that the juices fall in the bowl. Toss gently.
    3. Add the tomatoes, dill, chives, and ginger.
    4. Make the vinaigrette.
    5. Pour the vinaigrette over the salad and toss gently. Serve on a bed of watercress on a large platter.
6 portions

ORANGE VINAIGRETTE

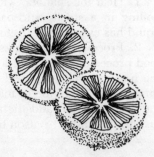

¼ cup fresh orange juice
2 tablespoons red wine vinegar
1 tablespoon Dijon-style mustard
1 cup mild olive oil
Freshly ground black pepper, to taste

"It takes four men to dress a salad: a wise man for the salt, a madman for the pepper, a miser for the vinegar, and a spendthrift for the oil."
—Anonymous

FULL MOON MENU

Green Gazpacho

Lobster Fiesta Salad
Cashew Sticks

Strawberry Hazelnut Torte

Chardonnay or
Mâcon-Villages

THE SALAD BOWL

The best green salads begin with a favorite, well-tended wooden salad bowl—a bowl that is never washed with soap and water, but rather wiped clean with paper towels after each use. This permits a slight residue of salad oil to permeate the wood and with time creates a well-seasoned salad bowl.

The best, most cherished salad bowls will build up a fine interior patina that will be faintly scented with all good things of salad making—garlic, mustard, pepper, and aromatic herbs. If you must wash the bowl, quickly rinse it under warm water, but the paper towel method is preferable for cleaning. Remember, oil and water don't mix.

We particularly like the early American cradle bowls that have survived the test of several generations of salad making. Another favorite is the burl bowl, handsomely carved from an old tree. Look for these treasures in rural antique stores. Short of antiques, a plain wooden bowl from a housewares store can be lovingly cajoled into becoming a time-worn, well-seasoned salad bowl.

Whisk the orange juice and vinegar in a small bowl until mixed. Whisk in the mustard; then gradually whisk in the oil. Continue to whisk until slightly thickened. Season to taste with pepper.

About 1½ cups

SHRIMP AND RASPBERRY SALAD WITH HARICOTS VERTS

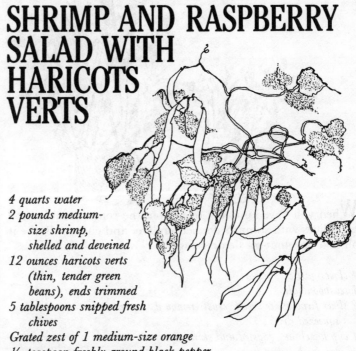

4 quarts water
2 pounds medium-
size shrimp,
shelled and deveined
12 ounces haricots verts
(thin, tender green
beans), ends trimmed
5 tablespoons snipped fresh
chives
Grated zest of 1 medium-size orange
½ teaspoon freshly ground black pepper
⅓ cup raspberry vinegar
1 teaspoon Dijon-style mustard
Salt and freshly ground black pepper, to taste
½ cup mild olive oil
1 cup fresh raspberries
1 bunch watercress, stems removed

1. Heat 4 quarts water to boiling in a large pot and drop in the shrimp. Boil 1 minute and drain in a colander. Let the shrimp cool completely in the colander.

2. Blanch the haricots verts in boiling water until bright green and just tender, about 1 minute. Drain, and drop into ice water to cool; drain and pat dry.

3. Toss the shrimp and green beans together in a large bowl. Add 4 tablespoons of the chives, the orange zest, and pepper. Toss gently.

4. Whisk the vinegar and mustard together in a small bowl. Season to taste with salt and pepper. Gradually whisk in the oil until thickened.

5. Pour ¾ cup of the vinaigrette over the shrimp salad and toss to coat. Add half the raspberries and very gently toss to combine.

6. Arrange the watercress on a serving platter and mound the salad in the center. Garnish with the remaining 1 tablespoon chives and remaining raspberries.

6 portions

LAMB AND FENNEL SALAD WITH HAZELNUT DRESSING

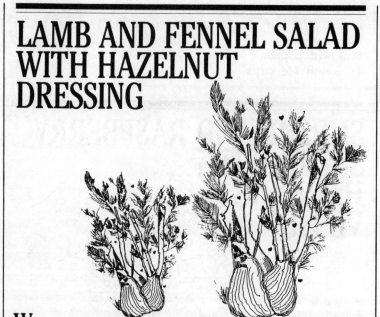

When you have lamb left over from the roast, combine the rare slices with spinach, fennel, endive, and chèvre. Bathe it all in a hazelnut-garlic dressing.

4 cloves garlic, minced
1 teaspoon salt
2 slices firm white bread, crusts removed, soaked in hot water and
*   squeezed dry*
1 cup hazelnuts, toasted and skinned
⅓ cup fresh lemon juice
⅓ cup olive oil
½ to ¾ cup water
Freshly ground black pepper, to taste
Spinach or romaine leaves to line 6 plates
1½ pounds sliced rare lamb
1 fennel bulb, cut diagonally into ½-inch pieces
1 Belgian endive, leaves separated, rinsed, and patted dry
8 ounces Montrachet or other soft mild chèvre cheese, crumbled

1. Mash the minced garlic with the salt to a paste in a small bowl. Add the bread and work in thoroughly until smooth.

2. Process the hazelnuts in a food processor fitted with a steel blade until ground. Add the garlic paste and process 5 seconds to combine. Add the lemon juice and oil and process to blend. With the machine running, slowly pour in enough of the water to thin the dressing to the consistency of heavy cream. Season to taste with black pepper.

3. Line 6 salad plates with the spinach leaves. Place a small shallow bowl of hazelnut dressing in the center of each salad.

4. Decoratively arrange the lamb slices, fennel pieces, and endive leaves in a circle around the dressing on each plate. Sprinkle each salad with some chèvre. Serve immediately.

6 portions

THE SALAD MAKINGS

For a great salad, the greens must be fresh, crisp, well rinsed, and well dried. While the greens should be chilled, a good vinaigrette should always be left to mellow at room temperature and tossed with the salad at the moment of serving.

Salad making is one of the most pleasurable, spontaneous, and creative moments in the whole gamut of cooking and menu planning. A pure green salad made from one head of perfect lettuce can be as memorable as a salad composed from a rainbow of leafy greens and vegetables. The secret is to use an artist's eye in assembling a salad that is the most complementary to the menu at hand. Wild native greens and imported European salad ingredients have infused new life into produce sections of markets across the country. Specialties like arugula, radicchio, and mâche are now almost as readily available in the Midwest as they are in New York and Europe.

We find the salads that receive the most raves from our guests are those that have a bit of whimsy. We like to scatter whole chives over the top of a salad and dot with the fringe of tender pink chive blossoms. Shredded radicchio and wild rose petals make another favorite combination. Mâche and the first spring violets are a savory mixture almost too pretty to eat. Don't be afraid to use your imagination, tempered with common sense and good taste as a guide.

THE GREEN LEAVES

Some of our favorite salad greens in combination include:

- ♥ Sliced fennel and crumbled Gorgonzola on a bed of watercress, tossed with an orange vinaigrette
- ♥ Endive, walnuts, and sliced apples, tossed with a walnut oil and honey cider vinaigrette
- ♥ Watercress, sliced pears, crumbled chèvre, and toasted hazelnuts, tossed with a hazelnut-oil–sherry vinaigrette
- ♥ Arugula, diced seeded tomatoes, and shredded smoked mozzarella, tossed with a balsamic vinaigrette
- ♥ Bibb lettuce, radish sprouts, violets, and chopped hard-cooked eggs with a Champagne vinaigrette
- ♥ Spinach, radicchio, and pomegranate seeds with a raspberry vinaigrette
- ♥ Belgian endive, grapefruit, and avocado with a lime and grapeseed-oil dressing

FENNEL

This is a bonus herb whose stalks make a great garden vegetable, cooked or raw, and whose feathery leaves are an anise-flavored herb. The seeds are wonderful, too, in breads, cookies, soups, and stews.

The Greek word for fennel is *marathon*, and the herb was a symbol of strength and praiseworthiness. The celebrated battle of Marathon in 490 B.C. was fought on a field of fennel.

ROASTED LAMB WITH FIG TAPENADE

A very gutsy spread made of figs, capers, anchovies, olives, and mustard dresses sliced rare-roasted lamb. To add a crisp fresh flavor, we've presented it on little platters decorated with Belgian endive and fresh lemon slices. Don't forget to sprinkle with chopped parsley!

½ cup chopped dried small figs
¼ cup brandy
⅔ cup water
½ cup pitted Niçoise olives
6 anchovy fillets
1½ tablespoons capers, drained
2 tablespoons fresh lemon juice
1 tablespoon Dijon-style mustard
1 cup best-quality olive oil
Freshly ground black pepper, to taste
3 tablespoons balsamic vinegar
Salt, to taste
36 slices (about 3 x 2 inches) rare-roasted lamb
2 Belgian endives, leaves separated, rinsed, and patted dry
Lemon slices (garnish)
Niçoise olives (garnish)
Fresh parsley sprigs (garnish)
Chopped fresh parsley (garnish)

1. Place the figs, brandy, and water in a small saucepan and simmer until the figs are tender, about 30 minutes. Drain.

2. Process the pitted olives, anchovies, capers, lemon juice, mustard, and cooked figs in a food processor fitted with a steel blade to make a thick paste. With the machine running, pour ½ cup of the oil in a thin steady stream through the feed tube to make a thick spread. Season to taste with pepper.

3. Mix the remaining ½ cup oil and the vinegar in a large bowl and season to taste with salt and pepper. Add the lamb, toss, and let stand 20 minutes at room temperature.

4. Arrange 6 endive leaves in a star pattern on each of 6 medium-size salad plates. Place a lemon slice in the center of each plate and top with an olive and parsley sprig.

5. Arrange the lamb slices in the intervals between the endive leaves. Place small spoonfuls of fig tapenade at the very tips of the endive leaves and larger spoonfuls over the ends of the lamb slices nearest the center of the plate.

6. Garnish with additional lemon slices, olives, and parsley sprigs, if desired. Sprinkle with chopped parsley. Serve immediately.

6 appetizer portions

MIDSUMMER'S VEGETABLES

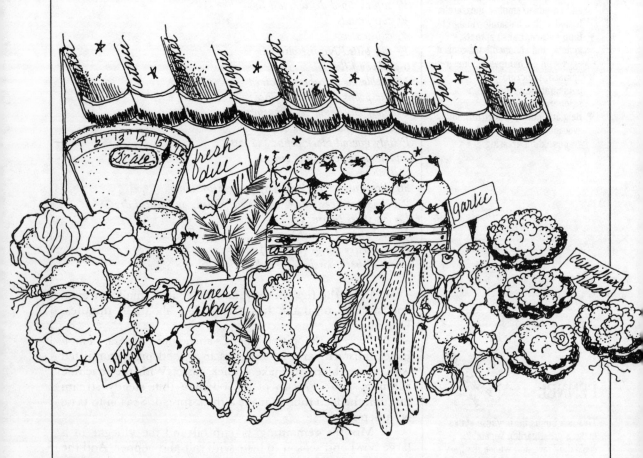

There is nothing more simple nor more memorable than the intense flavors of midsummer's vegetables. They set taste standards by which we judge all others the year round, and long for especially in the hot house depths of winter.

This is the one time of the year that we feel we all could become vegetarians without a moment's regret. Summer vegetable preparations should be uncomplicated to let every ounce of fresh flavor shine through.

NATURAL PRESENTATIONS

Although we do love casual entertaining in the summer, we also want to make our guests feel special. Putting a little effort into your summertime table is so easy with the abundance of summer's treasures. Focus on the natural simplicity of:

- ♥ A bunch of wild flowers in a milk pitcher.
- ♥ Antique straw baskets brimming with vine-ripened cherry tomatoes for nibbling.
- ♥ Linen napkins folded around zinnias from your garden.
- ♥ A table garden: Cluster bowls of garden peas, shiny peppers, baby carrots, and tomatoes for an edible centerpiece.
- ♥ Vases filled with leafy mint sprigs to adorn iced tea and lemonade.
- ♥ Using produce as containers— melons for soups, lemons for mayonnaises, lettuce for salads, tomatoes for stuffings.
- ♥ Pots of geraniums in full bloom with dark green ivy tucked around for a lovely table decor.
- ♥ Fresh herbs in little vases, piles of plums, peaches, strawberries, and raspberries in old straw baskets— your ingredients and your kitchen will never look more appealing.
- ♥ Filling the porch, terrace, and every nook and cranny in the house with flowers and herbs.
- ♥ Using seashells as containers for salt and pepper.
- ♥ Gilding the cake with lilies and the hors d'oeuvre tray with petunias. Surround the cookie plate with violets, the salad bowl with nasturtiums, and the breakfast table with morning glories.

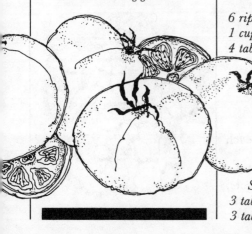

YELLOW OR RED TOMATO SAUTE

Tiny whole yellow tomatoes abound in a summer garden, and their golden color dazzles the eye. If you can't find them, red cherry tomatoes do quite nicely. This very simple preparation is lovely with beef or lamb.

1 tablespoon unsalted butter
1 tablespoon best-quality olive oil
2 cloves garlic, finely minced
4 cups fresh ripe yellow or red cherry tomatoes, stemmed
Salt and freshly ground black pepper, to taste
2 tablespoons finely chopped fresh parsley

1. Heat the butter and oil in a medium-size skillet over very low heat. Add the garlic and sauté for 1 minute.

2. Add the tomatoes and increase the heat to medium. Cook, shaking the pan frequently, just until heated through, 4 to 5 minutes. Do not overcook. Sprinkle with salt and pepper to taste.

3. Remove to a serving bowl and toss with the parsley. Serve immediately.

4 portions

BAKED TOMATOES STUFFED WITH COUSCOUS

The golden color of couscous along with the lightness of its grain makes it an attractive alternative to rice for stuffed tomatoes. The carrots, zucchini, and pine nuts add the colors and flavors of the Mediterranean.

6 ripe large tomatoes
1 cup water
4 tablespoons olive oil
2 teaspoons ground cumin
1 teaspoon curry powder
1 teaspoon Hungarian sweet paprika
½ cup couscous
¾ cup diced carrots
1 cup diced zucchini
¾ cup chopped red onion
2 teaspoons dried oregano
Salt and freshly ground black pepper, to taste
3 tablespoons chopped fresh Italian parsley
3 tablespoons pine nuts (pignoli)

1. Slice the tops from the tomatoes and scoop out the inner pulp from the shells. Discard the seeds but reserve the pulp. Lightly salt the insides of the tomatoes and let them drain upside down on paper towels while you prepare the filling.

2. Heat the water, 1 tablespoon of the olive oil, the cumin, curry, and paprika to boiling in a small saucepan. Stir in the couscous and continue to cook until most of the water has been absorbed, about 2 minutes. Remove from heat, cover the pot, and let stand 10 to 15 minutes.

3. Preheat oven to 350°F.

4. Dice the reserved tomato pulp into pieces the same size as the carrots and zucchini.

5. Heat the remaining 3 tablespoons olive oil in a skillet over medium heat. Add the onion, carrots, zucchini, and tomato pulp and sauté for 7 minutes.

6. Stir the oregano into the vegetables. Stir in the couscous and season to taste with salt and pepper. Stir in the parsley and pine nuts.

7. Spoon the couscous mixture into the tomato shells. Place in a baking pan.

8. Bake for 35 minutes, covering with aluminum foil if the couscous mixture seems to be drying out on top. Serve immediately.

6 portions

BABY ARTICHOKES PROVENCAL

A perfect little vegetable appetizer. Baby artichokes are cooked on a thick bed of carrots, leeks, and garlic. White wine and lemon juice add tartness, while creamy goat cheese blends everything together

18 baby artichokes
½ cup best-quality olive oil
3 large carrots, peeled and cut into small dice
3 leeks (white part and 3 inches green), well rinsed, dried, and
  chopped
4 cloves garlic, minced
Salt and freshly ground black pepper, to taste
½ cup dry white wine
1 tablespoon fresh lemon juice
4 ounces Montrachet or other soft mild chèvre
Niçoise or Ligurian olives (garnish)

1. Cut the stem and ¼ inch of the top from each artichoke. Trim the tough outer leaves with a scissors.

2. Heat the oil in a saucepan large enough to hold all the artichokes upright over medium-high heat. Add the carrots, leeks, and garlic and sauté, stirring frequently, for 10 minutes. Season to taste with salt and lots of black pepper.

IT'S ALL IN THE TOUCH

Experience will be the answer in the long run, but here are a few marketing guidelines for finding the choicest fruits and vegetables.

♥ LIFT lemons, oranges, limes. The heavier, the juicier—true for any citrus fruit.

♥ SQUEEZE peaches, plums, pears, avocados, tomatoes—gently! If they give slightly under pressure, they're ripe. Salad greens feel spongy when squeezed.

♥ THUMP eggplants, melons, pineapples, acorn squash, cucumbers to see if they're solid and meaty. It should sound like a thump on your wrist.

♥ TAP bread—a knuckle-rap should produce a hollow sound, telling you it's done.

♥ PAT cakes and muffins—if they spring back under a light touch, they're ready. Also check to see if they have shrunk away slightly from the sides of the pan.

♥ PRESS or PRICK a roast—firm means well done. If meat responds as in the cake test (soft yet resilient), it's medium rare. If rare, the juices will run red when pricked. If the juices are pink, it's medium; colorless means well done (overdone, in our book). Pork and fowl must be cooked until juices are clear.

♥ WIGGLE a drumstick—it should be tender to the touch, and the bone should jiggle around in its socket when it's done.

♥ NUDGE fish—it will bounce back under your fingers and flake with a fork when properly cooked.

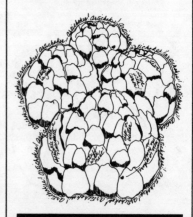

Celebrate the results of spring's hard work by setting a summer luncheon in the middle of your flower garden. Dazzle your friends with zucchini and zinnias, mussels and sweet marjoram, leafy homegrown greens, and tropical tarts.

3. Place the artichokes upright on the bed of vegetables and pour in the wine. Sprinkle the lemon juice over the tops of the artichokes. Cover the pan and simmer over medium-low heat for 20 to 25 minutes. Remove from heat and cool to room temperature.

4. Remove the artichokes from the vegetables and set aside. Crumble the chèvre into the vegetable mixture and fold gently together.

5. Spoon the vegetable mixture onto a platter or 6 individual serving plates. Arrange the artichokes on top of the vegetables, spooning a few vegetables over the tops. If you are serving on plates, allow 3 artichokes per serving. Garnish with olives and serve at room temperature.

6 portions

STUFFED BABY ZUCCHINI

a bowl of plum tomatoes

Baby vegetables are becoming more widely available, and these small zucchini make perfect hors d'oeuvres. We stuff ours with fresh ripe tomatoes, zucchini pulp, garlic, and parsley—a garden fresh ratatouille.

12 miniature zucchini
2 tablespoons mild olive oil
1 medium-size clove garlic, finely chopped
1 shallot, finely chopped
2 ripe Italian plum tomatoes, seeded and cut into ⅛-inch dice
2 tablespoons chopped fresh Italian parsley
1½ teaspoons chopped fresh thyme or ½ teaspoon dried
Freshly ground black pepper, to taste

1. Cut each zucchini lengthwise in half, leaving any blossoms on one of the halves. With the tip of a vegetable peeler, carefully scoop out the pulp, making a little shell. Reserve the pulp.

2. Heat the oil in a small skillet over low heat. Add the garlic and shallot and sauté 1 minute. Add the zucchini pulp, tomatoes, 1 tablespoon of the parsley, the thyme, and black pepper to taste. Cook, stirring frequently, for 5 minutes. Cool to room temperature.

3. Spoon the filling into the zucchini shells. Sprinkle with the remaining parsley. Arrange on a flat basket or platter and serve at room temperature.

24 pieces, 6 to 8 portions

BABY EGGPLANT, SUMMER TOMATO, AND BASIL CASSEROLE

16 baby eggplants (each 4 inches long)
4 cloves garlic, cut into slivers
4 medium-size bunches fresh basil, stems removed
Freshly ground black pepper, to taste
½ cup best-quality olive oil
2 tablespoons fresh lemon juice
4 ripe large tomatoes, cut into ¼-inch slices
7 tablespoons grated Parmesan cheese
1 bunch fresh thyme, leaves chopped, or 2 tablespoons dried thyme
2 tablespoons chopped fresh Italian parsley

1. Preheat oven to 425°F.

2. Cut the stems from the eggplants and cut each one lengthwise in half.

3. Place the eggplants, skin side down, on a cookie sheet. Make a slit in the center of each eggplant half and insert a garlic sliver and a small basil leaf. Sprinkle with pepper to taste and drizzle ¼ cup of the oil over all the eggplant.

4. Cover the pan tightly with foil and bake 20 minutes. Remove from the oven and turn the oven down to 350°F.

5. Place 1 layer of eggplant, skin side down, in a shallow 13 x 9-inch casserole. Sprinkle with 1 tablespoon of the lemon juice and pepper to taste. Arrange a layer of half the tomatoes over the eggplant and sprinkle with 3 tablespoons of the Parmesan. Sprinkle half the thyme evenly over the cheese and completely cover with a layer of basil. Drizzle with 2 tablespoons of the oil.

6. Repeat layers, using the remaining layer ingredients including all the Parmesan.

7. Cover the baking pan tightly with aluminum foil and bake 45 minutes. Garnish with the parsley and serve immediately.

8 portions

HAPPY RETURNS OF THE DAY

Birthdays are important to us all whether we admit it or not. To pamper someone all day long, start by serving best wishes and breakfast in bed, tuck tiny surprises around the bedroom, bath, in socks or pockets to discover while dressing, sneak a treat in his or her attaché case or purse, and arrange for something appropriate but special to be delivered to him or her during the day. Fill the evening with favorite foods, entertainment, and friends—by surprise or wish. Remember that the gifts most loved are those from the heart—a poem, a commitment of your time, a photograph—the more personal, the better.

RATATOUILLE WITH LEMON AND BASIL

A light, refreshing summer ratatouille. Make this dish when it's very hot and there's lots of fresh zucchini and basil in the garden. Cool with lemon juice and lemon zest.

About 1¼ cups best-quality olive oil
1 large eggplant, unpeeled, cut crosswise into 1-inch slices
1 large yellow onion, cut lengthwise into ¼-inch slivers
2 medium-size zucchini, cut lengthwise in half and then into 1-inch slices
5 large cloves garlic, minced
2 cups firmly packed whole basil leaves, plus additional for garnish
½ cup fresh lemon juice (2 lemons)
Coarsely grated zest of 2 lemons
¼ teaspoon salt
¼ teaspoon freshly ground black pepper
¼ cup chopped fresh Italian parsley

1. Heat ¾ cup of the oil in a heavy skillet over medium-high heat. Add several eggplant slices and sauté, turning occasionally, just until golden. Remove from the skillet, cut into 1-inch cubes, and place in a deep oven-proof casserole. Repeat with the remaining eggplant, adding additional oil if needed.
2. Preheat oven to 350°F.
3. Quickly sauté the onion and zucchini in ¼ cup of the oil in the skillet and remove to the casserole.
4. Add the garlic, 2 cups basil leaves, the lemon juice, lemon zest, salt, and pepper to the vegetables and stir to mix.
5. Bake covered for 1 hour.
6. Taste and adjust seasonings, and stir in the parsley.
7. Serve hot or at room temperature. Garnish with whole basil leaves.
8 portions

YELLOW PEPPER PUREE

This sunny pepper purée is enhanced by basil and garlic. It is wonderful served as a vegetable or perfect served cold with chilled fish or steak. Be sure it's in a clear glass bowl garnished with some basil leaves.

¼ cup best-quality olive oil
6 sweet yellow peppers, cored, seeded, and cut into ¼-inch dice
1 large yellow onion, chopped
2 cloves garlic, minced
2 tablespoons chopped fresh basil
Salt and freshly ground black pepper, to taste

SEAWORTHY FOOD

Greek sausages, goat cheese, and olives

Ratatouille with Lemon and Basil

Crusty peasant bread

Fresh peaches and figs

Valpolicella

You don't have to be sailing the Mediterranean to capture the spirit of the Greeks. This picnic basket of seaworthy food will bring to mind the hot white islands of Greece whether you are sailing the waters of the Atlantic, Pacific, or an inland lake. Play plenty of Greek music, dance, make noise, but don't get so carried away that you toss the plates overboard.

1. Heat the oil in a medium-size skillet over high heat. Add the yellow peppers, onion, and garlic and sauté for 10 minutes. Reduce the heat to low, cover the pan, and simmer for 30 minutes.

2. Transfer the pepper mixture to a food processor fitted with a steel blade; add the basil and salt and pepper to taste. Process until smooth. Remove to a saucepan and heat to boiling. Cook uncovered over medium-high heat, stirring frequently, until reduced and slightly thickened, 5 to 10 minutes. Serve hot, at room temperature, or cold.

6 portions

TEX-MEX STUFFED PEPPERS

The combination of three colors of peppers mirrors the boldness of the Texas spirit. The stuffing of jalapeño peppers, garlic, cumin, chicken, and cream cheese pays equal tribute to the big appetites cultivated in the Lone Star State.

4 sweet red peppers
4 sweet yellow peppers
4 green bell peppers
2 whole chicken breasts, poached, skinned, boned, and diced
6 scallions (green onions, white part and two-thirds green), chopped
2 jalapeño peppers, seeded and diced
2 cloves garlic, minced
12 ounces cream cheese, room temperature
2 eggs
3 tablespoons heavy or whipping cream
1 cup grated Monterey Jack cheese
1 tablespoon ground cumin
Salt and freshly ground black pepper, to taste
2 cups canned chicken broth

1. Slice the tops from the peppers and pull out the seeds and cores. Dice 1 pepper and its top of each color and set aside. Reserve the other 9 tops as well.

2. Drop the 9 remaining pepper shells into boiling salted water. Boil for 3 minutes. Drain and set aside.

3. Combine the diced peppers and chicken in a mixing bowl. Add the scallions, jalapeño peppers, and garlic and bind with the cream cheese by stirring with a wooden spoon. Stir in the eggs and cream, then the grated cheese. Season with the cumin and salt and pepper to taste.

4. Preheat oven to 350°F.

5. Place the pepper shells in a baking dish that will hold them snugly together. Spoon the filling into the peppers. Replace the tops and pour the broth around the peppers.

6. Bake until the filling is puffed and the peppers are soft and wrinkled but still intact, 1 hour. Serve immediately.

8 to 9 portions

"Those things are better which are perfected by nature than those which are finished by art."
—Cicero

TEQUILA

Tequila is the best known of all Mexican alcoholic beverages. Although it is often mistakenly believed to be distilled from cactus plants, in fact it comes from a different succulent called the blue agave, or *tequilana*.

In the old days, tequila was made in small stills, and the product was so often raw or unrefined that it developed quite a reputation for inducing hangovers. Fortunately, production has shifted to large distilleries which produce a product that can compete with the best of distilled spirits.

Tequila can be colorless or, if left to age in charred casks, pleasantly golden. Plain tequila is great in mixed drinks like the margarita or sunrise, while aged tequila should be drunk in the classic Mexican way: well chilled with a lick of salt and a squeeze of lime—the best way we know to alleviate the fiery sensations of hot Mexican dishes!

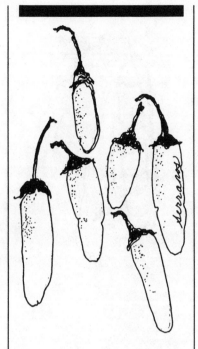

PEPPERS STUFFED WITH TOMATO, BASIL, AND CHEVRE

We often see peppers stuffed with rice mixtures, but here we've layered creamy chèvre, tomatoes, and fresh basil in green peppers and baked them for a light and colorful vegetable presentation. Serve with roasts, as an appetizer, or as a luncheon dish.

4 large green bell peppers, tops removed and reserved, cored and seeded
1 log (12 ounces) Montrachet or other soft mild chèvre, cut into 5 equal pieces
3 teaspoons chopped fresh Italian parsley
1 bunch fresh basil, stems removed (at least 16 large leaves)
2 ripe large plum tomatoes, cut into ¼-inch slices
Freshly ground black pepper, to taste
¼ teaspoon dried thyme
1 tablespoon best-quality olive oil
½ cup dry white wine

1. Preheat oven to 350°F.
2. Cut a very thin slice from the bottom of each pepper so it will stand straight.
3. Press 1 piece of the chèvre in the bottom of each pepper. Sprinkle the inside of each pepper with ½ teaspoon parsley and place 2 basil leaves in the bottom.
4. Divide the tomato slices evenly over the basil. Sprinkle with pepper to taste and the thyme.
5. Layer 2 more basil leaves in each pepper and drizzle ½ teaspoon oil over the basil in each pepper.
6. Crumble the last piece of chèvre on top of the peppers, and sprinkle with more black pepper and the remaining parsley. Replace the tops.
7. Rub the outside of the peppers with the remaining 1 teaspoon oil and place in a shallow baking dish just large enough to hold them. Pour the wine into the bottom of the dish.
8. Bake until tender, about 40 minutes. Serve immediately with roast lamb or veal or as a light luncheon dish.

4 portions

"Plant a radish
Get a radish
Never any doubt
That's why I love
   vegetables
You know what you're
   about!

Plant a turnip
Get a turnip
Maybe you'll get two
That's why I love
   vegetables
You know that they'll
   come true.''
—©Tom Jones &
Harvey Schmidt

NEW POTATOES WITH PEAS AND MINT

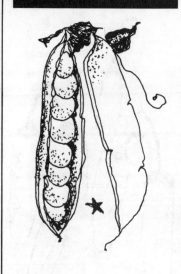

Tiny red-jacketed new potatoes and fresh mint are combined gently with crème fraîche in our delicate and refreshing summer potato salad. Sprinkle with fresh chives.

20 small new red potatoes, rinsed
⅓ cup olive oil
½ cup dry white wine
2 cups shelled fresh peas
2 cups Crème Fraîche (page 399)
½ cup chopped fresh mint leaves
3 tablespoons snipped fresh chives
Salt and freshly ground black pepper, to taste

1. Boil the potatoes in water to cover until tender but not mushy. Drain and cut into quarters, leaving skins on, while still hot.
2. Whisk the oil and wine together and drizzle over the hot potatoes in a large bowl. Stir to coat well. Let cool to room temperature.
3. Add the peas to the salad and then the crème fraîche, mint, and chives; toss gently to blend. Season to taste with salt and pepper.
4. Refrigerate for several hours before serving.

6 to 8 portions

POTATOES FONTECCHIO

A surefire favorite, we got this recipe from a former Silver Palate chef. Roasted new potatoes coated with lots and lots of garlic, mint, oil, and black pepper. Pure heaven.

5½ pounds red new potatoes
8 cloves garlic, finely minced
1½ cups best-quality olive oil
1 large or 2 small bunches fresh mint, stems removed, leaves finely chopped
2 tablespoons coarse (kosher) salt
Freshly ground black pepper, to taste

1. Preheat oven to 350°F.
2. Scrub the potatoes and prick each one about 6 times with a fork. Place in a shallow roasting pan and roast for 2 hours. Cut each potato in half.
3. Toss the potatoes with the garlic, oil, mint, salt, and pepper to taste in a large bowl. Let stand for 30 minutes before serving.

8 portions

MIDNIGHT AT THE OASIS

On a starry summer night when you are expecting late-arriving houseguests, plan a Midnight at the Oasis welcoming party. A widow's walk, a freshly mowed lawn, or a secluded beach cove is a perfect setting. Unfurl a magical Persian carpet, light deep eggplant-colored candles, and lay out a spread of sinful triple crème cheeses, plump dates, ripe melon wedges, and blushing peaches. Provide finger bowls of orange-flower water and offer snifters of ouzo and Sabra. Complete the mood with Ravi Shankar's music playing softly in the background.

THE BEST-DRESSED SALAD

The increasing availability of flavored oils, vinegars, and mustards inspires as much creativity in making dressings as in making salads. While we always love the combination of a good fruity olive oil with a rich wine vinegar, the French have opened our eyes to the merits of many subtler oils such as grapeseed, walnut, hazelnut, and almond oil.

As a general rule of thumb, the nutted oils should be used in simple combinations to let their distinctive flavors predominate. Grapeseed oil is a particularly good salad oil because it is light and subtle in flavor; use it in dressings that blend many ingredients such as garlic, mustard, flavored vinegars, and garden herbs. The choice of vinegar should be governed by rules similar to the ones used in selecting wine. Aged red wine vinegars, such as balsamic and Orleans, combine well with heavier fruity olive oils and robust salad greens. Sherry vinegar goes particularly well with salads that contain fruit and nuts; try combining it with a nutted oil. Milder vinegars, such as Champagne, white wine, and cider, combine well with lighter olive oils, shallots, tarragon, and mild greens. The wide variety of fruit vinegars require discretion but are particularly pleasant in the summer over both green and fruit salads: try tossing tiny blanched haricots verts with fresh raspberries and a simple dressing of walnut oil and raspberry vinegar. Finally, always remember to have the peppermill handy as an integral part of the salad course.

PATRIOTIC POTATO SALAD

Fresh garden herbs and vegetables join together in our midsummer potato salad. Dill, parsley, scallions, and carrots create a confetti effect that anticipates a celebration.

14 small new red potatoes, scrubbed clean
6 hard-cooked eggs, peeled and halved
1 medium-size carrot, peeled and grated
2 medium-size scallions (green onions, white part and 2 inches green), thinly sliced
3 tablespoons chopped fresh dill
2 tablespoons chopped fresh parsley
1 tablespoon caraway seeds
½ teaspoon salt
½ teaspoon freshly ground black pepper
¾ cup sour cream
¾ cup Hellmann's mayonnaise

1. Heat a medium-size saucepan of water to boiling. Add the potatoes and cook just until tender, 20 to 25 minutes. Drain, cool, and cut in half.
2. Combine the eggs, potatoes, carrot, and scallions in a large bowl. Add the dill, parsley, caraway, salt, and pepper and gently toss to combine.
3. Mix the sour cream and mayonnaise and gently fold into the potato mixture.
4. Refrigerate the salad several hours before serving to allow flavors to blend.

8 portions

LEEK FRITTATA

A pleasant Mediterranean twist on the classic omelette.

12 medium-size leeks
4 tablespoons (½ stick) unsalted butter
2 tablespoons olive oil
2 tablespoons fresh lemon juice
1 teaspoon sugar
7 eggs
½ cup chèvre or Crème Fraîche (page 399)
Salt and freshly ground black pepper, to taste
4 ounces cream cheese

1. Trim the root ends and a third of the green tops from the leeks. Rinse the leeks thoroughly to remove all of the sand and pat dry. Cut into ¼-inch slices.
2. Heat 3 tablespoons of the butter and the oil in a large skillet over medium heat. Add the leeks and sauté until

wilted. Stir in the lemon juice and sugar and simmer the leeks slowly in their own juices until very tender, about 30 minutes.

3. Preheat broiler.

4. Beat the eggs with the chèvre and season to taste with salt and pepper. Add the cooked leeks and combine thoroughly.

5. Butter a 10- to 12-inch cast-iron skillet or springform pan with the remaining 1 tablespoon butter. Pour in the egg-leek mixture and dot with the cream cheese.

6. Bake for 45 minutes. Serve warm or cold, cut into wedges.

6 appetizer portions or 4 main-course portions

LEEK LASAGNE

We've taken the notion of lasagne and translated it into a vegetable extravaganza. Blanched leeks serve as "noodles" layered alternately with a tomato-carrot-mushroom sauce and a creamy chèvre béchamel. Who needs pasta?

8 ounces fresh cultivated mushrooms
3 tablespoons olive oil
1 medium-size yellow onion, chopped
3 cloves garlic, minced
4 carrots, peeled and diced
1 can (16 ounces) tomatoes, drained
½ cup dry red wine
2 teaspoons dried thyme
Salt and freshly ground black pepper, to taste
¼ cup dried morels
12 medium-size leeks, roots trimmed, well-rinsed, and dried
4 tablespoons (½ stick) unsalted butter
6 tablespoons unbleached all-purpose flour
2 cups half-and-half
1 cup heavy or whipping cream
4 ounces Montrachet or other soft mild chèvre, crumbled

1. Trim the stems of the fresh mushrooms. Wipe mushrooms clean with a damp paper towel and dice. Heat the oil in a large cast-iron skillet over medium heat. Add the onion, garlic, carrots, and diced mushrooms and sauté for 10 minutes.

ONIONS

The vast family of onions, from chives, scallions, leeks, and shallots to the many varieties of the basic onion—Spanish, Italian, Bermuda, Walla Walla, Vidalia, Maui, pearl, Ebenezer, and globe—form a truly tear-inspiring array. Still, we can't imagine cooking without them and often use onions lavishly as the base of many of our favorite soups, stews, and roasts; or thinly sliced or chopped in salad combinations; or simply simmered slowly to highlight their natural sweetness.

Unfortunately, we don't believe in chopping onions in a food processor, as it tends to liquefy them—the basic chef's knife is still the best method. While everyone has a different theory on avoiding tears, we believe that chilling the onion before chopping will reduce tears by half, and we know that our lucky friends who wear contact lenses never cry at all . . . at least, over onions.

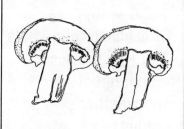

2. Add the tomatoes, wine, and thyme. Season to taste with salt and pepper. Simmer for 45 minutes.

3. Meanwhile, soak the morels in hot water to cover 30 minutes. Drain and cut in half. Add the morels to the skillet and simmer uncovered 15 minutes more.

4. Heat a large stock pot of lightly salted water to boiling. Add the whole leeks and simmer until tender, 15 to 20 minutes. Drain and rinse under cold running water until cool.

5. Melt the butter in a heavy saucepan over medium-low heat. Stir in the flour and cook 1 minute. Slowly pour in the half-and-half, whisking constantly to blend. When the sauce is thick and smooth, stir in the cream and heat just until hot. Stir in the chèvre and heat until melted. Season to taste with salt and pepper. Remove from heat.

6. Preheat oven to 350°F. Butter an 11 x 4-inch loaf pan.

7. Trim the leeks to 11 inches and separate the leaves. Line the bottom of the buttered pan with 2 layers of the leaves.

8. Spoon about 1 cup of the tomato-vegetable sauce evenly over the leeks and then top with another double layer of leaves. Top with 1 cup of the chèvre béchamel, spreading evenly. Repeat alternating layers until the pan is filled, ending with the béchamel.

9. Bake the lasagne until bubbling, about 45 minutes. Unmold the lasagne by inverting the pan onto a serving platter. Cut into slices and serve immediately.

6 to 8 portions

COARSE SALT

Coarse salt or kosher salt has many advantages over table salt. Because the grains are rough they do not melt on contact with other foods, making them perfect for sprinkling on greens, on pretzel or bagel dough before baking, and, of course, for coating the rim of a margarita glass. Table salt is treated with anti-clumping agents that allow it to seep into foods. Ironically, the larger crystals of kosher salt impart a less salty flavor because they cannot permeate the food.

Salt is an effective retainer of heat and moisture, and coarse salt can be used much like clay for baking foods, because it forms a crusty casing that seals in flavor and juices. It also absorbs melting fat and thereby provides a method of fat-free cooking.

Furthermore, the heat retention of salt reduces total cooking time by one-third to one-half. See—not everything about salt is bad.

QUE SERA SILK SALAD

Salting cabbage brings out a silklike texture without cooking. Enriched with fresh ginger, mint, and pink peppercorns, this is a beautiful and unusual salad.

1 large green cabbage, finely shredded
3 tablespoons coarse (kosher) salt
1 red onion, cut into thin rings
2 tablespoons finely minced fresh ginger root
½ cup fresh lemon juice
½ cup olive oil
½ cup chopped fresh mint leaves
1 ½ tablespoons pink peppercorns
Salt, to taste

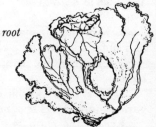

1. Sprinkle the cabbage with 2 tablespoons of the coarse salt in a large bowl. Let stand for 4 hours. Cover with ice water and let stand for 1 more hour. Rinse and drain the cabbage.

2. When the cabbage has been standing for 3 hours, sprinkle the onion with the remaining 1 tablespoon coarse salt. Let stand for 1 hour. Cover with ice water and let stand for 1 more hour. Rinse and drain.

3. Combine the cabbage and onion in a large mixing bowl.

4. Whisk the ginger, lemon juice, and oil together. Pour over the cabbage and onion and toss.

5. Stir in the mint and peppercorns. Taste and add salt if necessary.

6. Refrigerate for several hours before serving.

10 to 12 portions

STIR-FRY OF THREE CABBAGES

Because the cooked cabbages look like seaweed, this dish is an ideal accompaniment to seafood. If cooled to room temperature or chilled, it can be served as a vegetable rendition of a Chinese noodle salad.

2 tablespoons rice vinegar*
2 tablespoons soy sauce
1 tablespoon sesame oil*
2 teaspoons cornstarch
1 teaspoon sugar
2 cups finely shredded red cabbage
3 cups finely shredded Chinese cabbage
2 cups finely shredded green cabbage
3 tablespoons vegetable oil
3 cloves garlic, minced
1½ teaspoons chopped fresh ginger root
2 tablespoons sesame seeds
Several drops hot chili oil*

1. Mix the vinegar, soy sauce, sesame oil, cornstarch, and sugar in a small bowl and set aside.

2. Combine the cabbages in a large bowl with your hands.

3. Heat the vegetable oil in a wok over high heat. Add the garlic, ginger, and sesame seeds and stir-fry 1 minute.

4. Add the cabbages and stir-fry just until wilted and translucent, 4 to 5 minutes.

5. Pour in the reserved soy mixture and cook 1 minute more, tossing to coat. Sprinkle with the chili oil and toss.

Serve immediately.

6 portions

*available in some supermarkets, Oriental groceries, and other specialty food shops

" 'The time has come' the Walrus said,
To talk of many things
Of shoes and ships and sealing wax
Of cabbages and kings
And why the sea is boiling hot
and whether pigs have wings."
—Lewis Carroll

GONE FISHING

F ish is no longer the dreaded fare of Friday nights and religious fasts. Summertime brings the freshest catch as our thoughts turn toward the sea. We scramble to devour the first soft-shell crabs of the season, find that blackened redfish is becoming as common on restaurant menus as steak au poivre, con avid sportsmen friends into harpooning an extra swordfish or even hooking another bluefish, and rejoice in keeping fish odors out of the kitchen and over the outdoor grill. You'll hear no complaints about fish from us—we think it is perfect for light summer meals, especially when accompanied by our favorite chilled Chardonnays.

AN HERBY SUMMER GARDEN CLAMBAKE

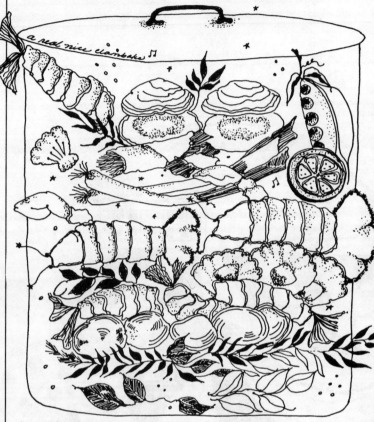

Bring a taste of the beach to your own kitchen stove. A lovely colorful mélange of lobster, shrimp, and scallops with summer vegetables in a fragrant broth of garden herbs. Serve over pasta or with hot crusty bread and lots of chilled white wine.

REAL NICE CLAMBAKE

Caesar Salad

An Herby Summer Clambake

Crusty French bread

Strawberry Hazelnut Torte

Sparkling Vouvray

1 pound littleneck clams, scrubbed
1 pound steamer (soft-shell) clams, scrubbed
1 pound mussels, scrubbed and bearded
½ cup vinegar
2 bunches fresh rosemary, stems removed
2 bunches fresh thyme, stems removed
2 bunches fresh oregano, stems removed
2 bunches fresh tarragon, stems removed
1 cup coarsely chopped shallots
8 large cloves garlic, peeled
2 teaspoons coarsely ground black pepper
4 cups water
4 cups dry white wine
4 medium-size leeks (1 ¾ pounds), well rinsed, dried, and white and light green part cut into thick julienne
2 fresh lobsters (1 ½ pounds each), cut into 6 pieces each, claws cracked
3 medium-size yellow squash (1 ¾ pounds), cut into ½-inch slices
12 fresh large plum tomatoes, cut in half
8 ounces snow peas, trimmed and stringed
1 teaspoon salt
1 pound medium-size shrimp, peeled and deveined
1 pound bay scallops
2 large shallots, finely chopped

"Fish, to taste right, must swim three times—in water, in butter, and in wine."
—Polish Proverb

"I'm fond of anything
that comes out of the
sea—and that
includes sailors."
—Janet Flanner

SALICORNIA

Salicornia is known as glasswort,
marsh samphire, *pousse-pied*. It was
once common in America, our first
president's favorite herb. Today it is
available only from Europe. It is a
crunchy, slightly salty, twiglike green
which grows in salt marshes. Look for
it, beg your merchant for it, then try
it raw, or steam it for 2 minutes, and
add a dash of olive oil and chopped
fresh basil. We love to use it as a bed
for fish or chicken.

1. To remove the sand from the clams and mussels, divide them between 2 large bowls, cover with water, and pour ¼ cup of the vinegar into each bowl. Let stand 30 minutes. Drain and rinse.

2. Cover the bottom of a 15-inch round deep pan with 1 bunch each of rosemary, thyme, oregano, and tarragon. Sprinkle with the coarsely chopped shallots, the garlic cloves, and 1 teaspoon of the pepper. Pour in the water and wine.

3. Cover the pan and slowly heat to boiling, about 10 minutes.

4. Remove from heat. Layer the littleneck clams and mussels in the pan. Cover with more thyme and rosemary and half the leeks. Place the lobster pieces evenly over the leeks and spread the squash and then the tomatoes evenly over all. Cover with half the remaining oregano.

5. Cover and simmer over low heat just until the clams open, about 10 minutes.

6. Remove from heat. Add the steamer clams, remaining thyme, oregano, and rosemary to the pan. Add the snow peas and remaining leeks and sprinkle with salt. Top with the shrimp and scallops. Toss gently with the remaining tarragon, 1 teaspoon pepper, and the finely chopped shallots. Cover and simmer, gently shaking the pan occasionally to distribute the juices without disturbing the layering, over medium heat until the steamer clams open and the shrimp and scallops are just tender, about 10 minutes.

7. Remove from heat. Let stand covered for 5 minutes before serving.

8. Serve over hot cooked angel hair pasta in bowls or with crusty French bread and chilled white wine.

8 to 10 portions

SHRIMP ON A BED OF SALICORNIA

A foil packet, which when opened, reveals an entire meal artfully arranged on a bed of brightly colored salicornia. The fragrance of the vegetables, herbs, lemon juice, and butter fills the room.

12 large shrimp
2 cups salicornia, ends trimmed (see Note)
4 ripe plum tomatoes, thinly sliced
6 tablespoons fresh lemon juice
2 large shallots, finely chopped
1½ tablespoons chopped fresh dill
1½ teaspoons dried tarragon
Freshly ground black pepper, to taste
1 unwaxed large cucumber
2 tablespoons unsalted butter
1 lemon, quartered

1. Preheat oven to 400°F.

2. Remove half the shell from each shrimp, leaving the shells attached at the tail end. Devein the shrimp.

3. Center a piece of aluminum foil that is about 2½ times longer than a cookie sheet on the cookie sheet. Arrange the salicornia in a bed on the foil. Arrange the tomato slices in a round pattern in the center of the salicornia.

4. Combine the lemon juice, shallots, dill, tarragon, and pepper to taste in a medium-size bowl. Add the shrimp and toss to coat.

5. Using a melon baller, cut balls from the unpeeled cucumber so that the dark peel is on one side. Try to avoid the seeds.

6. Arrange the shrimp on top of the tomatoes, pouring any extra juice from the bowl over the shrimp. Place the cucumber balls on top of the shrimp. Dot evenly with the butter. Gather the ends of the foil, folding the edges together to seal the package securely.

7. Bake for 15 minutes. Serve immediately with lemon quarters.

4 appetizer portions or 2 main-course portions

Note: Salicornia is available at specialty food shops. Because it is salty, you need not use any salt in the recipe. Arugula or watercress can be substituted for the salicornia.

LOBSTER RAGOUT

Very fresh light colors and flavors are combined in this ragout—a meal in itself. Serve with a watercress salad and chilled white wine such as a Chardonnay or Graves.

6 new red potatoes, peeled and quartered
½ cup (1 stick) unsalted butter
3 large shallots, finely diced (¾ cup)
2 lobsters (1½ pounds each), cut into 8 pieces each
1 hothouse cucumber, peeled (see Note)
4 medium-size leeks, well rinsed, dried, and cut into julienne
3 large or 6 medium-size plum tomatoes, seeded and cut into small dice
3 medium-size Belgian endives, leaves separated, rinsed, and patted dry
¼ cup chopped fresh dill
3 tablespoons snipped fresh chives
Grated zest of 2 oranges
Freshly ground black pepper, to taste

1. Cook the new potatoes in boiling salted water until tender. Drain and reserve.

CALIFORNIA WINES: MENDOCINO

This redwood valley lies to the north of Sonoma County. Fetzer, Parducci, Cresta Blanca, Husch, McDowell Valley, Milano, and Navarro are among the wineries in this area. Cresta Blanca Winery produced the first California wine to win an international competition, almost a century ago at the Paris Exposition of 1889. The vineyard now produces, among other wines, America's only vintage-dated brandy and a sparkling wine made entirely from Chardonnay grapes, considered to be one of California's first Champagne-style wines. Fetzer makes some outstanding vintage Zinfandels and Cabernets along with a good generic premium red. The McDowell Valley Vineyards produces wines exclusively from its own plantings, many of which are 30 to 70 years old. The winery makes a sophisticated Grenache Rosé harvested from 30- to 60-year-old vines.

CALIFORNIA WINES: CENTRAL COAST

The area south of San Francisco is home to much of the big-production California wine making. Almadén, Paul Masson, and Wente Brothers are located here. Despite the massive scale, the wines tend to be drinkable, consistent, and inexpensive. Ridge Vineyards is an exception to the mass production and is becoming known for bottling a limited amount of a superior late-harvest Zinfandel.

CLEANING SOFT-SHELL CRABS

Your fishmonger will clean the crabs for you. If that is not possible, you can do the job yourself. Begin by rinsing the live crabs thoroughly under cold running water. To kill a crab, snip off its head about ¼ inch behind its eyes. Then turn the crab on its back and lift and pull off the triangular apron on the lower part of the shell. Flip it over and peel back the points of the top shell and scrape out the spongy gills on both sides. Rinse the crab again and pat dry.

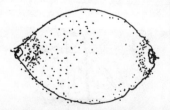

2. Melt the butter in a large heavy casserole over low heat. Increase the heat to medium-low and add the shallots and lobster pieces, leaving any coral or roe in the lobster. Sauté quickly, turning the lobster occasionally with a wooden spoon, until the shells turn red. Remove from heat.

3. Using a small melon baller, cut about 1½ cups balls from the cucumber, avoiding the seeds. Add the cucumber balls and leeks to the lobster. Cook covered 10 minutes over low heat, stirring once.

4. Add the potatoes, tomatoes, endives, dill, and 2 tablespoons of the chives. Toss to combine and cook covered another 5 minutes. Remove from heat.

5. Add the orange zest and season generously with pepper. Toss to combine.

6. Spoon onto a large platter and garnish with the remaining 1 tablespoon chives. Serve immediately with wooden serving utensils.

4 portions

Note: Hothouse cucumbers are also called English cucumbers. They are a long, thin variety, and often come wrapped in clear plastic.

SOFT-SHELL CRABS STERLING

One of the simplest and best preparations for soft-shell crabs we know. Soaking the crabs in the herb-milk mixture makes them extra plump, and sautéing them in lots of butter makes them extra crispy.

2 cups milk
1 tablespoon dried tarragon
8 soft-shell crabs, cleaned
1 cup unbleached all-purpose flour
Salt and freshly ground black pepper, to taste
½ to ¾ cup (1 to 1½ sticks) unsalted butter
Juice of 1 lemon
½ cup finely chopped fresh Italian parsley

1. Combine the milk and tarragon in a shallow bowl large enough to hold the crabs in a single layer. Add the crabs and let them soak in the milk at room temperature for 1 to 2 hours. (This makes the crabs very moist and plump.) Drain the crabs and discard the milk.

2. Season the flour with salt and pepper to taste and dredge each crab with the seasoned flour.

3. Heat ½ cup butter in a large sauté pan over medium-high heat. Add as many crabs as will fit in a single layer and sauté 4 to 5 minutes per side. Repeat with the remaining crabs, adding butter to the pan if needed.

4. Place the crabs on a large serving platter and sprinkle with lemon juice and parsley. Serve 2 per person.

4 portions

SWORDFISH STEAKS BROILED WITH OLIVADA AND ROUILLE

Swordfish can stand up to the hearty Mediterranean flavors of olives and rouille—a thick and spicy red pepper and garlic mayonnaise from Provence.

1 jar (8 ounces) olivada (Italian olive paste)*
6 swordfish steaks (about 8 ounces each), 1 inch thick
1 cup Rouille (recipe follows)
Fresh parsley sprigs (garnish)
Lemon wedges

1. Preheat broiler.
2. Spread a thin layer of the olive paste on one side of each swordfish steak. Top with a thicker layer of the rouille.
3. Place the steaks on a broiling pan and broil 6 inches from the heat until browned, 6 to 8 minutes.
4. Turn the steaks over and spread with another thin layer of the olive paste and a thicker layer of the rouille. Broil until the fish is firm and cooked through, 5 to 6 minutes.
5. Remove to a serving platter and garnish with parsley. Serve immediately with lemon wedges.

6 portions

*available in specialty food stores or see recipe, page 184

ROUILLE

4 cloves garlic, minced
1 teaspoon salt
1 teaspoon Hungarian sweet paprika
1 teaspoon cayenne pepper
½ teaspoon saffron threads
1 teaspoon fresh lemon juice
2 egg yolks
¾ cup olive oil
½ cup vegetable oil

COUNTRY CLUB SWIM MEET

Sarah's Summer Soup

Swordfish Steaks with Olivada and Rouille

Potatoes Fontecchio

Zucchini Sauté

Crusty French bread

Blueberry Pie with Cinnamon Lattice Crust

Sangría

SHORELINE GUESTS

Beach cottages attract houseguests all summer long—both those who are expected and those who show up by surprise. Smart hosts are always prepared, having planned out expandable menus, certainly in advance of the weekend, and maybe even in advance of the summer. But making guests feel comfortable is more than preparing good food. Also keep an assortment of summer straw hats within easy reach and a stack of bright towels on hand for your guests to take to the beach. Leave plenty of suntan oil and soothing lotions in the guest bathroom.

For the sports enthusiasts, be sure to reserve tennis courts and arrange challenging matches, or put together an interesting golf foursome. For the less energetic, organize a croquet or badminton tournament. Keep a tall pitcher of icy fresh lemonade in the shade.

If you're not using your beach house, consider its use a great gift to offer friends. Be sure to leave them a list of favorite restaurants, fun shops, bicycle paths, secluded beaches, beach permits, and picnic spots. Don't forget to leave the names and phone numbers of people to contact in case of any household crisis. Then put in your order for plenty of sunshine to make their stay perfect.

"How luscious lies the pea within the pod."
—Emily Dickinson

1. Mash the garlic, salt, paprika, cayenne, and saffron to a paste in a mortar with a pestle or with the back of a spoon in a mixing bowl. Let stand 5 minutes.

2. Whisk in the lemon juice and egg yolks. Add the oils, in drops at first and then in a thin stream, whisking constantly. The rouille should be the consistency of mayonnaise. Refrigerate covered until ready to use.

About 1½ cups

BAY SCALLOPS WITH ENDIVE AND THREE PEAS

Make this recipe at the height of the pea season, when they're so tender and green you barely have to cook them.

3 tablespoons unsalted butter
1 pound Belgian endives, rinsed, patted dry, and cut into
  ¼-inch slices
2 teaspoons sugar
2 cups heavy or whipping cream
Salt and freshly ground black pepper, to taste
2 pounds bay scallops
1 cup shelled fresh peas
1 cup lightly steamed snow peas
1 cup lightly steamed sugar snap peas

1. Melt the butter in a medium-size saucepan over medium heat. Add the endives and sauté for 5 minutes. Stir in the sugar and cook for another 5 minutes.

2. Pour in the cream and heat to boiling over high heat, stirring constantly. Reduce heat and simmer until the sauce is reduced by about half. Season to taste with salt and pepper.

3. Add the scallops and shelled peas to the cream mixture and cook over medium heat for about 4 minutes. Stir in the snow and sugar snap peas and cook 1 minute more. Serve immediately.

6 portions

BLACKENED REDFISH

Our version of an increasingly popular dish. Contrary to our usual accent on fresh herbs, dried herbs are essential to the blackening technique in this dish and we use lots of them. Another secret is to make sure the cast-iron skillet is very hot and the fish very cold. The ingredients in this American invention are quite straightforward; technique is everything.

2 cups (4 sticks) unsalted butter
½ cup fresh lemon juice
2 tablespoons dried thyme
2 tablespoons dried basil
1 ½ tablespoons coarsely ground black pepper
2 teaspoons red pepper flakes
Salt, to taste
6 red snapper or redfish (ocean perch) fillets (about ½ to ¾ pound each), skinned
Chopped fresh parsley (garnish)
Lemon wedges

1. Melt the butter in a medium-size saucepan. Stir in the lemon juice, thyme, basil, black pepper, red pepper, and salt to taste. Cook over low heat for 10 minutes. Remove from heat and pour into a shallow dish.

2. Dip both sides of each fillet into the butter mixture to coat thoroughly. Place the fillets on a plate, cover with plastic wrap, and refrigerate until cold, at least 1 hour. Reserve any remaining butter mixture. (The success of this technique depends on having well-chilled fish and a very hot skillet. Be prepared for smoke.)

3. Heat a large cast-iron skillet over high heat until a drop of water sizzles in the pan. Place 2 fish fillets in the skillet and cook quickly on each side to blacken, 1 to 2 minutes per side. Repeat with remaining fillets.

4. When all the fillets are cooked, add any remaining butter mixture to the pan and scrape up the browned bits stuck to the pan. Spoon over the fish fillets and garnish with parsley. Serve immediately with lemon wedges.

6 portions

CALIFORNIA WINES: SAN JOAQUIN VALLEY

The climate is hot in this valley east of San Francisco Bay. Enormous amounts of table wine are produced here by some of the giant vineyards, including Gallo, Guild Wineries, Franzia Brothers, and I.S.C. Wines of California.

This is a terrific menu for dinner around the pool on a warm summer night. We like to invite our guests early for water relays and races—a sure guarantee there'll be no leftovers!

CABANA DINNER

Cajun Chicken Morsels

Blackened Redfish

Baked Tomatoes Stuffed with Couscous

Que Sera Silk Cabbage

South-of-the-Border Breadsticks

Peanut Ice Cream

Rosé de Provence or White Zinfandel

CALIFORNIA WINES: MONTEREY COUNTY

The cool, damp, foggy climate here is just right for the growth of the "noble rot" fungus of the great French Sauternes. Monterey is a fairly new wine region and houses the Paul Masson, Chalone, Monterey, Monterey Peninsula, and Mirassou vineyards. The Riesling, Chenin Blanc, and Sauvignon Blanc (subject to noble rot) varietals are grown in Monterey County. The small Chalone vineyard produces an excellent Chardonnay and Pinot Noir.

CALIFORNIA SPARKLING WINES

Most of the best sparkling wines come from the Napa Valley. Schramsberg is probably tops, making an outstanding Crémant and Reserve, as well as a beautiful apricot-hued Blanc de Noir. California sparkling wines are made by the *méthode champenoise*, and a few French Champagne makers have recognized the area's potential and set up vineyards, including Domaine Chandon and Piper-Sonoma. These vintners use the classic French grapes, equipment, and methodology to produce delicious sparkling wines. Korbel, Almadén, and Hanns Kornell all produce lower-priced but reliable sparkling wines.

SPLASH BASS

With the bone removed this large fish is an easy preparation and spectacular presentation. Serve on a large oval platter surrounded with watercress or the best garden arugula. Accompany with chilled Italian white wine.

1 bass (8 to 8½ pounds), boned, with head and tail left on
Salt and freshly ground black pepper, to taste
2 lemons
5 large cloves garlic, finely chopped
2 tablespoons dried oregano
2 tablespoons dried rosemary
2 tablespoons small capers, drained
2 cups fresh Italian parsley leaves (2 small bunches)
2 ripe large tomatoes, cut into ¼-inch slices
2 tablespoons Basic Pesto (page 398)
3 or 4 fresh rosemary or thyme sprigs
6 tablespoons olive oil
1 cup dry white wine

1. Preheat oven to 350°F. Lightly oil a large shallow baking pan.
2. Carefully open the flaps of the bass and lay skin side down in the pan. Sprinkle generously with salt and pepper. Cut the zest from the lemons in thin strips and set aside. Squeeze the juice of both lemons over the fish.
3. Spread half the garlic, 1 tablespoon of the oregano, the dried rosemary, and half the capers evenly over the flesh. Chop the parsley and lemon zest together and sprinkle all but 2 tablespoons of the mixture over the fish. Sprinkle evenly with the remaining capers.
4. On one side of the fish, arrange the tomato slices, slightly overlapping, in a row. Spread the pesto over the tomatoes and grind more pepper on top.
5. Fold the fish back to its original shape and tie closed at 3 or 4 places with kitchen string.
6. Sprinkle with salt and pepper and then the remaining garlic, oregano, and parsley mixture. Top with the rosemary sprigs and then drizzle the oil and wine over the fish.
7. Bake, basting occasionally, until the fish flakes easily with a fork, 50 to 60 minutes.
8. Remove the fish from the pan carefully with a metal spatula. Place on a large fish platter and remove the strings. Spoon some of the pan juices on top and cut the fish into 12 to 14 pieces.
8 portions

GRILL CRAZY
SUMMER FLINGS AND FLAMES

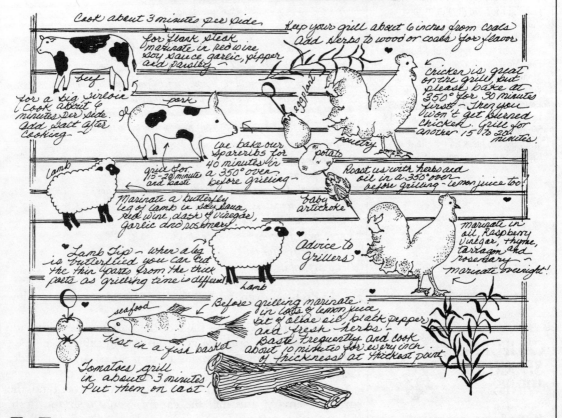

Cook about 3 minutes per side

for flank steak marinate in red wine soy sauce, garlic, pepper and parsley

beef

for a big sirloin I cook about 6 minutes per side. Add salt after cooking—

pork

Keep your grill about 6 inches from coals. Add herbs to wood or coals for flavor

eggplant

chicken is great on the grill, but please bake at 350° for 30 minutes first—Then you won't get burned chicken. Grill for another 15 to 20 minutes.

poultry

We bake our spareribs for 40 minutes in a 350° oven before grilling—

potato

Lamb

grill for 15-20 minutes and baste

Roast us with herbs and oil in a 350° oven before grilling—lemon juice too!

Marinate a butterfly leg of lamb in soy sauce, red wine, dash of vinegar, garlic and rosemary

baby artichoke

Advice to Grillers

marinate in oil, Raspberry Vinegar, thyme, tarragon and rosemary—marinate overnight!

Lamb Tip—when a leg is butterflied you can cut the thin parts from the thick parts as grilling time is different

lamb

seafood

Before grilling marinate in lots of lemon juice bit of olive oil, black pepper and fresh herbs. Baste frequently and cook about 10 minutes for every inch of thickness at thickest part

best in a fish basket

Tomatoes grill in about 3 minutes Put them on last!

Many chefs believe there is nothing new, or nouvelle, in cooking. They claim that you can't reinvent the wheel—and we have to agree as we trace the latest food craze for everything hot off the grill to the oldest method of cookery, the fire.

We've always been wild about the charred flavor of barbecued foods, and cooking outdoors over grills, spits, and pits has been as much a part of our summer activities as romantic flings and secret associations with old flames. Our metaphors tend to be as confused as the newfangled web of woods (mesquite or cherry), vines, and charcoals that tempt today's barbecue chefs. Our advice is to be adventuresome, try different methods, and remember that everything from your outdoor kitchen tastes better, so be ready for hearty appetites. Go grill crazy.

CAJUN HAMBURGERS

A spicy twist to the hamburger. Cool with sour cream.

2 pounds ground lean beef
1 green bell pepper, cored, seeded, and minced
½ cup chopped scallions (green onions)
3 cloves garlic, minced
2 teaspoons ground cumin
2 teaspoons dried oregano
1 teaspoon dried thyme
1 teaspoon paprika
Red pepper flakes, to taste
Salt, to taste
6 hamburger buns, toasted
Sliced tomatoes
Sour cream

1. Combine the beef, green pepper, scallions, and garlic in a mixing bowl. Add the cumin, oregano, thyme, paprika, and red pepper flakes and salt to taste, and mix until blended. Shape the meat into 6 patties.

2. Broil, fry, or grill the meat to desired doneness. Place the hamburgers on toasted buns and top with sliced tomatoes and sour cream.

6 portions

"What is patriotism but the love of the food one ate as a child?"
—Lin Yutang

BEST HAMBURGER STUFFED WITH BLUE CHEESE

One of our favorite combinations that oozes from the inside out with lots of melting blue cheese.

4 pounds ground lean beef
6 tablespoons snipped fresh chives
1 tablespoon chopped fresh basil
2 teaspoons dried oregano
⅔ teaspoon chili powder
½ teaspoon salt
¾ teaspoon freshly ground black pepper
1 pound blue cheese, crumbled

1. Gently mix all ingredients except the blue cheese and shape into 8 thick patties. Make a pocket in the center of each patty, fill with blue cheese, and cover the cheese with meat.

2. Broil, sauté, or grill for 5 minutes on each side for rare hamburgers.

8 portions

HAMBURGERS WITH SMOKED MOZZARELLA AND OLIVE PUREE

Not only is there a delicious surprise at the center of each burger, the rich olive spread makes for a special topping.

2 pounds ground lean beef
Salt and freshly ground black pepper, to taste
6 ounces smoked mozzarella, cut into 6 chunks
6 hamburger buns, toasted
¾ cup olivada (Italian olive spread)

1. Season the beef to taste with salt and pepper and divide into 6 parts. Form each part of the meat around a piece of mozzarella and shape into thick patties.
2. Broil, grill, or fry the hamburgers to desired doneness. Place the hamburgers on toasted buns and spread each burger with a thick layer of olivada.

6 portions

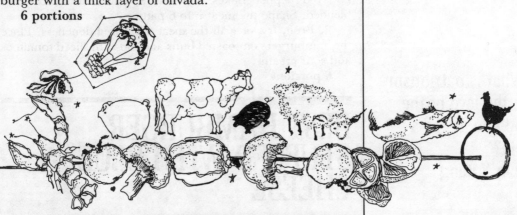

OLIVADA

If you cannot find prepared *olivada*, or olive spread, in a specialty food shop or Italian market, you can make your own. Pit 3 cups of imported black olives and process to a purée in a food processor fitted with a steel blade. Add about 2 tablespoons olive oil to bind, and process to a thick, smooth paste. Add more oil if needed. Season to taste with freshly ground black pepper.

STEAK TARTARE PATTIES

All the flavors that comprise steak tartare are combined in these delicious hamburgers.

2 pounds ground sirloin
½ cup chopped red onion
½ cup chopped fresh parsley
3 tablespoons capers, drained
⅓ cup Cognac
3 tablespoons Dijon-style mustard
2 raw egg yolks
Salt and freshly ground black pepper, to taste
12 hard-cooked egg yolks
⅓ cup mayonnaise
6 hamburger buns, toasted

SMOKE SIGNALS

There are two distinct methods of imparting a smoky flavor to food known as hot smoking and cold smoking. In the hot-smoking method the food is heated and cooked while it is bathed in smoke. In cold smoking, the food is salted in a spiced brine mixture first, then drained and smoked slowly—up to 10 hours—over hardwood chips. The salt acts as a preservative that eliminates the need for cooking. Cold-smoked foods last much longer than hot-smoked foods,

FUEL FOR THE FIRE

There are so many exotic wood chips and hardwood charcoals available these days, it seems a crime to use chemically treated briquette-type charcoal for your barbecue. We recommend trying:

MESQUITE—a dense hardwood tree that grows 30 to 40 feet high in the Southwest and Mexico. The wood is chopped and cured in sealed adobe structures to produce charcoal. It burns very hot and long and imparts a distinctive smokiness to foods. Chips are also available and must be soaked in water before being added to the fire at the moment of grilling.

HICKORY—responsible for the robust smoky flavor in the best barbecued ribs. It is available in chips, which should be soaked in water for 30 minutes before being distributed evenly over the fire. Be careful not to overdo the smokiness.

OAK—a widely available wood that burns long and slowly to produce a perfect glow for grilling.

FRUIT WOODS—wood from apple, cherry, peach, and other fruit trees imparts a pleasant sweetness and special aura to grilled foods. Flavors tend to be mild as opposed to smoky.

GRAPEVINES—the latest addition to the grilling craze, they burn very hot like mesquite and impart a light smokiness. Try combining with rosemary sprigs, thyme, dried fennel stalks, summer savory, or citrus peels to make grilled foods extra aromatic.

1. Combine the sirloin, onion, parsley, capers, Cognac, mustard, raw egg yolks, and salt and pepper to taste. Shape into 6 patties.

2. Broil, fry, or grill the hamburgers to desired doneness.

3. While the hamburgers are cooking, mash the 12 hard-cooked egg yolks and mix with the mayonnaise. Season to taste with salt and pepper.

4. Place the burgers on toasted buns and spread with a thick layer of the egg-yolk mayonnaise.

6 portions

CHEVRE-STUFFED LAMB BURGERS WITH RASPBERRY-MINT SAUCE

Try these burgers instead of hamburgers at your next outdoor barbecue. Lamb, chèvre, and mint make a delicious and unusual combination of flavors and textures. The raspberry vinegar in our mint sauce makes it special.

2 pounds ground lean lamb
Salt and freshly ground black pepper, to taste
8 ounces soft mild chèvre
Raspberry-Mint Sauce (recipe follows)

1. Season the ground lamb to taste with salt and pepper and divide the meat into 8 equal parts.

2. Shape about 1 ounce of the chèvre into a round nugget and mold one part of the lamb around the chèvre, enclosing it completely; then shape it into a thick patty. Repeat with the remaining lamb and chèvre.

3. Make the mint sauce.

4. Broil or grill the lamb burgers to desired doneness. Serve each burger with a few tablespoons of the mint sauce spooned over it.

8 portions

RASPBERRY-MINT SAUCE

1 ½ cups fresh mint leaves
⅓ cup white wine vinegar
2 tablespoons raspberry vinegar
1 tablespoon fresh lemon juice
3 to 4 tablespoons superfine sugar
Salt and freshly ground black pepper, to taste

Tear the mint leaves into coarse pieces and place in a shallow bowl. Add the vinegars and lemon juice. Stir in 3 to 4 tablespoons sugar, depending on how sweet you want the sauce, and season to taste with salt and pepper. Store covered in the refrigerator.

GRILLED SHORT RIBS OF BEEF

½ cup olive oil
½ cup red wine vinegar
5 large cloves garlic, crushed
½ cup chopped fresh Italian parsley
½ cup chopped fresh basil leaves, or 2 tablespoons dried
2 tablespoons dried oregano
2 teaspoons coarsely ground black pepper
1 teaspoon salt
4 pounds beef short ribs (about 8 pieces), 2½ to 3 inches wide and
    1½ inches thick

1. Combine the oil, vinegar, garlic, parsley, basil, oregano, pepper, and salt and pour over the ribs in a deep casserole. Refrigerate covered 6 hours, turning the ribs frequently.

2. Preheat oven to 350°F.

3. Bake the ribs in the marinade uncovered for 1 hour. Let stand until cool enough to handle.

4. Prepare hot coals for grilling.

5. Thread 2 rib pieces on each of 4 thin metal skewers, and grill 4 inches above the hot coals for 45 minutes, basting with the marinade and turning the ribs frequently. The meat should be quite tender. If necessary, grill a bit longer.

6. Serve immediately with a cold rice and vegetable salad and summer greens.

4 portions

GRILLED LAMB AND GREEN TOMATOES

In your summer garden you will always find some small green tomatoes; so pluck a couple of handfuls to grill with lamb and mushrooms.

½ cup raspberry vinegar
⅓ cup olive oil
¼ cup molasses
½ cup chopped fresh mint
½ teaspoon coarsely ground black pepper
¼ teaspoon salt
16 large mushroom caps, wiped clean
16 small green tomatoes
4 pounds leg of lamb, cut into 1½-inch cubes

1. Mix the vinegar, oil, molasses, mint, pepper, and salt in a large glass bowl. Add the mushrooms, tomatoes, and

WENDE'S BLOODY MARY

3 to 4 ounces vodka
½ teaspoon prepared horseradish
½ teaspoon Worcestershire sauce
1 large slice lemon
Dash Tabasco sauce
Dash celery salt
Freshly ground black pepper,
   to taste
8 ounces V-8 or tomato juice

Fill a large glass with ice. Add the vodka, horseradish, Worcestershire sauce, lemon, Tabasco, celery salt, pepper to taste, and the tomato juice in order and stir to mix.

1 drink

lamb and toss to combine. Cover and refrigerate, stirring occasionally, 3 to 4 hours.

2. Prepare hot coals for grilling.

3. Thread the mushrooms, tomatoes, and meat alternately on 8 long thin metal skewers. Reserve the marinade. Place the skewers on a grill 4 inches above the hot coals. Grill about 12 minutes, turning and basting with the marinade frequently. Serve immediately.

8 portions

FAMILY REUNION

Caesar Salad

Grilled Short Ribs of Beef

Baby Eggplant, Tomatoes, and Basil

Corn on the Cob with Jalapeño Butter

Peach Ice Cream

Barolo

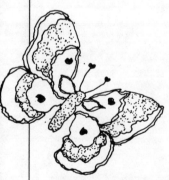

A great big family reunion with grandparents, cousins, aunts, and uncles is often a summertime event. With all those willing hands, it's a good idea to get everyone involved. Grill master and ice cream assistant are popular assignments, and don't forget about table setters, candle lighters, and salad tossers, too.

BUTTERFLIED LEG OF LAMB

1 cup dry red wine
¾ cup soy sauce
4 large cloves garlic, crushed
½ cup chopped fresh mint
2 tablespoons slightly bruised fresh rosemary or 1 tablespoon dried
1 tablespoon coarsely ground black pepper
1 butterflied leg of lamb (about 4 to 5 pounds)

1. Combine the wine, soy sauce, garlic, mint, rosemary, and pepper and pour over the lamb in a noncorrodible shallow baking pan. Refrigerate covered 6 hours, turning the lamb frequently.

2. Prepare hot coals for grilling.

3. Drain the meat but reserve the marinade. Grill the lamb 4 inches above the hot coals about 20 minutes on each side, basting frequently with the marinade. Check the lamb for doneness frequently after 30 minutes' grilling. Cut into very thin slices and serve immediately, accompanied by corn on the cob, sliced summer tomatoes, and a green salad.

8 portions

GRILLED CHICKEN WITH LEMON AND OLIVES

Crisp lemon-flavored chicken accented with garlic and black and green olives. Serve with grilled vegetables and bulgur. Present on a ceramic platter at an outdoor, noontime meal.

2 chickens (2½ to 3 pounds each), quartered
2 lemons, thinly sliced
12 cloves garlic, minced
1 cup olive oil
½ cup Cognac
Salt and freshly ground black pepper, to taste
1 cup Niçoise olives
½ cup Spanish or green olives

1. One day before serving, place the chicken pieces in a shallow dish. Combine the lemons, garlic, oil, Cognac, and salt and pepper to taste. Pour over the chicken and marinate overnight in the refrigerator, turning the pieces occasionally.

2. Prepare hot coals with some mesquite for grilling the chicken.

3. Remove the chicken from the marinade and grill several inches above the hot coals until the juices run clear when the thickest part of a thigh is pierced. When the chicken is almost done, heat the marinade with the olives over low heat until hot.

4. Transfer the chicken to a serving platter and spoon the olive mixture generously over the pieces. Serve immediately.

6 portions

CURRIED CHICKEN ON THE GRILL

This unexpected barbecue marinade, with peanuts and the slightly tart flavor of orange marmalade, forms a nutty coating on the chicken.

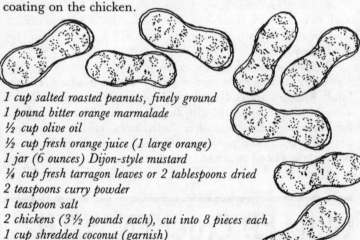

1 cup salted roasted peanuts, finely ground
1 pound bitter orange marmalade
½ cup olive oil
½ cup fresh orange juice (1 large orange)
1 jar (6 ounces) Dijon-style mustard
¼ cup fresh tarragon leaves or 2 tablespoons dried
2 teaspoons curry powder
1 teaspoon salt
2 chickens (3 ½ pounds each), cut into 8 pieces each
1 cup shredded coconut (garnish)
1 cup dried currants (garnish)

1. Combine the peanuts, marmalade, oil, orange juice, mustard, tarragon, curry powder, and salt in a bowl. Coat the chicken pieces thoroughly with this marinade. Place in a shallow roasting pan and refrigerate, turning the pieces occasionally, 4 to 6 hours.

2. Preheat oven to 350°F and prepare hot coals for grilling the chicken.

3. Bake the chicken with the marinade for 35 minutes. Remove the chicken from the marinade and grill 4 inches above the hot coals 8 to 10 minutes on each side, basting frequently with the marinade.

4. Remove the chicken to a large serving platter and sprinkle with the coconut and currants.

8 portions

MORE SUMMER CRAVINGS

. . . Tennis matches before the courts get crowded . . . jogging around the reservoir at dawn . . . the first cup of coffee on the beach . . . barbecued spareribs . . . taking a nap after an afternoon on the beach . . . parties lit entirely by candles . . . watermelon . . . Park Avenue at six in the morning on Sunday . . . crickets, lightning bugs, and fireflies . . . reading trashy novels at the beach . . . cucumbers . . . billowing spinnakers . . . an auction . . . holding cold bottles of beer to our faces . . . fresh mozzarella, basil, and tomatoes . . . vanilla ice cream for breakfast . . . discovering a berry patch . . . sliding down the dunes . . . Jeeps . . .

GRILLING TIPS

The key to the best and most tender flavor in grilling is a powerful, even source of heat. You should not start cooking until the coals have been burning long enough to be covered with gray ash. Be sure to allow at least 35 to 45 minutes after lighting for the ash coating to develop.

Make sure your grill is absolutely clean and free of residue from previous barbecues.

A marinade with olive oil will ensure that the meat or fish won't stick to the grill. If you're not marinating, it is wise to brush oil lightly over the meat or fish before placing it on the grill.

We like to precook many foods before grilling. It ensures that they will not dry out during a lengthy time over the coals but will still have the wonderful aroma and flavor that only outdoor grilling gives. This is especially true of chicken, spareribs, and whole roasts. We always allow at least 30 minutes of the total cooking time for basting and cooking over the coals.

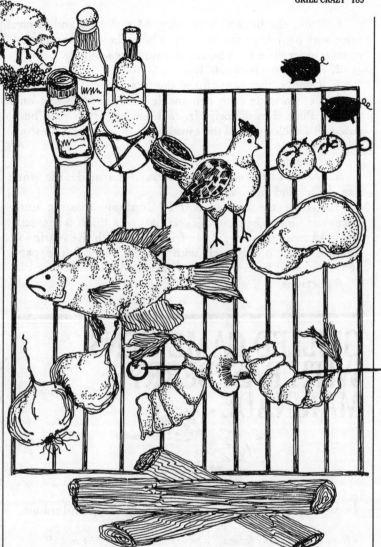

POUSSINS

Poussins are plump and meaty little chickens that have recently become very popular with savvy American restaurant chefs. These baby chickens are fed a special diet that contains no fish meal or chemical growth stimulants. Instead, they are fed a natural blend of corn, barley, and soy and allowed to roam freely (free range), as opposed to being cooped up in pens. They are killed at three weeks of age and hand-dressed in the old-fashioned farmhouse way. They are a delectable substitute in all recipes calling for Cornish game hens.

GAME HENS A LA PROVENCE

A marinade of oil and lemon juice combined with fresh basil gives the most aromatic flavor to these little birds. Finish your sauce with deep balsamic vinegar, lots of garlic, and *herbes de Provence*. Wonderful served hot or pack it for a picnic.

6 Rock Cornish hens (¾ to 1 pound each)
¾ cup olive oil
3 tablespoons fresh lemon juice
Salt and freshly ground black pepper, to taste
12 sprigs fresh basil
6 tablespoons Dijon-style mustard
3 tablespoons balsamic vinegar
6 cloves garlic, minced
1 tablespoon herbes de Provence

1. Rinse the hens and pat dry. Mix the oil and lemon juice and pour over the hens in a large bowl. Marinate at room temperature for 3 hours, turning occasionally.

2. Preheat oven to 450°F.

3. Remove the hens from the marinade; reserve the marinade. Sprinkle each hen inside and out with salt and pepper. Place 2 basil sprigs in each cavity. Truss each hen, rub with 1 tablespoon of the mustard, and place in a roasting pan.

4. Roast for 15 minutes.

5. Meanwhile, combine the reserved marinade, the vinegar, garlic, and *herbes de Provence*.

6. Reduce the heat to 350°F. Continue roasting until juices run clear when the thickest part of a thigh is pierced, about 45 more minutes. Baste frequently with the marinade mixture. Serve immediately with Yellow Pepper Purée (page 165) and sliced fresh tomatoes drizzled with a little olive oil.

6 portions

GRILLED GAME HENS WITH RASPBERRY MARINADE

These are a perfect size for someone to pick up and nibble.

6 Rock Cornish hens (about ¾ to 1 pound each), split in half
3 cups fresh or frozen raspberries, thawed if frozen
1 cup raspberry vinegar
¾ cup olive oil
2 bay leaves
1 tablespoon dried thyme
Salt and freshly ground black papper, to taste

1. One day before serving, rinse the birds and pat dry. Place the birds flat in a shallow dish.

2. Combine the raspberries and vinegar in a saucepan. Heat to boiling and boil for 1 minute. Remove from heat. Stir in the oil, bay leaves, and thyme. Cool to room temperature.

3. Pour the marinade over the birds and sprinkle with salt and pepper. Marinate overnight in the refrigerator, turning occasionally.

4. Prepare hot coals for grilling.

5. Remove the birds from the marinade and grill a few inches above the hot coals, basting occasionally with the marinade, until juices run clear when the thickest part of a thigh is pierced. Serve immediately.

6 portions

BLACK PEPPER

We crave freshly ground black pepper and always have a peppermill handy to twist over:

- ♥ Salad greens
- ♥ Fresh chèvres
- ♥ Sandwich butters, mustards, and mayonnaise
- ♥ Bloody Marys
- ♥ Strawberries, melons, and peaches
- ♥ Sliced garden tomatoes
- ♥ Raw oysters on the half shell
- ♥ Thinly sliced smoked fish
- ♥ Sardines
- ♥ Cold leftovers
- ♥ Chowders
- ♥ Cottage cheese and cream cheese
- ♥ Lamb chops and steaks just before they come off the grill

"Red skies in morning
Sailors take warning
Red skies at night
Sailors delight."

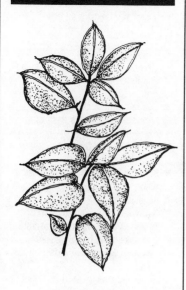

GRILLED JUMBO SHRIMP WITH PROSCIUTTO AND BASIL

This looks as beautiful as it tastes. Large shrimp marinated in white wine, olive oil, and basil are then wrapped in paper-thin slices of prosciutto and whole basil leaves before grilling.

1 cup dry white wine
1 cup olive oil
¼ cup fresh lemon juice
2 tablespoons Dijon-style mustard
½ cup chopped fresh basil
Freshly cracked black peppercorns
24 jumbo shrimp, peeled and deveined, tails left on
24 whole large basil leaves
24 thin slices prosciutto, fat trimmed

1. Combine the wine, oil, lemon juice, mustard, chopped basil, and peppercorns and pour over the shrimp in a shallow bowl. Marinate in the refrigerator at least 3 hours, turning the shrimp occasionally.

2. Prepare hot coals with a generous amount of mesquite for grilling the shrimp.

3. Remove the shrimp from the marinade; reserve the marinade. Wrap the middle of each shrimp first with a basil leaf and then with a slice of prosciutto. Thread 4 shrimp lengthwise starting at the head on each of 6 metal skewers.

4. Grill the shrimp, basting with the reserved marinade, for several minutes on each side. Serve immediately.

6 main-course or 24 appetizer portions

HERBED BLUEFISH FLAMED WITH GIN

This dish will delight the bluefish devotee. Fresh dill, sage, and rosemary tame the fish's strong flavor, and the flambéed gin makes it a show stopper!

2 tablespoons vegetable oil
1 whole bluefish (3 to 4 pounds), scaled and cleaned
Salt and freshly ground black pepper, to taste
½ cup gin
1 large or 2 small bunches fresh dill
4 sprigs fresh sage
4 sprigs fresh rosemary

1. Preheat oven to 375°F or prepare hot coals for grilling the fish.

2. Brush a large piece of heavy-duty aluminum foil lightly with the oil. Place the fish on top of the foil and sprinkle inside and out with salt and pepper. Wrap the fish in the foil and seal securely.

3. Place the fish on a baking sheet and bake for 15 minutes. Turn the fish and bake for 15 minutes more. Or grill the foil-wrapped fish about 4 to 5 minutes per side.

4. Heat the gin over low heat. Unwrap the fish and place the fish with its juices on a flame-proof platter. Arrange the herbs over the fish, pour on the gin, and flame it with a match.

5. Serve the fish with the flamed herbs immediately.

6 portions

SWORDFISH MARINATED WITH LIME AND CORIANDER

Tender swordfish steaks grilled over hot coals and flavored with fresh lime juice and coriander. For a low-calorie version, simply omit the butter and add more lime juice to taste.

3 pounds swordfish steaks
Juice of 3 limes
½ cup olive oil
¾ cup chopped fresh coriander
4 tablespoons (½ stick) unsalted butter, room temperature
Lime wedges

1. Place the swordfish steaks in a shallow bowl and sprinkle with the lime juice, oil, and ½ cup of the coriander. Marinate in the refrigerator for several hours, turning the fish occasionally.

2. Prepare hot coals with a generous amount of mesquite for grilling the fish.

3. Remove the fish from the marinade; reserve the marinade. Grill the fish, turning the steaks once and basting with the reserved marinade occasionally, just until the fish flakes easily with a fork.

4. Remove to a warmed serving platter. Spread the butter over the steaks and sprinkle with the remaining ¼ cup coriander. Serve immediately with lime wedges.

6 portions

LIME IS SUBLIME

♥ In daiquiris, gimlets, margaritas, gin and tonics, and bloody marys
♥ Combined with coconut milk and rum
♥ Rubbed around the edge of a Mexican beer with a dash of coarse salt
♥ Mixed with ale for British lager 'n' lime
♥ Sliced, stuck in the center with whole cloves, and floating in sangría.
♥ Squeezed over honeydew wedges wrapped with peppery prosciutto
♥ Squeezed over freshly sliced avocados along with a dash of hot sauce
♥ Squeezed over fresh fish filets both before and after grilling
♥ Mixed with olive oil and diced tomatoes as a marinade for steamed mussels
♥ Tossed with seeded cucumber balls and fresh coriander (cilantro)
♥ Drizzled over slices of papaya, mango, and pineapple
♥ Added to Mexican gazpacho, guacamole, and salsa
♥ Mixed with melted butter as a dip for lobster meat
♥ Substituted for lemon in a favorite lemonade recipe
♥ Made into marmalade
♥ Sprinkled on a cold compress for a hot summer day cool-off

THE VEGETABLE GRILL

For a stunning presentation in summer or winter, these vegetables glisten with both flavor and color. Don't worry about the weights—buy the number of vegetables called for and try to find them roughly all the same size. Be sure to pick the most beautiful colors and shapes. Rinse and pat each of the vegetables dry before starting.

2 cups fruity olive oil
1 cup dry white wine
8 medium-size garlic cloves, crushed
1 cup coarsely chopped fresh basil leaves
¼ cup fresh rosemary leaves or 2 tablespoons dried
1 teaspoon salt
1 teaspoon freshly ground black pepper
8 small new red potatoes
8 baby artichokes, stems trimmed
8 large shallots, peeled
8 small Italian eggplants
8 ripe plum or small tomatoes
8 pale green Italian frying peppers
4 small heads radicchio, cut in half
About 12 long sprigs fresh rosemary (3 bunches)

1. Combine the oil, wine, garlic, basil, rosemary, salt, and pepper in a bowl. Let stand covered for 1 hour.

2. Spread the potatoes, artichokes, shallots, and eggplants in a shallow roasting pan; combine the tomatoes, peppers, and radicchio in a large bowl. Pour 2 cups of the marinade over the vegetables in the roasting pan; pour the remainder over the vegetables in the bowl. Let stand covered for 4 hours, turning the vegetables occasionally.

3. Preheat oven to 400°F.

4. Uncover the roasting pan and bake the potatoes, artichokes, shallots, and eggplants, basting frequently, for 35 minutes.

5. Preheat broiler or prepare hot coals for grilling.

6. Remove the vegetables in the roasting pan and the bowl from the marinade. Combine; reserve the marinade.

7. Thread the vegetables through their centers on thin 16- to 18-inch skewers, placing each type of vegetable on its own skewer. Not all the vegetables will fit on a single skewer, so have extra skewers ready.

8. Twist 1 sprig of rosemary between the vegetables along the length of each skewer.

9. Broil or grill the vegetables about 6 inches from the heat, basting frequently with the marinade, until the peppers are blistering and the tomato skins pop, about 6 minutes on each side.

10. Arrange the skewers on a large serving platter and garnish with the remaining rosemary. Serve with a creamy chèvre, crusty bread, and a robust wine.

8 portions

SUMMER MEMORIES

*Creamy Chicken and
Jalapeño Nachos*

———

*Swordfish Marinated with
Lime and Coriander*

Stir-Fry of Three Cabbages

Potatoes Fontecchio

*Avocado with Raspberry
Vinaigrette*

———

Strawberry Hazelnut Torte

———

White Zinfandel

ICE CREAM SOCIALS

"The only emperor is ice cream."
Wallace Stevens

I n summertime, we all scream for ice cream. Make it a party, an old-fashioned event in a flowering garden or on a perfectly manicured lawn. Dress in white tie and frilly summer dresses, sport bonnets and parasols. Offer homemade waffle cones and every sundae topping imaginable. Frozen cream bombes, molds, cakes, and scoops will inspire nostalgia. Play big band music to inspire afternoon dancing. Sit back in a fancy wicker chair and enjoy your own side of paradise.

BIRTHDAY SURPRISES

Little surprises make it less painful and ever so much more delightful. The best of times is now.

♥ A bouquet of balloons filled with helium
♥ A salutation placed in the newspaper personal column
♥ Sky-written greetings
♥ Birthday banners for a home or office welcome
♥ Fewer candles for the cake than there are years
♥ A disc jockey dedication "Happy Birthday" song
♥ Rent space on a news sign or a billboard
♥ A trip—away from all the attention

"O, my luve's like a red, red rose,
That's newly sprung in June;
O, my luve's like the melodie
That's sweetly play'd in tune."
—Robert Burns

FRESH STRAWBERRY SORBET

3 cups hulled ripe strawberries
⅔ cup sugar
¼ cup fresh lemon juice
⅓ cup heavy or whipping cream
2 tablespoons framboise liqueur

1. Place the strawberries, sugar, and lemon juice in a food processor fitted with a steel blade and process until smooth. Pour in the cream and liqueur and process until blended.

2. Freeze in an ice cream maker, following manufacturer's instructions.

1 quart

LIME DAIQUIRI SORBET

2½ cups fresh lime juice (10 to 12 large limes)
Grated zest of 3 limes
1⅓ cups sugar
1 cup rum
½ cup water

Process all ingredients in a blender or food processor fitted with a steel blade. Freeze in an ice cream maker, following manufacturer's instructions.

1 quart

RASPBERRY BEAUJOLAIS SORBET

3 cups fresh raspberries
1 cup Beaujolais
2 tablespoons fresh lemon juice
½ cup sugar
¼ cup heavy or whipping cream

1. Place all the ingredients in a food processor fitted with a steel blade or a blender and process until smooth.

2. Freeze in an ice cream maker, following manufacturer's instructions.

About 1 quart

RICH APRICOT SORBET

2 cups dried apricots
2½ cups cold water
½ cup sugar
¼ cup amaretto liqueur
¼ cup heavy or whipping cream
2 tablespoons finely grated lemon zest

1. Place the apricots in a small saucepan and add water to cover by 1½ inches. Simmer uncovered over medium heat until the apricots are quite soft, about 45 minutes.

2. Drain the apricots and process in a food processor fitted with a steel blade until smooth. With the machine running, gradually pour in 2½ cups cold water. Add the sugar, liqueur, cream, and lemon zest and process until quite smooth.

3. Freeze in an ice cream maker, following manufacturer's instructions.

About 1½ quarts

CAPPUCCINO ICE CREAM

The essence of frothy cups of cappuccino in a refreshingly chilly form.

6 egg yolks
½ cup granulated sugar
3 tablespoons brown sugar
3 cups heavy or whipping cream
2 tablespoons instant coffee powder
1 cup very rich brewed espresso
3 tablespoons crème de cacao
2 teaspoons vanilla extract
1 teaspoon ground cinnamon

1. Beat the egg yolks, granulated sugar, and brown sugar in a medium-size bowl just until blended.

2. Heat the cream in a medium-size saucepan until almost boiling. Pour the cream in a thin stream into the egg yolk mixture, whisking constantly. Return the mixture to the saucepan and cook over medium-low heat to make a light custard, about 5 to 7 minutes. Do not allow to boil. Remove from heat.

3. Dissolve the instant coffee in the espresso. Stir in the crème de cacao, vanilla, and cinnamon and whisk into the custard. Refrigerate covered until cold.

4. Freeze in an ice cream maker, following manufacturer's instructions.

About 1 quart

FAVORITE ICE CREAM TOPPINGS

SWEET LIQUEURS—Cassis, Chambord, Grand Marnier, amaretto, fruit brandies

TOASTED NUTS—almonds, pecans, peanuts, cashews, hazelnuts, macadamias

THICK OLD-FASHIONED SAUCES— fudge and caramel

WHIPPED CREAM—with a little sugar and vanilla or almond extract

FRESH FRUIT—sliced bananas, kiwis, nectarines, peaches; strawberries, blueberries, raspberries, pineapple chunks

BERRY PURÉES—strawberry, raspberry, blackberry

CHOCOLATE—shaved bittersweet, cocoa powder, chocolate malt, white chocolate pieces, crumbled fudge brownies

CRYSTALLIZED FLOWERS—violets, roses, lilacs

STRAWBERRY PURÉE

A simple and delicious strawberry purée may easily be made by placing hulled strawberries in a food processor fitted with a steel blade and processing until smooth. Sweeten with a few tablespoons of confectioners' sugar to taste and a dash of lemon juice. Lavish over ice cream or other fresh berries.

PEACHES

Next to the apple, the peach is the most widely cultivated fruit tree in the world. When Madame Récamier, a great French beauty of the nineteenth century, was ill and refused all food, a dish of peaches in syrup and cream restored both her appetite and her will to live.

RICH VANILLA ICE CREAM

The name says it all—nothing more than heavy cream, egg yolks, sugar, and lots of pure vanilla. A little goes a long way.

3 cups heavy or whipping cream
2 vanilla beans
½ cup sugar
6 egg yolks

1. The night before you plan to make the ice cream, pour the cream into a small metal bowl and drop in one of the vanilla beans. Refrigerate covered overnight.

2. The next day, process the sugar and the remaining vanilla bean at high speed in a blender until the vanilla bean is finely pulverized. Whisk the sugar and egg yolks together in a medium-size bowl just to combine.

3. Heat the cream with the vanilla bean in a medium-size saucepan over medium heat until almost boiling. Discard the whole vanilla bean and pour the cream in a thin stream into the egg yolk mixture, whisking constantly. Return the mixture to the saucepan and cook over medium-low heat to make a light custard, 5 to 7 minutes. Do not allow to boil. Remove from heat and refrigerate covered until cold.

4. Freeze in an ice cream maker, following manufacturer's instructions.

About 1 ½ pints

PEACH ICE CREAM

1 ½ cups heavy or whipping cream
½ cup sugar
8 ripe medium-size peaches
3 tablespoons amaretto liqueur

1. Heat the cream and sugar in a medium-size saucepan over low heat just until the sugar dissolves. Let cool completely.

2. Drop the peaches, several at a time, into a large pan of boiling water and blanch for 2 minutes. Remove with a slotted spoon and let cool. Slip off the skins, cut the peaches in half, and remove the pits.

3. Process 6 of the peaches in a food processor fitted with a steel blade or a blender until smooth. Add the liqueur and process to combine. Mix the peach purée and cream mixture. Cut the remaining 2 peaches into ¼-inch dice and stir into the cream mixture.

4. Freeze in an ice cream maker, following manufacturer's instructions.

1 quart

SIESTAS, SUNSETS, AND STARGAZING

The summer sky hypnotizes us. The vibrant sun induces instant beach naps and city siestas. Sunsets recall the bright colors of the day in one last memorable explosion of snapdragon pink, zinnia orange, and buttery corncob yellow. A silvery night sky soothes and cools all with opalescent moon slivers and shooting stars. These are summer's most special moments, to be savored in secret, private places—cupolas, rooftops, and widow's walks; gazebos, greenhouses, and Jacuzzis; rowboats, beach blankets, and old-fashioned convertibles.

Good times don't always mean boisterous parties. They can be as simple as sharing a rich dessert while sipping Champagne and stargazing with someone very special.

MEZZALUNA

The mezzaluna is one of the most romantic cook's tools we know. It is an Italian chopping device shaped like a half-moon *(mezza luna)*. A knob is attached at each end, providing leverage to rock the blade back and forth. We think it is also one of the most practical culinary tools and know many who prefer it to a chef's knife.

Mezzaluna is also the name of one of our favorite New York restaurants. Florentine artists have covered every square inch of wall with half-moons—from the kitchen and the sky.

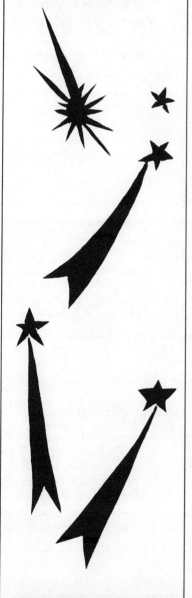

MEZZALUNA NUT COOKIES

Three of our favorite nuts are combined in these delicious half-moon cookies. For crispness, keep stored in a airtight container. Of course, they may not last that long! We love them.

⅓ cup skinned toasted hazelnuts
⅓ cup pecans
⅓ cup blanched almonds
2 cups unbleached all-purpose flour
Pinch salt
1 cup (2 sticks) unsalted butter, room temperature
1 cup confectioners' sugar
1 tablespoon vanilla extract
1 teaspoon almond extract
Granulated sugar for coating

1. Process the nuts, flour, and salt in a food processor fitted with a steel blade until the nuts are finely ground. Set aside.

2. Cream the butter and confectioners' sugar in a mixer bowl. Beat in the vanilla and almond extracts. Stir in the nut mixture thoroughly.

3. Wrap the dough in plastic wrap and refrigerate at least 1 hour.

4. Preheat oven to 350°F. Line cookie sheets with parchment paper.

5. Break off 1-inch pieces of the dough and shape by hand into 1½-inch crescents. Place on the prepared cookie sheets.

6. Bake the cookies until very lightly browned, about 15 minutes. Let the cookies cool a few minutes and then toss in a shallow bowl of granulated sugar to coat evenly. Store the cookies in an airtight container.

4 dozen cookies

CHOCOLATE AMARETTO MOUSSE

We love our Silver Palate chocolate mousse recipe so much that it's hard to think of changing the basic combination. This variation uses amaretto, almonds, and crème fraîche, but use your imagination for new flavors and textures.

1 ½ pounds semisweet chocolate chips
½ cup brewed espresso
½ cup amaretto liqueur
4 egg yolks
1 cup heavy or whipping cream, cold
¼ cup sugar
8 egg whites, room temperature
Pinch salt
1 cup lightly toasted sliced almonds
1 cup Crème Fraîche (page 399) to garnish

1. Melt the chocolate chips in a heavy medium-size saucepan over very low heat, stirring constantly. Stir in the espresso and then the liqueur. Let cool to room temperature.

2. Add the egg yolks, one at a time, beating thoroughly after each addition.

3. Whip the cream in a mixer bowl until thickened; gradually beat in the sugar and continue beating until stiff. Beat the egg whites with the salt in another mixer bowl until stiff. Gently fold the egg whites into the cream.

4. Stir about a third of the cream mixture thoroughly into the chocolate mixture; then scrape the remaining cream mixture over the lightened chocolate base and fold together gently. Fold in the almonds. Pour into 8 individual dessert cups or a serving bowl. Refrigerate covered until set, about 2 hours.

5. At serving time, pipe the crème fraîche decoratively over each mousse or pass the crème fraîche separately.

8 portions

CHOCOLATE MOUSSE VARIATIONS:

♥ Chocolate Hazelnut Mousse: Substitute ½ cup Frangelico for the amaretto liqueur and 1 cup chopped toasted hazelnuts for the almonds.

♥ Chocolate Macadamia Rum Mousse: Substitute ½ cup amber rum for the amaretto liqueur and 1 cup chopped toasted macadamia nuts for the almonds.

♥ Chocolate Raspberry Mousse: Substitute ½ cup framboise liqueur for the amaretto liqueur and lavish fresh raspberries over the crème fraîche at serving time.

♥ Chocolate Pecan Kahlúa Mousse: Substitute ½ cup Kahlúa for the amaretto liqueur and 1 cup chopped pecan pieces for the almonds.

✤ FLOWERS FROM THE SILVER PALATE

Fill old white and blue china bowls with garden roses in every shade of pink. Scatter some petals around the table.

Gather masses of pink, white, and fuschia cosmos from your garden and arrange loosely in a blue and white spatterware pitcher.

Tiny bunches of sweet William tied with pale green ribbons make beautiful bouquets for your guests to place in their pocket or pin in their hair.

THE SCAVENGER HUNT

Cream of Tomato Soup with Mint

Splash Bass

Potatoes Fontecchio

Yellow Pepper Purée

Blueberry Pie with Cinnamon Lattice Crust

Meursault or Chardonnay

BLUEBERRY PIE WITH CINNAMON LATTICE CRUST

A luscious pie brimming with cassis-soaked blueberries and topped with a pretty and spicy cinnamon lattice crust. A great pie to celebrate a hot day of blueberry picking.

PASTRY:

2 ½ cups unbleached all-purpose flour
5 tablespoons sugar
1 teaspoon ground cinnamon
½ teaspoon salt
6 tablespoons (¾ stick) unsalted butter, cold, cut into small pieces
6 tablespoons (¾ stick) unsalted margarine, cold, cut into small pieces
1 tablespoon fresh lemon juice
4 to 5 tablespoons ice water

FILLING:

2 quarts fresh blueberries
1 cup crème de cassis
Grated zest of 1 lemon
½ cup sugar
½ cup water
2 tablespoons fresh lemon juice
2 tablespoons cornstarch

"To know your ruling passion, examine your castles in the air."
—Archbishop Whately

MORE SUMMER CRAVINGS

. . . Circus clowns . . . sitting in a bar watching the sea . . . having the moon follow us down the beach . . . tennis at night . . . cantaloupe . . . inner tube races at the pool . . . our own rock in the sea . . . outdoor theater . . . dancing alot . . . grilled barbecue chicken . . . going blue-fishing . . . sailing around Manhattan at sunset . . . a summer fling . . . Cap d'Antibes in July . . . the Eden Roc . . . backpacking . . . learning to fly . . . cold fruit soups . . . a black-tie supper on the beach . . . drinking a glass of Champagne before bed . . . our own carousel . . . blueberry pie . . . blackberries . . . Coho salmon . . .

1. To make the pastry, process the flour, sugar, cinnamon, and salt in a food processor fitted with a steel blade just to combine. Add the butter and margarine and process until the mixture resembles coarse meal. With the machine running, add the lemon juice and ice water and process just until the dough gathers into a ball. Wrap in plastic wrap and refrigerate several hours or overnight.

2. To make the filling, combine the blueberries, crème de cassis, and grated lemon zest in a bowl. Cover and let stand several hours or overnight.

3. Drain the liquid from the blueberries into a small saucepan. Stir in the sugar, water, lemon juice, and cornstarch. Cook over medium heat, stirring constantly, until thickened and glossy. Pour over the blueberries and stir to combine.

4. Preheat oven to 350°F.

5. Roll out half the dough ⅛ inch thick on a lightly floured surface. Line a 9-inch pie plate with the dough. Trim and crimp the edges. Pour the blueberry filling into the pie shell. Roll out the remaining dough ⅛ inch thick and cut into ¼-inch-wide strips. Arrange the strips over the pie in a lattice pattern. Tuck the ends into the bottom shell.

6. Bake the pie until the crust is golden brown, about 45 minutes. Serve the pie warm or at room temperature with a dollop of rich vanilla ice cream.

8 portions

CHOCOLATE RASPBERRY TORTE

Two favorite and precious foods—fine bittersweet chocolate and raspberries—are paired in this dense flourless cake. The slow baking at a low temperature imparts an incredible chocolate density. The raspberry crème anglaise gives just the right contrast to make this a truly elegant dessert.

> "It may be that the stars of heaven appear fair and pure simply because they are so far away from us, and we know nothing of their private life."
> —Heinrich Heine

MIDSUMMER NIGHT'S DREAM

Pale Almond Gazpacho

Grilled Game Hens with Fresh Raspberry Marinade

Lemon Rice

Asparagus with Orange Pistachio Butter

Chocolate-Raspberry Torte

Tavel

CAKE:

1 pound best-quality bittersweet chocolate
14 tablespoons (1 ¾ sticks) unsalted butter
1 ½ cups sugar
10 eggs, separated, room temperature
¼ cup framboise liqueur
2 teaspoons vanilla extract

CREME ANGLAISE:

4 egg yolks, room temperature
½ cup sugar
2 cups milk, scalded
1 cup fresh raspberries, puréed and sieved

Fresh raspberries (garnish)

1. To make the cake, break the chocolate into small pieces and melt with the butter in a double boiler over simmering water. Stir in 1 cup of the sugar and heat until the sugar dissolves, about 3 minutes.

2. Beat the egg yolks in a large mixer bowl until blended. Beat in 1 cup of the warm chocolate mixture and then return to the chocolate mixture in the double boiler. Cook, stirring constantly, until slightly thickened, 3 to 4 minutes. Remove from heat and stir in the framboise and vanilla.

3. Preheat oven to 275°F. Butter a 9½-inch springform pan and lightly coat with sugar.

4. Beat the egg whites in a large mixer bowl just until beginning to stiffen. Gradually beat in the remaining ½ cup sugar, 1 tablespoon at a time, and continue beating until the peaks are stiff and glossy. Gently fold the egg whites into the chocolate mixture.

5. Pour the batter into the prepared pan. Bake until firm, about 3 hours. Let cool completely; then refrigerate until cold.

6. To make the crème anglaise, beat the egg yolks and sugar in a mixer bowl until thick and light. Gradually beat in the milk. Pour into a heavy saucepan and cook, stirring constantly, over low heat until the custard coats the back of the spoon. (This can take as long as 15 minutes.) Do not let it boil.

7. Remove the pan from the heat and place in a bowl of ice water to cool to room temperature. Stir in the raspberry purée. Refrigerate covered until ready to serve.

8. Cut the chocolate cake into thin wedges and serve on dessert plates. Spoon some of the crème anglaise around the cake and garnish with a few fresh raspberries.

12 to 14 portions

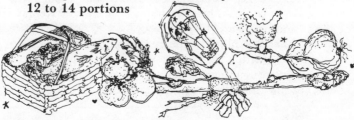

SOME BITTERSWEET NEWS

Bittersweet chocolate is often confused with unsweetened and semisweet chocolate. It is a slightly sweetened dark chocolate that contains less sugar than semisweet, and it is used primarily for baking. It produces luscious mousses, shiny chocolate curls for garnish, and an incredibly rich and dense chocolate cake.

If a recipe calls for bittersweet, then that is the chocolate to use. Never substitute unless the recipe tells you how to make the necessary adjustments.

RASPBERRY TARTS WITH PINE NUT CREAM FILLING

We think these are the most luscious raspberry tarts we've ever tasted. The pine nut filling has a mysterious affinity for the raspberries. Serve these for dessert at the end of a very special summer dinner.

PASTRY:

2 cups unbleached all-purpose flour
⅓ cup sugar
10 tablespoons (1 ¼ sticks) unsalted butter, cold, cut into small pieces
1 tablespoon water
1 tablespoon fresh lemon juice

FILLING:

¾ cup pine nuts (pignoli)
½ cup (1 stick) unsalted butter, room temperature
½ cup sugar
3 eggs
¼ cup unbleached all-purpose flour
2 tablespoons kirsch

TOPPING:

¾ cup apricot jam
¼ cup water
3 cups fresh raspberries

1. To make the pastry, process the flour, sugar, and butter in a food processor fitted with a steel blade until the mixture resembles coarse meal. Add the water and lemon juice. Using repeated pulses, process just until the dough starts to gather into a ball. Wrap in plastic wrap and refrigerate 1 hour.

2. Roll out the dough ⅛ inch thick on a lightly floured surface. Line eight 4½-inch tart pans with the dough. Trim and crimp the edges. Freeze for 15 minutes.

3. Preheat oven to 375°F.

4. Line the tart shells with parchment paper and weight with dried beans or pie weights. Bake on a baking sheet just until the edges begin to brown, about 15 minutes. Remove the beans and paper and let cool.

5. To make the filling, process the pine nuts in a food processor fitted with a steel blade until very finely chopped. Add the butter, sugar, eggs, flour, and kirsch and process 1 minute. Spoon the filling into the tart shells almost to the tops.

SUMMER FRUIT DESSERTS

♥ Lemon halves hollowed out and filled with lemon sorbet
♥ Raspberries and blueberries drizzled with cassis
♥ Poached whole apricots drizzled with amaretto and served with macaroons
♥ Raspberries sprinkled with balsamic vinegar and sugar to taste
♥ Sliced peaches with heavy cream
♥ Whole strawberries topped with melted white and dark chocolates
♥ A watermelon half hollowed out and filled with cantaloupe, honeydew, and watermelon balls
♥ Half a cantaloupe filled with fresh raspberries and served with lime wedges
♥ Cold Bing cherry soup with a dash of Grand Marnier, topped with Crème Fraîche
♥ Sliced nectarines and blueberries served over vanilla ice cream
♥ Wild strawberries with Devonshire cream
♥ Plum halves drizzled with cassis and brown sugar and then broiled
♥ Kiwi and raspberries with sprigs of fresh mint

6. Bake until the filling is puffed and brown and the shells are golden, 15 to 20 minutes.

7. Let cool to room temperature and then remove the tarts from the pans.

8. To make the topping, heat the apricot jam and water in a small saucepan until melted and smooth.

9. Dip each raspberry into the glaze to coat it, and arrange the raspberries over the tarts to cover completely. Serve within several hours.

Eight 4½-inch tarts

HEAVENLY ANGEL FOOD CAKE

This angel food cake makes a refreshing light dessert. For a change add any of the variations listed below.

1¼ cups sugar
1 cup cake flour
½ teaspoon salt
12 egg whites, room temperature
1 teaspoon cream of tartar
1 teaspoon vanilla extract

1. Preheat oven to 350°F.

2. Sift ¼ cup of the sugar, the flour, and salt together 3 times.

3. Beat the egg whites in a large mixer bowl until foamy. Sprinkle with the cream of tartar and beat until stiff but not dry. Beat in the vanilla. Then beat in the remaining 1 cup sugar, 1 tablespoon at a time. Beat until the peaks are stiff and glossy.

4. If you wish, add any of the variations to the sifted flour mixture. Gently fold the flour mixture into the egg white mixture.

5. Pour the batter in an ungreased 10-inch tube pan. Bake until the cake springs back when lightly touched, about 50 minutes. Invert the pan over the neck of a wine bottle. Let cool for several hours.

6. Run a knife around the side of the pan to loosen the cake and invert the cake onto a platter. Serve with Bittersweet Chocolate Sauce (page 99), if desired.

10 to 12 portions

VARIATIONS:

In step 4 add any of the following combinations to the sifted flour mixture:

♥ 1 cup finely chopped hard pink peppermint candies and 1 teaspoon ground cloves

♥ ½ cup finely chopped crystallized ginger

♥ 1 cup grated bittersweet chocolate

''When one has tasted watermelons one knows what angels eat.''
—Mark Twain

''The Queen of
  Hearts,
She made some tarts,
All on a summers day.
The Knave of Hearts,
He stole those tarts,
And gave them quite
  away!''
—Lewis Carroll

AUTUMN HUES

Autumn invigorates. A nip in the air, a crunch underfoot induce a flurry of activity. Nature and its inhabitants are caught up in the whirlwind of preparation. Trees send down many-hued showers of leaves, birds migrate south, and squirrel holes are stocked with hearty supplies of acorns. Gone are the lazy days of summer—children are bustled off to school, summer cottages are battened shut, gardens and grape-vines are harvested, and gardeners hurriedly plant their spring bulbs. The world is aglow while waiting for the arrival of Jack Frost. The awareness of nature's final curtain makes us live life to its fullest. We work hard, play hard, and find ourselves wishing that autumn could be three Septembers long.

Life in the city is as hectic as life in the country, and autumn is the finest time to be in a grand city such as New York or Paris. The city pulses with life and enjoys a cultural reawakening as museums, opera houses, theaters, and entertainments of every kind open for a new season. In Paris, in particular, the restaurant scene is infused with new excitement as many reopen with much fanfare after the long August vacations. Everybody wants a night out on the town. Yet don't despair if you're not on your way to New York or Paris. We've provided a show-stopping selection of soufflé recipes to make everybody feel they're following the social calendar.

The relentless pace of autumn concludes with a moment's peace and a time to give thanks for the abundance of good fortune that America has provided. While we like our lives to be filled with the unconventional, Thanksgiving is one time when we love to be tradi-tional.

OPENING NIGHT OPENERS

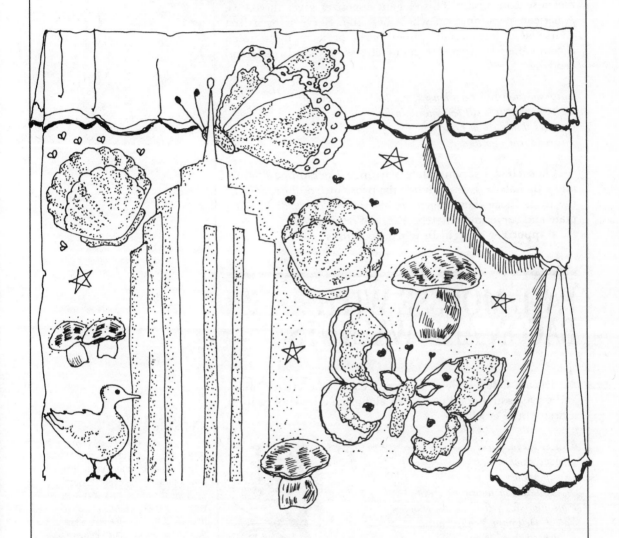

The electricity of opening night is contagious. Stars, directors, and investors scurry about backstage while the audience whispers out front in anticipation. Whether it be Broadway, local repertory, or a school play, butterflies abound.

Hosts and hostesses share similar opening night jitters when producing a party. Hors d'oeuvres open the night and set the stage for whatever follows. Having a spectacular collection is the first step in setting even the most flustered entertainers at ease.

PERSIMMONS AND FIGS DRAPED WITH PROSCIUTTO

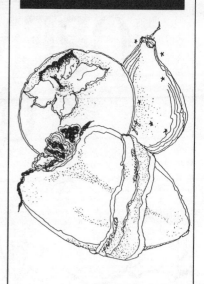

A wonderful fall combination that comes to the rescue when melon season is past. This elegant appetizer gives the native American persimmon a whole new life. Serve it as a first course at a formal fall dinner party or as a light lunch accompanied by rich Roquefort cheese, crusty bread, and red wine.

4 ripe medium-size persimmons, cut lengthwise in half
8 ripe purple figs, cut lengthwise in half
4 ounces thinly sliced prosciutto
4 lemons, cut into wedges

On each of 4 serving plates, arrange 2 persimmon halves and 4 fig halves. Evenly divide the prosciutto and drape over the fruit. Place the wedges of 1 lemon on one side of each plate and serve immediately. Pass the peppermill.

4 appetizer or light luncheon portions

PATE MOUSSE WITH BACON AND WALNUTS

A delicate chicken liver mousse. Toast some crusty bread and serve as an hors d'oeuvre or alongside a bowl of soup in a pretty little crock.

8 slices bacon, diced
1 pound chicken livers
½ cup brandy
¾ cup heavy or whipping cream
1 medium-size yellow onion, chopped
¼ cup Hellmann's mayonnaise
1 teaspoon dried thyme
Large pinch ground nutmeg
Salt and freshly ground black pepper, to taste
½ cup coarsely chopped walnuts
3 tablespoons chopped fresh Italian parsley
Crumbled crisp bacon and chopped fresh Italian parsley, or whole
  walnut meats and chopped parsley (garnish)

1. One day before serving, fry the diced bacon in a medium-size skillet until crisp. Remove from the pan with a slotted spoon and drain on paper towels.
2. Sauté the livers in the hot bacon fat over medium-high

PERSIMMONS

Persimmons are a lovely coral autumn fruit that can be found in the market from November through January. They yield a sensuous sweet pulp when fully ripe. Choose persimmons that are still underripe and allow them to soften on your kitchen window sill. They should be soft but not mushy, and if you eat one before it's ripe, be prepared to pucker because it will be chalky and sour. We like to bake them in puddings, combine them fresh with other fruit, and purée them for sorbets or as a sauce for French toast and waffles.

FIRST IMPRESSIONS

First impressions always count the most. With all of the work that goes into entertaining, it seems a shame that those first moments set the tone of the rest of the party, but it is so. That's why it is so important that it is the host who graciously welcomes guests at the door and gets the introductions flowing.

All of the senses need to be satisfied at once. Guests will be happy when they see flowers in the hallway; smell wonderful food, cozy cinnamon, or fresh aromas; hear the musical tones flowing through the air; feel the vibes that have been established for the party; and taste the liquid refreshment that is graciously and instantly offered.

Sometimes, to get the ball rolling, we ask our guests to make themselves a drink from a bar which has been set up, welcome them into the kitchen to help or watch the final cooking, or ask them to open the wine or change the record. Just make sure in this relaxed environment that you don't ask someone else to answer the doorbell. That's your job!

"The best of times is now
What's left of summer
But a faded rose?
The best of times is now."
—©Jerry Herman

heat until brown on the outside but still pink inside, 4 or 5 minutes. Remove from the pan and reserve.

3. Pour the brandy into the skillet over medium heat and stir, scraping loose browned bits on the bottom of the pan. Add the cream and heat to boiling. Reduce heat and simmer until reduced to about 1 cup.

4. Process the livers, onion, and reduced cream in a food processor fitted with a steel blade until smooth.

5. Add the mayonnaise, thyme, nutmeg, salt to taste, and lots of pepper. Process until smooth. Add the diced bacon, walnuts, and 3 tablespoons parsley and process just until blended.

6. Transfer the liver mixture to a crock or decorative serving dish and refrigerate covered overnight to allow the flavors to blend.

7. Garnish the pâté with crumbled bacon and parsley or walnuts and parsley. Serve with crusty bread or assorted crackers.

3 cups

PARK AVENUE PATE

A new dimension in country pâté. The recipe makes a lot, but extra pâtés can be wrapped tightly in foil and frozen. Serve with a crock of your favorite honey mustard.

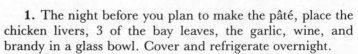

2 pounds chicken livers
12 bay leaves
6 cloves garlic, minced
1 cup dry white wine
½ cup brandy
1½ pounds bulk pork sausage
1 pound baked or boiled ham, cut into chunks
10 slices firm white bread
½ cup light cream
Grated zest of 2 oranges
1½ cups coarsely chopped pecans
Salt and freshly ground black pepper, to taste
1 pound sliced bacon

1. The night before you plan to make the pâté, place the chicken livers, 3 of the bay leaves, the garlic, wine, and brandy in a glass bowl. Cover and refrigerate overnight.

2. The next day, process the chicken livers with the liquid and bay leaves to a purée in a food processor fitted with a steel blade. Remove to a large mixing bowl.

3. Sauté the sausage in a large skillet over medium-high heat, crumbling it with a fork, just until it is no longer pink. Spoon off the excess fat and process the sausage in the food processor just until coarsely ground. Add to the liver mixture. Process the ham in the food processor until coarsely ground and add to the liver mixture. Stir until thoroughly combined.

4. Process the bread and light cream together in the food processor. Add to the meat mixture and mix well. Stir in the orange zest and pecans. Season to taste with salt and freshly ground pepper.

5. Preheat oven to 350°F.

6. Place 3 bay leaves in a row down the center of each of three 9 x 4-inch loaf pans. Arrange the bacon slices crosswise in each pan to line it completely. Pack the pâté mixture evenly into the 3 pans. Fold the ends of the bacon slices over the top. Cover each loaf pan completely with aluminum foil.

7. Place the 3 pans in a large baking pan. Pour hot water into the large pan to come halfway up the sides of the loaf pans. Bake for 1½ hours. Remove the pans from the water bath and let cool for 30 minutes.

8. Weight the pâtés overnight in the refrigerator by placing heavy cans or weights on small boards or pans that fit directly on the pâtés. Unmold the pâtés from the pans, wrap, and refrigerate until ready to serve.

Three 9 x 4-inch pâtés

MADEIRA PATE

A smooth, spreadable pâté, perfect with water biscuits or a crusty French bread. For a splendid winter supper, serve with Wintergreen Soup (page 360), bread, and a rich Burgundy.

½ cup (1 stick) unsalted butter
½ cup coarsely chopped shallots
2 cloves garlic, finely chopped
1 teaspoon dried tarragon
1 teaspoon dried rosemary, crumbled
½ teaspoon dried thyme
¼ teaspoon ground savory
½ cup chopped leafy celery tops
12 black peppercorns
2 bay leaves
6 cups water
1 pound chicken livers, well rinsed
¼ teaspoon ground allspice
½ teaspoon salt
½ teaspoon freshly ground black pepper
¼ cup Madeira

1. Melt the butter in a skillet over medium heat. Add the shallots, garlic, tarragon, rosemary, thyme, and savory and cook covered for 20 minutes.

2. Combine the celery tops, peppercorns, bay leaves, and water in a medium-size saucepan. Heat to boiling. Reduce heat and simmer uncovered for 10 minutes.

3. Add the chicken livers to the saucepan and simmer gently for 10 minutes. Do not overcook. Remove the livers to

Fall cheese and fruit platters are easy and great fun to put together. Use brightly colored birch, maple, and ash leaves to hold the cheese—big rounds of Canadian and Vermont Cheddars are favorites. This is one time when guests can cut away—be sure to pick up the crumbles from time to time so the platter always looks fresh and clean. Accompany the cheese with a wide assortment of unusual grapes—black, red, Concord—all in perfect clusters.

THE GUEST LIST

Creating an ambience of charm, warmth, and ease is the key to entertaining. What we love best are little dinners at home with friends. We ask only people we like—there are no ulterior motives or debts to pay. And positively no bores allowed.

A mix of ages, personality types, professions—new friends and old pals—is often the most successful. At the end of the evening, when you see them planning to get together again, you know your party's been a hit!

a mixing bowl with a slotted spoon and discard remaining contents of saucepan.

4. Add the herb mixture, allspice, salt, pepper, and Madeira to the livers and mix well. Process the liver mixture in small batches in a food processor fitted with a steel blade until smooth.

5. Remove the mixture to a decorative 2-cup crock. Refrigerate covered at least 6 hours. Let the pâté warm at room temperature 30 minutes before serving.

2 cups, at least 8 portions

SAUSAGE-STUFFED FRENCH LOAVES

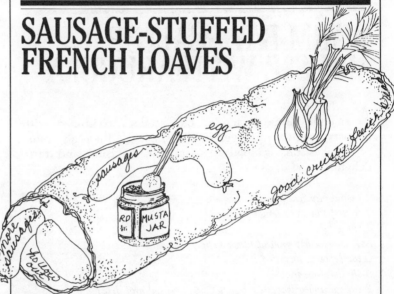

INDIAN SUMMER

We like to think of Indian summer as an intermezzo in the year—like a sorbet between seasons. Officially there should be a frost first, followed by warm days, but instead it vacillates—one moment cool and crisp, and the next as warm as a midsummer day, but always with an autumn mood. Perfect weather for enjoying outdoor cafés, tailgate picnics, antique hunting, fishing expeditions, hunting trips, long walks, and long, long games. The colors are rich and warm—forest greens, burnt oranges, deep reds, tobacco goldens, russets and browns. It is usually the first snowfall that draws the final curtain and forces us indoors.

A hearty sandwich that doubles as an hors d'oeuvre when thinly sliced. Great hot or cold. Perfect picnic fare, too.

2 fat, long loaves French bread
8 ounces bulk pork sausage
8 ounces ground beef chuck
1 medium-size yellow onion, diced
1 egg
1 teaspoon Dijon-style mustard
¼ cup chopped fresh Italian parsley
¼ teaspoon fennel seeds
Salt and freshly ground black pepper, to taste
2 tablespoons unsalted butter
2 cloves garlic, crushed

1. Preheat oven to 400°F.

2. Cut off the ends of the loaves and hollow out the loaves with your fingers. Process the soft bread in a food processor fitted with a steel blade to coarse crumbs. Reserve the bread ends.

3. Brown the sausage in a heavy skillet over medium heat. Add the beef and onion and cook until the beef is lightly browned.

4. Combine the bread crumbs, meat mixture, egg, mustard, parsley, fennel, and salt and pepper to taste in a large bowl. Spoon the mixture into the bread shells; attach the bread ends with small skewers.

5. Melt the butter over medium heat and stir in the garlic. Sauté for 30 seconds, then brush the loaves with the garlic butter and wrap in separate pieces of aluminum foil, leaving the foil open slightly at the top.

6. Bake until heated through, 15 to 20 minutes.

7. Cut into 1-inch slices for hors d'oeuvres or cut each loaf into 4 pieces for main-course servings.

8 main-course portions or 36 appetizer portions

WARM BAY SCALLOP MOUSSE WITH ARUGULA

A smooth purée of tender bay scallops combined with peppery arugula and layered with smoked salmon and mussels makes this seafood mousse both a visual and taste delight.

1 pound bay scallops
1 tablespoon fresh lemon juice
1 egg white
Salt and freshly ground black pepper, to taste
2 tablespoons unsalted butter
5 shallots, minced
2 cups arugula leaves (1 bunch), well rinsed and dried
1 teaspoon dried tarragon
½ teaspoon dried savory
Pinch ground nutmeg
1 cup heavy or whipping cream
⅔ cup Crème Fraîche (page 399)
4 ounces smoked salmon, thinly sliced
4 ounces smoked mussels
Tomato Beurre Blanc (recipe follows)

1. Place 12 of the scallops in a small bowl, sprinkle with a little of the lemon juice, and set aside. Process the remaining scallops in a food processor fitted with a steel blade, using repeated pulses, until puréed.

2. Add the egg white, the remaining lemon juice, and salt and pepper to taste. Process just until combined. Remove the mixture to a bowl and set in a larger bowl filled with ice. Chill the mixture, stirring occasionally, over the ice for 1 hour.

3. Melt the butter in a small saucepan over medium heat. Add the shallots and sauté about 5 minutes.

4. Reserve 3 whole arugula leaves to line the terrine and finely chop the remaining. Add the arugula, tarragon, savory, and nutmeg to the shallots. Season to taste with salt and pepper and cook 3 minutes. Set aside to cool.

5. When the scallop mixture has chilled for 1 hour, whisk in the heavy cream, 1 tablespoon at a time. Add the

IT'S YOUR PARTY

The most important person at your party is *you*. It isn't the guest of honor, your boss (whom you've never before invited home), the new board member at the museum, or your cousin who threw the best party of all time last week. It's not your mother's new husband, last week's love nor next week's—it's you.

It's your turn to be the star, producer, director, investor, stage manager, and critic. You set the tone from the moment your first guest arrives—no matter what's been burned, what didn't get delivered, or who canceled at the last moment. Here are the priorities as we see them:

• There's no need to be nervous. A nervous hostess will surely kill a party.

• Wear your favorite—and comfortable—clothes. Disappear an hour before your party, so you can dress and have one relaxed drink before everyone arrives.

• If there's a disaster in the kitchen, remember: you do not have to be a great chef to be a great host. Whatever happens, try to fix it without anyone noticing. If it is obvious, remember to laugh . . . these are your friends.

• Be at the door to greet each guest warmly—as though he or she were the most important person there and as though the party were being given just for them. Escort them into the room.

• Introduce each guest to at least someone, if not everyone. First and last names, please, and if you can give them a clue to their mutual compatability to start the conversation rolling, you're terrific.

• One of our favorite hostesses' laughter can be heard across the room. It is contagious, you know.

• Keep introducing people, stay alert, and inject titillating stories into conversations around the room, all the while maintaining a gracious calm, cozy, warm, and happy attitude.

crème fraîche in the same manner.

6. Process a third of the scallop mixture and all the arugula mixture in the food processor, using repeated pulses, until thoroughly combined.

7. Preheat oven to 375°F. Butter a 9 x 3-inch terrine or loaf pan.

8. Place the 3 arugula leaves decoratively across the bottom of the terrine. Pour half the scallop mixture over the leaves. Top with a layer of half the smoked salmon and place all the whole scallops and smoked mussels on top of the salmon. Cover with all of the arugula-scallop mixture. Top with another layer of the smoked salmon and then cover with the remaining scallop mixture.

9. Cover the terrine tightly with a piece of buttered aluminum foil and place in a baking pan filled with hot water to come halfway up the sides of the terrine. Bake for 1 hour.

10. Make the beurre blanc.

11. Remove the terrine from the water bath and let cool for about 10 minutes.* Invert onto a serving plate and cut into thick slices. Place a slice on each serving plate and spoon some sauce over each serving.

8 to 10 appetizer portions

*The mousse can also be cooled completely and reheated later by simmering individual slices in dry white wine in a shallow saucepan until the slices are slightly puffed and warmed through, about 10 minutes.

TOMATO BEURRE BLANC

1 cup fish stock, preferably homemade
1 cup dry white wine
1 ripe medium-size tomato, seeded and finely chopped
2 tablespoons finely chopped fresh basil
¾ cup plus 2 tablespoons (1¾ sticks) unsalted butter, cut into small pieces
Salt and freshly ground black pepper, to taste
2 teaspoons fresh lemon juice
1 tablespoon snipped fresh chives

1. Heat the stock, wine, tomato, and basil to boiling in a small saucepan over medium-high heat. Reduce heat to medium-low and cook, stirring occasionally, until the mixture is reduced to 1 cup.

2. Reduce heat to low and whisk in the butter, 1 piece at a time. Season to taste with salt and pepper and stir in the lemon juice. Just before serving, stir in the chives. Serve hot.

About 2 cups

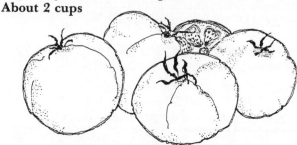

SAUERKRAUT, APPLE, AND STRING CHEESE SALAD

A perfect accompaniment to sausages or a charcuterie board.

2 egg yolks
2 tablespoons fresh lemon juice
2 tablespoons grainy mustard, such as Pommery
¾ cup best-quality olive oil
¾ cup vegetable oil
Salt and freshly ground black pepper, to taste
1 pound sauerkraut, rinsed and drained
1 large Granny Smith apple, peeled and coarsely grated
1 small red onion, finely chopped
8 ounces Armenian string cheese, pulled apart into strings
4 cornichons, coarsely chopped
1 tablespoon caraway seeds
Cornichons, sliced lengthwise (garnish)

1. Process the egg yolks, lemon juice, and mustard in a food processor fitted with a steel blade for 30 seconds. With the machine running, pour in the olive oil, then the vegetable oil in a thin steady stream through the feed tube to make a thick mayonnaise. Season to taste with salt and pepper.

2. Combine the sauerkraut, apple, onion, cheese, chopped cornichons, and caraway seeds in a large bowl. Toss thoroughly with enough of the mayonnaise to bind.

3. Transfer the salad to a serving crock and refrigerate until cold. Garnish the top with fanned cornichon slices and serve as an accompaniment to assorted charcuterie.

6 portions

apples and cabbage are yummy together

APPLE AND ONION TART

1 package active dry yeast
1 tablespoon plus 1 teaspoon sugar
1 cup warm water (105° to 115°F)
½ cup rye flour
2 tablespoons olive oil
1 teaspoon salt
2 cups unbleached all-purpose flour
12 tablespoons (1½ sticks) unsalted butter
2 tablespoons best-quality olive oil
3 cooking apples, peeled, cored, and cut into 1-inch pieces
1 head garlic, cloves peeled
2 Golden Delicious apples, peeled, cored, and thinly sliced
1 very large red onion, cut lengthwise in half and then crosswise into
    very thin slices
1 tablespoon ground coriander

"To offer wine is the most charming gesture of hospitality, and a host brings out for his guests the finest he has. Whether there are four wines or one, the gesture is the same."
—Alexis Lichine

✚ FLOWERS FROM THE SILVER PALATE

Gather large bunches of flowering herbs—oregano with its purple blossoms and basil with its white blossoms surrounded with silvery sage—and arrange the herbs in earthenware crocks.

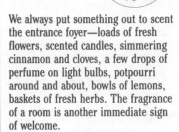

SCENTS

We always put something out to scent the entrance foyer—loads of fresh flowers, scented candles, simmering cinnamon and cloves, a few drops of perfume on light bulbs, potpourri around and about, bowls of lemons, baskets of fresh herbs. The fragrance of a room is another immediate sign of welcome.

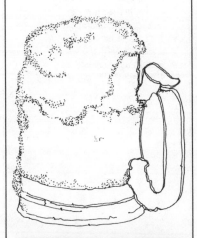

1. Combine the yeast and 1 teaspoon sugar in a large bowl. Stir in the water and let stand 5 minutes.

2. Whisk in the rye flour, cover the bowl, and let stand in a warm place for 20 to 30 minutes.

3. Stir in the 2 tablespoons olive oil, the salt, and all-purpose flour. Turn out onto a floured surface and knead until smooth and elastic, 7 to 10 minutes.

4. Place the dough in an oiled medium-size bowl and turn to coat the dough with oil. Cover and let rise in a warm place until doubled in bulk, about 1 hour.

5. While the dough is rising, make the apple-garlic purée. Heat 6 tablespoons of the butter and the best-quality olive oil in a medium-size saucepan. Add the cooking apples and the garlic. Simmer uncovered over low heat, stirring occasionally, until both the apples and garlic are very soft and falling apart, about 1 hour.

6. Let cool slightly; then purée in a food processor fitted with a steel blade.

7. Preheat oven to 375°F.

8. Punch the dough down and roll into a 15 x 9-inch rectangle on a lightly floured surface. Place on a baking sheet of the same size and crimp the edges decoratively with your fingers.

9. Spread the apple-garlic purée evenly over the dough.

10. Arrange the sliced apples and onions in alternating lengthwise rows over the purée.

11. Sprinkle the top with the 1 tablespoon sugar and the coriander. Dot the remaining 6 tablespoons butter evenly over the top.

12. Bake the tart until the crust is light brown and the apples are soft, about 45 minutes. Then broil the tart 6 inches from the heat to glaze the top, 4 to 5 minutes.

13. Serve the tart, cut into squares, warm or at room temperature.

12 portions

SCOTCH EGGS

Dream of an English pub while eating these hearty treats. They're fun to take along on a picnic or have with a cold glass of beer. Try both variations—the second is a surprise of Chinese tastes.

2 raw eggs
1 tablespoon Dijon-style mustard
2 cups fresh bread crumbs
8 hard-cooked eggs, peeled
1 pound bulk country-style sausage
Vegetable oil for frying

1. Beat the raw eggs and mustard together in a shallow bowl.

2. Place the bread crumbs in another shallow bowl.

3. Encase each hard-cooked egg completely in a thin layer of sausage, using both hands to mold the sausage around the egg.

4. Dip one sausage-encased egg first in the egg mixture and then coat with the bread crumbs. Set aside on a plate and repeat with the remaining eggs. Refrigerate covered at least 3 hours or overnight.

5. Heat 3 inches oil in a deep-fat fryer to 375°F. Fry 2 or 3 eggs at a time, turning occasionally, until quite well browned, 10 to 15 minutes. (You want to make sure the sausage meat is thoroughly cooked.) Remove them from the oil with a slotted spoon and drain on paper towels.

6. Serve the eggs, cut into quarters, at room temperature. Pass additional mustard if desired.

8 portions

SCOTCH EGGS CHINESE-STYLE

8 hard-cooked eggs, unpeeled but shells cracked all over
3 tablespoons soy sauce
2 whole star anise
2 bags Chinese black tea
2 raw eggs
1 tablespoon sesame mustard
2 cups fresh bread crumbs
2 tablespoons sesame seeds
1 pound bulk country-style sausage
2 teaspoons chopped fresh ginger root
2 teaspoons chopped garlic
Vegetable oil for frying

1. One day before serving, place the hard-cooked eggs, soy sauce, star anise, tea bags, and water to cover in a medium-size saucepan. Simmer the eggs uncovered for 25 minutes and then let stand overnight.

2. Beat the raw eggs and mustard together in a shallow bowl.

3. Combine the bread crumbs and sesame seeds in another shallow bowl.

4. Mix the sausage, ginger, and garlic.

5. Peel the hard-cooked eggs and proceed as directed in the recipe for Scotch Eggs.

8 portions

FALL SCAVENGER HUNT

At early fall gatherings, a scavenger hunt is great fun. Have everyone meet at your house to get the spirit rolling, then divide the group into teams, set the time limit, and give them their lists—a mixture of the possible and the impossible. Don't play the martyr: have dinner all prepared and put yourself on a team too. Just make sure you're the first one home to greet the returning scavengers with a warming supper.

Our scavenger hunt list:
♥ A bus token
♥ A letter sweater
♥ Graffiti
♥ Halved theater tickets
♥ A dried rose
♥ An original limerick
♥ A deflated football
♥ A restaurant menu
♥ Six whole nuts in the shell
♥ A wine label
♥ A history book
♥ A rock shaped like something identifiable
♥ Twelve leaves: three each of maple, hickory, elm, and apple
♥ A clump of moss
♥ Brass candlestick
♥ Something chocolate
♥ A copy of the *National Enquirer*

Raclette is a strong, yet delicious, cheese that is popular in Switzerland. We've often served the cheese with potatoes near an open fire, but here potatoes, cheese, and mustard are combined in little balls for a perfect hors d'oeuvre.

RACLETTE BEIGNETS

2 tablespoons unsalted butter
⅓ cup dry white wine
½ cup unbleached all-purpose flour
2 eggs
½ cup mashed cooked potato
¾ cup grated raclette cheese
1 tablespoon grainy Dijon-style mustard
Dash cayenne pepper
Salt and freshly ground black pepper, to taste
Vegetable oil for frying

1. Heat the butter and wine to boiling in a small saucepan over medium-high heat. When the mixture boils, add all the flour at once and stir until the flour is absorbed and the dough forms a ball. Continue cooking and stirring for about 1 minute to dry out the dough. Remove from heat and let stand 5 minutes.

2. Process the dough in a food processor fitted with a steel blade for about 10 seconds to break the dough into granules. Add the eggs and process until well blended and smooth.

3. Add the potato, cheese, mustard, cayenne pepper, and salt and pepper to taste. Process until thoroughly blended.

4. Heat 3 inches of vegetable oil in a deep-fat fryer to 375°F.

5. Using two teaspoons, shape and drop small bite-size balls of the batter into the hot oil. Fry 6 to 8 beignets at one time until golden brown. (The beignets will roll over by themselves when one side is browned.) Remove them from the oil with a slotted spoon and drain on paper towels. Serve warm in a basket lined with a starched napkin.

36 beignets

"Try to remember
The kind of
   September
When life was slow
And oh so mellow
Try to remember
The kind of
   September
When grass was green
And grain was
   yellow."
—©Tom Jones &
Harvey Schmidt

FULL MOON PASTRIES

A delicate cream cheese pastry stuffed with a rich garlic sausage thinly sliced. A dab of mustard inside adds the perfect touch.

Cream Cheese Pastry (recipe follows)
¼ cup Dijon-style mustard
12 ounces garlic sausage or any other hard spicy sausage, cut into
   ½-inch-thick slices
1 egg
2 teaspoons water

1. Make the pastry.
2. Preheat oven to 375°F. Lightly grease cookie sheets or line with parchment paper.

3. Keeping the remaining dough refrigerated, roll out 1 piece of the dough into a circle, about ⅛ inch thick, on a lightly floured surface. Cut into 2-inch circles and spread mustard on each circle.

4. Place a sausage slice on half the circles. Top with another circle and press the edges of the circles together. Place on the prepared cookie sheet. Repeat with the remaining dough, rerolling the scraps if desired, and remaining mustard and sausage.

5. Beat the egg and water in a small bowl and brush the egg wash over each pastry. Bake until golden brown, 15 to 20 minutes. Serve on small trays.

26 to 30 pastries

CREAM CHEESE PASTRY

6 ounces cream cheese, room temperature
1 cup (2 sticks) unsalted butter, room temperature
2 cups unbleached all-purpose flour
¼ teaspoon salt

1. Mix the cream cheese and butter with an electric mixer or wooden spoon until well blended. Add the flour and salt and mix thoroughly. Knead lightly and shape into a ball.

2. Cut the ball into quarters. Wrap in plastic wrap and refrigerate several hours or overnight.

CRESCENT PASTRIES WITH SHERRIED CRAB FILLING

Serve these on the same platter as Full Moon Pastries. The two make wonderful taste and shape contrasts.

Cream Cheese Pastry (recipe precedes)
1 tablespoon unsalted butter
2 shallots, finely chopped
1 ½ tablespoons unbleached all-purpose flour
1 cup milk, scalded
1 ½ tablespoons dry sherry
1 teaspoon tomato paste
1 teaspoon Worcestershire sauce
1 ½ teaspoons dried tarragon
1 teaspoon dry mustard
Pinch cayenne pepper
¼ teaspoon salt
⅛ teaspoon ground white pepper
8 ounces fresh or frozen crabmeat, drained and squeezed dry
2 tablespoons fresh lemon juice
2 tablespoons chopped fresh Italian parsley
1 egg
2 teaspoons water

FALL COLORS

While we usually admire the autumn foliage from the ground, or if we're lucky, from above in a small plane, other cultures have their own tricks. For instance, the Japanese tree-walk on tall stilts, getting closer to admire the leaves.

In the Middle Ages, European monks and hermits frequently retired to simple seats placed in the trees. And by the sixteenth century, the Italians, with their genius for pruning, had the most sensational idea of all: by judicious cutting of boughs and interweaving of branches, they converted the whole tree into an aboreal room.

TAPAS

Tapas is a wonderful Spanish custom that we are adopting with much gusto! Conversation and delicious food go hand in hand in Spain, so most Spaniards gather for a chat over a glass of wine and an array of small appetizers before both lunch and dinner. This sampling of appetizers is known as *tapas,* and it can range from simple to sophisticated.

While authentic Spanish tapas include dishes like garlic shrimp, spicy snails, grilled mushrooms, marinated mussels, and pork balls, we often borrow just the idea rather than the dishes, and instead serve lots of odds and ends of our own favorite nibbles in the same fashion. It's a great way to finish up the variety of foods after a guest-filled weekend and entertain the departing guests at the same time.

❖ FLOWERS FROM THE
SILVER PALATE

For a nonfloral autumn
centerpiece, mix
cranberries, whole nuts, and
polished lady apples in an
antique basket.

POTPOURRIS

We like to gather scented leaves,
herbs, and flowers throughout the
summer and late into fall to create
potpourri and fill the house with its
wonderful scent. When the leaves and
petals are dry, we put them in
individual airtight containers, label
them, and store them in a cool, dry
place until there is time to combine
them with spices and essences.
Remember to make potpourris well
ahead of Christmas, so they can ripen
for about a month before being
packaged in gift tins, jars, and
baskets.

1. Make the pastry.

2. Melt the butter in a medium-size saucepan over medium heat. Add the shallots and sauté for 2 minutes.

3. Add the flour and cook, stirring constantly, for 2 minutes. Gradually stir in the milk and boil, stirring constantly, until thickened, 5 to 7 minutes.

4. Add the sherry, tomato paste, Worcestershire sauce, tarragon, mustard, cayenne pepper, salt, and pepper. Simmer over low heat, stirring occasionally, for 5 minutes. Remove from heat and refrigerate covered several hours or overnight.

5. Toss the crabmeat with the lemon juice in a medium-size bowl. Add 1 cup of the cream sauce and fold gently to combine. Add the parsley and fold just until combined.

6. Preheat oven to 375°F. Lightly grease cookie sheets or line with parchment paper.

7. Keeping the remaining dough refrigerated, roll 1 piece of the dough into a circle, ⅛ inch thick, on a lightly floured surface. Cut into 3-inch circles.

8. Place a rounded teaspoon of the crab filling on the center of each pastry circle. Fold each circle in half and press the edges together with a fork. Place on a prepared cookie sheet. Repeat with the remaining dough, rerolling the scraps if desired, and remaining crab filling.

9. Beat the egg and water in a small bowl and brush the egg wash over each pastry. Bake until golden brown, 15 to 20 minutes.

32 to 40 pastries

BACON BITES

This is a simple, delicious hors d'oeuvre that leaves rather messy pans, but it is well worth the extra work. You'll almost never get enough of these to eat.

8 ounces sliced smoked bacon, preferably thick cut
1½ cups brown sugar
Honey mustard

1. Preheat oven to 375°F.

2. Separate the bacon slices. Place the brown sugar in a shallow bowl. Spread one side of each bacon slice with a thin layer of honey mustard. Dip both sides of each bacon slice in the brown sugar to coat thoroughly.

3. Place the bacon on a rack over a pan to catch the

drippings. (If smaller hors d'oeuvres are desired, cut the slices into halves or thirds.)

4. Bake in the upper third of the oven for 20 minutes. Finish browning the bacon under the broiler, watching closely.

5. Let cool slightly but not too long or the bacon will stick to the rack. Transfer to paper towels to drain. Serve at room temperature.

6 to 8 portions

Note: The bacon can be made in advance and refrigerated, but it must be reheated to melt the chilled fat and then cooled to room temperature before serving.

ASSORTED POTATO CHIPS

Homemade potato chips are a favorite. Ours are from two yummy potatoes—Idahos and sweet potatoes. The orange and golden brown chips look great in baskets lined with checked napkins. Sprinkle with some favorite herbs or spices.

3 sweet potatoes, peeled
3 Idaho baking potatoes, peeled
Ice water
Vegetable or peanut oil for frying
Salt

1. Cut the potatoes into ⅛-inch-thick slices. The easiest way to get wafer-thin slices is to use a mandoline with the slicing blade adjusted to the smallest possible setting. (If you do not have a mandoline, a very sharp knife and a steady hand will do.)

2. Soak the sweet potatoes and regular potatoes in separate bowls of ice water at least 3 hours or overnight in the refrigerator.

3. Preheat oven to 300°F. Heat vegetable oil in a deep-fat fryer.

4. Drain the potatoes and pat them dry. Fry the sweet and baking potatoes separately in batches in the hot oil until crisp. Drain on paper towels and sprinkle with salt.

5. To keep the chips very crisp, spread them out on a baking sheet and place in the oven while you fry the remaining chips.

6 portions

Variations: Lightly dust the sweet-potato chips with curry powder or sprinkle the regular potato chips with Italian herbs.

COUNTRY FARE

Autumn's chills bring sweater weather and robust appetites. There is no better time to savor hearty country foods and good jug wines. Crusty homemade breads and rich soups that capture the earthy flavors of the harvest are perfect accompaniments to fall foliage jaunts. These meals are complete with the added crunch of an apple or pear, a slab of farmhouse Cheddar, and a bottle of country wine. Inhale the autumn splendors with one last picnic set on a cozy blanket amidst milkweed pods and showers of maple leaves, beside crimson-hued bogs and moors, or along grassy cattail-bound ponds.

AUTUMN CELEBRATION SOUP

Rich orange rutabagas—one of our favorite turnips—blend beautifully with beef stock, carrots, and Hungarian paprika. The soup is highlighted with a dollop of sour cream and enlivened in texture by dark crispy bacon and caraway seeds.

6 tablespoons (¾ stick) unsalted butter
1 large yellow onion, chopped
2 tablespoons caraway seeds
2 cups rich Beef Stock (page 397; see Note) or canned beef broth
1 cup dry white wine
2 tablespoons Hungarian sweet paprika
2 to 2 ½ pounds rutabagas, peeled and cut into 1-inch cubes
2 Finnish yellow or all-purpose potatoes, peeled and cubed
4 carrots, peeled and sliced
8 to 10 cups water
3 cups milk
1 cup heavy or whipping cream
Salt and freshly ground black pepper, to taste
Sour cream (garnish)
Chopped crisp cooked bacon (garnish)

1. Melt the butter in a large stock pot over medium heat. Add the onion and caraway seeds and sauté until the onion is soft.

2. Stir in the stock, wine, and paprika. Add the rutabagas, potatoes, and carrots and pour in enough of the water to cover the vegetables by 1 inch. Heat to boiling. Reduce the heat and simmer until the vegetables are tender, 45 to 60 minutes.

3. Remove the soup from the heat and stir in the milk, cream, and salt and pepper to taste.

4. Purée the soup in batches in a blender or food processor fitted with a steel blade. Pour into a clean pot and gently heat until hot.

5. Ladle into soup bowls, dollop sour cream on each serving, and sprinkle with bacon.

8 portions

Note: For 2 cups rich stock, reduce 4 cups Beef Stock over high heat.

THE EARLS OF SANDWICH

♥ Slices of stuffed meat loaf on a baguette with extra stuffing and crisp Bibb lettuce
♥ Roasted red, yellow, and green peppers with garlic, olive oil, and Parmesan
♥ Smoked salmon, chèvre, lemon, dill, caraway, thyme, golden caviar, and black pepper on pumpernickel
♥ Apple slices with a nutty cheese spread on whole wheat
♥ Sliced hot giant shrimp with Rouille on a green purée (arugula and watercress) on warm homemade peasant bread
♥ Pears, Parmesan, and prosciutto with extra virgin olive oil and black pepper on crusty peasant bread
♥ Prosciutto, figs, sweet Gorgonzola, and chopped basil drizzled with olive oil and black pepper on pumpernickel
♥ Crisp thin bacon, tomatoes, arugula, and lemon mayonnaise on toast
♥ Black caviar, egg salad, and chopped dill on pumpernickel
♥ Soft-shell crabs, almonds, lemon juice, and mayonnaise on whole-wheat toast
♥ A triple crème cheese with Parma ham, persimmon (or apricot or mango), and black pepper drizzled with olive oil
♥ Parmesan-topped ratatouille on an Italian baguette; broiled until bubbly
♥ Beef filet, béarnaise, and watercress on a baguette
♥ Curried vegetable or chicken salad sprinkled with raisins and almonds and topped with a dollop of chutney in a pita
♥ Stilton, apples, and grilled sausages on a baguette

ROASTED CHESTNUT AND HAZELNUT SOUP

This very rich soup, the color of a brandy Alexander and as smooth as velvet, should be served in small cups and garnished with a dollop of crème fraîche.

1 pound raw chestnuts in shells
4 tablespoons (½ stick) unsalted butter
3 tablespoons chopped bacon
3 tablespoons chopped prosciutto
1 large yellow onion, chopped
5 ribs celery, chopped
2 carrots, peeled and chopped
1 teaspoon dried thyme
1 teaspoon dried chervil
Salt and freshly ground black pepper, to taste
1 cup dry white wine
6 cups Berta's Chicken Stock (page 396) or canned chicken broth
1 cup hazelnuts
1 cup milk
1 cup heavy or whipping cream
¼ cup brandy
Crème Fraîche to garnish (page 399)

1. Preheat oven to 350°F.

2. With a sharp knife, cut an X on the flat side of each chestnut. Bake in a roasting pan until both the outer shell and inner skin can easily be removed, 20 to 30 minutes. Let the nuts cool slightly and then shell them. Do not turn off the oven.

3. Melt the butter in a large stock pot over medium heat. Add the bacon, prosciutto, onion, celery, carrots, thyme, chervil, and salt and pepper to taste. Sauté until the vegetables begin to soften, about 10 minutes.

4. Add the wine and stock. Stir in the chestnuts. Heat to boiling. Reduce heat and simmer uncovered 45 minutes.

5. While the soup is simmering, toast the hazelnuts in the oven until they begin to turn brown, 15 to 20 minutes. Remove from the oven and rub the nuts back and forth in a kitchen towel to remove the skins. Let the nuts cool, then chop them coarsely by hand or in a food processor fitted with a steel blade and set aside.

6. When the soup has simmered for 45 minutes, remove it from heat and stir in the milk, cream, and brandy.

7. Purée the soup in batches in a blender or food processor fitted with a steel blade, adding a handful of hazelnuts to each batch. Pour into a clean pot, taste and adjust seasonings, and gently heat the soup until hot.

8. Ladle into small soup cups and garnish each serving with a dollop of crème fraîche.

6 portions

MELTING SANDWICHES

Grilled sandwiches seem to be more of a meal than regular ones. They remind us of Sunday-night suppers and watching Ed Sullivan. We also love them because they're goopy and delicious—worth the effort.

♥ Layer prosciutto and Provolone on Italian bread. Spread with Olive and Pistachio Pesto and broil until hot and bubbly.

♥ Spread crunchy celery rémoulade on rye bread; top with thin-sliced corned beef and even thinner Swiss cheese. Run under the broiler until bubbly.

♥ Combine Black Forest ham, ripe Brie, and your favorite mustard on raisin pumpernickel. Spread with butter and grill.

♥ Mix crisp-cooked broccoli, scallions, and toasted cashews with curry mayonnaise. Spread on English muffins, sprinkle with grated Parmesan, and broil until hot and bubbly.

♥ Layer turkey breast, avocado slices, and jalapeño Jack cheese on sourdough bread. Spread with butter and grill.

♥ Spread rye bread with mayonnaise, layer with sliced onion, tomato, mild green chiles, and two strips of cooked bacon. Top with Cheddar and broil, open face, until cheese is hot and bubbly.

Hazelnuts

SMOKY PUMPKIN SOUP

A deliciously unusual soup. Don't overlook the toasted seeds for garnish.

6 slices bacon, diced, cooked crisp, fat reserved
4 tablespoons (½ stick) unsalted butter
6 cups peeled cut-up pumpkin (1-inch pieces)
6 cups Beef Stock (page 397) or canned beef broth
½ cup Marsala
1 teaspoon dried thyme
Salt and freshly ground black pepper, to taste
Toasted Pumpkin Seeds to garnish (recipe follows)

1. Heat the bacon fat and butter in a stock pot over medium-high heat. Add the pumpkin and sauté for 15 minutes, stirring occasionally.

2. Pour in the stock and simmer covered until the pumpkin is very tender, about 30 minutes. Remove from heat.

3. Add the Marsala, thyme, and salt and pepper to taste. Process the soup in batches in a blender until smooth. Return to the stock pot.

4. Add the bacon. Simmer 10 minutes. Serve immediately, garnished with pumpkin seeds.

6 portions

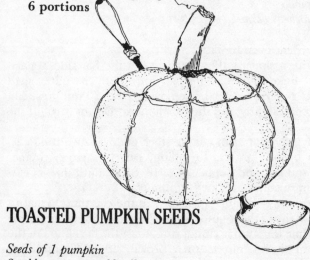

TOASTED PUMPKIN SEEDS

Seeds of 1 pumpkin
2 tablespoons vegetable oil
Salt, to taste

1. Rinse the seeds to remove strings and pulp and pat dry with paper towels. Spread the seeds on a baking sheet and let stand for several hours to dry.

2. Preheat oven to 350°F.

3. Toss the seeds with the oil and salt to taste. Toast the seeds in the oven, stirring every 5 minutes or so, until golden brown, about 25 minutes. Let cool completely. Taste and add more salt if needed.

4. Serve the pumpkin seeds as a snack or use as a garnish.

✤ FLOWERS FROM THE SILVER PALATE

An edible arrangement for autumn: purple kale and decorative pale green cabbages placed in shallow bowls of water. Add a pinch of sugar to the water to keep them fresh.

A PUMPKIN REMINDER

Everyone knows that Thanksgiving without pumpkin is like Christmas without Santa Claus, but don't limit it to your holiday table. Pumpkin is a very versatile member of the squash family, low in calories and available from early fall through early winter.

Try sautéing peeled chunks in butter with herbs or spices—we suggest a sprinkling of thyme, nutmeg, or cumin. Cook pieces in chicken stock; then purée them for Smoky Pumpkin Soup and garnish with Toasted Pumpkin Seeds (use a pumpkin shell as a tureen). Pumpkin works beautifully in tea breads, cheesecakes, waffles, pancakes, and, of course, in fluffy pie with lots of bourbon-flavored whipped cream.

SWEET-POTATO VICHYSSOISE

An unusual variation of vichyssoise. Hot or cold, this pale orange soup has an extremely comforting texture and flavor. Top the soup with our favorites—Peanut Noshes—or garnish it with a slice of fresh lime.

6 tablespoons (¾ stick) unsalted butter
4 leeks (white part only), well rinsed, dried, and sliced
6 cups Berta's Chicken Stock (page 396) or canned chicken broth
1 ½ cups dry white wine
3 large sweet potatoes, peeled and chopped
Grated zest and juice of 1 lime
1 cup milk
1 cup heavy or whipping cream
Salt and freshly ground black pepper, to taste
Peanut Noshes (page 102) or thin lime slices (garnish)

1. Melt the butter in a large stock pot over medium-high heat. Add the leeks and sauté until soft and transparent.

2. Add the stock, wine, and sweet potatoes. Heat to boiling. Reduce heat and simmer until the potatoes are tender, about 15 minutes.

3. Stir in the lime zest and juice, milk, and cream. Season to taste with salt and pepper.

4. Purée the soup in batches in a blender until very smooth.

5. If you are serving the soup hot, gently heat it and serve it with peanut noshes. If you are serving the soup cold, refrigerate it for several hours and serve it garnished with lime slices.

6 portions

TOMATO FENNEL SOUP

A great soup to make when the last of the basil has been bitten by frost and healthy bulbs of pale green fennel begin to appear in the market. Sprinkle steaming bowls of the soup with grated Fontina.

3 fennel bulbs (about 2 pounds)
1 cup (2 sticks) plus 2 tablespoons unsalted butter
1 large yellow onion, coarsely chopped
6 cloves garlic, minced
Salt and freshly ground black pepper, to taste
2 cans (35 ounces each) Italian plum tomatoes
½ cup Pernod
2 cups canned chicken broth

1. Cut the tops from the fennel bulbs and reserve the leafy tops. Coarsely chop 2 of the bulbs. Melt 1 cup butter in a large pan over low heat. Add the chopped fennel, onion, and 4 of the garlic cloves and cook until limp, about 15 minutes. Season with the salt and pepper, to taste.

2. Add the tomatoes with their liquid and simmer uncovered for 30 minutes.

3. Process the vegetable mixture in small batches in a food processor fitted with a steel blade or a blender, and then pass through a food mill. Return to the pan.

4. Finely chop the remaining fennel bulb. Melt 2 tablespoons butter in a small saucepan over medium heat. Add the fennel and sauté in the butter with the remaining 2 cloves garlic for 5 minutes.

5. Chop the leafy tops of the fennel. Add the sautéed fennel, leafy tops, Pernod, and chicken broth to the purée. Simmer until heated through, about 5 minutes. Serve immediately.

8 portions

SIPPETS

A sippet is a small piece of bread meant for dipping in liquid—a small sop. We love the term and think that a basket of sippets adds a bit of old-fashioned flair to Sunday night soup suppers. We like to make ours of triangles of pita bread. We spread them with a coating of butter, dot with aromatic herbs or freshly grated Parmesan, and toast lightly until crisp. Make a batch in advance and store them in an airtight container.

JULEE'S GARLIC AND ARUGULA SOUP

A simple, satisfying soup accenting two of Julee's favorite flavors—garlic and arugula.

7 tablespoons unsalted butter, room temperature
1 large yellow onion, coarsely chopped
2 heads (30 cloves) garlic, crushed
3 large Idaho potatoes, peeled and cut into ½-inch pieces
6 cups Berta's Chicken Stock (page 396) or canned chicken broth
1 teaspoon salt
½ teaspoon freshly ground black pepper
¼ cup fresh parsley leaves
2 cloves garlic, minced
½ cup heavy or whipping cream
3 bunches arugula, rinsed, patted dry, and leaves finely chopped

1. Melt 3 tablespoons of the butter in a Dutch oven over medium heat. Add the onion and 2 heads garlic and sauté until the onion is translucent, about 5 minutes.

2. Add the potatoes, stock, salt, and pepper. Heat to boiling. Reduce heat and simmer uncovered until the potatoes are tender, about 20 minutes.

3. Make a garlic-parsley butter for topping the finished soup. Process the remaining butter and the parsley in a food

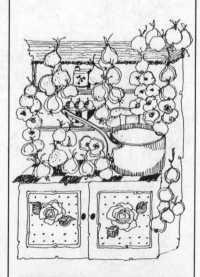

processor fitted with a steel blade until the parsley is finely chopped. Add the minced garlic and process just to combine. Spread the butter mixture on waxed paper and shape into a log. Freeze until ready to serve.

4. Process the soup in batches in a blender or a food processor fitted with a steel blade. Strain through a sieve back into the Dutch oven and reheat over low heat. Stir in the cream and taste and adjust seasonings. Stir in the arugula and simmer for 5 minutes.

5. Cut the garlic-parsley butter into thin slices. Ladle the soup into bowls and top each serving with a butter slice.

6 to 8 portions

COUNTRY AUCTION LUNCH

Wild Mushrooms Stuffed in Phyllo

Pheasant and Lentil Soup with cracklings

Apple and Onion Tart

Prunes in Zinfandel

Cabernet Sauvignon

The fall season is filled with bargains for hunters— garage sales, horse auctions, crafts fairs, farm equipment sales, and clothesline art shows. This can be a movable feast or an afternoon lunch in the shade of an apple tree.

PHEASANT AND LENTIL SOUP

The pheasant gives a deeper flavor to this soup than would chicken and is in perfect harmony with lentils.

1 pheasant (2 to 2½ pounds), ready to cook
1 orange or lemon, halved
Salt and freshly ground black pepper, to taste
8 slices bacon
1 medium-size yellow onion, chopped
2 leeks (white part only), well rinsed, dried, and chopped
4 carrots, peeled and chopped
3 cloves garlic, minced
1 teaspoon dried thyme
1 teaspoon dried rosemary
1 teaspoon dried chervil
2 quarts Berta's Chicken Stock (page 396)
1 pound lentils, soaked in water overnight and drained
½ cup heavy or whipping cream
1 cup finely chopped fresh Italian parsley
½ cup (or to taste) green Chartreuse

1. Preheat oven to 350°F.

2. Freshen the pheasant by rubbing it inside and out with the orange halves. Sprinkle the bird inside and out with salt and pepper.

3. Place 2 bacon slices in an X over the breast of the bird. Roast the bird in a roasting pan for 45 minutes, basting occasionally with the juices and fat in the bottom of the pan.

4. Meanwhile, dice the remaining bacon and sauté it in a large stock pot until crisp. Remove the bacon and set aside.

5. Add the onion, leeks, carrots, garlic, and herbs to the fat in the pot. Sauté until the onion and leeks are softened. Pour in the stock and heat to simmering.

6. Remove the bacon and as much skin as possible from the pheasant. Discard the bacon slices. Add the whole pheasant with the lentils to the stock pot. Simmer covered for 1¼ hours.

7. Remove the pheasant from the pot and let it cool.

8. Meanwhile, stir the cream into the soup and season to taste with salt and pepper. Purée the soup in batches in a food processor fitted with a steel blade or a blender and return to the stock pot.

9. When the pheasant is cool enough to handle, remove as much meat as possible from the bones. Finely chop the meat in a food processor fitted with a steel blade. Stir the meat, reserved bacon, and the parsley into the soup.

10. Cut the pheasant skin into ¼-inch dice and fry in a small frying pan over medium heat until the fat is rendered and the skin is crisp. Drain the pheasant cracklings on paper towels.

11. Heat the soup until hot. Just before serving, stir in Chartreuse to taste. Ladle the soup into bowls and sprinkle the pheasant cracklings over each serving.

8 to 10 portions

HEARTY BEEF AND VEGETABLE SOUP

T his is the kind of soup that fortifies one for a day of outdoor activity or nourishes the worst of winter colds. Comfort someone you love with a steaming bowlful.

3 medium-size leeks
1 tablespoon cider vinegar
1 cup (2 sticks) unsalted butter
2 carrots, peeled and cut into ½-inch pieces
3 ribs celery, cut into ½-inch pieces
1 small yellow summer squash, cut into ½-inch pieces
1 small zucchini, cut into ½-inch pieces
1 rutabaga (about 1 pound), peeled and cut into ½-inch pieces
2 large all-purpose potatoes, peeled and cut into ½-inch pieces
4 quarts Beef Stock (page 397)
3 pounds boiled beef from Beef Stock, coarsely shredded
Salt and freshly ground black pepper, to taste
3 ripe plum tomatoes, peeled, seeded, and chopped
1 cup cooked chick-peas (garbanzos)

STOCKING UP

Don't be unprepared for the occasional unexpected guest. Keep your kitchen shelves stocked with useful items that can be quickly transformed into appetizing treats. Such as . . .

♥ An assortment of crackers for cheese and hors d'oeuvres
♥ Unsalted and salted nuts—peanuts, pine nuts, Brazil nuts, almonds, pecans, walnuts, hazelnuts, macadamia nuts, and pistachios
♥ Dried figs, dates, apricots, apples, peaches, pears, and raisins
♥ Jars of roasted peppers, sardines, tuna, green and black olives, capers, and caviar
♥ Pickles—dill, sour, sweet, half-sours, gherkins, cornichons, halves, spears, and relishes
♥ Potato chips, pretzels, tortilla and corn chips
♥ Marinated and pickled vegetables, including carrots, string beans, mushrooms, cauliflower, broccoli, pearl onions, shallots, okra, and eggplant
♥ Chocolates, tea biscuits, Champagne wafers, sugared nuts
♥ Marmalades and jams, preserved fruits in liqueur, and chutneys
♥ Pretty cocktail napkins, toothpicks, and doilies to elevate any spur-of-the-moment effort into an affair to remember

COUNTRY WINES

Most hearty country food—garlicky sausages, game pâtés, pungent cheeses, thick soups, and crusty wheat breads—are best partnered by a simple wine. Save your Chassagne-Montrachet, Pétrus, and Dom Perignon for black-tie affairs and instead set a good jug of country wine into the earth and enjoy its simple charm.

Most country wines are delightfully light and fruity and are meant to be drunk young. This is the one instance when the most recent vintage is usually the best. California country wines tend to be generically named jug wines. Italian ones may be local wines without the D.O.C. label, and French country wines are actually regulated as *vins de pays.*

1. Cut the green tops and root ends from the leeks and discard. Cut the leeks lengthwise in half and soak in cold water to cover mixed with the vinegar for 15 minutes. Rinse, pat dry, and chop.

2. Melt the butter in a stock pot over low heat. Add the leeks, carrots, and celery and sauté until the vegetables are limp, about 15 minutes.

3. Add the yellow squash, zucchini, rutabaga, potatoes, stock, boiled beef, and salt and pepper to taste. Heat to boiling. Reduce heat and simmer uncovered until the rutabaga and potatoes are tender, about 20 minutes.

4. Stir in the tomatoes and chick-peas and simmer for 5 minutes. Serve immediately.

5 quarts, 18 portions

PURPLE PLUM AND BEAUJOLAIS SOUP

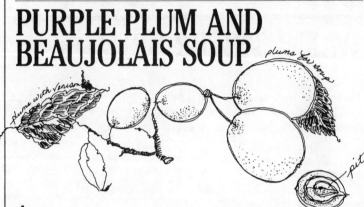

A special dessert soup, designed to take advantage of the happy season when purple plums are abundant.

5 pounds ripe purple plums, halved and pitted
3½ cups light fruity Beaujolais
2 cups water
2 medium-size oranges, thinly sliced
1 lemon, thinly sliced
8 whole cloves
2 pieces (3 inches each) cinnamon stick
2 tablespoons sugar
¼ teaspoon salt
¼ cup Grand Marnier
Grated zest of 1 orange (garnish)

1. Combine all ingredients except the Grand Marnier and orange zest in a large heavy pan over medium heat. Heat to boiling. Reduce heat to low and simmer covered for 1 hour. Let cool slightly.

2. Remove and discard the orange and lemon slices, cinnamon sticks, and cloves.

3. Process the plums and liquid in a food processor fitted with a steel blade until smooth. Strain through a sieve into a bowl.

4. Stir in the Grand Marnier. Refrigerate at least 4 hours before serving. Garnish with the orange zest.

8 to 10 portions

WALNUT BEER BREAD

A hearty and rustic bread that makes an excellent picnic lunch with cheese, especially goat's-milk cheese. Take your favorite full-bodied red wine along.

1½ cups warm beer
2 packages active dry yeast
4½ cups (or as needed) unbleached all-purpose flour
½ cup rye flour
2 tablespoons sugar
1 tablespoon salt
½ cup walnut oil
1 cup finely chopped yellow onion
¾ cup coarsely chopped walnuts
1 egg
2 teaspoons water
Fresh or dried rosemary

1. Heat the beer to 105° to 115°F and pour ½ cup into a small bowl. Stir in the yeast and let stand 10 minutes.

2. Mix the flours, sugar, and salt in a large bowl. Make a well in the center. Pour the yeast mixture, oil, and remaining 1 cup beer into the well and stir until blended.

3. Knead the dough on a floured surface until smooth and elastic, about 10 minutes, adding more flour if necessary.

4. Coat a large bowl with walnut oil. Place the dough in the bowl and turn to coat with oil. Cover with a damp towel and let rise in a warm place until doubled in bulk. (You can also let the dough rise overnight in a cool place or in the refrigerator.)

5. Punch the dough down and knead in the onion and walnuts until evenly distributed throughout the dough.

6. Divide the dough in half. Divide each half into thirds. Using your hands, roll each of the pieces into 12-inch long ropes. Braid 3 ropes together to form a loaf. Tuck the ends

ENGLISH CHEESES

The colors and flavors of British cheeses seem to have a natural affinity with autumn. Cheddars, Derbys, and Double Gloucesters remind us of the burnished foliage, while the fall harvest of pears and apples cries for a pairing with rich blue Stilton.

BLARNEY: A buttery yellow Swiss-style cheese from Ireland. Try it folded into an omelet with sautéed apple slices.

CHEDDAR: Originally made in England, Cheddar is now widely produced in Ireland, Australia, Canada, and the U.S. The best Cheddars are farmhouse (as opposed to factory) cheeses made from raw, unpasteurized milk, and aged anywhere from six months to two years. There's nothing like the flavor of a sharp nutty Cheddar to make us believe in the old saying, "An apple pie without the cheese is like a kiss without the squeeze."

CHESHIRE: A drum-shaped cheese thought to be the oldest English variety of Cheddar. It is more moist than Cheddar and has a slightly salty taste imparted from the cows that graze on the salty pastures of the Cheshire plain. Regular Cheshire is white; red Cheshire is dyed with annatto seeds.

DERBY: Another Cheddar-style cheese with a mild taste and flaky texture. Sage Derby is a favorite version, made by marbling the cheese with juice from sage leaves soaked in chlorophyll. We like to nibble it with fall fruits and nuts.

"Even if a farmer intends to loaf, he gets up in time to get an early start."
—Edgar Watson Howe

under and place on a 18 x 12-inch baking sheet. Repeat with the remaining dough, placing it on the same baking sheet. Cover and let rise until doubled in bulk, 45 minutes to 1 hour.

7. Preheat oven to 375°F.

8. Beat the egg and 2 teaspoons water in a small bowl. Brush the tops of the loaves with the egg wash and sprinkle with rosemary.

9. Bake until crusty and brown, 45 to 50 minutes. Cool in the pans for 10 minutes. Turn out onto wire racks and cool completely.

2 loaves

RICOTTA PEPPER BREAD

This is a good sandwich bread, but the dough also makes excellent dinner rolls.

½ cup milk, scalded and cooled to 115°F
2 packages active dry yeast
1 tablespoon sugar
6 tablespoons (¾ stick) unsalted butter, room temperature
2 cups ricotta cheese
2 eggs
2 teaspoons salt
2 tablespoons coarsely ground black pepper
½ cup snipped fresh chives
4 to 4½ cups unbleached all-purpose flour
1 egg (optional)
2 teaspoons water (optional)
Coarsely ground black pepper (optional)

1. Pour the milk into a large bowl and stir in the yeast and sugar. Let stand until foamy, about 5 minutes.

2. Beat the butter, ricotta, eggs, and salt into the yeast mixture with a whisk; then whisk in the pepper and chives.

3. Stir in enough of the flour, 1 cup at a time, to make a soft dough. Knead on a floured surface 5 to 10 minutes.

4. Place the dough in a buttered large bowl and turn to coat with butter. Cover the bowl with a damp towel and let rise in a warm spot until doubled in bulk, 1 to 1½ hours.

5. Punch the dough down and let it rise again for about 1 hour.

6. Butter a 12 x 4-inch loaf pan. Punch the dough down, shape it into a large loaf, and place in the loaf pan. Cover and let rise for 45 minutes.

7. Preheat oven to 350°F.

8. If desired, beat the egg and 2 teaspoons water in a small bowl, brush the top of the loaf with the egg wash, and sprinkle with black pepper. Bake until the loaf is nicely browned, about 45 to 50 minutes. Cool in the pan 10 minutes. Turn out onto a wire rack to cool completely.

1 large loaf

PORTUGUESE SWEET BREAD

A tradition in Portuguese communities, this bread makes a good breakfast served with butter and jam. It is also excellent toasted.

¼ cup warm water (105° to 115°F)
2 packages active dry yeast
⅔ cup plus 3 tablespoons raw sugar
½ cup Crème Fraîche (page 399)
6½ cups unbleached all-purpose flour
1½ teaspoons salt
Pinch ground nutmeg
7 eggs, room temperature
½ cup (1 stick) unsalted butter, room temperature
2 teaspoons water

1. Pour ¼ cup water in a small bowl. Stir in the yeast and 1 tablespoon of the sugar and let stand for 25 minutes.

2. Heat the crème fraîche in a small saucepan over low heat until melted, let cool slightly, then stir into the yeast mixture.

3. Mix 5 cups of the flour, the ⅔ cup sugar, salt, and nutmeg in a large bowl.

4. Make a well in the center of the flour mixture, pour the yeast mixture and 6 of the eggs into the well, and stir until blended. Stir in the butter.

5. Stir in enough of the remaining 1½ cups flour to make a soft dough. Knead on a floured surface until smooth and elastic, 15 to 20 minutes.

6. Place the dough in a buttered large bowl and turn to coat with butter. Cover with a damp towel and let rise in a warm place until doubled in bulk, 1 to 1½ hours.

7. Punch the dough down and divide it in half. Shape each half into a round ball and place in a buttered 2-quart soufflé dish. Cover and let rise until doubled in bulk, 1 to 1½ hours.

8. Preheat oven to 350°F.

9. Beat the remaining egg and 2 teaspoons water in a small bowl. Brush the dough with the egg wash and sprinkle the tops with the remaining 2 tablespoons sugar.

10. Bake until the top is dark and shiny, 30 to 40 minutes. If the bread seems to be getting too dark, cover with aluminum foil. Cool in the pan 10 minutes. Turn out onto wire racks to cool completely.

2 loaves

✜FROM THE SILVER PALATE NOTEBOOK

For the past several years, The Silver Palate has catered the opening of the Fall Antiques Show on a large pier in Manhattan. The surroundings are marvelous: a hundred dealers assemble from all over the country to display their prize pieces— their booths are perfect vignettes. Our job is to feed 1,000 people between 6 and 10 P.M. (the hungriest hours).

Every year we serve a different menu to match a theme. For a Pennsylvania Dutch theme, we draped the long, long tables with smoky blue and white striped cloths that hung to the floor and covered the tops with antique rag-rug runners—all in hues of blue, lavender, white, dusty green, and dusty rose. Sixteen-inch-high heart-shaped wooden candleholders, painted either dusty blue or dark red, were clustered at different spots along the table. Only tall beeswax candles were used, and, because they burn very quickly, we had hundreds as

BRAN BREAD WITH CINNAMON AND CURRANTS

Aromatic cinnamon bread with the healthful bonuses of bran and oatmeal. Try it slathered with apple butter.

½ cup orange liqueur
¾ cup dried currants
1 ¼ cups milk
1 cup water
½ cup (1 stick) unsalted butter
6 tablespoons pure maple syrup
8 cups unbleached all-purpose flour
2 cups unprocessed bran
1 cup quick-cooking oats
3 tablespoons brown sugar
2 tablespoons ground cinnamon
1 tablespoon salt
3 packages active dry yeast
4 eggs
2 teaspoons water
Cinnamon sugar (optional)

1. Pour the liqueur over the currants in a small bowl. Let stand at least 1 hour or overnight.

2. Heat the milk, 1 cup water, the butter, and syrup in a small saucepan to 120°F. All the butter need not be melted.

3. Mix 1½ cups of the flour, the bran, oats, brown sugar, cinnamon, salt, and yeast in a large mixer bowl. Gradually stir in the warm milk mixture. Beat with an electric mixer at medium speed for 2 minutes.

4. Add 3 of the eggs and ½ cup flour and beat 2 more minutes. Stir in the currants with the liqueur.

5. By hand, stir in enough of the remaining flour to make a stiff dough. Knead on a lightly floured surface until smooth and elastic, about 10 minutes.

6. Place the dough in a buttered large bowl and turn to coat with butter. Cover and let rise in a warm place until doubled in bulk, about 1 hour.

7. Punch the dough down and divide it in half. Roll out each half into a 15 x 9-inch rectangle. Starting at one short side, roll up each rectangle into a loaf and place in a buttered loaf pan. Cover and let rise in a warm place for 1 hour.

8. Preheat oven to 375°F.

9. Beat the remaining egg and 2 teaspoons water in a small bowl. Brush the top of each loaf with the egg wash. Sprinkle the tops with cinnamon sugar, if desired.

10. Bake until crusty brown, about 45 minutes. Cool slightly and remove from pans. Cool completely on wire racks.

2 loaves

backup. Flowers are always very important, but, as we were watching our budget, we found great antique laundry baskets and filled them with armloads of dried statice and dried hydrangeas, each basket a single color. The arrangements were at least 4 feet across and quite high. They provided gentle shocks of color—rose, purple, white, and pinky white. The walls behind the tables were hung with Amish quilts—dark greens, blues, roses. The effect was stunning.

RISING TO THE TOP
SOUFFLES AND NEW YORK

Many ambitious people think that New York is the place to be. They fanatically subscribe to the familiar line: If you can make it in New York, you can make it anywhere. Being right smack in the middle of the New York fever ourselves, we would have to agree. We love the glamour and glitz, culture and camouflage, diversions and diversity, professionalism and power struggles, hype and hierarchy, of this wonderfully mesmerizing metropolis.

We can think of no better way to celebrate rising to the top than with a display of culinary prowess. Soufflés are perfect congratulatory fare. They are spectacular, yet deceptively easy to prepare. Once you've mastered the art, your guests will be sure to make you the talk of the town.

WALL STREET SOUFFLE

An extra rich version of a cheese soufflé that will appeal to all tastes. A lovely blend of herbs makes this very special.

3 ½ tablespoons unsalted butter
3 ½ tablespoons unbleached all-purpose flour
1 ½ cups milk
⅓ cup dry white wine
6 egg yolks
1 tablespoon shallot or Dijon-style mustard
1 ½ teaspoons fines herbes (parsley, chives, tarragon, and chervil)
2 ½ cups grated Swiss or Gruyère cheese
Pinch ground nutmeg
Salt and freshly ground black pepper, to taste
6 egg whites, room temperature
Pinch cream of tartar

   1. Melt the butter in a heavy medium-size saucepan over medium heat. When it starts to foam, add the flour and cook, stirring constantly, 1 minute. Gradually whisk in the milk, then the wine. Cook, stirring constantly, until smooth and thick.
   2. Remove from heat and add the egg yolks, one at a time, whisking well after each addition. Stir in the mustard, *fines herbes,* and cheese. Season with nutmeg and salt and pepper to taste.
   3. Preheat oven to 375°F. Butter a 2-quart soufflé dish.
   4. Beat the egg whites and cream of tartar until stiff but not dry. Gently fold into the soufflé base. Pour into the prepared dish.
   5. Bake until well puffed and golden, about 45 minutes. Serve immediately.

   6 portions

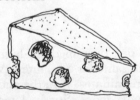 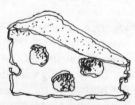

CHEESE SOUFFLE GRATINEE

A warming gratinée made light and fluffy with heavy cream.

Wall Street Soufflé (recipe precedes)
¾ cup heavy or whipping cream
1 ½ cups grated Swiss or Gruyère cheese

New York . . . oysters at Grand Central Station . . . a vest pocket park . . . softball in Central Park . . . Fifth Avenue franks . . . sesame noodles in Chinatown . . . the lighting of the Christmas tree in Rockefeller Center . . . the Madison Avenue art galleries . . . the aroma of roasting chestnuts . . . the Fifth Avenue stores . . . Soho . . . the Village Gate . . .

GRATIN DISHES

Baked foods that glisten with golden caramel-colored tops of melted cheese, toasted bread crumbs, or blistered rich white sauces have an irresistible appeal synonymous with French cooking. The French call the technique *au gratin* or *gratinée,* which means, quite simply, "burnt on top."
   Foods cooked in this manner are meant to be served in the dishes in which they were cooked. The best gratin dishes are made of heat-conducting materials like copper, porcelain, earthenware, and cast iron. They should be shallow rather than deep to ensure that each portion gets a healthy share of the crusty top. Many come with little side handles to facilitate carrying the bubbling dish straight from the broiler to the hungry and eager guests at the table.

1. Make the cheese soufflé. Let cool to room temperature, and then refrigerate covered until cold.

2. Preheat broiler.

3. Cut the soufflé into 2-inch slices and layer in a buttered au gratin dish. Pour the cream over the soufflé and top with the cheese.

4. Broil 5 inches from the heat until the cheese bubbles and browns slightly, about 10 minutes.

6 portions

RATATOUILLE AND CHEVRE SOUFFLE

The flavors of the Mediterranean come through in this unusual soufflé. Serve with peasant bread and a rich red wine.

2 tablespoons olive oil
1½ cups diced unpeeled eggplant
2 cloves garlic, minced
½ sweet red pepper, cored, seeded, and diced
3 anchovy fillets, finely chopped
2 tablespoons finely chopped sun-dried tomatoes (packed in oil)
*1 teaspoon minced fresh rosemary or ¼ teaspoon dried, plus
    additional for garnish*
3 tablespoons unsalted butter
¼ cup unbleached all-purpose flour
1½ cups milk
6 egg yolks
6 ounces soft mild chèvre, such as Montrachet
Salt and freshly ground black pepper, to taste
8 egg whites, room temperature
¼ teaspoon cream of tartar

1. Heat the oil in a sauté pan over medium-high heat. Add the eggplant and garlic and sauté for 5 minutes. Add the red pepper and sauté for 5 more minutes. Add the anchovies and tomatoes and sauté 1 minute more. Stir in 1 teaspoon rosemary and set aside.

2. Melt the butter in a heavy medium-size saucepan over medium heat. When the butter starts to foam, add the flour and cook, stirring constantly, for 1 minute. Gradually stir in the milk and cook, stirring constantly, until smooth and thick.

3. Remove from heat and add the egg yolks, one at a time, whisking well after each addition. Add 4 ounces of the chèvre and stir until the cheese melts. Heat the sauce briefly over low heat if it is not warm enough to melt the cheese.

4. Stir in the eggplant mixture, season to taste with salt and pepper, and set aside.

5. Preheat oven to 400°F. Butter a 2-quart soufflé dish.

FALL FILM FESTIVAL

*Persimmons and Figs
Draped with Proscuitto*

*Ratatouille and Chèvre
Soufflé*

Walnut Beer Bread

*Poached Pears with Ruby
Port Sabayon*

Beer or Merlot

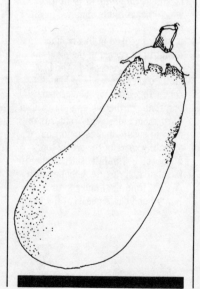

6. Beat the egg whites and pinch salt in a mixer bowl until foamy. Sprinkle with the cream of tartar and continue beating until the whites are barely stiff and stand in soft peaks. Do not overbeat, for they should not be dry. Gently fold the egg whites into the soufflé base.

7. Gently pour the batter into the prepared dish. Sprinkle the top with the remaining chèvre and additional rosemary.

8. Bake until well puffed and golden, 30 to 40 minutes. Serve immediately.

6 to 8 portions

AFTER THE THEATER SUPPER

Vivaldi's L'Autunno Pasta

Fulton Fish Market Soufflé

Luxembourg Salad

Poached Pears with Ruby Port Sabayon

Sauvignon Blanc

Sometimes it's more fun to take friends home after the theater for a midnight supper. It's important to maintain the evening's feeling of excitement. As soon as you're home, the food must be ready to go or ready to be cooked in front of your friends. Keep the tempo up with good aromas and have things ready to nibble on instantly.

FULTON FISH MARKET SOUFFLE

For a wonderful breakfast or brunch surprise, mix smoked fish into a gutsy soufflé. Don't forget the Bloody Marys.

4 tablespoons (½ stick) unsalted butter
½ sweet red pepper, cored, seeded, and diced
4 scallions (green onions, white part and 2 inches green), sliced
8 ounces smoked sablefish or finnan haddie, flaked
3 tablespoons unbleached all-purpose flour
1 ¼ cups milk
4 egg yolks
½ cup grated Swiss cheese
1 teaspoon crumbled dried savory
Salt and freshly ground black pepper, to taste
6 egg whites, room temperature
Pinch cream of tartar

1. Melt 2 tablespoons of the butter in a heavy small saucepan over medium-high heat. Add the red pepper and scallions and sauté for 5 minutes. Add the smoked fish and sauté for 10 more minutes. Set aside.

2. Melt the remaining 2 tablespoons butter in a heavy medium-size saucepan over medium heat. When it starts to foam, add the flour and cook, stirring constantly, for 1 minute. Gradually stir in the milk and cook, stirring constantly, until smooth and thick.

3. Remove from heat and add the egg yolks, one at a time, whisking well after each addition. Stir in the fish mixture, cheese, savory, and salt and pepper to taste.

4. Preheat oven to 400°F. Butter a 6-cup soufflé dish.

5. Beat the egg whites and pinch of salt until foamy. Sprinkle with the cream of tartar and continue beating until stiff but not dry. Gently fold the whites into the soufflé base. Pour into the prepared dish.

6. Bake until well puffed and golden, about 30 minutes. Serve immediately.

4 to 6 portions

ARUGULA SOUFFLE

3 tablespoons unsalted butter
¼ cup unbleached all-purpose flour
1 ½ cups light cream
6 egg yolks
4 bunches arugula, stems removed
½ cup crumbled soft mild chèvre
Pinch cayenne pepper
Pinch ground nutmeg
Salt and freshly ground black pepper, to taste
8 egg whites, room temperature
Pinch cream of tartar

   1. Melt the butter in a heavy medium-size saucepan over medium heat. When the butter starts to foam, add the flour and cook, stirring constantly, 1 minute. Gradually stir in the cream and cook, whisking constantly, until smooth and thick.
   2. Remove from heat and add the egg yolks, one at a time, whisking well after each addition.
   3. Process the arugula in a food processor fitted with a steel blade until finely chopped but not puréed. Measure 2 cups.
   4. Stir the arugula, cheese, cayenne, nutmeg, and salt and lots of black pepper to taste into the soufflé base.
   5. Preheat oven to 375°F. Butter a 2-quart soufflé dish.
   6. Beat the egg whites and pinch salt in a mixer bowl until foamy. Sprinkle with the cream of tartar and continue beating until the whites are stiff but not dry. Gently fold the whites into the soufflé base. Pour into the prepared dish.
   7. Bake until well puffed and golden, 35 to 45 minutes. Serve immediately.
   6 to 8 portions

PEAR AND BLEU DE BRESSE SOUFFLE

2 tablespoons unsalted butter
3 tablespoons unbleached all-purpose flour
1 cup half-and-half
4 egg yolks
5 ounces Bleu de Bresse, sweet Gorgonzola, or Stilton cheese
Salt and freshly ground black pepper, to taste
2 medium-ripe pears, peeled, cored, and very thinly sliced
1 tablespoon fresh lemon juice
2 tablespoons brandy, Poire Williams, or port
6 egg whites, room temperature
⅛ teaspoon cream of tartar

SOUFFLE DISHES

Although you could make a soufflé in any straight-sided, oven-proof dish, the tall sides of a soufflé dish are specifically designed to send the fluffy mixture dramatically upward as the heat of the oven causes the beaten egg whites to expand. The roundness of a soufflé dish ensures even heat penetration throughout the mixture so that it can rise to its maximum height.

   Additionally, the pretty porcelain and stoneware soufflé dishes double as decorative serving dishes. Keep in mind, however, that a soufflé baked in a stoneware dish should be removed from the oven sooner than one baked in porcelain, as a soufflé continues to cook once removed from the oven and stoneware is more heat-absorbent than porcelain.

   Most soufflé dishes come with a rim at the top. This is useful if you are making cold gelatin-based mousses or frozen desserts and wish them to look like mock soufflés. The effect is achieved by tying a paper collar, secured with string underneath the rim, around the dish to increase the height. Once the gelatin is set, the collar is removed to reveal a towering soufflélike dessert.

1. Melt the butter in a heavy medium-size saucepan over medium-low heat. When the butter starts to foam, add the flour and cook, stirring constantly, for 1 minute. Do not let it brown. Gradually stir in the half-and-half and cook, stirring constantly, until smooth and thick.

2. Remove from heat and whisk in the egg yolks, one at a time.

3. Crumble the cheese into the egg yolk mixture and stir until smooth. If the sauce is not warm enough to melt all of the cheese, heat it briefly over low heat. Season to taste with salt and pepper and set aside.

4. Sprinkle the sliced pears with the lemon juice and brandy.

5. Preheat oven to 400°F. Butter a 6-cup soufflé dish and coat with granulated sugar.

6. Beat the egg whites and pinch salt in a mixer bowl until foamy. Sprinkle with the cream of tartar and continue beating until the whites are barely stiff and stand in soft peaks. Do not overbeat the egg whites, for they should not be dry. Gently fold the egg whites into the soufflé base.

7. Set aside a few of the pear slices for decorating the top. Fan a third of the remaining pear slices in a thin layer on the bottom of the soufflé dish. Gently pour in a third of the batter. Top with another layer of pear slices and another third of the batter. Repeat the layers and arrange the reserved pear slices decoratively in the center of the soufflé.

8. Bake until well puffed and golden, 25 to 30 minutes. Serve immediately.

4 to 6 portions

PEAR AND HAZELNUT PRALINE SOUFFLE

An elegant blend of buttery pear purée and crunchy hazelnut praline. A most impressive way to end a formal dinner. Offer lots of freshly brewed coffee and Frangelico or Poire Williams cordials.

¾ cup coarsely chopped Hazelnut Praline (recipe follows)
4 tablespoons (½ stick) unsalted butter
3 firm ripe Anjou pears, peeled, cored, and sliced
½ cup sugar
2 tablespoons brandy
4 egg yolks
6 egg whites, room temperature
Pinch cream of tartar

1. Make the praline.

2. Melt the butter in a heavy medium-size saucepan over medium-low heat. Add the pear slices and sauté until quite soft, about 15 minutes.

3. Stir in the sugar and simmer until the pears begin to caramelize, 15 to 20 minutes.

4. Pour the pear mixture into a food processor fitted with a steel blade or a blender. Add the brandy and process until smooth. Place the purée in a medium-size bowl and beat in the egg yolks, one at a time. Stir in ½ cup of the coarsely chopped praline. Reserve the remaining praline for the top of the soufflé.

5. Preheat oven to 400°F. Butter a 2-quart soufflé dish and lightly coat with sugar.

6. Beat the egg whites with the cream of tartar until stiff but not dry. Gently fold into the soufflé base. Pour the batter into the prepared dish and sprinkle the top with the reserved praline.

7. Bake until puffed and golden, 35 to 40 minutes. Serve immediately.

6 portions

HAZELNUT PRALINE

1 ½ cups hazelnuts
½ cup sugar
2 tablespoons water
1 teaspoon vanilla extract
1 tablespoon unsalted butter

1. Preheat oven to 350°F.

2. Toast the hazelnuts on a baking sheet for 7 to 10 minutes. Rub the nuts against each other in a kitchen towel to remove the skins.

3. Slowly heat the sugar and water in a heavy medium-size saucepan to boiling. Then boil rapidly for 2 to 3 minutes, stirring occasionally with a wooden spoon. Remove from heat, add the nuts, and stir until evenly coated with syrup. The sugar will start to crystallize.

4. Return to medium heat to melt the sugar again and caramelize the nuts. Cook, stirring constantly with a wooden spoon, until the nuts begin to color. Stir in the vanilla. (If the

A CITY WEEKEND RETREAT

After a busy week, set aside a weekend to pamper yourself totally . . . in the city. You deserve it! Plan ahead, and on your way home from work on Friday night pick up a supply of your favorite self-indulgent foods. You may want to immerse yourself in cooking an intriguing new recipe, or you may just want a dinner of your favorite nibbling foods. Whichever, be sure to plan on a long bubble bath, and watch a favorite old movie.

Neither alarm clocks nor schedules are allowed this weekend. Sleep late and use the phone only to

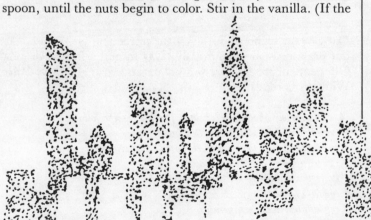

make calls to old friends whom you never find the time to talk to. This weekend no errands, laundry, or homework allowed. (Remember, you can have most anything delivered in the city.) But, don't forget to include some healthy exercise: squash, swimming, a softball game.

Spend Saturday lost in a novel, a sip or more of Champagne, and an intimate table for two at a hot new neighborhood restaurant.

Sunday is reserved for long hours in your bathrobe reading the *Times* (only the good sections) cover to cover, a bacon and eggs brunch, and snuggling with steaming mugs of coffee. Take an afternoon stroll through the park, a museum, or see a matinee performance. With the pressure off, play tourist.

Sunday evening is for savoring the last of Friday's food favorites, or if they are already devoured, then order in Chinese food. Go to bed early for a good night of sleep. You'll feel revitalized on Monday morning.

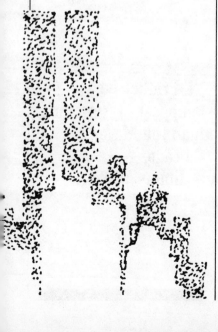

mixture begins to smoke, remove it immediately from the heat. Allow it to cool slightly before continuing.) Continue to cook and stir until the nuts turn a nice golden color. Remove from heat and stir in the butter.

5. Spread the praline mixture on an oiled piece of aluminum foil and let stand until completely cooled.

6. Break the cooled praline into pieces and process in a food processor fitted with a steel blade until coarsely chopped. Store the praline in an airtight container.

About 2½ cups

GINGERBREAD SOUFFLE

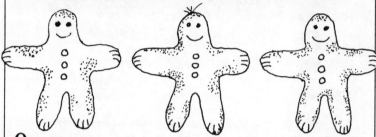

Old-fashioned gingerbread rises to new heights in this dramatic dessert.

6 tablespoons (¾ stick) unsalted butter
6 tablespoons unbleached all-purpose flour
1 cup milk
½ cup heavy or whipping cream
5 egg yolks
1 ½ cups packed light brown sugar
1 tablespoon ground ginger
1 teaspoon ground cinnamon
½ teaspoon ground nutmeg
¼ teaspoon ground cloves
2 tablespoons chopped crystallized ginger
7 egg whites, room temperature
Whipped cream (garnish)

1. Melt the butter in a heavy medium-size saucepan over medium heat. Whisk in the flour and cook 1 minute. Gradually stir in the milk and ½ cup cream. Cook, stirring constantly, until thick and smooth. Remove from the heat.

2. Add the egg yolks, one at a time, whisking well after each addition. Whisk in the brown sugar, breaking up the lumps, and continue whisking until the mixture is very smooth. Stir in the ground ginger, cinnamon, nutmeg, and cloves, and then the crystallized ginger.

3. Preheat oven to 425°F. Butter a 2-quart soufflé dish and coat lightly with sugar.

4. Beat the egg whites until stiff but not dry. Fold gently into the soufflé base. Pour into the prepared dish.

5. Bake until puffed and lightly golden, 35 to 40 minutes. Serve immediately with dollops of whipped cream.

8 to 10 portions

RICH CHOCOLATE SOUFFLE

A chocolate lover's dream. If the sheer purity of the main recipe doesn't satisfy you, experiment with the variations.

3 tablespoons unsalted butter
3 tablespoons unbleached all-purpose flour
1½ cups milk
1 pound best-quality bittersweet chocolate, broken into small pieces
¾ cup very strong brewed coffee
1 teaspoon vanilla extract
½ cup sugar
5 egg yolks
7 egg whites, room temperature
Pinch cream of tartar
Whipped cream

1. Melt the butter in a heavy small saucepan over low heat until foamy. Whisk in the flour and cook 1 minute. Gradually stir in the milk. Cook, stirring constantly, until thick and smooth.

2. Add the chocolate and heat, stirring constantly, over low heat until all the chocolate melts.

3. Stir in the coffee and remove from heat. Stir in the vanilla and ¼ cup of the sugar. Add the egg yolks, one at a time, whisking well after each addition.

4. Preheat oven to 375°F. Butter a 2-quart soufflé dish and coat with sugar.

5. Beat the egg whites with the cream of tartar until foamy. Beat in the remaining ¼ cup sugar, 1 tablespoon at a time. Beat until the peaks are stiff and glossy. Gently fold the egg whites into the soufflé base. Pour the batter into the prepared dish.

6. Bake for 40 minutes. Serve immediately with whipped cream.

6 to 8 portions

VARIATIONS:

♥ Process 1 cup toasted unsalted macadamia nuts and ¼ cup sugar in a food processor fitted with a steel blade until finely chopped. Add to the chocolate base just after it has been removed from the heat. Omit the ¼ cup sugar in step 3 but proceed as directed with the rest of the recipe.

♥ Add the finely grated zest of 1 orange and 2 tablespoons Grand Marnier to the chocolate mixture after it has been removed from the heat. Proceed with the rest of the recipe as directed. Serve with whipped cream flavored with Grand Marnier.

♥ Add 2 tablespoons of your favorite liqueur to the chocolate base and flavor the whipped cream with the same liqueur.

MUSICAL NOTES ♪

Get an opening-night autumn cocktail party started in the right spirit with lots of Cole Porter and favorite show tunes.

Complete the mood at a French dinner with the songs of Jacques Brel, Yves Montand, Edith Piaf, or Gershwin's *An American in Paris.*

Play lots of folk music at a country-style fall dinner—Judy Collins, Joni Mitchell, Peter, Paul, and Mary....

Keep the pace going after a night on the town with lots of jazz, rhythm and blues, or Motown sounds.

"I'd rather be a lamppost in New York than the Mayor of Chicago."
—Jimmy Walker

PASTAS WITH PEDIGREES

Americans are pasta crazy. More often than not, our curiosity leads us to explore dishes that are untraditional yet delicious. We always think a good thing can be made even better, so we've melted foie gras into ultrafine angel hair, stuffed giant pasta shells with garlicky French escargots, and saluted Vivaldi with a pasta extravaganza of four seasonal sauces. We think they are truly worthy of pedigrees.

VIVALDI'S FOUR SEASONS PASTAS

LA PRIMAVERA

A fresh and delicate pastel sauce of coral salmon and shrimp, pale purple shallots, and feathery green dill.

2 quarts water
1 lemon, cut in half
1 pound medium-size shrimp, shelled and deveined
1 pound bay scallops
8 ounces Nova Scotia smoked salmon, thinly sliced and shredded into
    2-inch pieces
2 cups mild olive oil
¼ cup fresh lemon juice
1 cup diced ripe tomatoes
½ cup chopped fresh dill
2 tablespoons finely chopped shallots
1 teaspoon freshly ground black pepper
Salt, to taste
1 pound linguine

1. Heat the water and lemon halves in a large saucepan over medium heat to boiling. Reduce the heat and add the shrimp. Simmer for 1 minute. Remove the shrimp with a slotted spoon and cool under cold running water. Pat dry and place in a large bowl.

2. Cook the scallops in the simmering water for 1 minute. Drain and cool under cold running water. Pat dry and add to the shrimp. Add the salmon.

3. Combine the oil, lemon juice, tomatoes, dill, shallots, and pepper in a separate bowl. Pour over the seafood and toss gently to combine. Let stand covered at room temperature for 1 hour or in the refrigerator up to 12 hours (warm to room temperature before serving).

4. Cook the linguine in boiling salted water until tender but still firm. Drain and toss immediately with the seafood sauce.

6 portions

PASTA IS SHAPING AMERICA

Everyone loves pasta, but it's important to pair the right pasta and sauce. Certain pastas are traditionally combined for favorite dishes: spaghetti with meatballs, lasagne with meat sauce, linguine with clam sauce, fettuccine alfredo.

We think common sense determines what shape of pasta to select. Thin and delicate pastas, such as angel hair, are made to carry lighter sauces. Curly pastas, such as fusilli, are great foils for mayonnaises and sauces and salads. Large shells and broad noodles are perfect for heavier foods such as sausage, broccoli, or chicken because they can sustain more weight. Filled pastas, such as tortellini and cappeletti, are terrific in preparations served in bowls, such as soups and entrées with thick sauces, because they're more robust.

BEAUJOLAIS NOUVEAU

Years ago this fruity French wine was such a local neighborhood specialty that it rarely ever made it into a corked bottle. Now it is an international phenomenon that makes November 15 the most important date on every wine lover's calendar. The difference between Nouveau and other Beaujolais wines is that Nouveau grapes are not crushed, but are left whole for each grape to undergo fermentation individually. The result is a light, fresh wine that is best drunk almost immediately—in the late fall and early winter. We like this seasonal wine served chilled, to accentuate its fruitiness and youth. Be sure to mark the date on your own calendar and reserve a case or two to tide you through the onset of winter.

In heaven, John Donne said, it is always autumn. There is probably nothing on earth that discloses the season's celestial side better than joining with good friends on a hunt for mushrooms, nuts, or game. Crisp fall breezes blow cares away, the rays of the sun bathe everyone in flattering light, and patience replaces rush as the order of the day.

L'ESTATE

We invented this pasta to preserve our favorite pesto flavors without having to put everything in the processor. A happy result with lots of texture and pizazz.

2 cups fresh basil leaves, cut into ¼-inch strips
5 ounces Parmesan cheese, cut into tiny squares
¾ cup pine nuts (pignoli), lightly toasted (page 57)
6 cloves garlic, crushed
2½ cups best-quality olive oil
Salt and freshly ground black pepper, to taste
1 pound linguine
Cherry tomato halves or tomato wedges (garnish)

1. Combine the basil, Parmesan, pine nuts, and garlic in a medium-size bowl. Pour the olive oil over all. Season to taste with salt and pepper. Let stand at room temperature for 3 hours.

2. Cook the linguine in boiling salted water until tender but still firm. Drain and toss immediately with the sauce. Place on a large serving platter and arrange the tomatoes around the edge.

4 portions

L'AUTUNNO

An unusual combination of ingredients makes one of the best new pasta dishes we've tried.

¾ cup best-quality olive oil
15 cloves garlic, 6 minced and 9 cut into thin slivers
1 cup dry white wine
1 tablespoon fresh rosemary or 1½ teaspoons dried
¾ cup dried apricots, cut into slivers
Salt and freshly ground black pepper, to taste
1 pound linguine
½ cup chopped fresh parsley

1. Heat the olive oil in a skillet over medium heat. Add the minced and slivered garlic and sauté just until browned.

2. Stir in the white wine. Reduce the heat and simmer uncovered for 5 minutes. Add the rosemary and apricots. Season with salt and pepper to taste. Simmer 5 to 10 minutes longer.

3. Meanwhile, cook the pasta in boiling salted water until tender but still firm; drain.

4. Place the pasta, sauce, and parsley in a serving bowl and toss to coat. Serve immediately.

4 to 6 portions

L'INVERNO

This dish is marvelous in cold weather and is easy to prepare ahead. The creamy St. André melts all over the pasta to create a luxurious sauce enriched by the smoky taste of Parma ham and the crunch of walnuts. Serve with a crisp green salad and a hearty red wine.

2 cloves garlic, finely minced
1 ½ cups large walnut pieces
1 pound St. André cheese, rind removed, cheese cut into irregular
    pieces
1 cup coarsely chopped fresh Italian parsley
8 ounces thinly sliced Parma ham, shredded
2 teaspoons salt
1 teaspoon freshly ground black pepper
1 cup plus 1 tablespoon best-quality olive oil
4 quarts water
1 pound dried linguine
Freshly grated Parmesan cheese

   1. Combine the garlic, walnuts, St. André, parsley, ham, ½ teaspoon of the salt, the pepper, and 1 cup oil in a large serving bowl. Let stand covered at toom temperature at least 4 hours.
   2. Just before serving, heat the water to boiling in a large pan. Add 1 tablespoon oil and the remaining 1 ½ teaspoons salt. Add the linguine and boil until tender but still firm, 8 to 10 minutes.
   3. Drain the pasta and immediately toss with the walnut sauce. Serve immediately. Pass the peppermill and Parmesan cheese.

   4 portions

ANGEL HAIR WITH FOIE GRAS AND DUCK CRACKLINGS

Light, airy, and elegant. Just perfect as an appetizer. If you cannot find fresh foie gras, a good tinned variety can take its place.

12 ounces angel hair pasta
8 ounces domestic duck foie gras roulade
½ cup (1 stick) unsalted butter
⅓ cup Cognac
1 cup duck cracklings*
Freshly ground black pepper, to taste

   1. Cook the pasta in boiling salted water until tender but still firm.

GOOSE GANDER

With a domestic foie gras industry beginning in New York State and imported foie gras becoming more widely available in specialty food stores across the country, it is important to become familiar with foie gras labeling distinctions. Foie gras is not all the same nor used in the same manner.

FRESH AMERICAN DUCK LIVER: The only fresh foie gras available in America, (federal regulations forbid the importation of fresh European foie gras). Americans have just begun to experiment with foie gras production, and a very good product comes from New York State. A special hybrid duck is "encouraged to eat" a select diet to produce the prized, rich liver. The livers are shipped to sellers in a vacuum pack, and most of the better stores will sell as much or as little as the customer desires.

   Fresh foie gras should be cut into thin slices, seasoned lightly with salt and pepper, and sautéed quickly over high heat without the addition of any extra fats or oils. It is one of the world's greatest delicacies and is best savored with a glass of Sauternes or Champagne on the grandest of occasions or holidays. Fresh foie gras has a shelf life of approximately 1 week.

IMPORTED FOIE GRAS: A whole duck or goose liver which has been semi-cooked before importation to comply with U.S. sanitary regulations. It is usually shipped in a vacuum pack and can be served without further cooking—chilled, sliced, and arranged on a plate with toast points and accompaniments such as sautéed pears, fresh raspberries, or cornichons. The Petrossian label is one of the best brands available in this country. Imported foie gras has a shelf life of 2 weeks.

ROULADE OR BLOC DE FOIE GRAS: Either the whole liver or pieces of liver, semi-cooked, flavored with spices and spirits, and molded into the shape of a round or square. It is available with or without black truffles in the center. Preservatives are added to prolong the shelf life; the better varieties are sold wrapped in foil, not tinned. Roulades or blocs last 2 to 3 weeks.

TINNED OR JARRED FOIE GRAS: These are made from fully cooked livers, usually a blend of pieces, seasoned and puréed together. The less expensive varieties are cooked right in the selling tin. This type of foie gras preparation does not require refrigeration, though it must be chilled for 12 hours prior to serving to obtain the proper consistency.

"No man is lonely while eating spaghetti."
—Robert Morley

2. Meanwhile, cut the foie gras into tiny (¼ inch) cubes and spread out on a piece of aluminum foil.

3. Melt the butter in a small saucepan. Stir in the Cognac and simmer several minutes. Be careful not to burn the butter.

4. Drain the pasta and toss immediately with the Cognac butter, foie gras, and duck cracklings. Grind pepper over the pasta and serve immediately.

6 appetizer portions

*To make duck cracklings, remove the skin of a 4-to 5-pound duck. Reserve meat for another use. Cut the skin into 1-inch pieces and sauté over medium heat until extra fat renders out and skin pieces are crispy, about 20 to 30 minutes.

ESCARGOT-STUFFED SHELLS

A wonderful twist on the usual escargots. Large pasta shells are filled with escargots in a stuffing of prosciutto, spinach, garlic, cream, and lots more—a wonderful meal.

11 tablespoons unsalted butter, room temperature
1 large yellow onion, cut into thin slivers
8 cloves garlic, minced
1 ¾ cups dry white wine
¼ cup Pernod
48 canned snails, drained and rinsed
4 ounces prosciutto, cut into julienne
2 packages (10 ounces each) frozen spinach, thawed and drained
1 cup heavy or whipping cream
Pinch ground nutmeg
Salt and freshly ground black pepper, to taste
¾ cup freshly grated Parmesan cheese
12 ounces large pasta shells
1 ½ cups fresh bread crumbs
3 tablespoons minced fresh parsley

1. Melt 6 tablespoons of the butter in a skillet over medium heat. Add the onion and sauté for 15 minutes.

2. Add the garlic, 1 cup of the wine, the Pernod, and snails. Cook until the liquid is reduced to about ¼ cup. Stir in the prosciutto and the spinach and cook 5 minutes more.

3. Add the cream, nutmeg, and salt and pepper to taste. Stir in the Parmesan. Keep warm while cooking the pasta.

4. Cook the pasta shells in boiling salted water until tender but still firm. Drain.

5. Preheat oven to 350°F. Butter a 13 x 9-inch baking pan with 2 tablespoons of the butter.

6. Fill each pasta shell with a heaping spoonful of the

snail stuffing and place, filled side up, in the pan.

7. Process the bread crumbs, parsley, and remaining 3 tablespoons butter in a food processor fitted with a steel blade until combined. Sprinkle the bread crumb mixture evenly over the shells. Drizzle the remaining ¾ cup wine over the shells.

8. Bake until the top is browned, 30 to 35 minutes. Serve immediately as a main course, or serve 1 or 2 as an appetizer.

6 to 8 main-course portions

SEAFOOD LASAGNE

A rich and creamy lasagne brimming with all our favorite shellfish. Using homemade noodles will make this dish worthy of your most important entertaining occasions.

SEAFOOD SAUCE:

3 tablespoons olive oil
1 large yellow onion, chopped
4 cloves garlic, minced
5 cups canned plum tomatoes (packed in tomato purée)
½ cup dry white wine
½ cup chopped fresh basil
2 teaspoons fennel seeds
Salt and freshly ground black pepper, to taste
1 cup heavy or whipping cream
2 tablespoons Pernod
1 pound medium-size shrimp, shelled, deveined, and poached briefly
1 pound scallops, poached briefly
3 dozen mussels, steamed and shelled
2 dozen littleneck clams, steamed and shelled

1 ¼ pounds lasagne noodles, preferably fresh tomato noodles

FILLING

3 cups ricotta cheese
8 ounces cream cheese, room temperature
2 eggs
1 package (10 ounces) spinach, cooked, drained, and chopped
1 pound cooked lump crabmeat, shredded
1 sweet red pepper, seeded, cored, and diced
1 bunch scallions (green onions), sliced
½ cup chopped fresh basil
Salt and freshly ground black pepper, to taste
1 ½ pounds mozzarella cheese, thinly sliced

SATURDAY NIGHT BUFFET

Sauerkraut, Apple, and String Cheese Salad

Seafood Lasagne

Spinach and Bacon Salad

Chestnut Mousse

Date and Fig Bars

Chianti

BIG TEN FOOTBALL PARTY

Plan a Sunday afternoon of touch football and beer with only the most reticent allowed to act as cheerleaders. Have Big Ten sweatshirts for all and plenty of school pennants around. Decorate the "goal post" and play tapes of Big Ten College football songs.

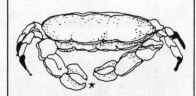

1. To make the seafood sauce, heat the oil in a large skillet over medium-high heat. Add the onion and garlic and sauté for 5 minutes. Add the tomatoes with the purée and cook for 5 minutes more. Stir in the wine, basil, fennel seeds, and salt and pepper to taste. Simmer uncovered over medium heat for 45 minutes, stirring occasionally.

2. Stir the cream into the sauce and then the Pernod. Stir in all the shellfish and simmer 5 minutes. Remove from the heat.

3. Preheat oven to 350°F.

4. Cook the lasagne noodles in boiling salted water until tender but still firm. Drain and cool under cold running water.

5. To make the filling, beat the ricotta, cream cheese, and eggs in a mixing bowl with a wooden spoon until smooth. Stir in the spinach, crabmeat, red pepper, scallions, basil, and salt and pepper to taste.

6. Butter a large rectangular baking pan. Spread a thin layer of the sauce without any shellfish on the bottom of the pan. Cover with a layer of noodles. Top with half the filling, then half the seafood sauce. Cover the sauce with a layer of the mozzarella.

7. Place another layer of noodles over the mozzarella and spread with the remaining filling. Top with another layer of mozzarella. Add a final layer of noodles and then the remaining seafood sauce. Cover with the remaining cheese.

8. Bake the lasagne until bubbling and browned, about 50 minutes. Let stand for 10 minutes before serving.

10 to 12 portions

THE FALL MARATHONS

The Greeks said "Celebrate the body, but nourish the mind."

Three thousand years after that first foot race at Olympus, Americans have caught the fever of running with the wind. Whether it is sprinting around the football field, or joining the Boston, New York, or Bay to Breakers Marathon, or training on the beach for the Olympics, those who are running have health, strength, and good luck.

Each year thousands compete in late October in New York's five-borough marathon. And each year pasta is on the menu the night before, as runners load up—for once without guilt—on carbohydrates.

BOLOGNESE SAUCE

This meaty Italian tomato sauce is made extra spicy with hot Italian sausage. Serve over a hearty pasta, like thick spaghetti, ziti, or corkscrews, and pass a bowl of freshly grated Parmesan.

2 pounds hot Italian sausages
2 pounds ground beef
½ cup (1 stick) unsalted butter
1 large yellow onion, cut into ¼-inch dice
1 medium-size green bell pepper, seeded, cored, and diced
2 ribs celery, cut into ¼-inch dice
2 cans (28 ounces each) Italian plum tomatoes
1 bay leaf
3 tablespoons dried oregano
2 tablespoons dried basil
2 teaspoons salt
1 teaspoon freshly ground black pepper
1 cup dry red wine
2 cans (6 ounces each) tomato paste
⅛ teaspoon ground cinnamon

1. Cut the sausage into ½-inch cubes and brown in a heavy skillet over medium heat. Drain and set aside.

2. Brown the ground beef in the same skillet over medium heat. Drain and set aside.

3. Melt the butter in a large saucepan over medium heat. Add the onion, green pepper, and celery and sauté until limp, about 5 minutes.

4. Stir in the sausage, beef, tomatoes with liquid, bay leaf, oregano, basil, salt, and pepper. Simmer covered for 30 to 40 minutes. Stir in the wine, tomato paste, and cinnamon and simmer covered for 15 minutes.

5. Let stand at least 30 minutes before serving but preferably overnight. Reheat before serving.

6 to 8 portions

SUN-DRIED TOMATO PASTA SAUCE

A good basic spicy pasta sauce for a cool evening meal. Serve with a crisp arugula salad. For a heartier sauce, slices of quickly fried pepperoni can be added just before serving.

¼ cup oil from the jar of sun-dried tomatoes
4 tablespoons (½ stick) unsalted butter
1 large yellow onion, chopped
3 ribs celery, minced
3 carrots, peeled and minced
3 cloves garlic, minced
1 teaspoon fennel seeds
2 cans (28 ounces each) tomatoes, undrained
¾ cup chopped sun-dried tomatoes (packed in oil)
1 cup dry white wine
Salt and freshly ground black pepper, to taste

1. Heat the oil and butter in a large saucepan over medium-high heat. Add the onion, celery, carrots, garlic, and fennel seeds and sauté for 15 minutes.

2. Stir in the canned tomatoes, sun-dried tomatoes, wine, and salt and pepper to taste. Simmer uncovered for 1 hour, stirring occasionally.

3. Transfer the sauce to a food processor fitted with a steel blade and process with repeated pulses until blended but not smooth. Tiny chunks should still remain.

4. Serve the sauce over a hearty pasta, such as thick spaghetti or ziti, with freshly grated Parmesan cheese.

6 to 8 portions

SUN-DRIED TOMATOES

Imported sun-dried tomatoes from Italy are one of our current cravings. The technique of preserving the tomatoes is similar to the one used to turn a grape into a raisin or a plum into a prune. Red ripe tomatoes at their peak of perfection are set out in the hot Italian sun to shrivel and dry. They are then packed in fruity Italian olive oil and sometimes seasoned with a secret blend of herbs.

Sun-dried tomatoes have become so popular in America that many inferior grades have recently appeared on the market. Beware of those not packed in oil and sold at a considerably lower price, as they often don't reconstitute beyond the state of tough shoe leather. Look for tomatoes that are packed in oil and are bright red rather than brownish. Pumate San Remo from Liguria is one of our favorite brands.

We love the explosive concentrated flavor of sun-dried tomatoes in sauces, salads, and sandwiches, and tossed with basil and slices of fresh mozzarella cheese.

THE AUTUMN HUNT

After the laziness of the summer months, we welcome the activity of autumn. We get caught up in it, like the animals squirreling away hibernation treats and birds flocking south in graceful formations. We too want to join in the action. Now is the time to gather chestnuts and hickory nuts from under gnarled old trees, to rescue wild mushrooms from the first killing frosts, to savor the sweet delicacy of New England bay scallops, and to reap the benefits of the fall hunting season. Whether your hunt takes place in thick woods and marshlands or in the traffic of congested city markets, the cooking aromas of these dishes are sure to evoke the wonder of all outdoors.

WILD MUSHROOM TART

This tart embodies the essence of autumn with the sweet cider, the woodsy mushrooms, and the smoky mozzarella.

PASTRY:

1½ cups unbleached all-purpose flour
¾ teaspoon salt
½ cup (1 stick) unsalted butter, cold,
    cut into small pieces
3 tablespoons ice water

FILLING:

1 cup apple cider
¾ cup dried porcini
¼ cup best-quality olive oil
1 small yellow onion, minced
4 ounces fresh wild mushrooms (such as shiitake or chanterelles),
    well rinsed, dried, and sliced
8 ounces fresh cultivated mushrooms, wiped clean and sliced
¼ cup applejack
Salt and freshly ground black pepper, to taste
½ cup chopped fresh Italian parsley
4 eggs
¾ cup heavy or whipping cream
¾ cup shredded smoked mozzarella
½ cup grated Parmesan cheese

1. To make the pastry, process the flour, salt, and butter in a food processor fitted with a steel blade until the mixture resembles coarse meal. With the machine running, pour the ice water through the feed tube in a thin, steady stream and process just until the dough holds together. Wrap in plastic wrap and refrigerate 1 hour.

2. Preheat oven to 375°F.

3. Roll out the dough ⅛ inch thick on a lightly floured surface. Line a 9-inch tart pan with removable bottom with the dough. Trim and crimp the edges. Freeze for 10 minutes.

4. Line the shell with aluminum foil and weight with dried beans or pie weights. Bake for 20 minutes. Remove the beans and foil and set aside to cool.

5. To make the filling, heat the cider to boiling and pour over the dried porcini in a small bowl. Let stand 30 minutes.

6. Heat the oil in a medium-size skillet. Add the onion and wild and fresh mushrooms and sauté for 10 minutes. Add the porcini with the liquid, the applejack, and salt and pepper to taste. Cook uncovered over low heat for 20 minutes. Remove from heat and stir in the parsley.

7. Reset oven at 375°F.

8. Beat the eggs and cream together and stir in the

"If you think you are a mushroom—jump into the basket."
—Russian Proverb

RECONSTITUTING DRY MUSHROOMS

The taste of wild mushrooms can still be yours even if fresh varieties are not available at any of your markets and wandering in the woods is not your thing. Several kinds are available in dried form, usually imported from Europe. When they are properly reconstituted by soaking, the flavor and texture are as good—though different—as those of the fresh.

Buy from a reputable dealer, and preferably one who offers his wares in bulk; dried mushrooms can be invaded by worms and other insects, and a wary shopper will examine them closely. Rinse them thoroughly under cold running water and soak them in water or, more wisely, a liquid that you will be able to incorporate into the recipe, thus saving every bit of elusive flavor. Madeira, white wine, red wine, port, brandy, Cognac, and chicken stock are the best choices.

After soaking, dried mushrooms are usually chopped and sautéed in butter to bring out their full flavor before being added to a dish. We have learned to combine an ounce or two of dried with a pound or more of sautéed sliced cultivated mushrooms; the exchange of flavors and textures benefits both, and the result is a generous quantity of wild mushroom flavor with a minimum of expense.

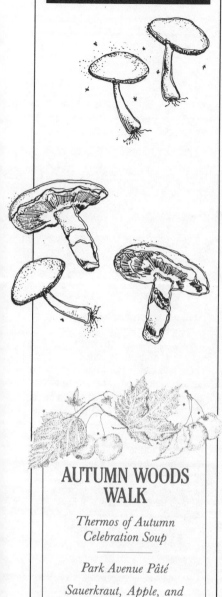

cheeses. Combine the egg and mushroom mixtures and pour into the tart shell.

9. Bake the tart for 30 minutes. Cool 5 minutes, then cut into wedges and serve immediately.

6 portions

WILD MUSHROOM PASTRIES

A woodsy *duxelles* is prepared with tawny port, fresh shallots, and butter. Chanterelles, shiitake, and oyster mushrooms make the base. We wrap tiny bits in phyllo, decorate with a mushroom slice, and bake until golden. These deserve to be served on a silver platter.

½ cup (1 stick) unsalted butter
2 large shallots, minced
6 ounces fresh chanterelles, well rinsed and patted dry
6 ounces fresh shiitake mushrooms, well rinsed and patted dry
6 ounces fresh oyster mushrooms, well rinsed and patted dry
¼ cup tawny port
Salt and freshly ground black pepper, to taste
1 pound phyllo dough, thawed if frozen, cut crosswise in half
1½ cups (3 sticks) melted unsalted butter

1. Melt the ½ cup butter in a large saucepan over medium heat. Add the shallots and sauté for 2 minutes.

2. Add the mushrooms, reserving several small ones, and sauté for 2 minutes. Add the port, reduce the heat, and simmer until all the liquid evaporates, about 20 minutes.

3. Remove from heat and process in a blender or food processor fitted with a steel blade until finely minced. Season the *duxelles* to taste with salt and pepper.

4. Preheat oven to 350°F.

5. Brush one side of 1 phyllo sheet with butter, roll it up diagonally, and shape into a tight spiral.

6. Place 1 teaspoon *duxelles* in the center of the spiral and press deeply into the dough. Place the filled spiral on a baking sheet lined with aluminum foil. Continue rolling and filling with the remaining *duxelles* and phyllo.

7. Cut the reserved mushrooms into slices. Top each pastry with a mushroom slice, brush with butter, and bake until golden brown, about 20 minutes.

8. Present these delicate pastries on a round platter or flat basket.

About 36 pastries

AUTUMN WOODS WALK

Thermos of Autumn Celebration Soup

Park Avenue Pâté

Sauerkraut, Apple, and String Cheese Salad

Wild Mushroom Tart

Grapes, apples, and pears

Zinfandel

Spend the afternoon walking in the woods when the trees are their most glorious. Take along classical music tapes, read poetry aloud, or just listen to nature's own music.

RISOTTO PORCINI CASSEROLE

Risotto is a wonderful dish to serve as a main course or with a highly flavored fish or lamb. Porcini add a rich deep taste and this version doesn't require the constant last-minute attention that is so characteristic of risottos.

2 ounces dried porcini
8 tablespoons (1 stick) unsalted butter
2 bunches scallions (green onions),
*   chopped*
3 carrots, peeled and minced
2 cups Italian Arborio rice
½ cup dry white wine
4 to 5 cups Beef Stock (page 397) or canned beef broth
1 pound fresh cultivated mushrooms, wiped clean and sliced
3 cloves garlic, minced
¾ cup chopped fresh parsley
Salt and freshly ground black pepper, to taste
2 cups freshly grated Parmesan cheese
1 cup heavy or whipping cream
2 eggs
Pinch ground nutmeg

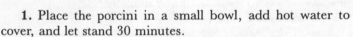

1. Place the porcini in a small bowl, add hot water to cover, and let stand 30 minutes.

2. Melt 4 tablespoons of the butter in a 10 to 12-inch skillet over medium heat. Add the scallions and carrots and sauté for 10 minutes. Add the rice and cook, stirring to coat with the butter and vegetables, for 1 minute. Drain the porcini, strain the liquid through cheesecloth, then pour it over the rice. Add the wine and enough of the stock to completely cover the rice. Simmer covered over low heat, adding more stock as needed, until the rice is tender but still firm, about 30 minutes.

3. While the rice is cooking, melt the remaining 4 tablespoons butter in a medium-size skillet over medium heat. Add the porcini and cultivated mushrooms and sauté for 10 minutes. Stir in the garlic and parsley and simmer uncovered 10 minutes. Season to taste with salt and pepper.

4. Preheat oven to 350°F. Butter a 2-quart baking dish.

5. Spread half the rice in the bottom of the baking dish. Top with all the mushrooms. Sprinkle 1 cup of the Parmesan over the mushrooms and top with the remaining rice.

6. Whisk the cream, eggs, and nutmeg together and pour evenly over the rice. Sprinkle with the remaining 1 cup Parmesan.

7. Bake until the top is puffed and brown, about 30 minutes. Let cool several minutes before serving.

8 portions

TRUFFLES

Truffles are a precious commodity. They're fungi, either black or white, and are shaped like little nuggets of coal. Most of the world's truffles come from the Périgord region of France, where they're rooted out by trained pigs. The Piedmont region of Italy yields the famous white truffle.

Truffles are now being cultivated in the U.S. Although terribly expensive, a little goes a long way. We store fresh white truffles in the refrigerator, buried in a container of white rice. Still, they must be used within a week. (The rice will have absorbed some of the truffle's heady flavor, so cook it up and enjoy.)

PORCINI

Porcini are the great Italian mushroom. In Tuscany they often grow as large as toadstools and are broiled whole as an entrée. We most often find porcini here in their dried form—but don't think this is an inferior substitute. Drying actually intensifies their unique flavor.

BAY SCALLOPS

Bay scallops are one of the greatest native American delicacies. The anticipation for the opening of scallop season in autumn rivals that of the springtime quest for shad roe. Great debates take place as to which East Coast bay harbors the sweetest. The issue is further complicated by deep-ocean voices that claim sea scallops are the sweetest of them all. Never ones to let regional pride interfere with pure enjoyment, we think the fresher the sweeter and like to eat our scallops raw, just popped from the shell, with a sprinkling of fresh lemon juice.

Chefs and connoisseurs pursue both the Long Island bay scallop, where the season runs from September 17 through the end of March, and the Nantucket bay scallop, where the season opens November 1 and runs to the end of March. During these months the harbors and bays are jammed with boats and fishermen dredging for scallops. A few brave souls even don wet suits and scan the chilly depths of the ocean floor in search of these succulent jewels. Whatever the method, scalloping is grueling work, making these bivalves an expensive and precious commodity.

There are all sorts of regulations governing the bay scallop industry. Fishing temperatures, zones, and licenses, as well as size, age, and amounts of scallops that can be gathered in a single day are all governed by specific laws. After the scallops are dredged, sorted, and packed in bushels, they must be opened and removed from the shell before being sold to fish markets or restaurants.

Nantucketers who are not professional fishermen enjoy a special treat: the month of October is reserved for family scalloping only. Residents attired in old clothing and waders, armed with rakes and pushers, tow bushel baskets affixed to inner tubes to gather their shoreline harvests. The bushel basket is the family limit, and from the head of the town harbor to the eel grasses of Madaket, friends and family gather to share in the excitement of this pre-season bounty.

BROILED BAY SCALLOPS ON THE HALF SHELL

A delicious appetizer, attractively presented and simple to prepare.

Fresh bay scallops
Vermouth
Pernod
Olive oil
Chopped garlic
Chopped fresh parsley
Freshly ground black pepper

1. Preheat broiler.
2. For each hors d'oeuvre, place 2 scallops in the center of a bay scallop shell. Spoon 2 teaspoons vermouth, 1 teaspoon Pernod, and 2 teaspoons olive oil over the scallops. Sprinkle with a little garlic, parsley, and pepper.
3. Place the shells on a baking sheet. Broil 6 inches from the heat just until browned and cooked, about 3 minutes. Let cool slightly before serving, in the shells.

SCALLOPS WITH VODKA AND CREME FRAICHE

Fresh bay scallops combined with northern accents of fresh dill, vodka, and crème fraîche. Serve with toothpicks as an hors d'oeuvre or in individual scallop shells as an entrée.

1 pound bay scallops
3 tablespoons vodka
1 teaspoon finely grated lemon zest
2 tablespoons chopped fresh dill
¾ cup Crème Fraîche (page 399)
Paprika

1. Toss the scallops with the vodka, lemon zest, and dill in a bowl. Transfer to an au gratin dish large enough to hold the scallops in a single layer. Spoon the crème fraîche over the scallops and sprinkle lightly with paprika.
2. Refrigerate covered at least 3 hours but no longer than 24 hours.
3. Preheat broiler.
4. Broil the scallops 6 inches from the heat until the top is well browned and the scallops are just cooked, 4 to 5 minutes. Serve immediately.

8 appetizer or 4 main-course portions

a pair of quails

QUAILS BAKED IN PEAR HALVES

A most elegant and unusual presentation. Tiny quail nestled in pear halves are sprinkled with cinnamon and napped with a sauce of brandy, honey mustard, and cream.

6 large underripe pears
Ground cinnamon
12 quail, ready to cook
Salt and freshly ground black pepper, to taste
¾ cup dried currants
1 cup (or as needed) brandy
¼ cup plus 2 tablespoons honey mustard
1¼ cups heavy or whipping cream
Fresh Italian parsley sprigs (garnish)

1. Cut the pears in half and core. Using a melon scoop, partially hollow out the inside of each pear half to make a nest for each quail. Sprinkle the inside of each pear half lightly with cinnamon.

2. Pat the quails dry inside and out with paper towels. Sprinkle them with salt and pepper inside and out. Place each quail in a pear half and place the pears in a shallow bowl. Sprinkle with currants and pour 1 cup brandy over all. Let stand at room temperature for 1 hour.

3. Preheat oven to 425°F.

4. Remove the quails and pears from the bowl. Drain off the brandy and reserve. Stuff each quail with about 1 tablespoon of the currants. Spread a thin layer of the ¼ cup mustard over each quail.

5. Place the pears in a shallow roasting pan and set each quail back in its pear shell. Bake until the quail are done, 25 to 30 minutes.

FALL MUSEUM OPENING

Autumn Celebration Soup

Quails Baked in Pear Halves

Radicchio salad

Risotto Porcini Casserole

Chestnut Mousse

Sauvignon Blanc

FAIR GAME

The great gastronome Brillat-Savarin defined game as "those animals which live in the woods and field in a state of natural freedom, and which are still good to eat." While game is traditionally wild, today increasing amounts are being farm-bred to meet the demand. Game animals fall into four categories:

WATERFOWL—flourish and are hunted in almost every state. The principal members are geese and mallard ducks.

UPLAND GAME—includes partridge, quail, grouse, pheasant, guinea hens, squab, and woodcock. These are the birds that are readily available in specialty markets; they are commercially raised on farms under semiwild conditions.

BIG GAME—includes deer, bear, antelope, elk, moose, and boar.

SMALL GAME—includes hare, rabbits, squirrels, and raccoons.

6. Remove the pears and quail to a warmed serving platter. Measure the reserved brandy, add more if needed to make ½ cup, and pour it into the roasting pan. Heat over medium heat, stirring constantly, until hot. Stir in the cream and cook the sauce until it begins to thicken. Whisk in the 2 tablespoons mustard and taste and adjust seasonings.

7. Pour enough of the sauce over each quail to drip down and form a small pool around each pear. Garnish with parsley sprigs and serve immediately.

12 first-course or 6 main-course portions

AFTER-THE-HUNT DINNER

Roasted Chestnut and Hazelnut Soup

Golden Roast Pheasant

Glazed Lady Apples and Onions

Potato and Celery Root Purée

Pear Tart with Poire Williams

Chocolate Truffles

White Burgundy

There is something so satisfying about sitting down—in black tie, perhaps, surrounded by silver, crystal, and the best china available—to a meal of fresh game. The group that hunts is always wise to include among its number at least one high-caliber culinary artist to work miracles in the kitchen.

GOLDEN ROAST PHEASANT

Quickly and simply prepared, this bird is just the right size for a dinner for two.

1 orange
1 pheasant (about 2½ pounds), ready to cook
Salt and freshly ground black pepper, to taste
½ teaspoon rubbed sage
¼ teaspoon paprika
3 cloves garlic, peeled
3 sprigs fresh parsley
4 tablespoons (½ stick) unsalted butter, room temperature
3 slices bacon
1 cup dry white wine
½ cup golden raisins

1. Preheat oven to 350°F.

2. Cut the orange in half. Squeeze the juice from 1 orange half into the cavity of the pheasant and over the skin. Rub the bird inside and out with salt, pepper, sage, and paprika. Cut the remaining orange half in half and place, along with the garlic and parsley, in the cavity of the bird.

3. Spread the butter over the breast and place the bird breast side up, in a shallow roasting pan. Lay the bacon crosswise over the breast.

4. Cover the pheasant with aluminum foil and bake for 45 minutes.

5. Meanwhile, heat the wine to boiling in a small saucepan over high heat. Add the raisins, remove from heat, and let stand for 45 minutes.

6. Remove the foil and pour the wine and raisins over the pheasant. Bake uncovered, basting frequently, until the juices run clear when a thigh is pierced with a sharp skewer, about 45 minutes.

7. Remove the pheasant with the bacon to a small serving platter. Spoon some raisin sauce over the top and pour the remaining into a sauceboat. Serve immediately.

2 portions

ROASTED DUCK BREASTS WITH CRANBERRY GLAZE

This is a very simple and delicious preparation. Arrange the slices of duck breast like a fan on a small platter. Spoon more cranberry glaze over the duck and serve with a beet purée.

1½ cups cranberry coulis (from Sliced Oranges with Cranberry Coulis, page 339)
6 whole duck breasts, boned, skin left on
Salt and freshly ground black pepper, to taste

1. Make the cranberry coulis.
2. Preheat oven to 450°F.
3. Place the duck breasts, skin side up, on a roasting rack in a roasting pan. Sprinkle with salt and pepper.
4. Roast the breasts for 15 minutes. Remove from the oven. Reduce the heat to 300°F.
5. Spoon 1 cup of the cranberry coulis over the duck breasts. Roast for 10 more minutes.
6. Cut the breasts diagonally into slices. Fan the slices on individual serving plates or a serving platter. Spoon the remaining cranberry coulis over the slices and serve immediately.

6 portions

HEARTY PEASANT DUCK

We've roasted bright orange rutabagas with our duck. The luscious flavor of the duck juices comes through the rutabagas, and all is sprinkled with caraway seeds.

2 fresh ducks (4 to 5 pounds each), with giblets and necks
Salt and freshly ground black pepper, to taste
2 small yellow onions, quartered
4 ribs celery with leafy tops, broken in half
2 tablespoons olive oil
2 large rutabagas, peeled and cut into 1½-inch pieces
1 cup apple or pear juice
2 tablespoons caraway seeds

1. Preheat oven to 450°F.
2. Rinse the ducks and pat dry. Sprinkle the cavities with salt and pepper. Place 1 onion and 2 celery ribs in each cavity. Truss the ducks and place in a large roasting pan.
3. Rub the ducks with the olive oil and sprinkle all over with salt and pepper. Place the giblets and necks in the bottom of the roasting pan.
4. Roast for 30 minutes.
5. Remove the pan from the oven. Scatter the rutabagas

"IN"-CANDESCENCE

Candelight makes everyone and everything look more attractive. Therefore, you should make it an integral entertaining element, since it can ensure your reputation as a sensational host. We often light a party house only with candles.

Keep in mind that it is the candlesticks that are the most important part of the candlelight statement. Brass or silver makes a setting more formal, while ceramic holders convey more of a casual, country style.

If you entertain a lot, you might experiment with different candle arrangements. We have a friend who likes to place his candlesticks at the four corners of a table, so they won't block anyone's view during a meal as center arrangements are apt to do. He also prefers tall, flamboyant, beeswax candles that soar above eye level and create a translucent effect when they burn.

You might want to take them off the table completely and instead line a mantelpiece with a grouping of candles of varying heights. Or you might want to choose a different color for every month—lavender candles for April, bachelor-button blue for June, pumpkin for November.

Remember that candles always make a setting and moment intimate and memorable—but also remember that candle wicks should always be charred before guests arrive. Unlit wicks are considered a sign of inhospitality.

in the bottom of the pan and toss to coat with the accumulated duck fat. Pour the apple juice over the rutabagas. Sprinkle the caraway seeds over the ducks and rutabagas.

6. Return the ducks to the oven and roast until the juices run clear when the thickest part of the thigh is pierced, about 1 hour. Stir the rutabagas and baste the ducks frequently. Let stand several minutes before carving. Serve the ducks surrounded with the rutabagas on a large serving platter. Discard the necks and giblets.

6 portions

BRAISED GOOSE WITH PORT AND VEGETABLES

The very simple stuffing makes this preparation unusual. Perfect for the winter, it is slowly cooked in chicken stock and ruby port.

½ cup (1 stick) unsalted butter
1 large yellow onion, peeled and thinly sliced
4 carrots, peeled and thinly sliced
4 ribs celery, coarsely chopped
4 cloves garlic, minced
2 teaspoons dried thyme
3 bay leaves
1 goose (9 to 11 pounds), with giblets and neck
Salt and freshly ground black pepper, to taste
¼ cup unbleached all-purpose flour
4 cups Berta's Chicken Stock (page 396)
2 cups ruby port
1 pound mushrooms, wiped clean and sliced
1 cup chopped fresh parsley

1. Preheat oven to 450°F.

2. Melt the butter in a large skillet over medium heat. Add the onion, carrots, celery, and garlic and sauté until softened, about 5 minutes. Add the thyme and bay leaves and sauté 10 minutes more.

3. Coarsely chop the goose giblets and add the giblets to the vegetables. Stir in the mushrooms and cook 5 minutes more. Stir in the parsley and remove from the heat.

4. Rinse the goose and pat dry. Sprinkle the cavity with

salt and pepper. Spoon a third of the vegetable mixture into the cavity. Truss the goose and place the goose and the neck in a deep roasting pan.

5. Roast the goose for 20 minutes.

6. Meanwhile, add the flour to the remaining vegetable mixture and cook a few minutes to thicken. Stir in the stock and port. Season to taste with salt and pepper. Heat to boiling, stirring constantly. Remove from heat.

7. Reduce oven heat to 350°F. Remove the goose from the oven and spoon the vegetable mixture around the goose. Continue roasting about 20 minutes per pound, basting with the pan juices occasionally.

8. Remove the goose from the oven and let stand 10 minutes before carving. Discard the vegetables from the cavity of the goose. Carve the goose and serve with the braised vegetables.

6 portions

FRIED RABBIT WITH SWEET MUSTARD

A simple and delicious rabbit preparation, this is great hot but perhaps even better cold as an unusual variation on cold fried chicken. The honey mustard adds a special sharpness.

1 rabbit (3 to 3½ pounds), cut into 8 pieces
2 large eggs
½ cup honey mustard, plus additional for dipping
1½ cups unbleached all-purpose flour
1 tablespoon salt
2 teaspoons freshly ground black pepper
1 tablespoon paprika
½ cup (1 stick) unsalted butter
Chopped fresh Italian parsley (garnish)

1. Rinse the rabbit pieces and pat dry.

2. Beat the eggs and ½ cup mustard in a shallow bowl. In a second shallow bowl, mix the flour, salt, pepper, and paprika.

3. Dip each rabbit piece first in the egg mixture and then coat with the flour mixture.

4. Melt the butter in a skillet large enough to fit all the rabbit pieces in a single layer over medium heat. Add the rabbit and brown well on all sides. Reduce the heat to low and cook covered, turning the pieces occasionally, until tender, about 30 minutes.

5. Transfer the rabbit to a warmed serving platter, sprinkle with parsley, and serve with additional honey mustard for dipping. If you wish, refrigerate the rabbit and serve cold.

4 portions

TAILGATE PICNIC

Bloody Marys

Thermoses of Smoky Pumpkin Soup

Fried Rabbit with Sweet Mustard

Patriotic Potato Salad

June's Apple Crisp Cheddar cheese

Old-Fashioned Oatmeal Cookies

Mulled cider

For the big football game, put together a large group of friends and rent a bus. Serve plenty of Bloody Marys in spill-proof cups and fancy little bags of nuts on the ride to the stadium. At the stadium, spread out plaid blankets for a grand tailgate picnic and make sure your guests have a very good time. Buy them programs and pompoms and seat them in groups according to their favorite team. Have the mulled cider for the return trip and sing all the way home.

For a sparkling Saturday night sit-down dinner, a little formality heightens expectations and puts people at their best. After dinner, serve Chartreuse and watch the conversation fly.

BRAISED RABBIT WITH CHARTREUSE

The strong herb flavor of Chartreuse complements the mild gaminess of rabbit. Serve to adventurous friends.

1 rabbit (3 to 3½ pounds), cut into 8 pieces
6 tablespoons (¾ stick) unsalted butter
8 shallots, minced
2 cloves garlic, minced
⅓ cup plus 1 tablespoon green Chartreuse
1 teaspoon dried tarragon
1 teaspoon dried thyme
Salt and freshly ground black pepper, to taste
¾ cup (or as needed) Berta's Chicken Stock (page 396)
½ cup Madeira
½ cup Crème Fraîche (page 399)
2 cups sliced fresh mushrooms
Chopped fresh Italian parsley (garnish)

1. Rinse the rabbit pieces and pat dry. Melt 4 table-spoons of the butter over medium heat in a skillet large enough to fit all the rabbit pieces in a single layer. Add the rabbit and sauté until the underside is browned. Turn the pieces to brown the other side; add the shallots and garlic to the skillet. Cook until the second side is browned, about 5 minutes.

2. Pour ⅓ cup Chartreuse into the skillet and warm it. Standing way back, flame the Chartreuse (the flames may soar quite high). When the flames have subsided, season with the tarragon, thyme, and salt and pepper to taste.

3. Pour in the stock and Madeira, cover the pan, and simmer until the rabbit is tender, 45 minutes to 1 hour. Check the pan from time to time and add more stock if all the liquid has evaporated. When the rabbit is tender, remove it from the pan and keep warm in the oven.

4. Stir the crème fraîche into the pan juices and simmer until the sauce is thick and glistening. At the same time, sauté the mushrooms in the remaining 2 tablespoons butter in a separate skillet. Taste the sauce, adjust the seasoning, and stir in the remaining 1 tablespoon Chartreuse.

5. Add the rabbit and mushrooms to the sauce and turn the pieces to coat with sauce. Garnish with parsley and serve immediately.

4 portions

AMERICANS IN PARIS

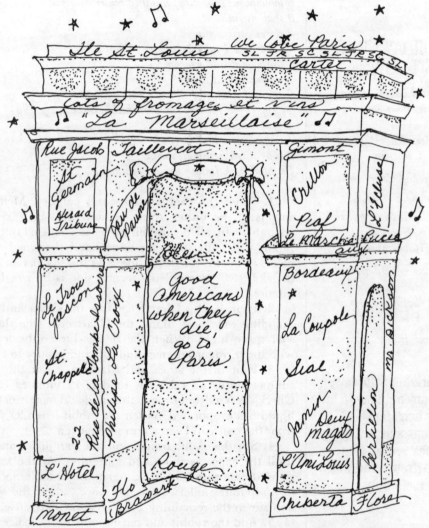

No matter how much we learn about food and cooking, we are continually amazed by the French. While we celebrate the coming of age of food in America, we never stop craving trips to France both to reaffirm the strength of traditional cooking methods and to glimpse the future through three-star crystal balls. From crêpes to *coq au vin*, from crocks of onion soup to cassoulets, the French lead the way, and we are forever indebted to them for remaining an endless source of inspiration and sophistication.

"I love Paris in the
spring time,
I love Paris in the fall,
I love Paris in the
summer
When it sizzles,
I love Paris in the
winter
When it drizzles.
I love Paris every
moment
Every moment of the
year."
—©Cole Porter

CHABLIS

Genuine Chablis comes from the
quiet, vine-covered village of Chablis
in France and is far superior to the
white wines that have borrowed its
name the world over. The best of the
true Chablis is one of the finest white
wines in the world. Only 5,000 acres
of Chardonnay vines are entitled to
the Chablis or Petit Chablis
appellation. The best Chablis is called
Grand Cru, meaning "great growth,"
and in all Chablis only seven
vineyards are entitled to this coveted
label—Les Clos, Blanchots, Valmur,
Grenouilles, Vaudésir, Les Preuses,
and Bourgros. Chablis wines have a
gold-green color, the fruity aroma of
the Chardonnay grape, and a flinty
taste.

ONION SOUP LES HALLES

Homemade beef stock is a must for perfecting this popular
French soup. Cognac and a dash of mustard make our
version extra special. The lavish topping of three cheeses
further distinguishes this soup from ordinary bistro fare.

SOUP:

4 tablespoons (½ stick) unsalted butter
2 tablespoons olive oil
6 cups sliced yellow onions
4 cloves garlic, minced
1 teaspoon sugar
⅓ cup Cognac
1 tablespoon Dijon-style mustard
½ teaspoon dried thyme
3 tablespoons unbleached all-purpose flour
3 quarts Beef Stock (page 397)
1½ cups dry white wine
Salt and freshly ground black pepper, to taste

CROUTONS:

8 thick slices French bread
4 tablespoons (½ stick) unsalted butter, room temperature
4 tablespoons olive oil
3 cloves garlic, minced

CHEESE GRATINEE:

8 ounces Gruyère, shredded
8 ounces smoked mozzarella, shredded
4 ounces freshly grated Parmesan cheese

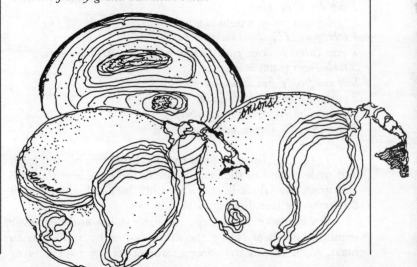

1. To make the soup, heat the butter and oil in a large stock pot. Add the onions and cook over high heat, stirring occasionally, for 15 minutes. Add the garlic and sugar. Reduce heat to medium and cook, stirring occasionally, until the onions are golden brown, about 40 minutes.

2. Pour in the Cognac, warm it, and flame with a match. When the flames subside, add the mustard and thyme. Stir in the flour and cook, stirring frequently, for 3 minutes.

3. Gradually stir in the stock and wine. Season to taste with salt and pepper. Simmer uncovered over medium heat for 1 hour.

4. Preheat oven to 350°F.

5. To make the croutons, spread one side of each bread slice with 1½ teaspoons butter and 1½ teaspoons oil. Sprinkle with the garlic. Toast the prepared side only on a baking sheet until crusty and golden, 12 to 15 minutes.

6. Combine the 3 cheeses for the gratinée.

7. Preheat broiler.

8. Ladle the hot soup into 8 oven-proof soup bowls to fill three-fourths full. Float a crouton in the center of each bowl. Top each bowl lavishly with the cheeses. Broil 6 inches from the heat until the cheese is melted and bubbling, about 4 to 5 minutes. Serve immediately.

8 portions

CREPE RAMEKINS

An unusual and richly flavored dish of little crêpes layered with prosciutto, salami, and Gruyère cheese. All is held together with a grainy mustard sauce. Serve in the center of a bright plate with the sauce spooned over and around the crêpes. Pass the peppermill.

2 cups unbleached all-purpose flour
½ teaspoon salt
4 eggs
1 cup dry white wine
5 tablespoons melted unsalted butter
4 tablespoons (½ stick) unsalted butter
2 cups Crème Fraîche (page 399) or heavy or whipping cream
3 tablespoons grainy mustard
Salt and freshly ground black pepper, to taste
5 ounces prosciutto, thinly sliced
8 ounces Gruyère cheese, thinly sliced
8 thin slices Hungarian or Genoa salami

1. Mix the flour and salt in a medium-size mixing bowl and make a well in the center. Break the eggs into the well and gradually whisk in the wine until blended; then stir in the melted butter. Let stand 10 minutes.

2. Lightly butter a large cast-iron skillet and heat over medium-high heat. Drop the crêpe batter by spoonfuls to make small crêpes the same diameter as the ramekins or

FRENCH CHEESE

The French produce over 300 cheeses, each a reflection of variations in soil, climate, vegetation, and local tastes. From the milk of cows, goats, and sheep, from the green flats of Normandy to the Alps, from little farms and giant cooperatives, the varieties have led the diplomatic Churchill, De Gaulle, Roosevelt, and Sartre each to have been attributed the saying: "A country with 325 cheeses can't be governed." Who knows—but while the average American enjoys approximately 18 pounds of cheese per year, the Frenchman puts away 42!

Much was said about French cheeses in our first book, so we needn't repeat it here. What is new is the recent availability of French raw-milk cheeses in this country. The U.S. Department of Agriculture forbids the importation of cheese made from unpasteurized milk and aged less than 60 days, but fortunately a few bold importers have managed to get these wonderful raw-milk cheeses into the country. While pasteurization may make cheese safe by U.S. sanitary standards, it also kills all the organisms that give a cheese its essential earthy character. Pasteurized cheeses tend to be bland and a poor representation of the inimitable quality of the best French cheeses. Once you've tasted a true raw-milk Brie or Camembert, you'll have really tasted cheese.

Paris . . . the beauty overwhelms . . . the Tuileries . . . the flower stalls . . . the Louvre . . . the sidewalk cafés . . . the style . . . Bertillon . . . the aura of Piaf, Hemingway, Picasso . . . the bateau mouche . . . La Coupole . . . the oyster shuckers . . . crêpes . . . the Arc de Triomphe on Bastille Day . . . riding western style in the Bois de Boulogne . . . Pré Catelan . . . a Charlie Chaplin mime outside of Deux Magots . . . the love of country . . .

"When you are a young French man, you drink Beaujolais. With each decade you mature as do your wines—Bordeaux, Burgundy, Cognac, Armagnac, and in your seventies, Marc de Bourgogne. But when you are French, your whole life you drink Champagne."
—Phillippe la Croix

small soufflé dishes you intend to use. You should be able to cook 6 to 8 crêpes at a time. Cook until the bottom side is golden, about 1 minute. Continue until all the batter is used.

3. Heat the crème fraîche to boiling in a small saucepan to thicken slightly. Remove from heat and stir in the mustard. Season to taste with salt and pepper.

4. Preheat oven to 375°F. Butter 8 individual soufflé dishes or ramekins.

5. Spoon a little of the mustard sauce into the bottom of each prepared dish. Place 1 crêpe on top. Top the crêpe with a thin slice of the prosciutto and a thin slice of the Gruyère. Spoon a little more of the mustard sauce over the cheese.

6. Place another crêpe on top, pressing it down lightly. Top with a slice of the salami and then another slice of the Gruyère. Spoon more of the sauce over the top.

7. Place a third crêpe on top and repeat the prosciutto, cheese, and sauce layer.

8. Top with a final crêpe and cover with more of the mustard cream sauce and one last slice of Gruyère.

9. Bake on a large baking sheet for 20 minutes and then, leaving temperature set at 375°F, broil them 6 inches from the heat until browned, 5 to 7 minutes. Let cool 5 minutes.

10. Holding each dish with a pot holder, run a narrow spatula around the edges. Invert onto warmed individual serving plates. Surround with the remaining mustard sauce and serve immediately.

8 portions

COQ AU VIN

There are many versions of this French classic; ours is a meal in itself. Don't assume that any old wine will do for this dish. We have chosen a St. Julien here, but you can use another hearty red wine that is a personal favorite.

10 slices bacon, diced
2 chickens (2½ to 3 pounds each), quartered
16 small (1 inch) white pearl onions, peeled
6 scallions (green onions, white and green parts), sliced
1 head garlic, cloves separated and peeled
1 pound mushrooms, wiped clean and quartered
3 tablespoons unbleached all-purpose flour
3 cups St. Julien Bordeaux or other good-quality red wine
1 cup Berta's Chicken Stock (page 396) or canned chicken broth
1 teaspoon dried thyme
Salt and freshly ground black pepper, to taste
16 small new potatoes
12 ounces baby carrots, peeled
Chopped fresh parsley (garnish)

1. One day before serving, fry the bacon in a large Dutch oven until crisp. Remove the pieces from the pan, drain on paper towels, and reserve. Brown the chicken pieces in batches in the hot bacon fat. Set the chicken aside.

2. Add the onions, scallions, and garlic to the pan and sauté over medium-high heat for 5 minutes. Add the mushrooms and sauté 5 minutes more.

3. Sprinkle the flour over the vegetables and cook 1 minute. Slowly pour in the wine and stock, stirring constantly. Season with the thyme and salt and pepper to taste. Heat to boiling. Remove from heat; add the bacon, chicken, and potatoes, and distribute evenly. Refrigerate covered overnight.

4. The next day, let the *coq au vin* warm to room temperature before baking.

5. Preheat oven to 350°F.

6. Bake covered in the oven for 1 hour. After 1 hour, add the carrots and stir to distribute. Bake for 50 minutes. The chicken should be almost falling off the bone and the vegetables tender.

7. Spoon the *coq au vin* onto large plates, serving everyone 2 potatoes, 2 onions, and plenty of carrots. Sprinkle with fresh parsley.

8 portions

BLACK BEAN "CASSOULET" SOUP

Our black bean soup is a Silver Palate staple. In this recipe we've dressed it up with lots of hot and garlicky sausages, sweet red peppers, a bit of brown sugar, and unusual spices. This makes a meal when served with a crisp, tart green salad.

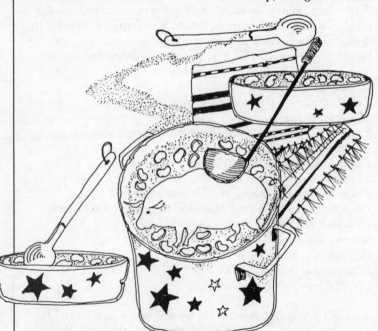

BISTRO FOOD

We don't think bistro food should be limited to France or to wine bars. The conviviality it portrays is something that we'd like to be part of everyday American eating habits. A loaf of crusty bread, a wonderful cheese, something to nosh, and a glass of wine . . . What more could you ask for? Because we're most often "grabbing a bite"—here are some of our suggestions.

A glass of wine, a loaf of bread and . . .

♥ White radishes, sweet butter, Niçoise olives, and chèvre

♥ The first spring salad Niçoise

♥ Bélon oysters, sweet butter, and freshly ground black pepper

♥ Smoked trout, Granny Smith apple slices, and lemon mayonnaise

♥ Country pâté, cornichons, pickled cherries, and green peppercorn mustard

♥ Gravlax, smoked salmon, poached salmon, and dill mustard

♥ Pot au feu with six mustards

♥ Parma ham, olives, and sweet mustard

♥ Hot garlic sausage, green peppercorn mustard, mixed green salad

♥ Grilled beef with small new potatoes

♥ Herb-grilled herring, mustard mayonnaise, and crudités

♥ Sardines, lemon juice, and mayonnaise

♥ Boudin blanc stuffed with pistachios

♥ Country pâté, cornichons, garlic mayonnaise, and Dijon mustard

♥ Rillettes and spinach pâté

♥ Grilled garlic cloves, chèvre, and carpaccio

♥ Grilled sausage, hot potato salad, and mustard

♥ Sliced roast pheasant and mushrooms on toast

♥ Boudin blanc and boudin noir, mustard, and french fries

FOREVER FRANCE

Crêpe Ramekins

Black Bean Cassoulet Soup

Mâche with Sautéed Pears

Crusty French bread

Chocolate Soufflé

Hermitage

FAVORITE PARIS RESTAURANTS

THREE-STAR DINING
L'Archestrate
Le Bernardin
Michel Rostang
Le Pré Catelan
Jamin
BISTROS AND BRASSERIES
Chez L'Ami Louis
Chez Georges
Brasserie Stella
Brasserie Flo
Au Pied de Cochon
Chez Robert
Chez Josephine
Cartet
Brasserie Lipp
GREAT BARS
The Ritz Bar
Crillon Bar
Plaza Athénée
American Bar
Bristol Bar
L'Hôtel Bar

---

2 pounds dried black (turtle) beans
1¼ cups best-quality olive oil
3 cups diced yellow onions
12 cloves garlic, crushed
1 very meaty ham bone or 2 smoked ham hocks
8 quarts water
3½ tablespoons ground cumin
2 tablespoons dried oregano
3 bay leaves
1 tablespoon coarse (kosher) salt
1 tablespoon freshly ground black pepper
Pinch cayenne pepper
8 tablespoons chopped fresh Italian parsley
1¾ to 2 pounds fresh garlic sausage
6 sweet Italian sausage links, cut into 1-inch pieces
6 hot Italian sausage links, cut into 1-inch pieces
1 pound bratwurst, cut into 1-inch pieces
3 medium-size sweet red peppers, cored, seeded, and diced
¼ cup dry sherry
3 tablespoons dark brown sugar
2 tablespoons fresh lemon juice
Sour cream

1. Soak the black beans in water to cover overnight.

2. Heat 1 cup of the oil in a large heavy stock pot over low heat. Add the onions and garlic and sauté until the onions are limp, about 10 minutes.

3. Drain and rinse the beans and add to the stock pot. Add the ham bone and 6 quarts of the water. Stir in the cumin, oregano, bay leaves, salt, pepper, cayenne, and 3 tablespoons of the parsley. Heat to boiling. Reduce heat to medium and cook uncovered at a slow rolling boil for 2 hours, skimming foam from the top and stirring occasionally to prevent sticking.

4. Place the garlic sausage in a medium-size saucepan and add the remaining 2 quarts water. Heat to boiling. Reduce heat to low and simmer for 40 minutes. Drain. Remove casings and cut into ½-inch slices.

5. Heat the remaining ¼ cup oil in a large heavy skillet over medium heat. Add the Italian sausages and sauté until browned. Remove the sausages with a slotted spoon.

6. In the same skillet, sauté the bratwurst until browned. Remove with a slotted spoon.

7. After 2 hours of cooking, process 2 cups of the beans in a food processor fitted with a steel blade until smooth and return to the pot. Continue to cook for 30 minutes.

8. Add all the sausages and the red peppers and cook for another 30 minutes.

9. Remove the ham bone from the soup, shred the meat and return to the pot. Stir in the sherry, sugar, and lemon juice.

10. Cook over medium heat until the beans are very soft and the soup is thick, 30 to 45 minutes. Stir in the remaining 5 tablespoons chopped parsley. Taste and adjust seasonings.

11. Ladle the soup into soup bowls and dollop each serving with sour cream.

16 portions

WHITE SAUSAGE RAGOUT

This white sausage ragout is a refreshing change, cooked with celery, fresh tomatoes, and lots of dill and parsley. The whole garlic cloves are soft and sweet. Serve with a light red wine or a deep white Burgundy.

¼ to ½ cup best-quality olive oil
3 pounds veal sausages and pork sausages, cut into 1-inch slices
3 cups 1-inch pieces celery
2 cups water
12 whole garlic cloves, unpeeled
1 pound ripe plum tomatoes, quartered
1 cup canned chicken broth
1 cup Fresh Tomato Sauce (page 397)
10 large fresh basil leaves or 1 teaspoon dried
½ cup plus 2 tablespoons chopped fresh Italian parsley
½ cup chopped fresh dill
Salt and freshly ground black pepper, to taste

1. Heat ¼ cup oil in a large skillet over medium-high heat. Add the sausages and cook until browned. Remove to a heavy casserole.

2. In the same skillet, sauté the celery for 5 minutes, adding more oil if needed. Add the celery to the casserole.

3. Heat the water to boiling in a small saucepan. Drop in the garlic and simmer over medium heat for 5 minutes. Drain, rinse under cold running water, and slip the peels off. Add the garlic to the casserole.

4. Add the tomatoes, broth, tomato sauce, basil, ½ cup parsley, the dill, and salt and pepper to taste to the casserole. Simmer covered over medium heat for 10 minutes. Remove the cover and stir well. Simmer uncovered, stirring occasionally, for 20 minutes.

5. Serve over angel hair pasta, accompanied by a crisp green salad.

6 to 8 portions

BURGUNDY

The art of making wine has been going on for over 2,000 years in Burgundy, and it is a fine art indeed.

The vineyards of Burgundy are planted along a stretch of sloping land known as the Côte d'Or. The wines vary from the rich and velvety reds of Gevrey-Chambertin and Nuits-Saint-Georges, to the fruity light reds of Beaujolais, Fleurie, Mercurey, to the celebrated dry whites of Meursault, Corton-Charlemagne, Chassagne-Montrachet, and Chablis, to the lighter whites of Mâcon and Pouilly-Fuissé.

The vineyards of Burgundy are often small and frequently are tended by a number of growers. The bottling system is different than that of Bordeaux, where each château has one owner. While the names of Burgundies come from the villages where the grapes are grown, the grapes are often sold off to *négociants* who mix and match the grapes of different growers. Thus it is important to find a négociant whose product you like and trust. While you may have tasted a Morey-Saint-Denis you like, for example, its quality may differ from one négociant to another, even though the name remains the same. Some of the better négociants are Bouchard Père et Fils, Louis Jadot, Louis Latour, Joseph Drouhin, and Georges Duboeuf.

There are also estate-bottled wines in Burgundy. Look for *mis au domaine* or *mis en bouteilles par le propriétaire* on the label to distinguish these bottles. They are likely to be the best and most expensive Burgundies.

The rich reds of Burgundy come from the Pinot Noir grape, the lighter Beaujolais-style wines come from the Gamay grape, and most of the whites come from the Chardonnay grape. The Pinot Blanc grape is also grown, and the Aligoté produces the wine thought to blend best with cassis to produce the classic aperitif kir.

The wines of Burgundy have glamorous-sounding names. However, it should be kept in mind that most of these evocative names are one and the same as the names of the tiny and picturesque villages that make up the Côte d'Or.

BORDEAUX

Bordeaux is the most important wine region in France and is considered by many to be the wine capital of the world. It is a diverse area that produces a multiplicity of different types of wine. The city of Bordeaux is in the center of the region banded by two rivers, the Dordogne and the Garonne, which meet and flow into the Gironde, which in turn descends 50 miles into the Atlantic Ocean. Thus, most of the wines of Bordeaux are river wines, with the majority of reds produced north of the city and of whites produced to the south. Médoc, Saint-Emilion, and Pomerol are the major areas that produce red Bordeaux. Graves, Sauternes, and Barsac are known for whites, ranging from very dry to sweet dessert wines. There is a strict hierarchy to wine classification in Bordeaux, and only five estates have earned the aristocratic *premier cru* title— Château Lafite, Château Margaux, Château Latour, Château Haut-Brion, and Château Mouton-Rothschild. The classification dates from 1855 and is confusing, to say the least, when one considers that perhaps the best and most famed Bordeaux wine, Château Pétrus, has never been classified.

Red Bordeaux wines are made chiefly from three varietals: Cabernet Sauvignon, Cabernet Franc, and Merlot. White Bordeaux wines are made from the Sémillon, Sauvignon Blanc, and Merlot Blanc grapes. Almost all Bordeaux are made from blending varieties of grapes according to the theories and tastes of different growers. Most Bordeaux on the market are either a regional bottling of a Bordeaux Rouge or Bordeaux Blanc or a specific château bottling. The latter tend to be the better wines as they are always made from a single harvest at one vineyard. Wines bottled at a particular château will be labeled *mis en bouteilles au château* and are guaranteed to be authentic.

There are over 2,000 different châteaux in Bordeaux and it is impossible to make an accurate listing here. Our advice is to enjoy red and white Bordeaux table wines as reliable everyday wines, and seek out the advice of a reputable wine merchant concerning grand or vintage Bordeaux for special occasions.

POTATO AND CELERY ROOT PUREE

The concentrated flavor of celery root adds a real zest to the blandness of potatoes. This is one of our very favorite vegetable combinations. Serve it with a roast meat dish.

9 large potatoes, peeled and diced
2 pounds celery root (celeriac), peeled and diced
6 tablespoons (¾ stick) unsalted butter, room temperature
½ cup heavy or whipping cream
Salt and freshly ground black pepper, to taste

1. Place the potatoes in a large saucepan and add water to cover. Heat to boiling. Reduce heat and simmer over medium heat until tender. At the same time, simmer the celery root in water to cover in another saucepan until tender. Drain the potatoes and celery root separately.

2. Place the potatoes in a mixer bowl. Cut the butter into small pieces and add to the potatoes. Beat with an electric mixer until fluffy. Beat in the cream. Process the celery root in a food processor fitted with a steel blade or a blender until puréed and add to the potatoes. Beat until blended. Season with salt and pepper to taste. Serve immediately.

6 to 8 portions

PRUNE AND ARMAGNAC PUREE

Marvelous prunes plumped and blended with Armagnac and black pepper. Serve stuffed in one half of a baked, scooped-out sweet potato shell (fill the other half with Sweet Potato and Banana Purée; page 288).

1 pound pitted prunes
3 tablespoons unsalted butter
⅓ cup Armagnac
Freshly ground black pepper, to taste
Thin strips lemon zest (garnish)

1. Place the prunes in a medium-size saucepan and add water to cover. Simmer uncovered over medium heat for 30 minutes. Drain.

2. Process the prunes, butter, Armagnac, and lots of freshly ground pepper in a food processor fitted with a steel blade until smooth. Serve immediately, garnished with lemon zest.

6 portions

SASSY GINGER SALUTE

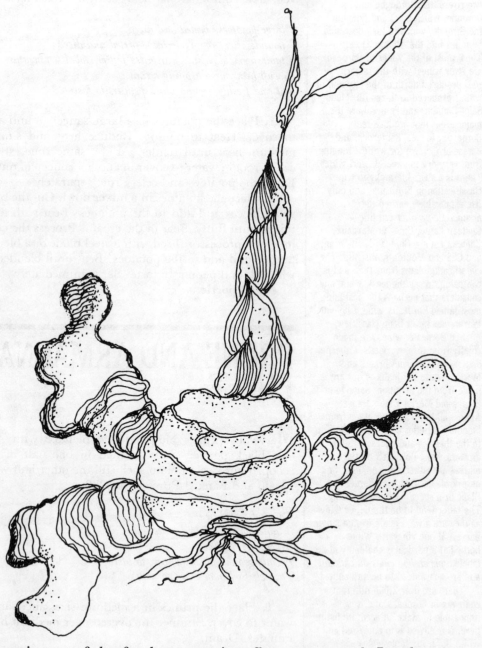

Ginger is one of the freshest, zestiest flavors around. Its clean taste punches up recipes and gives them sass. Be adventurous with fresh, ground, and crystallized ginger—if you've limited it to ginger-bread, you're doing your cooking an injustice.

GINGER DRUMSTICKS

These chicken drumsticks make great hors d'oeuvres or wonderful lunchtime eating.

24 chicken drumsticks
1 cup soy sauce
⅓ cup sesame oil*
½ cup sesame mustard*
3 tablespoons fresh lemon juice
2 cups fresh bread crumbs
1 tablespoon chopped fresh ginger root
2 teaspoons chopped fresh garlic
Salt and freshly ground black pepper, to taste

1. Marinate the drumsticks overnight in the soy sauce in the refrigerator.
2. Preheat oven to 350°F.
3. Drain the chicken and place in rows on a large baking sheet. Using a pastry brush, brush each drumstick with a thin coating of the sesame oil.
4. Whisk the mustard and lemon juice together and brush generously over each drumstick.
5. Combine the bread crumbs, ginger, and garlic and sprinkle evenly over the top and sides of each drumstick. Sprinkle with salt and pepper.
6. Bake 1 hour, covering with aluminum foil if the drumsticks get too brown. Serve warm or at room temperature.

24 chicken drumsticks

*available in Oriental or specialty food shops

"Man loves company even if it is only that of a small burning candle."
—Georg Christoph Lichtenberg

GINGER

Ginger has a sharp and pungent flavor that marries well with many foods. Its beautiful fragrance is most familiar to us in Oriental cuisine, where ginger is an integral flavoring, but it also has enjoyed popularity in the Western world—the British love their ginger marmalade, Americans their gingerbread.

Ginger comes in several forms— as fresh ginger root, in crystallized chunks, and dried and ground. Ground ginger is the best for baking; crystallized is delicious in chutneys and desserts or with after-dinner coffee. Ginger root is wonderful for cooking when you want intense flavor. The root is fibrous and should be peeled and then either cut into rounds, grated, or finely minced. Store fresh ginger root in a cool, dark place or in the refrigerator.

VEAL SCALOPPINE WITH GINGER AND LIME

A pungent sauce for veal scaloppine. The ginger adds spice, while the lime and pink peppercorns lend a subtle sweetness and pretty pink and green pastel colors.

1 large lime
6 tablespoons confectioners' sugar
½ cup water
1 pound veal scallops, pounded thin
3 tablespoons unbleached all-purpose flour
Salt and freshly ground black pepper, to taste
4 tablespoons (½ stick) unsalted butter
1 cup Berta's Chicken Stock (page 396) or veal stock
1½ tablespoons finely chopped fresh ginger root
1 tablespoon pink peppercorns*

1. Cut the zest of the lime into a fine julienne. Squeeze the juice from the lime and reserve. Combine the lime zest, sugar, and water in a small saucepan. Heat to boiling. Reduce the heat and simmer uncovered until most of the water has evaporated and the zest has candied in the clear syrup, 15 to 20 minutes. Do not let the zest brown. Remove from the heat and set aside.

2. Lightly coat the veal scallops with the flour seasoned to taste with salt and pepper. Melt 2 tablespoons of the butter in a large skillet over high heat. Add the veal scallops and quickly sauté 1 to 2 minutes per side. Remove to a serving platter and keep warm while making the sauce.

3. Add the stock, ginger, reserved lime juice, and the peppercorns to the skillet. Heat to boiling and cook, stirring occasionally, until reduced by about half. Whisk in the remaining 2 tablespoons butter and season to taste with salt and pepper.

4. Pour the sauce over the scaloppine and garnish with a few strips of the candied lime zest. Serve immediately.

4 portions

*available in specialty food shops

WHOLE CHICKEN BAKED IN SALT

Baking in salt creates an extremely moist chicken. The lemon and ginger cooked in the bird's cavity perfumes the bird. Serve lots of lemon wedges on the side.

2 tablespoons vodka
1 roasting chicken (3½ to 4 pounds), ready to cook
1 piece (2 inches) fresh ginger root, cut into 8 pieces
1 lemon, cut into 8 pieces
3 scallions (green onions), coarsely chopped
4 pounds coarse (kosher) salt

1. Rub 1 tablespoon of the vodka into the large cavity of the chicken. Place the ginger, lemon, and scallions in the cavity and tie the legs securely together.

2. Rub the remaining tablespoon of vodka over the outside of the chicken. Let stand until the skin dries, about 1 hour.

3. Wrap the chicken in a double thickness of cheesecloth, tying the ends over the breast.

4. Heat the salt in a large wok over high heat, stirring frequently, until the salt is hot to the touch, 7 to 10 minutes. Remove all but about 1 inch of the salt to a bowl.

5. Place the chicken, breast side up, on top of the salt in the wok. Cover completely with the remaining hot salt.

6. Cover the wok and cook the chicken over medium-low heat for about 2 hours. Test for doneness by scraping away

GIVE MY REGARDS TO BROADWAY

Escargot-Stuffed Shells

Flank Steak with Garlic-Ginger Sauce

Risotto Porcini Casserole

Braised and Glazed Leeks

Poached pears with Ruby Port Sabayon

Côte Rôtie or Brunello di Montalcino

Hold a "Give My Regards to Broadway" Party with each guest portraying a favorite Broadway musical star. Cover the walls with old theater posters and encourage after-dinner performances by any guests who are willing.

the salt near one thigh and piercing it with a knife to see if the juices run clear.

7. When the chicken is done, carefully lift it out of the wok by the cheesecloth knot on the top of the bird. Carefully unwrap the cheesecloth and transfer the chicken to a serving platter. Carve and serve immediately.

4 portions

FLANK STEAK WITH GARLIC-GINGER SAUCE

Garlic-Ginger Sauce (recipe follows)
1 flank steak (2 pounds)
1 tablespoon soy sauce
1 tablespoon sesame oil

1. Make the sauce.

2. Preheat broiler.

3. Sprinkle both sides of the steak with the soy sauce and sesame oil and rub into the meat.

4. Broil 6 inches from the heat for 5 to 7 minutes per side, depending on desired doneness. Cut the steak diagonally into thin slices.

5. Overlap 5 or 6 slices on each serving plate and top with several spoonfuls of the garlic-ginger sauce. Serve hot or at room temperature.

6 portions

GARLIC-GINGER SAUCE

¾ cup olive oil
6 cloves garlic, finely minced
3 tablespoons chopped fresh ginger root
4 large carrots, peeled and cut into small dice
5 scallions (green onions, white part and 2 inches green), sliced
1 cup dry white wine
½ cup water
1 tablespoon dried oregano
Pinch red pepper flakes
½ cup chopped fresh Italian parsley
Salt and freshly ground black pepper, to taste

1. Heat the oil in a medium-size skillet over medium heat. Add the garlic, ginger, and carrots and sauté for 10 minutes.

2. Stir in the scallions and sauté 2 minutes more. Add the wine, water, oregano, and red pepper flakes and simmer uncovered over low heat for 30 minutes.

3. Stir in the parsley and season to taste with salt and pepper.

3½ cups

CANDIED GINGER BISCUITS

Serve these flavorful crunchy biscuits with pork, turkey, or chicken. They're terrific for sandwiching leftover baked ham and great hot out of the oven with unsalted butter.

½ cup (1 stick) unsalted butter, room temperature
⅓ cup packed brown sugar
2 tablespoons molasses
¼ cup apple cider or juice
2 cups unbleached all-purpose flour
1 tablespoon ground ginger
½ teaspoon baking soda
½ cup finely minced candied (crystallized) ginger

1. Cream the butter and sugar in a mixer bowl. Beat in the molasses, then the apple cider.
2. Combine the flour, ground ginger, baking soda, and candied ginger. Stir into the butter mixture with a wooden spoon. Wrap in plastic wrap and refrigerate 1 hour.
3. Preheat the oven to 350°F. Lightly grease a cookie sheet.
4. Roll out the dough ¾ inch thick on a lightly floured surface. Cut into rounds with a 1½-inch biscuit cutter and place on the prepared cookie sheet. Gather up the scraps, reroll, and cut as many biscuits as possible from the remaining dough.
5. Bake until lightly browned, about 15 minutes.
16 to 20 biscuits

THREE-GINGER COOKIES

We are absolutely crazy about ginger. These cookies—with ground ginger, fresh ginger, and crystallized ginger—satisfy our cravings.

¾ cup (1½ sticks) unsalted butter, room temperature
1 cup packed dark brown sugar
¼ cup molasses
1 egg
2¼ cups unbleached all-purpose flour
2 teaspoons ground ginger
2 teaspoons baking soda
½ teaspoon salt
1½ tablespoons finely chopped fresh ginger root
½ cup finely chopped crystallized ginger

1. Cream the butter and brown sugar in a large mixer bowl. Beat in the molasses and then the egg.
2. Sift the flour, ground ginger, baking soda, and salt

FALL FRUIT DESSERTS

♥ Plums simmered in Zinfandel, topped with orange and lemon zest
♥ Seedless grapes topped with sour cream and brown sugar, lightly broiled
♥ Three types of grapes macerated in Sauternes
♥ Pear halves baked with brown sugar, Poire Williams, and chopped hazelnuts
♥ Apples baked with maple syrup
♥ A bowl of Concord grapes and a bowl of peanuts in the shell
♥ Wedges of Macoun, Empire, Cortland, and Golden Delicious apples served with chilled glasses of Late Harvest Riesling
♥ Applesauce and homemade cookies
♥ Poached pears and gingerbread
♥ Crenshaw melon wedges drizzled with port

"The highest form of bliss is living with a certain degree of folly."
—Erasmus

together. Stir into the butter mixture with a wooden spoon until blended. Add the fresh and crystallized gingers and stir until well mixed.

3. Refrigerate the dough covered at least 2 hours or overnight.

4. Preheat oven to 350°F. Grease cookie sheets.

5. Shape the dough into 1-inch balls and place about 2 inches apart on the cookie sheets. Bake until browned, 10 minutes.

6. Remove to wire racks to cool completely.

3½ to 4 dozen cookies

LEMON-GINGER COOKIES

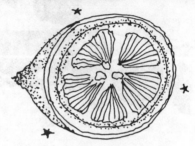

Another tempting ginger cookie with the tart complement of lemon. These snaps are very fragile but well worth the effort. Serve with tea, fruit, or sorbet.

½ cup (1 stick) unsalted butter, room temperature
2 tablespoons brown sugar
⅔ cup granulated sugar
Finely grated zest of 1 lemon
Juice of 1 lemon
¼ cup pure maple syrup
1 teaspoon orange extract
1 cup cake flour
1 teaspoon ground ginger
½ cup finely chopped crystallized ginger

1. Preheat oven to 325°F. Line cookie sheets with aluminum foil and butter the foil.

2. Cream the butter and sugars in a large mixer bowl. Beat in the lemon zest and juice and maple syrup and then the orange extract.

3. Sift the flour and ground ginger together. Add the crystallized ginger and toss to coat. Stir into the butter mixture.

4. Drop teaspoons of the batter 3 inches apart on the cookie sheets. Be sure to leave plenty of space for the cookies to spread. Bake the cookies for 12 to 15 minutes, watching closely so that they do not burn. They will be thin and lacy.

5. Let the cookies cool on the sheets about 4 minutes and then remove with a thin metal spatula to wire racks to cool completely.

4 dozen cookies

MORE AUTUMN CRAVINGS

...Log cabins...jumping in a pile of leaves...*shabu shabu*...baked apples...McDonald's french fries ...antique dollhouses...herby baked baby eggplants...Dr. Zhivago ...big woolly sweaters...opening a bottle of Pétrus...fried eggs with *pancetta*...Sarabeth's Goldi Lox Omelet...New York is Book Country Sunday...red cabbage and apples ...to be cozy...Concord grapes... bay scallops with fresh lime...wild rice...gravy...

"How do they taste? They taste like more." —H.L. Mencken

APPLES AND PEARS

We can't imagine autumn without crunchy apples and elegant pears. While these fruits epitomize the season with their skins of burnished hues, they also remind us of the comforts of our childhood and Mom's cooking. We remember the joys of coming home from school to a big pot of warm homemade applesauce, and Saturday suppers that ended with steaming spoonfuls of brown betty. Whether old family favorites or new inventions, recipes with apples and pears always fill us with a cozy sense of delicious contentment.

BAKED CHICKEN WITH CIDER AND APPLES

This chicken is highlighted by the crisp tingle of the apple cider marinade and the sweetly mellow flavor of the apple slices. It's an easy and delicious dinner for friends and family.

2 chickens (2½ to 3 pounds each), quartered
2 cups apple cider
1 cup unbleached all-purpose flour
1 tablespoon ground ginger
2 teaspoons ground cinnamon
Salt and freshly ground black pepper, to taste
3 tablespoons brown sugar
⅓ cup applejack
2 apples, cored and cut into thin wedges

Make a fruit centerpiece special by taking care to polish each fruit individually. Nothing looks more enticing than a big basket of shiny red apples or an earthenware bowl of deep purple plums.

1. One day before serving, place the chicken pieces in a shallow dish. Pour the cider over the chicken and marinate overnight in the refrigerator, turning the pieces occasionally.

2. Preheat oven to 350°F.

3. Remove the chicken from the cider but reserve the cider. Mix the flour, ginger, cinnamon, and salt and pepper to taste in a shallow bowl. Dredge the chicken with the flour mixture and place skin side up in a shallow baking pan.

4. Bake the chicken for 40 minutes.

5. Meanwhile, combine the reserved cider, the brown sugar, applejack, and apple slices.

6. Pour the marinade mixture over the chicken and bake 25 minutes more, basting occasionally with the pan juices. Serve immediately.

6 portions

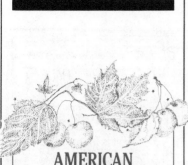

AMERICAN COUNTRY MENU

Wild Mushroom Tart

Baked Chicken with Cider and Apples

Bulgur Pilaf

Baked Kumquats and Parsnips

Spicy Layer Cake

Apple Cider

American folk art has such charm that its spirit makes your home immediately cozy and warm. You might want to create an American country ambiance with bright quilts as tablecloths, and herb wreaths as centerpieces. Roll up the carpets and have a good old-fashioned hoedown with American music spanning the decades.

"All millionaires love a baked apple."
—Ronald Firbank

JUNE'S APPLE CRISP

A simple, crunchy, old-fashioned apple recipe that is a most comforting conclusion on a chilly autumn evening.

5 Granny Smith apples, peeled, cored, and thinly sliced
1½ tablespoons fresh lemon juice
1 cup unbleached all-purpose flour
1 cup sugar
1½ teaspoons ground cinnamon
½ teaspoon salt
½ cup (1 stick) unsalted butter, cold, cut into pieces

1. Preheat oven to 350°F. Grease an 8-inch cake pan.

2. Place a layer of apple slices in the pan and sprinkle with some of the lemon juice. Repeat the layers until all the apples are in the pan. Lightly press down on the apples to even them.

3. Process the flour, sugar, cinnamon, and salt in a food processor fitted with a steel blade just to combine. Add the butter and process, using repeated pulses, until the mixture resembles coarse meal.

4. Press the crumb mixture evenly over the apples, making sure the edges are well sealed.

5. Bake until the top is golden and the apples are tender, about 1 hour. Serve warm with ice cream.

6 portions

GRANNY SMITH SORBET

Serve between courses of a formal autumn dinner to clear the palate.

5 medium-large Granny Smith apples, peeled, cored, and diced
½ cup fresh lemon juice
¾ cup sugar
1½ cups water
2 tablespoons Calvados

1. Process the apples and lemon juice in a food processor fitted with a steel blade until smooth. Add the sugar, water, and Calvados and process until thoroughly blended.
2. Freeze in an ice cream maker, following manufacturer's instructions.

4½ cups

POACHED APPLES STUFFED WITH GORGONZOLA

The luscious combination of apples, cheese, and wine takes on a new sophistication in this dessert.

2 cups Marsala
2 cups sweet red wine
2 cups water
1 cup sugar
3 tablespoons fresh lemon juice
2 strips lemon zest
2 tablespoons ground coriander
6 Golden Delicious apples, peeled
Sauternes Sabayon (page 108)
6 ounces sweet Gorgonzola

1. Combine the Marsala, red wine, water, sugar, lemon juice, lemon zest, and coriander in a large deep saucepan. Heat to boiling and add the apples. Poach uncovered for 20 minutes. Cool completely in liquid.
2. Meanwhile, make the sabayon.
3. Remove the cooled apples from the poaching liquid and core them from the bottom with an apple corer, leaving the tops with the stems intact. Stuff the hollow of each apple with 1 ounce of the cheese.
4. Place each apple on an individual dessert plate, stem end up, and spoon the sabayon over and around the apple. Serve with a knife and fork.

6 portions

PICKING PEARS

ANJOU: a good eating and cooking green pear, available October through June.

BARTLETT: a widely available eating and cooking pear with a classic bell shape and greenish-yellow speckled skin.

BOSC: a longer pear with a distinctly tapered neck and sandy-textured golden brown skin. The creamy ivory interior makes it a good eating and cooking pear.

COMICE: a rotund pear with thick green skin and flesh that is sweet, juicy, and buttery all at once—our favorite eating pear.

FORELLE: the perfect pear for the partridge, this slender golden variety with its blush of red reminds us of a Christmas tree ornament.

PASSE CRASSANE: a new pear from California that is gaining in popularity and tastes like a cross between an Anjou and Comice.

RED BARTLETT: the same as a regular Bartlett, but with an enticing bright red skin.

SECKEL: the tiniest pear, with reddish skin. We like it in chutneys and spiced conserves.

HOMEMADE APPLESAUCE

Just like Julee's dad Frank used to make. This applesauce is delicious when served still warm, but it is also nice cold, especially with oatmeal cookies.

20 Granny Smith apples, peeled, cored, and cut into chunks
1 ½ cups apple cider
½ cup packed brown sugar
1 tablespoon ground cinnamon
½ teaspoon ground nutmeg

1. Place the apples in a large saucepan and pour in the cider. Simmer uncovered over medium-high heat for 40 minutes, stirring every 5 minutes or so to prevent sticking.

2. Stir in the sugar, cinnamon, and nutmeg and continue to cook, stirring to break down the apples, until it is a chunky sauce.

About 7 cups

PEAR TART WITH POIRE WILLIAMS

A beautiful open tart filled with overlapping layers of thinly sliced pears and fortified with a sprinkling of potent Poire Williams.

PASTRY:

1 cup unbleached all-purpose flour
½ cup (1 stick) unsalted butter, cold, cut into small pieces
1 ½ tablespoons sugar
Pinch salt
2 to 3 tablespoons ice water

FILLING:

5 medium-ripe pear halves, peeled and cored
5 tablespoons sugar
4 tablespoons (½ stick) unsalted butter
1 tablespoon Poire Williams or other pear liqueur

GLAZE:

⅓ cup apricot jam
2 tablespoons Poire Williams

GARNISH:

Whipped cream
Poire Williams

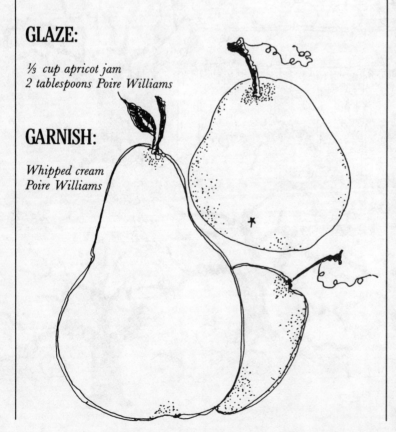

FRUIT GRATINEES

An elegant way to serve fresh fruit for dessert is to fill individual gratin dishes with colorful arrangements of seasonal fruit, cover with *Sauternes* or *Ruby Port Sabayon,* and place them under the broiler for a few minutes. The fruit will stay fresh and cool while the sugar and cream in the sabayon caramelize to form a golden brown custard.

Special effects and accents may be added by infusing julienne strips of orange, lemon, or lime peel with intense color and flavor. Place the strips of julienne peel in a small saucepan and cover with a few tablespoons of green crème de menthe. Cook over medium heat until the peel is slightly candied and most of the liquid has evaporated. The result will be a deep green mint-flavored strip. The same technique can be used with grenadine to obtain brilliant red strips. The peels should be drained and then scattered on top of the sabayon as an accent.

Use your imagination to create arrangements inspired by your favorite artists. Here are some of our favorite combinations:

MATISSE

Fill each gratin dish with 2 wedges of quartered kiwi fruit, 2 sections pink grapefruit, 2 wedges nectarine, and 2 wedges of peach. Ladle enough Sauternes Sabayon to cover fruit. Dot with 5 fresh raspberries, 2 strips grenadine-infused fruit peel, 2 strips crème de menthe–infused fruit peel. Place gratin dishes on a baking sheet 6 inches from a preheated broiler. Broil until lightly browned, about 2 minutes. Serve immediately.

PICASSO–BLUE PERIOD

Fill each gratin dish with 2 wedges of quartered purple plum, ½ cup blueberries, and ⅓ cup blackberries. Cover fruit with *Ruby Port Sabayon* and dot with a few strips of blue-curaçao–infused lemon peel. Place gratin dishes on a baking sheet 6 inches from a preheated broiler. Broil until puffed and browned, about 2 minutes. Serve immediately.

SEURAT

Fill each gratin dish with blueberries, raspberries, blackberries, and *fraises des bois* (or regular strawberries cut into blueberry-size dice) arranged in a single layer of alternating colors. Cover with *Sauternes Sabayon*. Finely mince ½ tablespoon crème-de-menthe–infused citrus peel and ½ tablespoon grenadine-infused citrus peel, and scatter this on the sabayon to give a pointillistic effect. Place gratin dishes on a baking sheet 6 inches from a preheated broiler. Broil until puffed and golden, 1 to 2 minutes. Serve immediately.

VAN GOGH

Arrange 2 fruit "flowers" in each gratin dish using peach or nectarine slices in a circular overlapping pattern. Fill the centers with a hulled large strawberry or a few raspberries. Cover the fruit with *Sauternes Sabayon*. Arrange julienne strips of grenadine-infused citrus peel in a round petal pattern following the lines of the fruit slices. Place gratin dishes on a baking sheet 6 inches from a preheated broiler. Broil until puffed and golden, 1 to 2 minutes, Serve immediately.

"The gentlemen did like a drop too much ... more Port than was exactly portable."
—Thomas Hood

1. To make the pastry, process the flour, butter, sugar, and salt in a food processor fitted with a steel blade until the mixture resembles coarse meal. With the machine running, add enough of the water for the dough to gather into a ball. Remove from the machine, dust with a little flour, and wrap with plastic wrap. Refrigerate at least 1 hour.

2. Roll out the dough into a 12-inch circle on a lightly floured surface. Line a 9-inch tart pan with the dough. Trim and crimp the edges. Prick the bottom of the dough with a fork. Freeze while the filling is being prepared.

3. Preheat oven to 400°F.

4. To make the filling, cut each of the pear halves crosswise into slices as thin as possible, maintaining the shape of the pear half by keeping the slices in place. Fan 4 of the pear halves in the tart shell, filling in the gaps with the fifth pear half. (The slices should be arranged so that they look like a large blossom.)

5. Sprinkle the pears with the sugar. Cut the butter into small bits and dot the pears with the butter. Sprinkle with the Poire Williams.

6. Bake until the pears are caramelized and the crust is well browned, 50 to 60 minutes. Let cool 10 minutes.

7. While the tart is baking, make the glaze. Heat the apricot jam and Poire Williams in a small saucepan until melted and smooth. Spoon the glaze over the baked tart.

8. Cut the tart into wedges and serve warm, topped with a dollop of whipped cream flavored to taste with Poire Williams.

6 to 8 portions

RUBY PORT SABAYON

The perfect accompaniment to peeled Comice pears that have been gently poached in a bottle of California red wine laced with cinnamon sticks and lemon zest and sweetened to taste with sugar.

3 egg yolks
½ cup superfine sugar
⅔ cup ruby port
Several thin strips of lemon zest

1. Whisk the egg yolks and sugar together in a heavy large saucepan. Cook, whisking constantly, over medium-low heat until thick and creamy, about 7 minutes.

2. Place the pan in a larger pan filled with simmering water. Slowly whisk in the port and lemon zest. Continue to whisk until the mixture froths to almost triple in volume and is pale pink-brown in color.

3. Serve immediately or place in a large bowl of ice water and whisk until cold. Store covered in the refrigerator up to 3 days.

3 cups

AMERICA GIVES THANKS

Thanksgiving is the most traditional menu of the year for American families. However creative we are in celebrating the bounty of autumn, we still choose to serve the dinner of the Pilgrims, *sans* muskets . This is the time for families and old friends to gather and give heartfelt thanks for our very remarkable country.

ROAST TURKEY WITH GRAND MARNIER APRICOT STUFFING

Grand Marnier Apricot Stuffing (recipe follows)
1 turkey (about 21 pounds), ready to cook
2 oranges, cut in half
1 teaspoon dried thyme
Salt and freshly ground black pepper, to taste
2 cups (4 sticks) butter, room temperature

1. Make the stuffing.
2. Preheat oven to 450°F.
3. Rinse the turkey inside and out and pat dry. Squeeze the juice of the oranges all over the turkey and in the neck and body cavities. Spoon the stuffing loosely into the cavities. Set aside any extra stuffing. Sew up the cavities or close with small trussing skewers.
4. Place the turkey on a roasting rack in a roasting pan. Sprinkle all over with the thyme and salt and pepper to taste. Spread the butter all over the turkey. Turn breast side up in the pan and cover the pan with aluminum foil.
5. Place the turkey in the oven and reduce the heat to 325°F. Roast for 3 hours. Remove the foil and roast, basting occasionally, until the juices run clear when the meaty part of a thigh is pierced with a sharp skewer, about 2 more hours. Bake the leftover stuffing in a baking dish at 325°F for 30 minutes.
6. Let the turkey stand, covered with foil, for 15 minutes before carving.

12 to 14 portions

GRAND MARNIER APRICOT STUFFING

A Thanksgiving stuffing laced with many of our favorite ingredients.

1 cup diced dried apricots
1 ½ cups Grand Marnier
Turkey liver and heart
1 cup (2 sticks) unsalted butter
2 cups coarsely chopped celery
1 large yellow onion, chopped
1 pound bulk pork sausage
1 pound herb stuffing mix
1 cup slivered almonds
2 cups Berta's Chicken Stock (page 396) or canned chicken broth
½ teaspoon dried thyme
Salt and freshly ground black pepper, to taste

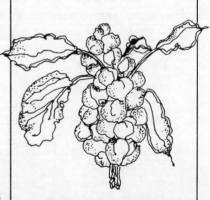

1. Place the apricots and 1 cup of the Grand Marnier in a small saucepan. Heat to boiling. Remove from the heat and set aside. Simmer the turkey liver and heart in water to cover in a small saucepan for 5 minutes; set aside to cool

2. Melt ½ cup of the butter in a large skillet over medium heat. Add the celery and onion and sauté for 10 minutes. Transfer to a large mixing bowl.

3. Cook the pork sausage in the same skillet, crumbling with a fork, until it is no longer pink. Remove from the heat and add to the celery mixture.

4. Add the stuffing mix, apricots with liquid, and almonds. Finely dice the turkey livers and heart and add to the stuffing mixture. Stir to combine.

5. Heat the remaining ½ cup butter and the stock in a small saucepan just until the butter melts. Pour over the stuffing mixture and add the remaining ½ cup Grand Marnier. Stir well to moisten the stuffing. Season with the thyme and salt and pepper to taste.

Enough for a 21- to 24-pound turkey

BRUSSELS SPROUTS WITH MAPLE AND WALNUT VINAIGRETTE

Combined with nuts and maple syrup this vegetable glistens and reminds us of family gatherings—all the good warm times.

4 cups Brussels sprouts
4 tablespoons sherry vinegar
4 tablespoons pure maple syrup
1 tablespoon Dijon-style mustard
½ cup walnut oil
Pinch freshly grated nutmeg
Salt and freshly ground black pepper, to taste
1 cup coarsely chopped walnuts

1. Cut an X in the bottom of each Brussels sprout. Steam until tender but still firm.

2. Meanwhile, whisk the vinegar, maple syrup, and mustard together. Gradually whisk in the oil. Season with the nutmeg and salt and pepper to taste.

3. Toss the hot Brussels sprouts with the walnuts and vinaigrette. Serve immediately.

8 portions

THANKSGIVING WINE

On Thanksgiving we like to serve an American wine. And although turkey is a member of the poultry family, it is a bird of such robust flavor that our choice is Zinfandel, California's most distinctive contribution to wine making. It has the deep, red, sturdy taste of berries and spices.

Our other choices for turkey would include Beaujolais Nouveau, a California Chardonnay, Merlot, or perhaps a Cabernet Sauvignon. If you prefer white, Champagne lightens the meal, as does a Sauvignon Blanc.

CALIFORNIA ZINFANDEL

Zinfandel is considered the "mystery vine of California," as it grows nowhere else in the world and seems to grow effortlessly all over the Golden State.

Zinfandel was considered a table wine, often used in blends, until the wine explosion in the 1960s. Then growers realized the grape's potential for producing a noble wine and began to plant it in the best locations in prime wine districts, and vinified it with skill and care. The grape offers a wide range of possibilities for vinifying, and the price of California Zinfandels tends to vary from some of the least expensive varietals to one of the most expensive California wines.

Many Zinfandels are fruity, light wines similar to Beaujolais, while the newer Zinfandels are being produced as big, deep, memorable wines worthy of California's best labels. Late harvest Zinfandels tend to be truly extraordinary wines with hefty bouquets of melted chocolate and wild raspberries and the sweetness of port. They do not go well with main dishes and are best served with dried fruits and freshly cracked nuts. Look for Mayacamas and Ridge vineyards.

THANKSGIVING POTATOES

The combination of butter, cream cheese, and sour cream make these mashed potatoes super rich and a special treat on Thanksgiving. We guarantee that they'll become a welcome addition to your family's traditional meal.

9 large baking potatoes, peeled and diced
½ cup (1 stick) unsalted butter, room temperature
12 ounces cream cheese, room temperature
¾ cup sour cream
½ teaspoon ground nutmeg
Salt and freshly ground black pepper, to taste

1. Place the diced potatoes in a large saucepan and add water to cover. Heat to boiling. Reduce heat and simmer over medium heat until tender. Drain.

2. Place the potatoes in a mixer bowl. Cut the butter and cream cheese into small pieces and add to the potatoes. Beat with an electric mixer until light and fluffy. Beat in the sour cream. Season with the nutmeg and salt and pepper to taste.

3. Serve immediately or reheat in a buttered casserole at 300°F for 20 minutes, if you want to prepare them in advance.

8 portions

GLAZED LADY APPLES AND ONIONS

An original and delicious way to use fashionable little lady apples.

6 tablespoons (¾ stick) unsalted butter
16 white pearl onions (the size of the apples), peeled
16 lady apples, peeled and cored with a round corer
1½ tablespoons sugar
2 tablespoons brandy
2 teaspoons ground coriander
Salt and freshly ground black pepper, to taste
½ cup sliced almonds

1. Melt the butter in a medium-size sauté pan over medium-low heat. Add the onions and sauté until softened and lightly browned, 15 to 20 minutes.

2. Add the apples and sprinkle with the sugar. Increase the heat to high; cook, shaking the pan constantly, just until the onions and apples are caramelized. Add the brandy, coriander, and salt and pepper to taste. Reduce the heat to medium and simmer uncovered until tender but not mushy, about 10 minutes.

3. Preheat broiler.

4. Remove the onions and apples to an au gratin dish and sprinkle with the almonds. Broil until the almonds are browned, about 1 minute. Serve immediately.

8 portions

SWEET POTATO AND BANANA PUREE

Perfect to serve with pork or game.

8 cups peeled, diced sweet potatoes
3 ripe bananas
6 tablespoons (¾ stick) unsalted butter
2 tablespoons rum
1 tablespoon brown sugar
¼ teaspoon ground nutmeg
Salt, to taste
1 cup toasted sliced almonds

1. Place the sweet potatoes in a medium-size saucepan and add water to cover. Cook covered until very tender; drain.

2. Cut the bananas into 1-inch pieces and purée in a food processor fitted with a steel blade. Add the hot sweet potatoes, 4 tablespoons of the butter, the rum, and brown sugar. Process until smooth. Add the nutmeg and salt to taste; process just to blend. Keep warm.

3. Melt the remaining 2 tablespoons butter in a small skillet. Add the almonds and sauté until lightly browned. Sprinkle with a little salt. Top each serving of the sweet potato purée with a generous amount of the toasted almonds.

8 portions

CRANBERRY LATTICE PIE

Cranberries and apricots are a deliciously tart combination for this pie. The sweetness comes from amaretto liqueur. Serve hot with whipped cream or vanilla ice cream.

CALIFORNIA PINOT NOIR

Pinot Noir is the grape that gives red Burgundies their extraordinary reputation. It has been hard to grow in California: genetically a delicate and unstable vine, very sensitive to both frost and sunburn, it is also subject to a variety of molds and diseases. Even in the best of health, the Pinot Noir vines do not produce a high yield of grapes.

Some people believe that the grape will never be grown successfully in the U.S.; yet Americans continue to have great expectations for the prized grape of Burgundy, and it is a best-seller in wine shops across the country. American Pinot Noirs tend to be clean-tasting and fruity but much less substantial than their French counterparts. American growers keep hoping for the big "breakthrough" that will make grand Pinot Noirs possible. In the meantime, these vineyards produce some very good Pinot Noir wines: Beaulieu; Carneros Creek Winery; Caymus; Firestone; Heitz Wine Cellars; Robert Mondavi; Joseph Swan; Fetzer; Freemark Abbey; Charles Krug; Zaca Mesa.

"On Thanksgiving Day all over America, families sit down to dinner at the same moment—halftime."
—Anonymous

CRUST:

2 cups unbleached all-purpose flour
¼ cup sugar
2 teaspoons ground cinnamon
Pinch salt
¾ cup (1 ½ sticks) unsalted butter, cold, cut into small pieces
2 egg yolks
2 hard-cooked egg yolks
Grated zest of 1 lemon

FILLING:

3 cups cranberries
12 dried apricots, quartered
1 ¼ cups sugar
½ to ¾ cup water
⅓ cup amaretto liqueur

GLAZE:

1 egg
2 teaspoons water
¼ cup slivered almonds

CALIFORNIA CABERNET SAUVIGNON

The Cabernet Sauvignon grape is California's leading red varietal and the darling of wine collectors and connoisseurs. California Cabernet is often compared with Bordeaux, since the principal grape is the same as many of the great château wines—Lafite, Margaux, Mouton-Rothschild, and Haut-Brion. In fact, Cabernet Sauvignon is often stored in the cellar for several years to age in the same fashion as many a fine Bordeaux.

The warmer suns of California make the Cabernet Sauvignon a more voluptuous wine than its Bordeaux counterparts. It may also be successfully drunk much younger than many Bordeaux. Look for: Heitz Martha's Vineyard; Beaulieu; Freemark Abbey; Robert Mondavi Reserve; Simi Reserve; Jordan; Clos du Val; Stag's Leap; Burgess Cellars.

1. To make the crust, process the flour, sugar, cinnamon, salt, butter, raw and cooked egg yolks, and the lemon zest in a food processor fitted with a steel blade until the dough gathers into a ball. Wrap in plastic wrap and refrigerate 1 hour.

2. To make the filling, combine the cranberries, apricots, sugar, and ½ cup water in a medium-size saucepan. Cook uncovered over medium heat, stirring occasionally, for 15 minutes. (If the mixture seems too dry, add an additional ¼ cup water.) The cranberries should be popped. Add the liqueur and simmer for 15 minutes more.

3. Preheat oven to 375°F.

4. Divide the dough in half. Roll out 1 piece to a 13½-inch circle on a lightly floured surface. Line a 12-inch tart pan with removable bottom with the dough. Trim the edges.

5. Spread the cranberry filling in an even layer in the bottom of the tart shell. Roll out the remaining dough ⅛ inch thick. Cut into ¼-inch-wide strips and arrange in a lattice pattern on the top of the pie. Trim the edges.

6. To make the glaze, beat the egg and water together. Sprinkle the top of the pie with the almonds and brush with the egg wash.

7. Bake until the top is golden and the filling is bubbling, about 45 minutes. Let cool and serve at room temperature.

10 to 12 portions

OLD-FASHIONED APPLE PIE

PASTRY:

1 ¾ cups unbleached all-purpose flour
3 tablespoons sugar
Pinch salt
⅓ cup lard, cold, cut into small pieces
6 tablespoons (¾ stick) unsalted butter, cold, cut into small pieces
3 to 4 tablespoons ice water

FILLING:

3 pounds McIntosh apples, peeled, cored, and cut into ½-inch slices
½ cup sugar
1 tablespoon fresh lemon juice
2 teaspoons ground cinnamon
½ teaspoon ground nutmeg
½ cup heavy or whipping cream

1. To make the crust, place the flour, sugar, and salt in a food processor fitted with a steel blade. Add the lard and butter and process until the mixture resembles coarse meal. With the machine running, add enough of the ice water through the feed tube for the dough to gather into a ball. Wrap the dough in plastic wrap and refrigerate 1 hour.

2. To make the filling, toss the apples, sugar, lemon juice, cinnamon, nutmeg, and cream together.

3. Preheat oven to 450°F.

4. Divide the dough in half. Roll out 1 piece to an 11-inch circle on a lightly floured surface. Line a 9-inch pie plate with the dough, leaving the edge untrimmed.

5. Spoon the apple filling into the pie shell. Roll out the remaining dough into another 11-inch circle. Carefully place over the top of the pie. Trim and crimp the edges. (The excess dough can be used for decorating the top of the pie, if desired.) Cut 4 steam vents in the top of the pie.

6. Bake 20 minutes. Reduce the heat to 375°F and bake for 40 minutes more. Serve the pie warm or at room temperature.

8 to 10 portions

FALL FRUIT AND CHEESE COMBINATIONS

- ♥ Concord grapes with Doux de Montagne
- ♥ Persimmons and sweet Gorgonzola
- ♥ Seedless red grapes and Vacherin
- ♥ Oranges, ricotta, and cranberry bread
- ♥ Anjou pears and peppery Boursin
- ♥ Emperor apples, Caerphilly, and sweet cider
- ♥ Italian purple plums and Saga
- ♥ Blackberries, beach plums, and St. André
- ♥ Prunes, Stilton, and port
- ♥ Pears, Tomme, and a bowl of lightly toasted hazelnuts
- ♥ Jonathan apples, farmhouse Cheddar, and roasted peanuts
- ♥ Homemade applesauce with spiced caraway cheese and assorted hard sausages

RAVE REVIEWS

After a fortuitous opening and a substantial second act, everyone loves a happy ending. More often than not, the final tastes of the evening are the ones that linger on and conjure up rave reviews. Make sure your final act—the dessert course—lives up to the rest of the menu. Pamper your guests with smooth spoonfuls of fruity mousses, spicy slices of old-fashioned layer cakes, and buttery mouthfuls of favorite cookies. And be prepared for cries of *Encore!*

SPICY LAYER CAKE

An old-fashioned layer cake to satisfy hearty appetites on chilly autumn evenings.

CAKE:

30 pitted prunes, cut into quarters
⅓ cup brandy
1 cup (2 sticks) unsalted margarine, room temperature
1 cup packed dark brown sugar
1 cup granulated sugar
4 eggs
3 ¼ cups sifted unbleached all-purpose flour
2 teaspoons baking powder
1 teaspoon baking soda
1 teaspoon ground cinnamon
1 teaspoon ground cardamom
½ teaspoon ground nutmeg
½ teaspoon ground cloves
½ teaspoon salt
1 ¼ cups buttermilk
1 teaspoon vanilla extract

FROSTING:

½ cup (1 stick) unsalted butter, room temperature
8 ounces cream cheese, room temperature
1 teaspoon vanilla extract
4 cups confectioners' sugar
1 tablespoon grated lemon zest
Fresh lemon juice

Lemon zest strips or whole poached prunes (garnish)

1. To make the cake, place the prunes in a medium-size saucepan. Add the brandy and enough water to cover by ½ inch. Simmer until the prunes are plump and tender, about 20 minutes.

2. Preheat oven to 350°F. Butter and flour two 9-inch cake pans.

3. Cream the margarine and the sugars in a large mixer bowl. Add the eggs, one at a time, beating well after each addition.

4. Sift the flour, baking powder, baking soda, cinnamon, cardamom, nutmeg, cloves, and salt together. Drain the prunes, reserving ½ cup of the cooking liquid. Add the flour mixture alternately with the buttermilk and prune cooking liquid to the butter mixture, beating well after each addition. Beat in the vanilla and stir in the prunes.

5. Pour the batter into the prepared pans. Bake until the cake springs back when lightly touched in the center, 35 to 40 minutes. Let cool 10 minutes. Invert onto wire racks and

FOR A SOOTHING EVENING MENU

Wild Mushroom Pastries

Vivaldi's L'Inverno Pasta

Arugula and Radicchio Salad

Crusty French bread

Apricot Mousse

Puligny-Montrachet

Invite friends to join you on a local color tour—either a walk through the woods or a long drive in the country before dinner. Then set a fall table that epitomizes earthly delights. Use autumn-colored linens with a basket of dried leaves and hydrangeas as a centerpiece, wooden-handled flatware, and pewter candlesticks and mugs. After dinner, serve coffee and nuts by the fire. Lemon and orange twists, fancy sugar cubes, steamed milk, and cinnamon sticks can accompany the coffee, along with an assortment of cordials.

cool completely.

6. To make the frosting, beat the butter, cream cheese, and vanilla in a mixer bowl until smooth. Gradually beat in the confectioners' sugar. Add the lemon zest and beat until blended. Beat in a few drops of lemon juice if the frosting is too thick.

7. Frost the layers, side, and top of the cake. Use any extra frosting to pipe a decorative design on the cake, if desired.

8. Refrigerate until cold. Remove from the refrigerator 30 minutes before serving. Garnish with lemon zest or whole poached prunes.

10 to 12 portions

APRICOT MOUSSE

A light and refreshing mousse laced with the subtle hint of orange. Serve this mousse with a plate of assorted cookies.

8 ounces dried apricots
1 envelope unflavored gelatin
2 tablespoons cold water
2 egg yolks
½ cup sugar
2 tablespoons orange liqueur
2 cups heavy or whipping cream, cold

1. Place the apricots in a medium-size saucepan and add water to cover by 1 inch. Let stand for 30 minutes. Then heat to boiling. Reduce the heat and simmer uncovered until the apricots are tender, 20 to 25 minutes.

2. Meanwhile, soften the gelatin in the cold water in a small bowl.

3. Process the hot apricots with the cooking liquid and the gelatin in a food processor fitted with a steel blade until smooth. Set aside to cool.

4. Beat the egg yolks, sugar, and liqueur in a mixer bowl until blended. Transfer to the top of a double boiler. Whisk over simmering water until the mixture is hot to the touch and lightly thickened. Cool to room temperature.

5. When both the egg yolk and apricot mixtures are cooled, mix them together.

6. Whip the cream until fairly stiff and fold into the apricot mixture.

7. Spoon the mousse into goblets or a serving bowl. Refrigerate covered several hours.

8 to 10 portions

A wine drinker, being at table, was offered grapes at dessert. "Thank you," he said, pushing the dish away from him, "but I am not in the habit of taking my wine in pills."
—Brillat-Savarin

CHESTNUT MOUSSE

6 egg yolks, room temperature
½ cup sugar
1 cup chestnut purée
1 tablespoon brandy or Cognac
1 cup heavy or whipping cream, cold

1. Beat the egg yolks in a mixer bowl until thickened and pale yellow.
2. Gradually beat in the sugar and continue to beat until the mixture forms a ribbon when the beater is lifted, about 10 minutes.
3. Add the chestnut purée and mix until blended. Mix in the brandy.
4. Whip the cream in another mixer bowl until soft peaks form. Gently fold the cream into the chestnut mixture.
5. Spoon the mousse into individual serving bowls or a large serving bowl. Refrigerate covered for 3 to 4 hours before serving.

6 to 8 portions

Everyone loves a happy ending . . . and autumn is a time when you want to be pampered just a little bit more. We like our sweets sweet but not cloying, with fruit flavors, autumn spices, and crunchy textures that come through loud and clear. Serve them with hot cider, frothy cappuccino, mulled wine, or warmed brandy.

PRUNES IN ZINFANDEL

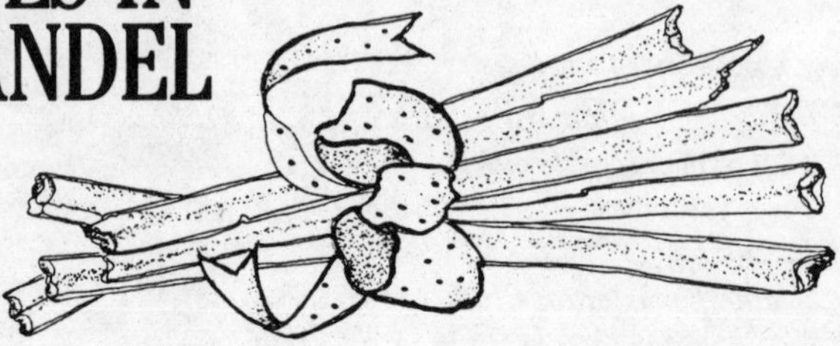

A wonderful end to a hearty meal, simple yet elegant. For a change of pace, try these prunes as a fruit starter for brunch on a leisurely Sunday.

2 pounds large prunes
3 bottles (750 ml) California Zinfandel (good but not expensive)
¾ cup sugar
2 medium-size oranges, thinly sliced
2 lemons, thinly sliced
½ vanilla bean
1 medium-size cinnamon stick

1. Soak the prunes in cold water to cover for 2 hours. Drain.
2. Heat the wine, sugar, oranges, lemons, vanilla bean, and cinnamon stick in a large Dutch oven or stock pot to boiling. Add the prunes and heat again to boiling. Remove from the heat. Let stand for 8 hours. Do not chill.
3. Spoon the sauce over the fruit in individual serving bowls.

10 portions

THE FINAL CURTAIN

The fall vegetable harvest is timed around Jack Frost, whose arrival pulls the final curtain down on the garden. Cold weather can come in a flash—so we find it best to consult our copy of the *Farmer's Almanac*.

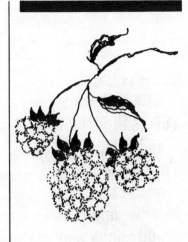

RASPBERRY–SHERRY VINEGAR PUREE

This is a beautiful rose-colored sauce with a hint of sherry. Serve over fresh figs or other fruit, pound cake, bread puddings, or French toast. Or eat as is using a tiny spoon.

3 cups fresh raspberries
2 tablespoons sugar
3 tablespoons sherry vinegar

Process the raspberries, sugar, and vinegar in a blender or a food processor fitted with a steel blade until smooth. Strain through a fine-mesh sieve. Refrigerate until cold.

1¾ to 2 cups

MORE AUTUMN CRAVINGS

...Brussels sprouts on the stalk... the Cloisters...pink shirts on men anywhere...venison...outdoor-café weather...the first frost...crisp days alternating with midsummer days...wild mushrooms...long walks...acorn squash...the first bite of an apple...pumpkin mousse ...cranberry conserves...pear sorbet...peanuts...cinnamon toast ...garlic...

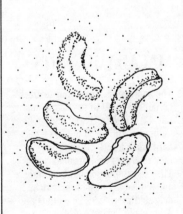

CASHEW BUTTER COOKIES

1 cup cashew butter (prepared or see step 1 below)
½ cup (1 stick) unsalted butter, room temperature
½ cup packed dark brown sugar
½ cup granulated sugar
1 egg
1½ cups sifted unbleached all-purpose flour
1 teaspoon baking soda
½ teaspoon salt
2 tablespoons dark rum
½ teaspoon vanilla extract
1 cup coarsely chopped roasted cashews
½ cup old-fashioned rolled oats

1. If you are not using prepared cashew butter, make your own by processing 1 cup unsalted roasted cashews and 2 tablespoons vegetable oil in a food processor fitted with a steel blade or a blender until the mixture forms a thick, smooth paste.

2. Preheat oven to 350°F. Grease cookie sheets.

3. Cream the butter and sugars in a large mixer bowl. Beat in the egg and then the cashew butter.

4. Sift the flour, baking soda, and salt together. Stir into the butter mixture with a wooden spoon. Stir in the rum and vanilla extract and then the chopped cashews and the oats.

5. Shape the dough into 1-inch balls and place 2 inches apart on the prepared cookie sheets. Flatten the balls with a fork dipped in warm water, making a crisscross pattern.

6. Bake until golden, 12 to 15 minutes. Remove to wire racks to cool completely.

4 to 5 dozen cookies

OLD-FASHIONED OATMEAL COOKIES

Next to chocolate chip, oatmeal cookies are America's favorite. Pecans, raisins, and dates make these both extra moist and healthy. Be sure to keep the cookie jar filled.

1 cup (2 sticks) unsalted butter, room temperature
1½ cups packed dark brown sugar
3 tablespoons honey
2 eggs
1½ cups unbleached all-purpose flour
1 tablespoon ground cinnamon
1 teaspoon salt
4 cups old-fashioned rolled oats
1½ cups chopped pecans
¾ cup raisins
¾ cup chopped dates

1. Preheat oven to 375°F. Lightly butter cookie sheets.
2. Cream the butter and brown sugar in a large mixer bowl. Beat in the honey and eggs until smooth.
3. Sift the flour, cinnamon, and salt together. Stir into the butter mixture with a wooden spoon.
4. Add the oats, pecans, raisins, and dates and stir until well mixed.
5. Shape the dough into 2-inch balls. Place about 9 balls on each cookie sheet and then flatten each one with the palm of your hand to make large cookies.
6. Bake until lightly browned, about 15 minutes. Immediately remove the cookies to wire racks to cool completely.
2 dozen large cookies

CHUNKY CREAM CHEESE AND MACADAMIA NUT COOKIES

½ cup (1 stick) unsalted butter, room temperature
8 ounces cream cheese, room temperature
¾ cup packed dark brown sugar
Finely grated zest of 1 orange
2 teaspoons vanilla extract
1½ cups unbleached all-purpose flour
2 teaspoons baking powder
¾ cup coarsely chopped macadamia nuts

1. Beat the butter and cream cheese in a large mixer bowl until light and fluffy. Beat in the brown sugar and then

"This is the land of milk and honey,
This is the land of sun and song, and
This is a world of good and plenty,
Humble and proud and young and strong."
—©Jerry Herman

MACADAMIA NUTS

The expression "tough nut to crack" certainly applies to the macadamia nut. Produced in Hawaii and California, this regal nut has a very hard outer husk—which is why they're always sold preshelled. They're gaining popularity both here and abroad because of their rich, delicate flavor. Macadamia nuts are delicious in baking, sprinkled on chicken salads and fruit desserts, and are terrific teamed with chocolate.

the orange zest and vanilla extract.

2. Sift the flour and baking powder together and stir into the butter mixture with a wooden spoon. Stir in the macadamia nuts. Refrigerate the dough at least 1 hour or overnight.

3. Preheat oven to 400°F. Lightly butter cookie sheets.

4. Drop heaping teaspoons of the dough 2 inches apart onto the prepared cookie sheets and flatten slightly with the back of a spoon.

5. Bake until lightly browned, 8 to 10 minutes. Remove to wire racks to cool completely.

4 dozen cookies

DATE AND FIG BARS

These bar cookies are incredibly moist and chewy and are wonderful on their own or served with a dollop of ice cream.

1 cup (2 sticks) unsalted butter, room temperature
2 cups packed dark brown sugar
2 eggs
2 teaspoons vanilla extract
2½ cups old-fashioned rolled oats
2¼ cups unbleached all-purpose flour
1 teaspoon baking powder
2 teaspoons ground cinnamon
1 teaspoon salt
1 cup chopped skinned toasted hazelnuts
1 cup pitted dates
¾ cup chopped dried figs
3 tablespoons granulated sugar
2 tablespoons grated lemon zest
2 tablespoons brandy

1. Cream the butter and brown sugar together in a large mixer bowl. Add the eggs, one at a time, beating well after each addition. Beat in the vanilla.

2. Stir in the oats, flour, baking powder, cinnamon, salt, and hazelnuts with a wooden spoon.

3. Place the dates and figs in a medium-size saucepan and add water to cover by 1 inch. Simmer until tender, about 20 minutes. Drain; process the fruit, granulated sugar, lemon zest, and brandy in a food processor fitted with a steel blade until smooth.

4. Preheat oven to 350°F.

5. Pat two-thirds of the oatmeal mixture in the bottom of a 9-inch square baking pan. Spread the date purée over the top. Crumble the remaining oatmeal mixture over the date purée.

6. Bake for 25 to 30 minutes. Cool completely and cut into 16 squares.

Sixteen 2-inch bars

"Cuisine is when things taste like themselves."
—Curnonsky

FIGS

These small, luscious fruits are bursting with soft, sweet flavor. Beautiful to behold with their green, brown, or purple skins, they're one of autumn's finest fruits. We like to eat figs fresh, combined with soft cheeses and smoked hams, in fruit gratinées, or soaked in liqueur. We also love the dried variety, and use them in stuffings, in fresh fruit salads as a texture contrast, and in cookies and confections.

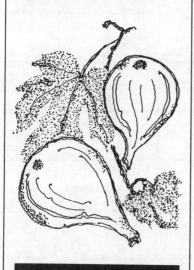

WINTER WONDERLAND

We love the magic of winter, especially in the North— the purity of a snowy landscape, the drama of a wind-swept sky, the adventures of skiing and sledding, and all the spirited celebrations of the long holiday season. As the bitter cold makes our cheeks rosy and our appetites hearty, the instinct to nourish is at its keenest. No sooner have the final bits of Thanksgiving turkey been transformed into the last leftover variation than the hectic holiday schedule is upon us. Every event seems to center on good food and spirits, and we love all the festive preparation.

Meals are super-special at this time of year. The house is decorated with wreaths, garlands, and candles, hosts and guests are dressed to the nines, and the table sparkles with pearly linens, china, and crystal.

New Year's brings an end to a month of glorious feasting with one last splurge of oysters, caviar, and foie gras. Champagne corks pop like the grand finale of a fireworks display— and then we are left to settle into the heart of winter with invigorating ski weekends and comforting fireside dinners.

THE DINNER PARTY

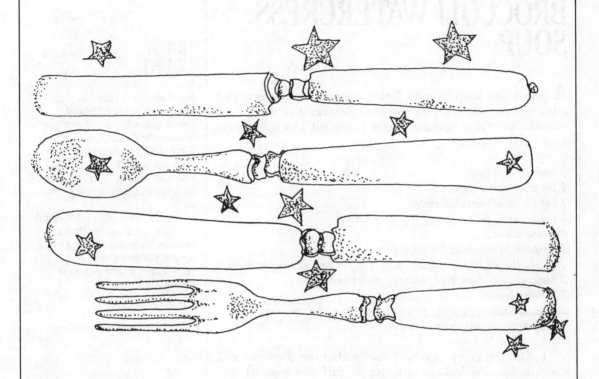

The holiday season brings on the urge to entertain lavishly. With everything looking festive—evergreen boughs, holly, and mistletoe decorating every nook and cranny—it is the perfect time of the year for a formal dinner party. People want to get dressed up and show off their fancy clothes, and you want to share the warmth of the holiday hearth with your friends.

Our dinner menus are rich and spectacular. In the true spirit of giving, we pull out all the stops for these occasions. First courses of creamy steaming soups and salmon caviar salads create the aura of formality. Tenderloin of beef melts in the mouth while venison ragout delights with its ruby color and distinctive flavors. Vegetables glisten in smooth purées and fluffy gratinées. Desserts are sublime—intensely chocolate dacquoise and cloudlike maple hazelnut mousse. Champagne flows in fountains and voluptuous red wines swirl in crystal goblets. 'Tis the season!

DINNER AT EIGHT

BROCCOLI-WATERCRESS SOUP

A pale green soup of mild leeks, peppery watercress, and crunchy broccoli. Potatoes and heavy cream give the soup a smooth, satisfying texture, while blanched broccoli florets lend a crisp contrast.

3 medium-size leeks
1 teaspoon cider vinegar
1 cup (2 sticks) unsalted butter
1 medium-size yellow onion, coarsely chopped
1 tablespoon salt
1 teaspoon freshly ground black pepper
2 quarts Berta's Chicken Stock (page 396) or canned chicken broth
2 medium-size all-purpose potatoes, peeled and sliced
2 bunches broccoli
2 bunches watercress, stems removed, rinsed, and patted dry
½ cup heavy or whipping cream

1. Cut the green tops and root ends from the leeks and discard. Cut the leeks lengthwise in half and soak in cold water to cover mixed with the vinegar for 15 minutes. Rinse, pat dry, and coarsely chop.

2. Melt the butter in a stock pot over very low heat. Add the leeks, onion, salt, and pepper and cook until the vegetables are limp, about 15 minutes.

3. Add the stock and potatoes and simmer uncovered for 15 minutes.

4. Trim the ends of the broccoli stalks and discard. Slice the stalks. Measure and reserve 1 cup florets. Add the remaining florets with the sliced stalks to the soup and simmer for 10 minutes. Remove from the heat, stir in the watercress, and let stand for 2 minutes.

5. Process the soup in small batches in a food processor fitted with a steel blade or a blender, then pass through a food mill. Whisk in the cream in a slow stream. Warm the soup over low heat.

6. Blanch the reserved florets in boiling water for 1 minute.

7. Ladle the soup into serving bowls and garnish with the reserved florets.

8 to 10 portions

GUEST COUNT

Never ever try to entertain more people than you honestly feel comfortable with—it will surely be a disaster. For dinner parties we prefer between six and twenty-four. Buffets work well up to thirty. Cocktails—with staff—can be any number. Grand sit-downs and balls—the sky's the limit.

Do remember that people need not come in pairs—only Noah's animals. You're not matching guests for life, just giving them dinner. Who cares if there's an extra man or woman?

"The most indispensable quality in a cook is punctuality, and no less is required of a guest."
—Brillat-Savarin

YOU ARE INVITED...

Rules about invitations are much more relaxed these days, and originality and creativity are more often appreciated than etiquette-perfect engravings. Some of our favorite new ideas are:

♥ To use a calendar grid as an invitation with the appropriate party date highlighted and a mixture of cute information and pertinent facts intermingled on the other calendar squares.

♥ Printing invitations on shiny silver Mylar with hot-colored ink for a gala occasion like Champagne and caviar on New Year's Eve.

♥ Weaving colorful ribbon through contrasting vellum paper and printing the ribbon itself with pertinent party facts.

♥ Making a patchworklike invitation for a country-style party by alternating squares of tiny print material with squares of paper cut in graduating sizes. Print all the party information on the squares of paper.

♥ To add to a pre-celebration spirit, fill the invitation envelope with multi-colored tissue-paper confetti.

♥ To indicate a surprise party, seal the envelope with a big sticker that says "Shh...."

♥ Have an invitation printed in your own handwriting style rather than in the standard printer's type.

♥ Have a fireworks or stargazing invitation printed on synthetic plastic in a sparkle pattern.

♥ Print a boat picnic invitation in nautical red, white, and blue with anchors and yachting flags.

♥ Announce a come-meet-the-new-baby party as "A Star is Born," and fill the envelope with little stick-on stars from the local five and dime.

LUXEMBOURG SALAD

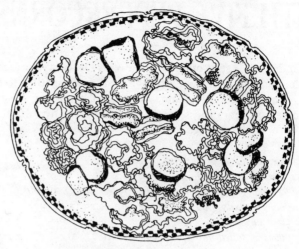

This salad was inspired by one we ate at a favorite New York restaurant. Leafy greens, crisp bacon lardoons, and sautéed croutons—all coated with a rich mustard vinaigrette. A perfect luncheon—or serve before grilled steak and potatoes.

12 thick slices bacon, cut into 1-inch pieces
4 slices day-old bread, cut into 1-inch squares
Luxembourg Dressing (recipe follows)
9 cups torn salad greens (a combination of leafy lettuces and chicory)
1 ½ cups crumbled blue cheese

1. Fry the bacon pieces in a medium-size skillet until crisp. Drain on paper towels and reserve the fat in the skillet.

2. Sauté the bread slowly in the hot bacon fat until crisp and browned.

3. Make the salad dressing.

4. Combine the salad greens, bacon, croutons, and blue cheese in a salad bowl. Add the dressing, toss, and serve immediately.

6 portions

LUXEMBOURG DRESSING

4 cloves garlic, finely minced
⅓ cup balsamic vinegar
2 tablespoons fresh lemon juice
1 ½ tablespoons Dijon-style mustard
1 ½ tablespoons mixed salad herbs (parsley, chives, tarragon, and chervil)
1 cup olive oil
Salt and freshly ground black pepper, to taste

Whisk the garlic, vinegar, lemon juice, and mustard together in a mixing bowl. Whisk in the herbs. Gradually whisk in the oil. Season to taste with salt and pepper.

About 1 ½ cups

TENDERLOIN OF BEEF WITH FIVE PEPPERCORNS

The tenderloin is split open, spread with Dijon-style mustard and blended peppercorns, and then tied back together so that it slices like a beef roulade. The quick roasting ensures moistness and tenderness, and you need serve with nothing more than the pan juices.

1 beef tenderloin (3 to 4 pounds), fat trimmed
3 tablespoons Dijon-style mustard
1½ tablespoons green peppercorns (packed in water), drained
3 tablespoons coarsely ground 5-peppercorn blend (see Note)
8 fresh large sage leaves
2 tablespoons unsalted butter, room temperature
Salt, to taste
4 bay leaves

1. Preheat oven to 425°F.
2. Using a sharp knife, make a cut lengthwise down the center of the tenderloin through two-thirds of the thickness. Spread the meat open and flatten slightly with a meat pounder.
3. Spread the mustard in a thin layer over the opened tenderloin. Scatter the green peppercorns evenly over the opened meat and press into the meat lightly with your hands. Sprinkle 1 tablespoon of the peppercorn blend evenly over the opened meat. Place the sage leaves in a row down the center.
4. Shape the tenderloin back to its original shape and tie closed at several places. Rub the outside of the tenderloin with the butter. Press the remaining peppercorn blend onto the outside surface of the tenderloin and sprinkle with salt to taste. Place seam side down in a shallow roasting pan and slip the bay leaves underneath the strings on the top of the roast.
5. Roast the meat for 45 to 55 minutes for rare meat. Let stand 10 minutes before carving. Cut away the strings and slice the meat. Serve with a bit of the pan juices spooned over the slices.

6 to 8 portions

Note: Mix equal parts of green, black, white, and pink peppercorns and whole allspice in a peppermill, and coarsely grind.

peppercorns grow
in little bunches

✤FLOWERS FROM THE
SILVER PALATE

For dinner at eight, don't forget long-stemmed white roses with a couple of dark red ones intermingled. Place in a tall cut-glass vase.

'TIS THE SEASON

Broccoli Watercress Soup

Tenderloin of Beef with Five Peppercorns

Gratinée of Cauliflower

Curried Carrots

Luxembourg Salad

Dacquoise with Chocolate Ganache

Gevrey-Chambertin

GRATINEE OF CAULIFLOWER

Cauliflower with its snowy clusters seems best as a winter vegetable. We've tempered its purity with just enough sinfully rich cream and cheese to make this wonderful dish for holiday entertaining.

6 tablespoons (¾ stick) unsalted butter
4 cloves garlic, minced
4 ounces thinly sliced prosciutto, cut into thin strips
Florets of 1 large head cauliflower, cut into ¼-inch lengthwise slices
2 tablespoons unbleached all-purpose flour
1 ½ cups heavy or whipping cream
Pinch cayenne pepper
Salt and freshly ground black pepper, to taste
1 ½ cups grated Swiss cheese
½ cup chopped fresh parsley

1. Preheat oven to 350°F.
2. Melt the butter in a large skillet over medium heat. Add the garlic and sauté 2 minutes. Stir in the prosciutto and sauté 2 minutes more.
3. Add the cauliflower and cook just until it begins to lose its crispness, 3 to 4 minutes.
4. Stir in the flour and then the cream. Blend well. Season with the cayenne and salt and pepper to taste. Heat to boiling and immediately remove from heat.
5. Pour the cauliflower into a shallow au gratin dish. Top with the cheese and parsley. Bake until the top is lightly browned and bubbling, about 30 minutes. Serve immediately.
6 to 8 portions

CURRIED CARROTS

A very simple carrot dish is made special with curry powder and brown sugar. Tartness is added with a sprinkle of lemon juice. Garnish with crisp pecans.

12 medium-size carrots, peeled and cut into 1-inch lengths
6 tablespoons unsalted butter, room temperature
2 tablespoons best-quality curry powder
¼ teaspoon salt
¼ teaspoon freshly ground black pepper
¼ cup fresh lemon juice
2 tablespoons brown sugar
1 cup pecans, toasted and chopped

1. Place the carrots in a heavy large saucepan and add cold water to cover. Cook over medium-high heat just until tender, 15 to 20 minutes. Drain and return to the pan.

2. Mix the butter, curry powder, salt, and pepper and add to the carrots. Heat over very low heat, tossing to coat the carrots with the butter mixture. Add the lemon juice and brown sugar. Heat, tossing occasionally, until the carrots are glazed. Sprinkle with the chopped pecans. Serve immediately.

6 to 8 portions

DACQUOISE WITH CHOCOLATE GANACHE

This dessert is a chocolate extravaganza. Feathery light layers of chocolate meringue are alternated with rich and thick chocolate ganache, delicate whipped cream, and sumptuous coffee buttercream.

MERINGUES:

¾ cup ground almonds
¼ cup unsweetened cocoa powder
1 cup confectioners' sugar
6 egg whites, room temperature
⅔ cup superfine sugar

GANACHE:

4 ounces best-quality bittersweet chocolate
½ cup heavy or whipping cream, scalded
1½ tablespoons rum
½ cup heavy or whipping cream, cold

BUTTERCREAM:

1 cup granulated sugar
⅓ cup water
6 egg yolks, room temperature
1 cup (2 sticks) unsalted butter, room temperature
3 tablespoons instant coffee powder
2 tablespoons hot brewed coffee

WHIPPED CREAM:

1 cup heavy or whipping cream, cold
3 tablespoons confectioners' sugar
1 tablespoon instant coffee powder
2 tablespoons rum
½ cup toasted sliced almonds (garnish)

"At a dinner party one should eat wisely but not too well, and talk well but not too wisely."
—W. Somerset Maugham

THE ART OF RELAXING

Too often cooks make the mistake of trying too hard. The evening becomes one of ornate course after ornate course: too much food, too many sauces.

Today it's important to relax. The idea is to have fun with less-demanding meals. No longer is it required that as each course appears at the table, conversation stop and the food be admired. After all, as Jean Cocteau said, "Elegance is the art of not astonishing."

CREATURE COMFORTS

- Make sure you've asked your guests about any dietary restrictions.
- Don't forget to set up a good system for keeping guests' coats organized.
- Have artificial sweeteners or sugar substitutes on hand for guests who don't use sugar.
- Keep your dining room cool (around 65°) until the guests come in. We can't stand overheated dining rooms. Have we all not sweltered while the candles melted and the window remained hermetically sealed?
- If a guest arrives by taxi, take note and be prepared to have one ready at departure time.
- Stack extra hand towels and a pretty flower arrangement in the powder room.

"Americans are just beginning to regard food the way the French always have. Dinner is not what you do in the evening before something else. Dinner is the evening."
—Art Buchwald

1. To make the meringues, preheat oven to 300°F. Cut three 8-inch circles from waxed paper or parchment paper. Lightly butter and flour 2 baking sheets, place the paper circles 2 inches apart on the sheet, and butter and flour the paper circles.

2. Using repeated pulses, process the almonds, cocoa, and confectioners' sugar in a food processor fitted with a steel blade to mix thoroughly.

3. Beat the egg whites in a mixer bowl until just beginning to stiffen. Gradually beat in 2 tablespoons of the superfine sugar and continue beating until the egg whites are stiff. Gradually add the remaining superfine sugar, beating at a low speed. Gently fold in the almond mixture.

4. Carefully spoon the meringue into a pastry bag fitted with a plain ½-inch tip. Pipe the meringue in a spiral to completely fill each of the 3 circles. If you have meringue left, change the tip on the bag to a star tip and pipe small stars onto the baking sheets between the large circles. The small meringues will be used later for decorating the dacquoise.

5. Bake the meringues until dry but not browned, about 1 hour. The meringues can be prepared up to 1 week in advance. Let cool, then wrap and store in a dry place.

6. To make the ganache, melt the chocolate in the top of a double boiler over simmering water. Remove the pan from the water and stir in the scalded cream. Whisk until smooth and then blend in the rum. Refrigerate covered until firm but not hardened, about 4 hours.

7. Remove the ganache to a large mixer bowl and beat until light and fluffy.

8. Beat the cold cream until it forms soft peaks and fold into the ganache. Refrigerate covered until ready to use.

9. To make the buttercream, combine the sugar and water in a heavy saucepan and heat to boiling. Cook without stirring to 250°F on a candy thermometer.

10. Meanwhile, beat the egg yolks in a mixer bowl until thick. Pour in the sugar syrup in a thin steady stream, beating constantly. Continue beating until the mixture cools, about 10 minutes.

11. Beat in the softened butter, 1 tablespoon at a time. Dissolve the instant coffee in the brewed coffee and beat into the buttercream. Refrigerate covered until firm but still spreadable.

12. To make the whipped cream, beat the cream until it starts to hold peaks. Beat in the sugar, instant coffee, and rum and continue beating until quite stiff. Refrigerate.

13. To assemble the dacquoise, place one meringue layer on a serving platter and spread with a thin layer of the buttercream. Cover with a smooth layer of all the ganache. Top with a second meringue layer and spread with the whipped cream. Top with the last meringue layer.

14. Spread the side and top of the dacquoise with the remaining buttercream. Using a pastry bag, pipe any remaining buttercream in a decorative pattern over the top.

15. Sprinkle the top with the almonds and decorate the side with meringue stars if you made them.

16. Refrigerate at least 1 hour before serving.

10 to 12 portions

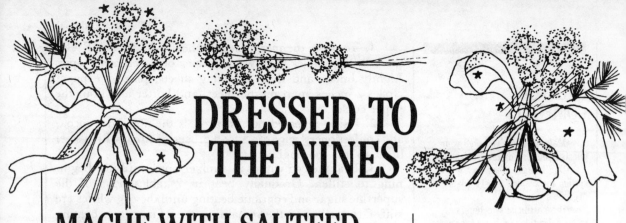

DRESSED TO THE NINES

MACHE WITH SAUTEED PEARS

The fragile flavor of mâche and succulent texture of warm pears create a delicate and sophisticated salad perfect for an elegant dinner party.

1 shallot, finely chopped
1 clove garlic, finely chopped
⅓ cup sherry vinegar
1 tablespoon Dijon-style mustard
1 teaspoon dried thyme
1 cup plus 3 tablespoons best-quality olive oil
Salt and freshly ground black pepper, to taste
8 cups mâche (lamb's lettuce) leaves
4 ripe medium-size Anjou pears

1. Several hours before serving, mix the shallot, garlic, vinegar, mustard, and thyme in a mixing bowl. Gradually whisk in the 1 cup oil. Season to taste with salt and pepper. Let stand at room temperature for several hours.

2. Just before serving, arrange the mâche on 8 salad plates.

3. Peel the pears, cut in half, core, and cut into thinly sliced fans. Heat the 3 tablespoons oil in a skillet large enough to fit 8 pear halves over medium heat. Carefully place the fanned pear halves in the skillet and gently sauté for 4 to 5 minutes.

4. Using a spatula, carefully transfer each pear half to the center of each plate of mâche. Quickly whisk the dressing to combine and spoon some over each salad. Serve immediately.

8 portions

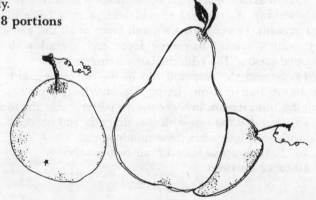

SALMON CAVIAR AND WHITE BEAN SALAD

1 pound dried white beans, soaked overnight and drained
2 quarts water
1 bunch arugula, stems removed, rinsed, and patted dry
¾ cup best-quality olive oil
¼ cup fresh lemon juice
Salt and freshly ground black pepper, to taste
1 red onion, finely chopped
4 ounces salmon caviar
Lemon slices (garnish)

1. Heat the beans and 2 quarts water in a large pan to boiling. Reduce heat and simmer gently covered until cooked but not mushy, about 45 minutes. Drain the beans and let them cool 10 minutes.

2. Reserve several whole arugula leaves for garnish and finely chop the remaining by hand or in a food processor fitted with a steel blade. Whisk the oil and lemon juice together and then whisk in the chopped arugula. Season to taste with salt and pepper. Place the warm beans in a mixing bowl and dress the beans with the vinaigrette. Add the onion and toss to combine.

3. Gently stir in all but 1 tablespoon of the salmon caviar. Remove to a serving platter and decorate the top with the whole arugula leaves. Place small clusters of the caviar at the sides of each leaf to resemble holly leaves and berries. Place the lemon slices around the edge of the platter. Serve warm or at room temperature.

8 to 10 portions

WELCOMED GUESTS

During the holidays, there's more "dropping in" than usual—delivering gifts, picking up children. During this season we usually have a fire going day and night—it is cozy for us and welcoming for guests. A pot of mulled wine or cider simmers away to permeate the air with good smells, and bowls of spiced nuts are always out as instant appetite appeasers. Not to be caught unawares, we make up several little baskets of assorted Christmas goodies to give to friends and relatives who stop by.

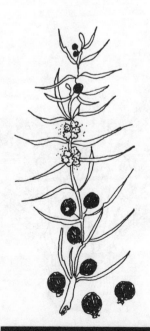

RUBY VENISON RAGOUT

4 pounds venison, cut into 2-inch cubes
1 cup red wine vinegar
2 cups red Bordeaux
1 tablespoon whole black peppercorns
6 juniper berries, slightly crushed
8 cups water
4 cups purple pearl onions (20 ounces)
4 slices bacon
8 tablespoons (1 stick) unsalted butter
2 tablespoons potato starch
1½ pounds fresh ripe purple plums, pitted
1 cup canned beef broth
2 tablespoons brown sugar
1 cup dried small figs or large figs cut into pieces
2 tablespoons red currant jelly

1. Combine the venison, vinegar, 1 cup of the wine, the peppercorns, and juniper berries in a large glass bowl. Marinate covered in the refrigerator for 5 hours.

2. Heat the water to boiling in a large saucepan over medium heat. Add the onions and cook for 5 minutes. Remove from heat and drain. Trim the ends and slip the skins off.

3. Drain the venison, reserving the marinade, and pat dry.

4. Fry the bacon in a large heavy casserole to render the fat. Remove the bacon pieces and reserve. Add 2 tablespoons of the butter to the bacon fat and heat over medium-high heat. Add the venison, a few pieces at a time, and brown on all sides. Add up to 4 tablespoons butter as needed. Place the browned venison in a large bowl.

5. When all the venison has been browned, pour the reserved marinade into the casserole and boil for 3 minutes, scraping up all the browned bits.

6. Sprinkle the potato starch over the venison and toss well to coat. Return to the casserole.

7. Add the remaining 1 cup wine, the plums, broth, brown sugar, figs, and bacon. Simmer covered over low heat, stirring occasionally, until the meat is almost tender, about 1½ hours.

8. Remove the cover and stir in the onions and jelly. Simmer uncovered 30 minutes.

9. Using a large slotted spoon, remove all the solids from the casserole to a bowl. Whisk the remaining 2 tablespoons butter into the casserole and boil over high heat until the sauce is reduced by a third, about 10 minutes.

10. Return the solids to the sauce and stir well.

11. Remove to a deep serving bowl and serve with lots of hot buttered noodles.

8 portions

CREAMY FENNEL PUREE

A staple vegetable in Italy, fennel is still somewhat unknown to Americans. Introduce fennel at your table with this creamy, pale green purée that surprises with its faint anise flavor, and you'll be sure to create an instant fennel following.

½ cup (1 stick) unsalted butter
9 cups coarsely chopped fennel stalks and bulb, feathery leaves removed (1 large bulb)
½ cup heavy or whipping cream
2 tablespoons Pernod
½ teaspoon fennel seeds
Salt and freshly ground black pepper, to taste

1. Melt the butter in a large skillet over low heat. Add the chopped fennel and toss to coat with the butter. Cover the

PUREES

Purées are often mistaken for baby food, but it would be a shame to waste them on a yet unrefined palate! They can taste even better than the original vegetable or fruit. To purée means, literally, to purify a substance into a liquid or semi-liquid state. When you purée you reduce it by mashing, and then often by straining, so all that is left is the ''pure'' food— no strings, seeds, or pits.

One of the most imaginative ways to cook vegetables is to purée them in combination with fruits, nuts, herbs, peppers, and spices.

Another effective way to cook with purées is to use them as thickeners. They add extra flavor as they thicken, without adding excessive calories. For instance, a purée of apples and pears can be used in place of the traditional custard or pastry cream to line a tart; the result is a fresh-tasting low-fat dessert.

CENTER STAGE

Here are some of the pretty table things we like to have share center stage. Remember, you want them to be lower or higher than eye level and—depending on what they are— perhaps removed before guests are seated.

- ♥ All-white flowers mixed in vases or in individual containers.
- ♥ A miniature flower arrangement at each place setting.
- ♥ A bed of leaves or moss down the center of the table, layered with masses of wild flowers.
- ♥ Branches of dogwood, cherry, and apple blossoms, or wild berries.
- ♥ Baskets filled with fresh herbs.
- ♥ Seashells filled with sand or water and miniature blossoms.
- ♥ A selection of raw fruits and vegetables you've used in preparing the meal—perhaps in miniature.
- ♥ A basket of dried herbs and flowers.
- ♥ A grapevine wreath filled with a variety of fresh grapes. By surrounding the outer edges with fresh grape leaves and a variety of cheeses, you will have an edible centerpiece.
- ♥ Dried fresh pasta as a natural bed for stuffed mushrooms or quail eggs.
- ♥ Beloved objects from travels that suit the dinner theme.

skillet and cook slowly until the fennel is quite tender, about 30 minutes.

2. Process the fennel in batches in a food processor fitted with a steel blade, adding some of the cream and Pernod to each batch. Stir in the fennel seeds and salt and pepper to taste. Serve immediately or warm gently in a saucepan just before serving.

8 portions

BULGUR PILAF WITH GREEN PEPPERCORNS

A good accompaniment to beef dishes.

6 tablespoons (¾ stick) unsalted butter
1 small yellow onion, diced
2 cups bulgur
4 cups Berta's Chicken Stock (page 396)
2 tablespoons green peppercorns (water packed), finely chopped
1 teaspoon salt
½ cup chopped fresh parsley

1. Melt the butter in a large saucepan over medium heat. Add the onion and sauté until translucent, about 5 minutes.

2. Add the bulgur and stir to coat with the butter. Cook until the bulgur colors slightly, about 5 minutes.

3. Add the stock, peppercorns, and salt and cook, partially covered, until the bulgur is tender, about 15 minutes.

4. Remove the cover and fluff with a fork. Fold in the parsley and serve immediately.

8 portions

MAPLE-HAZELNUT MOUSSE

D elicious and unusual contrast of textures. The silkiness of the mousse and the pleasant crunch of the praline is superb. Serve with pear slices drizzled with a little maple syrup.

Hazelnut Praline (page 242)
9 egg yolks, room temperature
¾ cup pure maple syrup
1½ cups heavy or whipping cream, cold
3 egg whites, room temperature
Pinch cream of tartar

1. Make the praline.

2. Beat the egg yolks and syrup in a mixer bowl until the mixture forms a slowly dissolving ribbon when the beaters are lifted. Transfer to the top of a double boiler and whisk over simmering water until the mixture is very thick, about 3 minutes. Remove and let cool completely.

3. Beat the cream until stiff. In a separate bowl with clean beaters, beat the egg whites with the cream of tartar until stiff but not dry. Gently fold the whipped cream into the cooled maple custard; then fold in the egg whites and then the praline.

4. Spoon the mousse into 8 goblets and refrigerate covered several hours.

8 portions

GERMAN CHOCOLATE LACE COOKIES

The ingredients of one of our favorite cakes used to make an equally tempting cookie.

½ cup (1 stick) unsalted butter, room temperature
½ cup (packed) brown sugar
2 tablespoons dark rum
¼ cup heavy or whipping cream
4 ounces semisweet chocolate, chopped
¼ cup unbleached all-purpose flour
⅛ teaspoon baking soda
¼ teaspoon salt
1 cup quick-cooking oats
½ cup shredded coconut
½ cup chopped pecans

1. Preheat oven to 350°F. Grease and flour cookie sheets.

2. Cream the butter and sugar in a mixer bowl until light and fluffy, about 5 minutes. Beat in 1 tablespoon of the rum.

3. Heat the cream to boiling in a small saucepan. Reduce heat and stir in the remaining 1 tablespoon rum. Simmer for 2 to 3 minutes. Remove from heat and stir in the chocolate until it melts and mixture is well blended. Beat ⅓ cup of the chocolate mixture into the butter mixture.

4. Sift the flour, baking soda, and salt together. Stir into the butter mixture. Fold in the oats, coconut, and pecans.

5. Drop rounded teaspoons of the batter 2 inches apart onto the prepared cookie sheets. Bake for 8 minutes. Remove from the oven and let cool on the cookie sheets for 5 minutes to harden. Remove cookies to wire racks to cool.

6. Drizzle the remaining chocolate mixture over the cookies in a lacy pattern.

25 large cookies

"Often, admiring a chef and getting to know him is like loving goose liver and then meeting the goose."
—George Lang

SILVER BELLS

FOIE GRAS SAUTEED WITH RASPBERRIES

Foie gras is becoming readily available in specialty shops, and this combination is simply sensational.

1 fresh domestic duck foie gras (about 1½ pounds)
Salt and freshly ground black pepper, to taste
2 tablespoons unsalted butter
1½ cups fresh or frozen raspberries, thawed and drained if frozen
3 tablespoons raspberry vinegar
⅓ cup Sauternes
Sugar if necessary

1. Cut the foie gras into ¼-inch slices. Sprinkle both sides of each slice lightly with salt and pepper. Melt the butter in a heavy skillet over medium-high heat. Add the foie gras and quickly sauté until lightly browned on both sides. Remove to a platter and keep warm.

2. Discard all but 1 tablespoon of the fat from the skillet. Return the skillet to high heat and stir in the raspberries, vinegar, and Sauternes. Add pepper to taste. Cook, stirring constantly, until smooth and somewhat thickened. Taste the sauce. If the raspberries are too tart, add a little sugar.

3. Pour the sauce over the foie gras and serve immediately, accompanied by chilled Sauternes.

6 appetizer portions

ARUGULA AND CHEVRE SALAD WITH TRASTEVERE DRESSING

Our version of a favorite salad from a small Italian restaurant in Julee's neighborhood.

Trastevere Dressing (recipe follows)
8 cups arugula leaves (4 bunches)
6 ounces Montrachet or other soft mild chèvre, crumbled
¼ cup balsamic vinegar

1. Make the dressing.

2. Divide the arugula leaves between 6 salad plates. Sprinkle the chèvre and then the vinegar over the salads. Top each salad with a generous dollop of the dressing and serve immediately.

6 portions

TRASTEVERE DRESSING

8 ripe medium-size tomatoes
1 small yellow onion, cut lengthwise into fine slivers
3 cloves garlic, minced
2 cups best-quality olive oil
Salt and freshly ground black pepper, to taste
2 tablespoons fresh lemon juice
1 teaspoon sugar

1. Seed the tomatoes placing the seeds in a sieve set over a medium-size saucepan. Press the tomato seeds to extract the juice. Dice the pulp and add it to the saucepan. Add the onion and garlic to the saucepan, pour in the oil and stir to blend. Season with salt and lots of freshly ground pepper to taste. Stir in the lemon juice and sugar.

2. Let stand in a warm place (on top of the stove or in the oven over a pilot light) for several hours to allow the flavors to blend.

4 cups

PARSLIED RACK OF LAMB

This elegant cut of lamb cooks quickly and multiplies easily for crowds, with each rack serving two people. Make as many as required, keeping the cooked racks warm in a 200°F oven (if you have a second oven) or covered, on top of the stove.

1 trimmed rack of lamb (about 1 ¾ pounds)
2 tablespoons olive oil
Salt and freshly ground black pepper, to taste
½ cup finely chopped fresh parsley
3 cloves garlic, finely minced
½ cup fresh French bread crumbs
1 teaspoon finely grated lemon zest
3 tablespoons melted unsalted butter

ANNIVERSARIES

Private or shared with friends and family—anniversaries are cherished celebrations. Just the simplest touches, like the little things couples do together to make a perfect relationship, make this a special celebration.

♥ First — Paper
♥ Second — Cotton
♥ Third — Leather
♥ Fourth — Linen or silk
♥ Fifth — Wood
♥ Tenth — Tin
♥ Fifteenth — Crystal
♥ Twentieth — China
♥ Twenty-fifth — Silver
♥ Thirtieth — Pearl
♥ Fortieth — Ruby
♥ Fiftieth — Gold
♥ Sixtieth — Diamond
♥ Seventy-fifth — Diamond

1. Preheat oven to 500°F.

2. Rub the rack of lamb with the oil and then sprinkle with salt and pepper.

3. Place the lamb, meat side down, on a rack in a roasting pan. Roast in the upper third of the oven until browned, 8 to 10 minutes.

4. Meanwhile, combine the parsley, garlic, bread crumbs, and lemon zest. Turn the rack meat side up and pat the parsley mixture evenly over the meat. Drizzle with the butter, then return to the oven and roast for 5 minutes more for rare meat.

5. Carve the rack and serve immediately.

2 portions

PARSNIP AND PEAR PUREE

The elusive flavor of parsnips melts with buttery pears in this ultra-smooth purée. Sour cream enriches the mixture, and a dash of Cognac adds spirit. The final result is like soft buff-colored velvet.

6 cups coarsely chopped parsnips (about 3 large)
4 tablespoons (½ stick) unsalted butter
2 Anjou pears, peeled and coarsely chopped
1 tablespoon Cognac
½ cup sour cream
¼ teaspoon ground allspice
Salt and freshly ground black pepper, to taste

1. Place the parsnips in a medium-size saucepan and add water to cover. Heat to boiling. Reduce heat and simmer covered until tender, about 20 minutes. Drain.

2. Meanwhile, melt the butter in a small skillet over medium heat. Add the pears and sauté for 5 minutes. Add the Cognac and cook, stirring frequently, for 15 minutes.

3. Process the parsnips and pears in a food processor fitted with a steel blade until smooth. Add the sour cream, allspice, and salt and pepper to taste and process just to blend. Serve immediately or warm gently over low heat just before serving.

6 to 8 portions

A winter anniversary seems to call for an intimate at-home gathering, perhaps just before the holidays when spirits are naturally high. The season's rich colors and textures add grace and warmth: silver and ivory, white velvet and deep green taffeta, crimson silk, and above all, candlelight. Write out the invitations by hand, for a personal touch, and mix family and friends at cozy round tables.

PARSNIPS

At one time, parsnips were as popular as carrots, but they were overshadowed when the potato was brought to Europe from the New World by the early explorers. They are a sweet and richly flavored vegetable, available in the depths of winter—and deserve more attention.

CHOCOLATE CHESTNUT TORTE

CAKE:

18 ounces semisweet chocolate, broken into small pieces
1 cup granulated sugar
½ cup brandy
6 tablespoons (¾ stick) unsalted butter
3 egg yolks, room temperature
5 eggs, room temperature
⅓ cup heavy or whipping cream
2 tablespoons cornstarch
2 cans (15½ ounces each) whole chestnuts, drained and puréed

FROSTING:

6 ounces semisweet chocolate, broken into small pieces
¼ cup water
1 tablespoon instant coffee powder
1 cup (2 sticks) unsalted butter, room temperature
3 egg yolks
2 teaspoons maple extract
1 cup sifted confectioners' sugar
12 marrons glacés (optional)

1. Preheat oven to 300°F. Butter a 10-inch springform pan.

2. To make the cake, combine the chocolate, sugar, brandy, and butter in a medium-size saucepan. Heat over medium-low heat stirring constantly, until the chocolate melts.

3. Beat the egg yolks, eggs, cream, and cornstarch in a mixer bowl until light, about 3 minutes. Then beat in the chocolate mixture and the chestnuts thoroughly. Pour the batter into the prepared pan.

4. Bake for 1 hour 15 minutes. Cover the top of the cake with aluminum foil and bake for 45 minutes more. Remove from the oven and let cool completely. Remove from the pan.

5. To make the frosting, heat the chocolate, water, and coffee powder in a small saucepan over low heat, stirring until the chocolate is melted and the mixture is smooth. Set aside to cool.

6. Cream the butter in a mixer bowl until light and fluffy; then beat in the egg yolks, one at a time. Beat in the maple extract. Beat in the cooled chocolate mixture, then the confectioners' sugar. Refrigerate the frosting until thick enough to spread.

7. Frost the top and side of the cake smoothly. If you want, make 12 lavish frosting stars, using a pastry bag fitted with a large star tip, around the edge of the top of the cake. Top each star with a *marron glacé.*

12 very rich portions

An elegant cake to grace a buffet table. Do use the *marrons glacés*—they give the cake a festive holiday look and are delicious with their sugar coating.

"'Tis an ill cook that cannot lick his own fingers."
—William Shakespeare

DINNER'S FINALE

When the conversation is going well, think of serving coffee at the table, rather than breaking up to go into another room.

On the other hand, moving to another room keeps up the pace, lets people stretch their legs, and allows the party to begin all over again. We do like to keep things moving!

You may choose to have dessert at the table and coffee and brandies in the living room, in the library, or on the terrace. The coffee must be piping hot, and don't forget to offer freshly ground decaffeinated. Make the liqueurs the best you can afford, and have cigarettes and chocolates within easy reach.

NUTCRACKER SWEET OPEN HOUSE

Share your sugarplum fantasies with friends and neighbors at a holiday open house. Set the stage: abundant decorations of Christmas greens, Tchaikovsky and a table laden with delectable confections. Guests can join in singing Christmas carols, decorating the tree, making popcorn chains, enacting Dickens's *A Christmas Carol* . . . pleasures for children of all ages, and a happy and relaxed way to celebrate the season together.

MARNO'S POPCORN

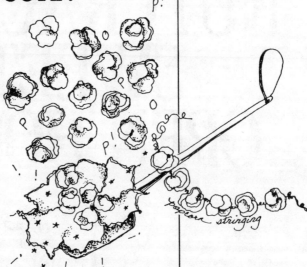

popcorn stringing

This candied popcorn is nice and crunchy, not too sweet, and positively addictive. It's a terrific snack with a mug of chilled apple cider or hot buttered rum.

1½ cups sugar
½ cup water
½ cup molasses
3 tablespoons unsalted butter
2 tablespoons vinegar
½ teaspoon salt
½ teaspoon baking soda
2 quarts popped popcorn

1. Combine the sugar, water, molasses, butter, vinegar, and salt in a heavy small saucepan. Cook over medium-high heat to 260°F on a candy thermometer or until a small amount forms a hard ball when dropped in ice water.

2. Remove from the heat and stir in the baking soda. The mixture will bubble up and then look creamy. Pour it over the popcorn in a large bowl and stir to coat. Spread on a lightly greased cookie sheet and cool completely, about 1 hour.

2 quarts popcorn

CANDIED CLEMENTINES

In France, candied citrus peels are often served at the end of a formal meal. Offer these to your guests as a special touch after retiring to the parlor for Cognac and cordials.

4 cups water
2½ cups sugar
3 tablespoons Grand Marnier
8 unpeeled Clementines, cut into ⅛-inch slices

1. One day before serving, heat the water, sugar, and Grand Marnier in a medium-size saucepan to boiling. Add the Clementines and simmer until tender but not mushy, 30 to 45 minutes.

2. Remove from heat and let stand in syrup overnight.

3. Drain and serve. The candied slices can also be dipped in melted bittersweet chocolate or used as a garnish for other fruit.

8 portions

WREATHS

Wreath making is an ancient and honored art that originated about a thousand years before Christ. A crown of oak leaves adorned the warrior, ivy rewarded the poet, and statesmen were dignified under their laurels. Only men of distinction wore these crowns, never laymen.

At Christmas the wreath or circle is symbolic of immortality. It may be made of laurel, oak, olive, parsley, palm, or poplar; with orange blossoms, myrtle, rosemary, or daffodils; of statice, yarrow, pine cones, grapevines, magnolia leaves, dried herbs, or holly. Greet the winter holidays with your own imaginative wreath for an extension of the holiday spirit.

DECK THE HALLS

To help bring out the child in all of us:

♥ Drape mantels, staircases, and doorways with holly, mistletoe, rosemary, and white candles.

♥ Put sprigs of green around wall hangings and chandeliers.

♥ Mound apples, lemons, grapes, oranges, pineapples, and pine cones in pretty bowls.

♥ Use juniper berries, aspen flowers, chestnuts, magnolia leaves, pine cones, and rose hips everywhere.

♥ Set a children's table with miniature rocking horses, gingerbread houses, bread-dough men, tiny trees and wreaths, and let tiny teddy bears hold the place cards.

♥ Tuck herb bundles into the evergreen tree and then dust it with sparkling fairy dust, snow, baby's breath, or angels hair.

♥ Ask family members to give one another something that doesn't cost money.

♥ Light the house only with candlelight.

♥ Fill the house with bright red amaryllis plants or force lots of paperwhite narcissus.

♥ Trim a tree with glorious Japanese fans.

♥ Transform your tree with white roses, snowberries, white velvet bows, baby's breath, and white candles.

♥ Toss herbs or cinnamon, hickory or apple chips, on the fire for sweet scents.

♥ Leave hay and carrots for Santa's reindeer and a treat for Santa.

♥ Hide an almond in the Christmas Eve cake to determine who opens the first gift the next morning.

♥ Keep miniature filled stockings on hand for drop-in guests.

CHRISTMAS PUDDING CANDY

These heavenly morsels make wonderful gifts during the holiday season.

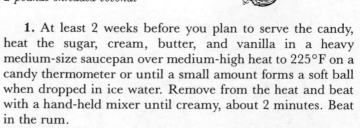

3 cups sugar
1 cup heavy or whipping cream
2 teaspoons unsalted butter
1 teaspoon vanilla extract
¼ to ½ cup dark rum
3 cups chopped almonds
1 pound dates, chopped
1 pound figs, chopped
8 ounces raisins
2 pounds shredded coconut

1. At least 2 weeks before you plan to serve the candy, heat the sugar, cream, butter, and vanilla in a heavy medium-size saucepan over medium-high heat to 225°F on a candy thermometer or until a small amount forms a soft ball when dropped in ice water. Remove from the heat and beat with a hand-held mixer until creamy, about 2 minutes. Beat in the rum.

2. Stir in 2 cups of the almonds, the dates, figs, raisins, and 1 pound of the coconut. Shape the dough into balls the size of small golf balls. Roll half the balls in the remaining coconut and the other half in the remaining almonds.

3. Let the candy ripen in airtight containers at room temperature for 2 weeks before serving.

100 candies

VIENNESE CHRISTMAS TREES

There are over 1,500 pastry shops in Vienna—and an almost equally staggering number of specialty confections. These nutty cookies—which we've cut into Christmas tree shapes—are typical of the riches.

1 ¼ cups (2 ½ sticks) unsalted butter, room temperature
⅔ cup granulated sugar
2 cups unbleached all-purpose flour
1 cup ground almonds
¾ cup skinned toasted hazelnuts, ground
1 teaspoon ground cinnamon
1 cup seedless raspberry jam
Confectioners' sugar for dusting

1. Cream the butter and granulated sugar in a mixer bowl until light and fluffy. Using a wooden spoon, beat in the flour, almonds, hazelnuts, and cinnamon to make a slightly stiff dough. Wrap in plastic wrap and refrigerate at least 1 hour.

2. Preheat oven to 350°F. Lightly grease cookie sheets.

3. Roll out the dough ⅛ inch thick on a lightly floured surface. Cut out 24 trees with a 2½- to 3-inch tree-shaped cookie cutter. Place the trees on the prepared cookie sheets.

4. Cut out another 24 trees with the same cutter. Using a ¼-inch round cutter (such as a plastic drinking straw), cut out a few holes in each of the second batch of trees. Place this batch on lightly greased cookie sheets. If there is any extra dough, roll it out, then cut out an even number of trees. Make holes in half of them.

5. Bake both kinds of trees until lightly browned, 10 to 12 minutes. Remove to wire racks to cool completely.

6. When the cookies have cooled, spread the solid trees with a thin layer of the raspberry jam. Dust the trees with the holes with confectioners' sugar and place on the jam-coated trees.

2½ to 3 dozen cookies

VIENNESE COFFEEHOUSES

Vienna is the quintessential city for indulgence in exquisite pastries and richly brewed cups of coffee, and it is the elegant coffeehouse that is the most typical Viennese institution. The first coffeehouse was opened in the seventeenth century, when attacking Turks retreated and left behind sacks of coffee beans, which were instantly put to profitable use.

Sitting for hours over a steaming cup of coffee, away from the cares of the day, proved habit-forming and soon became an integral part of every Viennese person's life. Some coffeehouses were sacred to washerwomen and coachmen, while others became the favorite meeting spots of philosophers and politicians. Differentiations always remained distinct, and a café once chosen became a second home for life.

We think a coffeehouse is a fine place to be in snowy weather, be it along the banks of the Blue Danube or just around the corner. They are wonderful meeting spots—we can never figure out if it is good talkers that create the ambience in our favorite spots, or whether the coffeehouse itself breeds great conversation.

COGNAC SUGARPLUMS

A spirited little gem of a cookie that goes well with rich brewed coffee and the final nightcap of a holiday evening.

6 ounces semisweet chocolate bits
½ cup sugar, plus additional for coating
¼ cup light corn syrup
⅓ cup Cognac
2 ½ cups finely ground vanilla wafers
1 cup finely chopped pecans
Candied red and green cherry halves (garnish)

1. Melt the chocolate in the top of a double boiler over simmering water. Stir in ½ cup sugar, corn syrup, and Cognac. Stir in the wafer crumbs and nuts to make a pastelike mixture.

2. Roll into 1-inch balls. Roll each ball in additional sugar. Press a red or green cherry half into the center of each ball.

3. Store in an airtight container. These cookies improve with age.

4 dozen cookies

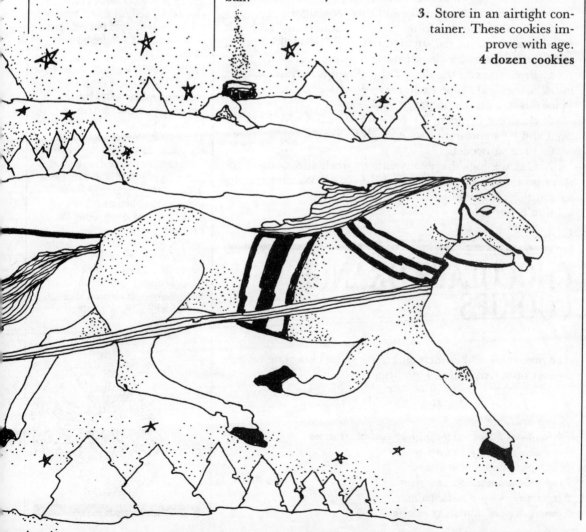

GRANNY REESMAN'S MANDELBROT

When it was time for a cup of tea, there was always a piece of *mandelbrot* in Sheila's house to dip in it. This not-too-sweet toasted bread is perfect with a cup of hot chocolate, too.

3 eggs, room temperature
1 cup sugar
⅓ cup vegetable oil
1 teaspoon vanilla extract
2¾ cups unbleached all-purpose flour
2 teaspoons baking powder
1 teaspoon ground cinnamon
¼ teaspoon salt
½ cup chopped walnuts

   1. Preheat oven to 350°F. Grease a cookie sheet.
   2. Beat the eggs and sugar in a mixer bowl until light and fluffy. Add the oil and vanilla and mix thoroughly.
   3. Sift the flour, baking powder, cinnamon, and salt together and add to the sugar mixture. Mix until blended, adding the nuts as the dough starts to come together.
   4. Briefly knead the dough on a floured surface. Divide into 2 pieces and shape each piece into a log, 3 inches wide. Place the logs on the prepared cookie sheet.
   5. Bake until golden, 30 to 35 minutes. Remove from the oven and let stand until cool enough to handle.
   6. Preheat broiler.
   7. Cut the logs diagonally into ½-inch slices. Broil the slices on the cookie sheet just until toasted. Watch carefully so that they do not burn.
   6 to 8 portions

CHOCOLATE-ORANGE COOKIES

The pistachios add crunch and make these chocolate-orange cookies taste like Italian Florentines.

½ cup (1 stick) unsalted butter
⅓ cup light corn syrup
2 tablespoons frozen orange juice concentrate, thawed
1 tablespoon finely grated orange zest
⅔ cup packed dark brown sugar
1 cup unbleached all-purpose flour
1 cup finely chopped pistachio nuts
6 ounces chopped bittersweet chocolate

HOLIDAY CHEESE WREATHS

SPICY CHEESE WREATH: Place 8 ounces softened cream cheese, 4 ounces sharp Cheddar cheese, 4 ounces Monterey Jack cheese with jalapeño peppers, and 2 ounces Stilton or blue cheese in a food processor fitted with a steel blade. Process until soft and well blended and remove to a mixing bowl. Fold in 2 ounces finely chopped Hot and Spicy Nuts (page 341). Line a small decorative ring mold with a double thickness of cheesecloth. Add the cheese mixture to the mold and pat down firmly and evenly. Cover the mold and refrigerate overnight. When ready to serve, invert the mold onto a serving platter and peel off the cheesecloth. Sprinkle with 2 more ounces finely chopped Hot and Spicy Nuts and garnish with fresh greens.
12 portions

SWEET CHEESE WREATH: Place 1 pound softened cream cheese, 4 ounces softened unsalted butter, ½ cup maple syrup, and 1 teaspoon Cognac in a food processor fitted with a steel blade. Process until smooth and remove to a mixing bowl. Fold in 1 cup chopped pecans. Line a small decorative ring mold with a double thickness of cheesecloth. Add the cheese mixture to the mold and pat down firmly and evenly. Cover the mold and refrigerate overnight. When ready to serve, invert the mold onto a serving platter and peel off the cheesecloth. Sprinkle with 2 tablespoons shredded coconut and 2 tablespoons finely chopped almonds. Garnish with sprigs of parsley.
12 portions

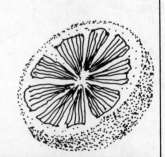

THE HOLIDAY BUFFET

♥ Potted narcissus are glorious at holiday time. Sparkle your table with these delicate starlike flowers. Be sure they're in little clay pots.

♥ Your table linens will create an overall effect at first glance. For a cozy feeling use an old red and white American quilt over the table. Roll silverware in white linen napkins and tie each one with a large dark green velvet bow. Stand them up in a fairly deep old basket, and you'll have created another centerpiece. Another approach is to cover your table with an old lace cloth—even a crocheted bedspread. Red and white checked linen napkins would be lovely here, tied with silver ribbon. Remember, though, to limit this to a non-food table if the covers are precious.

♥ Gather all your candlesticks, shine them up, and place them among the food on the table. Don't use scented candles because it detracts from the luscious aromas of the food.

♥ Fill a large wooden bowl with piles of clementines. These are easy to eat—no seeds—and arrive in the markets in December.

♥ Fill your prettiest little bowls with whole nuts in their shells and place a different style of nutcracker in each bowl.

♥ Always keep an eye on your buffet table to keep it crisp and clean looking. Pick up used glasses, plates, napkins, and nut shells as soon as possible.

♥ Present cookies beautifully in antique baskets lined with white lace liners. Combine all different shapes and types of cookies. At a large buffet party they are much easier to eat than sliced cakes. Make plenty—everyone loves cookies. Cut star shapes, decorate some with little silver balls, and sprinkle others with powdered sugar. You're creating a winter fantasy.

♥ As people walk in the door be sure to have the *Nutcracker Suite* playing, candles lit, and if possible a fire roaring. The first guest will feel that the party has already started.

1. Heat the butter, corn syrup, orange concentrate, orange zest, and sugar in a medium-size saucepan over medium heat to boiling. Remove from heat and gradually stir in the flour and nuts. Let cool completely and then stir in the chocolate. (If the mixture is warm, it will melt the chocolate.)

2. Preheat oven to 375°F. Line cookie sheets with aluminum foil and butter the foil.

3. Drop level teaspoons of the batter 3 inches apart on the prepared cookie sheets. Bake until golden, 8 to 10 minutes.

4. Let cool 5 minutes and then remove to wire racks to cool completely.

4 dozen cookies

ROCKY MOUNTAIN-CHIP COOKIES

We love the way chocolate dresses up these chewy cookies. Be sure you don't overbake them because they do harden as they cool.

½ cup (1 stick) margarine, room temperature
½ cup (1 stick) unsalted butter, room temperature
1 cup packed dark brown sugar
1 cup granulated sugar
2 eggs, lightly beaten
2 tablespoons milk
2 teaspoons vanilla extract
2 cups sifted unbleached all-purpose flour
1 teaspoon baking powder
1 teaspoon baking soda
1 teaspoon salt
2 cups quick-cooking oats
12 ounces semisweet chocolate chips
1 cup coarsely chopped walnuts

1. Cream the margarine, butter, and both sugars in a large mixer bowl until light and fluffy. Add the eggs, milk, and vanilla and beat until blended.

2. Sift the flour, baking powder, baking soda, and salt together and add to the butter mixture. Stir just until blended. Stir in the oats. Fold in the chocolate and walnuts.

3. Refrigerate the dough covered for at least 1 hour.

4. Preheat oven to 350°F. Grease cookie sheets.

5. Shape the dough into balls, using a rounded teaspoon for small cookies or a scant tablespoon for large. Flatten slightly into rounded disks. Place 2 inches apart on the prepared baking sheets. Bake until the edges are slightly browned but the cookies are still white, 8 to 10 minutes.

6. Remove from the oven and let cool on the sheets for 5 minutes. Remove to wire racks to cool completely.

100 small or 50 large cookies

OLDE ENGLISH TRIFLE

The traditional British dessert is a festive blend of rich flavors. Layer it decoratively in a favorite glass bowl and sit back and enjoy Christmas—the whole dessert can be prepared ahead of time.

1 Sara Lee pound cake (10 ¾ ounces), thawed
½ cup seedless raspberry jam
1 cup coarsely broken amaretti
1 cup Marsala
3 tablespoons granulated sugar
1 ½ tablespoons cornstarch
3 egg yolks
2 ½ cups milk
1 teaspoon vanilla extract
2 cups heavy or whipping cream, cold
3 tablespoons confectioners' sugar
½ teaspoon almond extract
1 cup toasted sliced almonds
Candied red cherries or fresh strawberries (garnish)

1. Cut the cake into ¼-inch slices and spread out flat on a surface to dry for several hours. Spread a thin layer of the jam on half the cake slices. Top with the remaining cake slices. Cut the cake sandwiches into 1-inch cubes and scatter in a large glass bowl.

2. Add the amaretti crumbs and toss together. Sprinkle with the Marsala and toss to coat.

3. Whisk the granulated sugar, cornstarch, and egg yolks together in a saucepan. Whisk in the milk in a thin, steady stream. Cook, stirring constantly, over medium heat until thickened to the consistency of a custard. Remove from heat and whisk in the vanilla. Let cool completely.

4. Pour the cooled custard over the cake mixture.

5. Whip the cream in a chilled bowl until soft peaks form. Beat in the confectioners' sugar and almond extract and continue beating until stiff. Pipe the flavored cream over the top of the trifle using a pastry bag, or spoon it over decoratively. Scatter the almonds over the top. Refrigerate, covered with plastic wrap, until ready to serve, up to 3 days.

6. Spoon the trifle into glass bowls and garnish with candied cherries.

8 to 10 portions

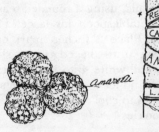

VANILLA

Vanilla is one of the most familiar flavorings in our everyday foods, yet few of us ever stop to appreciate how many taste treats it actually enhances. Vanilla comes from a rare species of the orchid family which produces a suitable bean only on a single day once a year. If the day is missed, a whole year must pass before another bean can be harvested. Once the bean is picked, it is immediately dipped into boiling water to stop its growth. Then it is placed in the sun to cure for six to nine months, inducing the subtle chemical changes that give vanilla its unique qualities.

Beware of artificial vanilla made from vanillin—the flavor can't compare to the real thing. In addition to using vanilla extract in many baked goods and sweets, we like to stash a whole bean in our sugar canister to intensify the flavor in baking or to jazz up the spoonful in our morning coffee.

HOLLY BERRIES

The essence of Christmastime, holly was originally hung over doorways as the herb of the fairies. Hollies are native to Cape Cod and some trees now living may well have been there when the Pilgrims landed. Today it brings cheer to all, and a sprig carried home from church brings good luck, life everlasting, friendship, hope, and festivity.

CHOCOLATE-RASPBERRY CAKE

This untraditional cake was created to please a chocolate fanatic on her wedding day. Dense, Sachertorte-like layers are brushed with melted raspberry jam and liqueur, and the whole cake is frosted with a shiny bittersweet glaze. Fresh raspberries and flowers decorate it elegantly.

CAKE:

12 ounces semisweet chocolate
2 cups (4 sticks) unsalted butter, room temperature
2 cups confectioners' sugar, sifted
16 egg yolks, room temperature
2 cups unbleached all-purpose flour, sifted
3 tablespoons framboise liqueur
20 egg whites, room temperature

GLAZE:

¾ cup seedless raspberry jam
2 tablespoons framboise liqueur

FROSTING:

1 ½ cups heavy or whipping cream
⅓ cup light corn syrup
9 ounces semisweet or bittersweet chocolate, broken into small pieces
1 ½ ounces unsweetened chocolate, finely chopped

GARNISH:

1 pint fresh raspberries
Fresh flowers

    1. To make the cake, preheat oven to 300°F. Butter 3 cake pans, 10, 8, and 6 inches; line the bottom of each pan with parchment paper and butter the paper.
    2. Melt the chocolate in the top of a double boiler over simmering water. Set aside to cool. Cream the butter in a large mixer bowl until light and fluffy. Beat the cooled chocolate into the butter. Beat in the confectioners' sugar. Add the egg yolks, one at a time, beating well after each addition. Stir in the sifted flour until well blended. Stir in the liqueur.
    3. Beat the egg whites until stiff but not dry and fold gently into the batter. Pour into the prepared pans.
    4. Bake until the center is firm and the cake has pulled away from the side of the pan, 45 minutes to 1 hour,

THE ART OF HOUSE GIFTS

Giving and receiving house gifts can be tricky—timing and appropriateness are important to the giver, and attention and graciousness key to the recipient.
    If the gift is presented upon arrival at a party, do so quietly, and make sure it needs little immediate attention. For example, bring fresh flowers already arranged in a vase, or better, send some earlier in the day. If the gift is wine, mention that it is for the cellar and not for the meal, so the host does not feel obliged to use it. There are a multitude of other options: books, homemade gifts of food or folly, a framed photograph of an earlier party, the latest hot game, a much-longed-for cooking gadget, a record.
    When you are given a house gift, don't let your thanks disappear amidst the introductions, taking of coats, offers of drinks, and so on. A momentary and thoughtful aside is all that is necessary to accept a gift graciously—but a note or a phone call the next day never hurts. If the gift is wrapped, leave the opening until after the party.

depending on the size of the layers. Let cool and then turn out of the pans. Peel off the parchment paper.

5. To make the glaze, heat the jam and liqueur, stirring occasionally, just until melted and smooth.

6. Cut each cake layer horizontally in half and brush the cut sides with the glaze. Put the layers together again and brush the top and side of each layer with glaze.

7. Cut 3 cardboard circles exactly the same size as each cake layer. Place the cake layers on their cardboard circles and assemble the tiered cake.

8. To make the frosting, heat the cream and corn syrup to boiling. Immediately remove from heat and stir in both chocolates. Cover and let stand for 5 minutes; then stir to melt the chocolate completely. If the chocolate is not completely melted, stir the mixture over very low heat. Let cool to barely warm.

9. Place the cake on a wire rack over waxed paper to catch the dripping frosting. Pour the frosting over the cake, starting at the top center and letting the frosting cascade over the layers. Fill in any missed spots with a narrow metal spatula, if necessary. Let the frosting set at least 1 hour. Store in a cool place until ready to serve but no longer than 1 day.

10. Just before serving, decorate the layers with the fresh raspberries and flowers.

35 portions

CRANBERRY-CURRANT CONSERVE TART

Our tart and chunky cranberry conserve makes a perfect filling for this holiday tart, which is baked on a fragile cookielike crust. Serve warm with a dollop of sour cream.

PASTRY:

½ cup (1 stick) unsalted butter, cold, cut into small pieces
2 cups sifted unbleached all-purpose flour
⅓ cup sugar
¼ teaspoon salt
2 eggs, lightly beaten

FILLING:

2 ½ cups Cranberry Currant Conserve

TOPPING:

3 tablespoons unsalted butter, room temperature
¼ cup sugar
½ cup finely chopped walnuts
Finely minced zest of 1 orange
About ½ cup unbleached all-purpose flour

CRANBERRY CURRANT CONSERVE

1 thin-skinned orange, seeds removed, cut into eighths
1 pound fresh cranberries
½ cup dried currants
2 cups firmly packed dark brown sugar
1½ cups raspberry vinegar
1 teaspoon ground cinnamon
½ teaspoon ground cloves
½ teaspoon salt
⅛ teaspoon freshly ground black pepper
1 cup coarsely chopped walnuts

1. Process the orange in a food processor fitted with a steel blade until coarsely chopped.

2. Combine the chopped orange with all the remaining ingredients except the walnuts in a heavy saucepan. Simmer, uncovered, until all the cranberries have popped open, 10 to 12 minutes. Skim any foam from the top. Remove from heat and stir in the walnuts.

3. Pack conserve not being used immediately into hot sterilized jars and process in a boiling water bath.
Makes 6 half pints.

1. To make the pastry, cut the butter into the flour with a pastry blender. Stir in the sugar, salt, and eggs to make a soft dough. Refrigerate, wrapped in plastic wrap, for 1 hour.

2. Make the cranberry currant conserve.

3. To make the topping, cream the butter and sugar in a small mixer bowl. Stir in the walnuts and orange zest. Stir in just enough of the flour to make a crumbly mixture.

4. Preheat oven to 350°F.

5. Roll out the dough on a lightly floured surface. Line a 10-inch tart pan with removable bottom with the pastry, and prick it all over with a fork.

6. Spread the conserve evenly in the tart shell. Sprinkle the topping over the conserve, concentrating it in the center.

7. Bake until golden brown, 40 to 50 minutes. Cool slightly and remove the side of the pan. Serve warm.

6 to 8 portions

At holiday time the Silver Palate phones are buzzing with calls for help with office parties and large private Christmas parties. People want food that's easy to eat—and plenty of it. We always refer to it as "lush and abundant." It must also look festive.

Dramatic presentations are appropriate at this time, therefore serve whole cheeses, such as Corolle, St. André, or Stilton. Corolle is great because it has a hole in the center—you can create a cheese wreath. Fill the center with Hot and Spicy Nuts and surround the cheese with deep green holly leaves with red berries. Don't forget to cut out the first wedge of cheese.

WHITE CHOCOLATE MOUSSE WITH FRANGELICO

A sumptuous combination of white chocolate and hazelnut liqueur, topped with a dusting of cocoa for a striking color contrast.

8 ounces best-quality white chocolate, broken into small pieces
½ cup (1 stick) unsalted butter
6 eggs, separated, room temperature
1 cup sifted confectioners' sugar
½ cup Frangelico liqueur
2 cups whipping cream, cold
Pinch cream of tartar
Unsweetened cocoa powder or grated dark chocolate (garnish)

1. Melt the white chocolate and butter in a small saucepan, stirring constantly. Set aside.

2. Beat the egg yolks, sugar, and liqueur until the mixture forms a slowly dissolving ribbon when the beaters are lifted. Pour the mixture into the top of a double boiler and cook, whisking constantly, over simmering water until very thick, about 3 minutes.

3. Remove to a large mixing bowl. Whisk in the white chocolate mixture and stir until smooth and cool.

4. Beat the cream until the peaks are stiff. In a separate bowl with clean beaters, beat the egg whites with the cream of tartar until stiff but not dry. Gently fold the egg whites into the chocolate mixture; then fold in the whipped cream. Refrigerate covered until set, about 3 hours.

5. Spoon the chilled mousse into individual ramekins or goblets. Sprinkle with cocoa or grated chocolate.

10 to 12 portions

CHRISTMAS EVE

Christmas Eve is our favorite part of Christmas. It embodies the essence of anticipation, a moment that is still and expectant. Presents lie wrapped and beribboned beneath a glowing tree, and the crackle of the yule log beckons us all to gather around and feel the warmth of the season. The frantic holiday pace is winding down, and we have time to dream of a white Christmas ahead.

Wassail bowls and nutmeg-speckled eggnogs fill us with good cheer, while the mingling aromas of Christmas spices, savory rib roasts, and plentiful evergreens add to the excitement. The evening ends as stockings are hung with care, and for a moment the idea of Santa Claus becomes very real indeed.

CHRISTMAS EVE

Christopher Wren Gems

Roast Beef Laurels

Yorkshire Pudding

Cornmeal Gnocchi with Sage

Roasted potatoes

Spinach, Avocado, and Pomegranate Salad

Olde English Trifle

Hermitage

CHRISTOPHER WREN GEMS

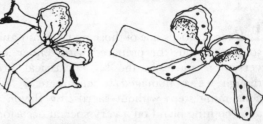

Dried figs and dates come to life when plumped in Marsala. The cream cheese filling abounds with hazelnuts, and all is wrapped in prosciutto. (Make sure the prosciutto you use isn't too salty.) Serve hot on a small silver platter and sprinkle with lemon juice.

8 ounces Calimyrna figs
8 ounces pitted large dates
1 cup plus 1 tablespoon Marsala
8 ounces cream cheese, room temperature
½ cup hazelnuts, toasted and chopped
8 ounces prosciutto, thinly sliced
Juice of ½ lemon
Lemon or lime slices (garnish)
Chopped fresh Italian parsley (garnish)

1. Cut the figs in half and combine with the dates in a small bowl. Cover with 1 cup Marsala and let stand at least 1 hour.

2. Process the cream cheese, hazelnuts, and 1 tablespoon Marsala in a food processor fitted with a steel blade until blended. Refrigerate until cold.

3. Drain the figs and dates, reserving the Marsala. Slit each date down the center and open each fig half along the cut side to form a pocket. Fill each fig and date with a heaping teaspoon of the cream cheese mixture.

4. Preheat oven to 350°F.

5. Cut strips of prosciutto slightly smaller than the dates and figs are long and wrap 1 strip around each stuffed fruit. Sprinkle with some of the reserved Marsala as you work to keep the prosciutto from drying out.

6. Place the wrapped figs and dates on a baking sheet and bake until heated through, 7 to 10 minutes. Let cool slightly, arrange on a serving dish, sprinkle with lemon juice, and garnish with lemon slices and parsley.

About 50 hors d'oeuvres

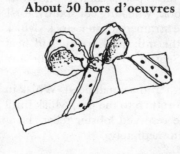

✤ FLOWERS FROM THE SILVER PALATE

Tie bunches of mistletoe with shiny silver and red satin ribbon and put one at each place setting with a place card tucked in.

LOBSTER BISQUE

Lobster bisque is one of those extravagant and quintessential soups that must be prepared with tender loving care. Our version is made in the basic classical French tradition, though we've managed to eliminate a few of the time-consuming steps without sacrificing flavor. Savor this rich and soothing blend on a very special occasion.

2 gallons water
2 live lobsters (1 to 1 ¼ pounds each)
6 tablespoons (¾ stick) unsalted butter
⅓ cup Cognac
½ cup plus 3 tablespoons chopped shallots
2 cloves garlic, minced
3 tablespoons tomato paste
2 ½ cups dry white wine
1 teaspoon dried tarragon
½ teaspoon dried thyme
Pinch red pepper flakes
2 bay leaves
3 tablespoons unbleached all-purpose flour
2 ½ cups milk
¾ cup heavy or whipping cream
Salt and freshly ground black pepper, to taste
2 egg yolks

1. Heat the water in a large stock pot to boiling. Drop in the lobsters and cook covered for 12 minutes. Remove the lobsters from the pot; reserve 4 cups of the water. Let the lobsters cool.

2. When the lobsters are cool enough to handle, crack the shells and remove all the lobster meat. Finely dice the meat and set aside. Reserve the shells.

3. Melt half the butter in a large skillet over medium heat. Add the lobster shells and pour in the Cognac. Heat until the Cognac is warm, then flame it with a match. When the flames subside, stir in ½ cup shallots, the garlic, tomato paste, wine, reserved cooking liquid, the tarragon, thyme, red pepper flakes, and bay leaves. Simmer uncovered for 30 minutes. Strain through a sieve into a bowl.

4. Melt the remaining 3 tablespoons butter in a stock pot over medium-high heat. Add 3 tablespoons shallots and sauté 2 minutes. Add the flour and cook, whisking constantly, for 1 minute. Gradually whisk in the strained lobster stock; whisk until well blended. Whisk in the milk and cream and heat over medium heat until hot. Season to taste with salt and pepper.

5. Whisk the egg yolks together in a small bowl. Whisk in ½ cup of the hot soup and then return to the pot; whisk until thoroughly blended. Stir in the reserved lobster meat. Heat for several minutes and serve immediately.

6 very rich portions

PARTY PRESENTS

Give a little present to each of your guests. Collect miniature shopping bags and fill them with little homemade jams, perfumed soaps, a potpourri sachet, and put them at each place setting.

RED AND GREEN CHRISTMAS SALAD

10 cups torn spinach leaves
1 medium-size avocado, pitted, peeled, and thinly sliced
Seeds of 1 pomegranate
1 cup Warm Champagne Vinegar Dressing (recipe follows)

1. Place the spinach leaves in a large salad bowl and arrange the avocado slices in a circle around the edge of the salad. Place the pomegranate seeds in the center of the salad.

2. Make the warm dressing.

3. Pour 1 cup of the dressing over the salad at the table, toss, and divide between salad plates.

8 portions

WARM CHAMPAGNE VINEGAR DRESSING

1 cup Champagne vinegar
2 tablespoons sugar
1 ½ tablespoons unbleached all-purpose flour
2 teaspoons dry vermouth
1 teaspoon Dijon-style mustard
1 egg, beaten
3 tablespoons heavy or whipping cream
2 cups olive oil
Salt and freshly ground black pepper, to taste

1. Combine the vinegar, sugar, flour, vermouth, and mustard in a small saucepan. Heat to simmering over medium heat.

2. Gradually whisk in the egg and cream over low heat. Whisk in the oil in a thin steady stream. Season with salt and pepper to taste. Remove from the heat.

3 cups

MUSICAL NOTES

Maintain the formal mood throughout a fancy dinner party with the music of Mozart, Beethoven, and Bach playing softly in the background.

Set the mood for a Winter Escape dinner with calypso music or the exotic sounds of Ravi Shankar's sitar.

On a cold winter night, curl up in front of the fire with a steaming bowl of soup—and some Brahms in the background.

Complete the seductive atmosphere on Valentine's Day with romantic music—Chopin's preludes, Liszt's *Hungarian Rhapsodies*, Tchaikovsky's *Romeo and Juliet*, or Ravel's *Boléro*.

ROAST BEEF LAURELS

GOAT CHEESE POPOVERS AS YORKSHIRE PUDDING

First, refer to the Goat-Cheese Popover recipe on page 59. Substitute ⅓ cup hot roast beef fat for the walnut oil. Pour the fat into a 13 x 9-inch Pyrex dish. Pour in the popover mixture and crumble the goat cheese evenly over the top. Place in a preheated 400°F oven and bake until puffed and golden, 45 to 55 minutes. Serve immediately.

A standing rib roast is classic and beautiful when served at winter holiday festivities surrounded by dark green holly. We've puréed garlic and placed it over the roast before baking it with lots of red wine. Be sure to serve the juices!

2 heads garlic, cloves peeled
1 teaspoon salt
1 standing rib roast of beef (6½ pounds), fat trimmed in one strip and reserved
12 bay leaves
Salt and freshly ground black pepper, to taste
2 cups red wine

1. Preheat oven to 450°F.
2. Process the garlic in a blender or a food processor fitted with a steel blade to a purée. Add 1 teaspoon salt to the garlic and process to a paste. Pat the garlic paste in an even layer over the top and sides of the roast. Place the bay leaves evenly over the garlic.
3. Place the trimmed strip of fat over the garlic and bay leaves. Tie in place with kitchen string. Sprinkle the roast all over with salt and pepper. Place in a roasting pan; pour the red wine in the bottom of the pan.
4. Roast for 20 minutes. Reduce the heat to 350°F. Roast about 18 minutes per pound for rare or 22 minutes per pound for medium done. Let stand 5 minutes before carving.

8 portions

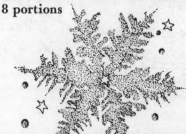

CORNMEAL GNOCCHI WITH SAGE

This is simply delicious with a standing rib roast. Buy an extra bunch of silvery fresh sage for garnish.

2 cups milk
½ cup water
1 cup fine yellow cornmeal
1 teaspoon salt
8 tablespoons (1 stick) unsalted butter
2 eggs, lightly beaten separately
12 fresh sage leaves
½ cup unbleached all-purpose flour
1½ cups freshly grated Parmesan cheese

1. Heat the milk and water in a medium-size saucepan to boiling. Remove from heat and gradually stir in the cornmeal and salt, mixing well. Cook over low heat, stirring constantly, until smooth and quite thick, about 15 minutes.

2. Remove from heat and add 1 tablespoon of the butter and 1 egg. Stir quickly to blend. Lightly moisten a cookie sheet with water and spread the cornmeal mixture in an even ½-inch layer. Let cool to room temperature.

3. Meanwhile, dip each sage leaf in the remaining beaten egg and then coat with the flour. Heat 3 tablespoons of the remaining butter in a sauté pan over medium heat. Add the dipped leaves and sauté until golden on both sides. Drain on paper towels.

4. Preheat oven to 350°F. Butter an au gratin dish with 1 tablespoon of the remaining butter.

5. Cut the gnocchi into rounds with a 1½-inch biscuit cutter. Arrange the gnocchi in slightly overlapping rows in the prepared dish. Crumble the sage leaves over the gnocchi. Dot with the remaining 3 tablespoons butter. Sprinkle the Parmesan over the top.

6. Bake until puffed and brown, about 25 minutes. Serve immediately.

6 to 8 portions

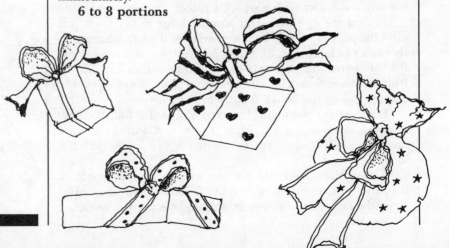

ST. NICHOLAS CAKE

This has become a holiday tradition in our store. It's the only fruitcake we've ever liked because it's chock-full of dates, walnuts, and cherries, bound together with only a minimum of batter.

pit in a date

8 cups pitted whole dates (about 3 pounds)
8 cups walnut halves (about 1 ¾ pounds)
1 cup candied cherries (about 6 ounces)
½ cup unbleached all-purpose flour
6 eggs, separated, room temperature
¾ cup granulated sugar
¾ cup packed dark brown sugar
6 tablespoons (¾ stick) unsalted butter, melted
4 ½ tablespoons heavy or whipping cream
2 tablespoons vanilla extract
2 teaspoons grated orange zest
½ teaspoon almond extract
1 ½ cups whole-wheat flour
2 ½ teaspoons baking powder

1. Preheat oven to 325°F. Butter three 9 x 5 x 3-inch loaf pans. Line the bottoms and sides with foil and butter the foil generously.

2. Combine the dates, walnuts, and cherries in a very large bowl or roasting pan. Sprinkle with the all-purpose flour and toss to coat well, separating the dates with your fingers.

3. Combine the egg yolks and the sugars in a large mixer bowl; beat until light and fluffy. Beat in the butter, cream, vanilla, orange zest, and almond extract. Mix the whole-wheat flour and baking powder thoroughly in a small bowl; stir into the batter with a wooden spoon.

4. Beat the egg whites in another large mixer bowl just until the peaks are stiff. Fold a quarter of the egg whites into the batter to lighten it, and then fold in the remaining. Pour the batter over the date mixture and mix well to coat all the fruit and nuts. Spoon into the prepared pans, dividing evenly and mounding the batter slightly in the pans.

5. Cover the pans with buttered aluminum foil. Bake 40 minutes; remove the foil from the tops. Continue baking until the centers are firm to the touch, 15 to 20 minutes longer.

6. Cool the cakes in the pans on wire racks. Remove from the pans; wrap tightly in aluminum foil. The fruitcake can be eaten the next day or stored in a cool place up to 2 weeks.

3 cakes

HOLIDAY CAKES

A day arrives in November, and somehow people know—it's fruitcake weather! The kind of work we all like best begins with buying cherries and citron, ginger, butter, dates, walnuts, and many eggs and spices.

Eggbeaters whirl, spoons spin round in bowls of butter and sugar, vanilla sweetens the air, ginger spices it; melting, nose-tingling odors saturate the kitchen, suffuse the house, drift out to the world on puffs of chimney smoke. Cakes to be laced with whiskey over the next month bask on windowsills and shelves . . . all awaiting the holiday season.

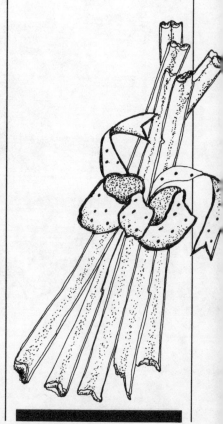

CHRISTMAS MORNING BREAKFAST

We used to have a rule when we were little: if you woke first on Christmas morning you could sneak down and open one present—but then you had to wait. It was deciding which present to choose that kept us up all night. Once the family was up—it seemed to take forever—and all the gifts exchanged, we helped Dad make a great big Christmas breakfast.

"Now Christmas is
  come
Let's beat up the
  drum,
And call all our
  neighbors together,
And when they
  appear,
Let us make them
  such cheer."
—Washington Irving

EGGNOG FRENCH TOAST

There couldn't be a more perfect or simple way to begin Christmas morning than with eggnog toast. Because the eggnog is already prepared, you have plenty of time to peek into stockings and open Christmas presents.

2 cups prepared eggnog
12 thick slices stale firm white bread
8 tablespoons (1 stick) unsalted butter

1. Pour the eggnog into a shallow bowl and dip the bread slices into the eggnog, turning to coat both sides.
2. Melt 2 tablespoons of the butter in a skillet over medium-high heat. Add 2 or 3 slices of the bread and fry until golden on both sides. Repeat with the remaining bread and butter.
6 portions

SURPRISE FLAPJACKS

An unusual variation of an all-American favorite. The aroma of these on the griddle will send everyone scurrying to the breakfast table.

1 ½ cups whole-wheat flour
1 cup unbleached all-purpose flour
1 cup old-fashioned rolled oats
½ cup yellow cornmeal
1 tablespoon baking powder
2 teaspoons baking soda
1 teaspoon salt
¾ cup (1 ½ sticks) unsalted butter, cold, cut into small pieces
4 eggs
4 cups buttermilk
½ cup honey
1 cup chopped pecans
Melted butter

   1. Process the whole-wheat flour, all-purpose flour, oats, cornmeal, baking powder, baking soda, and salt in a food processor fitted with a steel blade until well blended. Add the butter and process until the mixture resembles coarse meal.
   2. Beat the eggs and buttermilk together in a large mixing bowl. Beat in the honey. Stir in the flour mixture and then fold in the chopped pecans.
   3. Heat a pancake griddle and brush it with melted butter. Ladle the batter onto the griddle to make 6-inch pancakes. Cook until golden on both sides. Serve with butter and maple syrup.
   6 to 8 portions

MAPLE-WALNUT MUFFINS

Incredibly moist muffins with an interesting texture of walnuts, chopped dates, and rolled oats. These keep well and make lovely gifts for family and friends.

1 ⅓ cups chopped walnuts
3 tablespoons unsalted butter, room temperature
2 eggs
1 cup heavy or whipping cream
1 ⅓ cups pure maple syrup
1 teaspoon maple extract
1 ½ cups unbleached all-purpose flour
1 ½ cups old-fashioned rolled oats
1 tablespoon ground cinnamon
2 teaspoons baking powder
1 teaspoon baking soda
1 cup chopped pitted dates

CHRISTMAS MORNING BREAKFAST

Mimosas

Sliced Oranges with Cranberry Coulis

Eggnog French Toast

Maple-cured bacon

Santa Lucia Buns

Cappuccino

1. Preheat oven to 350°F. Line 20 muffin cups with paper liners.

2. Toss the walnuts and butter together on a baking sheet and toast in the oven for 10 to 15 minutes, stirring occasionally. Set aside. Keep the oven on.

3. Beat the eggs, cream, 1 cup of the maple syrup, and the maple extract together in a mixing bowl.

4. Combine the flour, oats, cinnamon, baking powder, and baking soda. Stir into the egg mixture just until combined. Stir in the dates and 1 cup of the toasted walnuts.

5. Fill each muffin cup three-fourths full with the batter. Sprinkle the tops with the remaining walnuts and drizzle with the remaining syrup. Bake for 20 minutes. Poke a toothpick into the center of a muffin. If it comes out dry, the muffins are done.

20 muffins

CHRISTMAS COFFEE CAKE

A delicious cake to showcase the fruits of the season.

4 tablespoons (½ stick) unsalted butter, room temperature
1¼ cups sugar
2 eggs, separated, room temperature
1 teaspoon vanilla extract
1½ cups plus 2 tablespoons unbleached all-purpose flour
2 teaspoons baking powder
½ cup buttermilk
2 cups peeled, sliced fresh fruit
1 cup chopped walnuts
4 tablespoons melted unsalted butter
1½ teaspoons ground cinnamon

1. Preheat oven to 375°F. Grease and flour a 9-inch cake pan.

2. Cream the butter and ¾ cup of the sugar in a large mixer bowl until light and fluffy. Add the egg yolks and beat well. Add the vanilla and beat until blended.

3. Sift 1½ cups flour and the baking powder together. Add the flour mixture alternately with the buttermilk to the butter mixture, beating well after each addition and beginning and ending with the flour mixture.

4. Sprinkle 2 tablespoons flour over the fruit in a separate bowl and toss to coat.

5. Beat the egg whites until stiff and fold into the batter. Pour the batter into the prepared pan and arrange the fruit over the top.

6. Combine the remaining ½ cup sugar, the walnuts, melted butter, and the cinnamon in a small bowl. Pat the mixture gently over the fruit.

7. Bake until a cake tester inserted in the center of the cake is withdrawn clean, 35 to 45 minutes. Cool in the pan on a wire rack and serve slightly warm.

8 portions

SANTA LUCIA BUNS

"Santa Lucia Buns"
a Swedish Christmas

Wagon Wheels

Twists

Goat Horns

These rich saffron buns are traditionally served in Sweden on December 13, when the eldest daughter in the household wears a wreath of candles and wakes everyone to steaming coffee and warm Santa Lucia buns. The whimsical shapes—wagon wheels, Santa twists, goat horns, and the standard Lucia bun—are fun to make. These are sure to become a favorite part of your family's Christmas traditions.

1 cup light cream
¾ cup sugar
½ cup (1 stick) unsalted butter
1 teaspoon saffron threads
1 teaspoon salt
2 packages active dry yeast
¾ cup warm water, 105° to 115°F
5½ cups unbleached all-purpose flour
3 eggs
½ cup golden raisins
1 cup ground almonds
¼ cup dark raisins
2 teaspoons water

Lucia Buns

HOLIDAY TRADITIONS

As the holidays approach, the days grow shorter and we bundle up, anxious to get home where it's cozy and warm. To our minds these holidays are the most festive occasions of the year—when you gather in your family and your most cherished friends. Dinner parties, buffets, open houses, holiday balls, fireside picnics, Champagne and dessert parties—you need to pace yourself. It's the time when extra effort needs to be sustained; good humor glosses over any mood, and sensitivity and love prevail. Good food and drink are at the heart of holiday entertaining, and imagination is the key to survival.

1. Heat the cream just until hot, but not boiling, in a medium-size saucepan. Remove from heat. Add the sugar, butter, saffron, and salt, and stir until the butter is melted. Let cool to room temperature.

2. Stir the yeast into the warm water in a large mixing bowl. Let stand until foamy, about 5 minutes.

3. Stir the cream mixture into the dissolved yeast. Using a wooden spoon, stir in 2½ cups of the flour; beat until smooth. Beat in 2 of the eggs, the golden raisins, and ground almonds. Gradually incorporate the remaining flour, first stirring with the spoon and then mixing with your hands. The dough will be fairly soft.

4. Turn the dough out onto a lightly floured surface and knead until smooth and elastic, 5 to 10 minutes.

5. Place the dough in a large buttered bowl and turn to coat with butter. Let rise, covered with a damp towel, in a warm place until doubled in bulk, about 1½ hours.

6. Punch the dough down and place on a lightly floured surface. Cut into 20 pieces. Roll the dough into ropes on a work surface and shape on greased cookie sheets in any of the ways that follow.

DECK THE HALLS BREAKFAST

Sliced Oranges with Cranberry Coulis

Sunny Baked Eggs

Surprise Flapjacks

Spicy Breakfast Sausage

Maple Walnut Muffins

Hot chocolate

''My ship has sails that are made of silk It's decks are trimmed with gold Of jam and spice there's a paradise In the hold.''
—©Kurt Weill & Ira Gershwin

7. Cover the buns with a damp towel and let rise until doubled in bulk, about 45 minutes.

8. Preheat oven to 375°F.

9. Mix the remaining egg and the 2 teaspoons water. Just before baking, brush the buns with the egg wash.

10. Bake until golden brown, 12 to 15 minutes. Remove to wire racks to cool. Serve warm or at room temperature with plenty of butter.

About 10 large or 20 small buns

WAGON WHEELS: Roll 2 pieces of dough into 10-inch ropes, ½ inch wide. Place the 2 strips side by side on the cookie sheet. Pinch all but the ends together and coil each of the 4 ends to resemble the diagram. Press a dark raisin in the center of each coil.

SANTA TWISTS: Roll 1 slightly smaller piece of dough into an 8-inch rope, ½ inch wide. Coil the ends in opposite directions, making an S that resembles the diagram. Press a dark raisin into the center of each coil.

SANTA LUCIA BUNS: Roll 2 pieces of dough into 10-inch ropes, ½ inch wide. Make an X with the ropes. Coil each end counterclockwise to resemble the diagram. Press a dark raisin in the center of each coil.

GOAT HORNS: Roll 1 piece of dough into a 10-inch rope, ½ inch wide. Make a V and coil each end to make horns that resemble the diagram. Press a dark raisin in the center of each coil.

SLICED ORANGES WITH CRANBERRY COULIS

A terrific breakfast compote for Christmas morning.

1½ pounds fresh cranberries
1¼ cups sugar
1 cup fresh orange juice
Grated zest of 1 orange
½ cup water
⅓ cup orange liqueur
6 oranges, peels and white membranes removed, cut into ½-inch slices

1. Simmer the cranberries, sugar, and orange juice uncovered in a medium-size saucepan for 15 minutes.

2. Add the orange zest and water. Simmer uncovered another 15 minutes, stirring occasionally.

3. Strain the cranberry mixture through a fine-mesh sieve. Stir in the liqueur. Let cool to room temperature.

4. On each of 6 dessert plates, make a pool of the cranberry coulis. Fan a sliced orange on each cranberry pool; spoon a little more cranberry coulis over the oranges.

6 portions

CHRISTMAS DAY DINNER

Dinner on Christmas Day is the culmination of the holiday feasting. After all the presents have been opened, the final treat of the day—a delicious meal—tempts us with its wafting aromas. We like a traditional dinner of succulent scalloped oysters, fruity roast goose, and an elegant Strawberry-Hazelnut Torte. The pace of Christmas Day is slow, with plenty of time for listening to favorite Christmas music, catching up with family and friends, and sharing a formal dinner toward the end of the day. There is no need to rush, for Christmas comes but once a year.

Adding a little spice just before a meal begins is an excellent way to stimulate the taste buds and whet the appetite. We love this recipe made with one favorite nut or a combination of many. We often warm them just a bit in the oven before serving in a ceramic crock, an antique basket, or an art deco silver bowl .

HOT AND SPICY NUTS

2 tablespoons unsalted butter
1 tablespoon Worcestershire sauce
¼ teaspoon ground cumin
½ teaspoon celery salt
½ teaspoon garlic powder
⅛ teaspoon cayenne pepper
½ teaspoon seasoned salt
1 ½ cups mixed unsalted roasted nuts
1 tablespoon coarse (kosher) salt

1. Preheat oven to 325°F.

2. Melt the butter in a medium-size saucepan over low heat. Add the remaining ingredients except the nuts and coarse salt. Simmer over low heat for several minutes to combine flavors.

3. Add the nuts and stir until evenly coated. Spread on a baking sheet and bake for 15 to 20 minutes, shaking the pan occasionally.

4. Toss the nuts with the coarse salt and let cool. Store in an airtight container.

1 ½ cups

SCALLOPED OYSTERS

1 pint shelled, undrained oysters
1 ½ cups crushed Ritz crackers
½ cup (1 stick) unsalted butter, melted
2 teaspoons fresh lemon juice
Salt and freshly ground black pepper, to taste
¾ cup heavy or whipping cream
1 tablespoon dry sherry
Dash Worcestershire sauce

1. Preheat oven to 350°F.

2. Drain the oysters; measure ½ cup juice and reserve.

3. Combine the crackers, butter, lemon juice, and salt and pepper to taste. Sprinkle a third of the crumb mixture in the bottom of a buttered 3-cup au gratin dish. Arrange half the oysters over the crumbs. Sprinkle another third of the crumb mixture over the oysters and top with the remaining oysters.

4. Whisk the cream, reserved oyster juice, the sherry, and Worcestershire sauce together and pour over the oysters. Sprinkle with the remaining crumb mixture.

5. Bake for 40 minutes. Serve immediately.

6 portions

CHRISTMAS GOOSE

A most unusual stuffing in a traditional holiday bird. The tart cranberries and kumquats balance in flavor and texture with the pork sausage and crunchy pistachios. An orange-flavored liqueur blends the flavors all together. Goes best with a wonderful red Burgundy wine.

1 pound bulk pork sausage
½ cup (1 stick) unsalted butter
1 large yellow onion, chopped
5 ribs celery, coarsely chopped
1½ cups dry white wine
1 bag (1 pound) dried herb stuffing
12 ounces fresh cranberries
1 jar (9 ounces) kumquats, drained and quartered
½ cup shelled pistachio nuts
¼ cup Cointreau or Grand Marnier
2 eggs, lightly beaten
Salt and freshly ground black pepper, to taste
1 goose (9 to 11 pounds)
1 lemon, halved
1 teaspoon ground allspice
½ cup pure maple syrup

1. Sauté the pork sausage in a large skillet, crumbling it with a fork, just until it is no longer pink. Transfer to a large mixing bowl.
2. Melt the butter in the same skillet over medium heat. Add the onion and celery and sauté about 10 minutes. Stir in the wine and cook 1 minute more. Add the herb stuffing to the sausage, pour the vegetable mixture over all, and stir to combine thoroughly.
3. Add the cranberries, kumquats, and pistachios to the stuffing and stir to combine. Moisten the stuffing with the Cointreau and eggs. Season to taste with salt and pepper.
4. Preheat oven to 450°F.
5. Rinse the goose and pat dry. Rub inside and out with the cut lemon. Sprinkle the cavity with salt and pepper.
6. Loosely stuff the bird and then truss. (Extra stuffing can be baked in a greased casserole for about 40 minutes at 350°F.) Fill a roasting pan with ½ inch water. Place the goose in the pan and sprinkle with the allspice, salt, and pepper.
7. Roast the goose for 20 minutes. Reduce the heat to 350°F. Continue roasting until juices run clear when the thickest part of the thigh is pierced, about 20 minutes per pound. Baste first with the syrup and then the accumulated pan juices.
8. Remove from the oven and let stand about 10 minutes before carving.

6 portions

Wouldn't it be fun to live in a place called Santa Claus, Noel, or the North Pole? There is Noel, Missouri; Silver Bell, Arizona; Joy, Illinois; Evergreen, Alabama; Snowflake, Arizona; and Santa Claus, Indiana. But the most fun of all would be to live in the North Pole. There's one in Colorado and one in New York, but to us, it's the one in Alaska that is the real frosty little town.

Absolutely beautiful—yellow and red onions and green and white leeks baked with a mild Havarti cheese, a spicy Boursin, and a nutty Gruyère. The cheese melts and sweetens the mixture beautifully. A perfect accompaniment to meat or poultry, or serve it as a vegetable luncheon entrée with a chilled white Burgundy.

CHRISTMAS TREE DECORATIONS

HARVEST TREE—trim with fruits and nuts, homemade decorations, crabapples, ribbons, miniature baskets and cornucopias, straw figures and a Swedish straw star.
SPICE TREE—decorate with pomanders tied with gay tartan ribbons and tiny silver bells, spice balls, and nosegays of rosemary. Add whole nutmegs and cinnamon sticks, gingerbread men, frosted cookie stars, bright red and gold foil ornaments, and lots of candy canes.
FRIENDS' TREE—hold annual trim-the-tree parties, asking all who are invited to make an ornament to place on the tree. Over the years it will fill with happy mementos.
CHILDREN'S TREE—sparkling with popcorn and cranberries, with felt and wooden cutouts of snowmen, doves, hearts, horses, and angels shining with sequins . . . and lots of chocolate chip cookies strung on ribbons.
BIRDS' TREE—after you've enjoyed your tree indoors, instead of throwing it out, use it as a bird feeder by trimming it with orange slices, popcorn or cranberry ropes, and birdseed purses.

THREE-ONION CASSEROLE

3 tablespoons unsalted butter
2 large yellow onions, thinly sliced
2 large red onions, thinly sliced
4 medium-size leeks, well rinsed, dried, and thinly sliced
Salt and freshly ground black pepper, to taste
1 ½ cups grated Havarti
2 packages (5 ounces each) Boursin with herbs, crumbled
1 ½ cups grated Gruyère
½ cup dry white wine

1. Preheat oven to 350°F. Butter an 8-cup baking dish with 1 tablespoon of the butter.
2. Make a layer in the baking dish, using a third each of the yellow onions, red onions, and leeks. Sprinkle the layer lightly with salt and pepper. Top with the Havarti and make 1 more layer of the onions and leeks, seasoning each with salt and pepper. Top this layer with the Boursin. Layer the remaining onions and leeks and top with the Gruyère. Dot the top with the remaining 2 tablespoons butter. Pour the wine over all.
3. Bake for 1 hour. Cover the top with aluminum foil if it gets too brown. Serve immediately.
6 portions

BAKED KUMQUATS AND PARSNIPS

A winter bounty of fruits and vegetables. Garnish with a few fresh kumquat leaves for a splash of winter green.

1 pound parsnips, peeled and cut diagonally into ¼-inch slices
2 pears, peeled and sliced
12 kumquats, seeded and sliced crosswise
4 tablespoons (½ stick) unsalted butter, melted
3 tablespoons brown sugar
3 tablespoons fresh orange juice
1 tablespoon orange liqueur

1. Preheat oven to 350°F.
2. Arrange the parsnips and pears in alternating rows in a 10-inch oval or square au gratin dish. Insert the sliced kumquats evenly throughout all the rows.
3. Mix the butter, brown sugar, and orange juice and liqueur in a small bowl until smooth. Pour the mixture evenly over the sliced parsnips, pears, and kumquats.
4. Cover the dish with aluminum foil and bake for 45 minutes. Uncover and bake 15 minutes to brown the top.
6 portions

STRAWBERRY HAZELNUT TORTE

Crunchy layers of hazelnut biscuits filled with lightly whipped cream and fresh ripe strawberries make this a very sophisticated version of the American classic. Be sure to assemble just before serving so that the biscuits don't become soggy. Try it with fruit other than strawberries—such as raspberries, blueberries, or peaches.

BISCUITS:

½ cup (1 stick) unsalted butter, room temperature
½ cup granulated sugar
⅔ cup skinned toasted hazelnuts, finely ground
1 ¼ cups unbleached all-purpose flour

FILLING:

1 ½ cups heavy or whipping cream, cold
2 tablespoons confectioners' sugar
2 tablespoons framboise liqueur
1 pint fresh strawberries, hulled
Confectioners' sugar

1. To make the biscuits, cream the butter and sugar in a mixer bowl until light and fluffy. Add the nuts and flour and beat just until blended. Divide the dough into 3 equal parts.

2. Preheat oven to 375°F. Lightly butter 2 large cookie sheets.

3. Pat 1 piece of the dough ¼ inch thick on the bottom of an 8-inch springform or tart pan with your hands. Invert onto one of the cookie sheets and remove the pan bottom. Repeat with the remaining dough, making three 8-inch circles. Refrigerate for about 15 minutes.

4. Bake the biscuits until lightly golden, about 10 minutes. As soon as you remove them from the oven, cut each circle with a long knife into 8 equal wedges.

5. Just before serving, whip the cream until stiff. Beat in the 2 tablespoons sugar and liqueur. Slice the strawberries.

6. Place 1 layer (8 wedges) of the hazelnut biscuit on a serving platter and spread with a third of the whipped cream. Top with half the strawberries. Carefully place another layer of the biscuit on top, making sure to line up the wedges evenly with the layer below. Spread with another third of the whipped cream and top with the remaining strawberries. Top with the final hazelnut biscuit, again lining up the wedges.

7. Spoon the remaining whipped cream into a pastry bag fitted with a star tip. Pipe rosettes along the rim of the biscuit. Dust with confectioners' sugar and serve.

8 portions

NEW YEAR'S EVE

N ew Year's Eve is a last chance to be decadent and outrageous before the moral resolves of the New Year hold sway. Our elegant menu tempts with caviar, oysters, and Champagne and deserves black ties and sequined gowns. Heighten the evening's drama by encouraging guests to wear fancy-dress masks to maintain the mystery until midnight. Be sure to get all the mischief out of your system before the clock strikes twelve, for with the first strains of "Auld Lang Syne," masks and old habits must be tossed aside to begin the year anew.

GOLDEN CAVIAR SOUFFLE

Golden caviar has become widely available and very popular in the past few years. This soufflé is elegant on its own, but it can be further embellished with a hollandaise or beurre blanc sauce and topped with additional caviar.

2 tablespoons unsalted butter
3 tablespoons unbleached all-purpose flour
1 cup half-and-half
4 egg yolks
½ cup golden caviar
⅓ cup snipped fresh chives
Finely grated zest of 1 lemon
2 tablespoons vodka
Freshly ground black pepper, to taste
8 egg whites, room temperature
Pinch salt
¼ teaspoon cream of tartar

1. Melt the butter in a heavy medium-size saucepan over medium heat. When the butter starts to foam, add the flour and cook, stirring constantly, for 1 minute. Gradually stir in the half-and-half and cook, whisking constantly, until smooth and thick.

2. Remove from heat and add the egg yolks, one at a time, whisking well after each addition. Gently stir in the caviar, chives, lemon zest, vodka, and pepper. Set aside.

3. Preheat oven to 400°F. Butter a 6-cup soufflé dish.

4. Beat the egg whites and salt in a mixer bowl until foamy. Sprinkle with the cream of tartar and continue beating until the whites are barely stiff and stand in soft peaks. Do not overbeat the egg whites, for they should not be dry. Gently fold the whites into the soufflé base. Pour gently into the prepared dish.

5. Bake until well puffed and golden, 15 to 20 minutes. (Be careful not to overcook this soufflé or the caviar will no longer be crunchy but rubbery instead.) Serve immediately.

6 portions

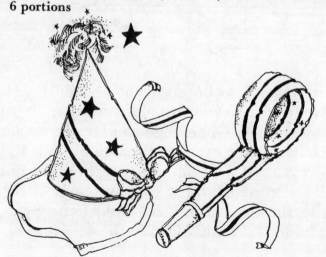

BLACK, WHITE, AND SILVER NEW YEAR'S EVE

Broiled Oysters with Arugula and Champagne Sabayon

Golden Caviar Soufflé

Chicken Breasts in Champagne

Ruby Radishes

Nutted Wild Rice

Spinach and Bacon Salad

Kumquat Citrus Tarts

French Champagne

''Why, then the world's mine oyster, Which I with sword will open.''
—William Shakespeare

CAVIAR

BELUGA: Comes from the largest sturgeon. These fish weigh up to 1,750 pounds and the females must mature more than 20 years before yielding eggs for caviar. Beluga eggs are the largest and most delicate, with a creamy and distinctive flavor that is pure paradise.

OSSETRA: Comes from a smaller sturgeon weighing 60 to 220 pounds. The female can produce eggs after maturing 12 to 15 years. The eggs are of a medium grain and firm texture. The taste is tart and fruity, some say even nutlike. These eggs are best added to sauces just at the end of cooking, as they can withstand minimal amounts of heat.

SEVRUGA: Comes from the smallest and most abundant sturgeon. The female produces eggs within 7 years. It has the fishiest flavor of the caviars, though it is similar in texture to Beluga. Sevruga caviar has a wonderful affinity for raw oysters.

PRESSED: Made from the damaged eggs of all three sturgeon caviars, pressed together into a stiff licorice-colored concentrate. It takes 5 pounds of regular caviar to produce 1 pound of pressed. The essence of caviar flavor abounds, while the price is half that of other caviars. Pressed caviar is delicious spread on buckwheat blinis with a dollop of sour cream.

OTHER CAVIARS OR ROES

SALMON ROE: Probably the best budget alternative to sturgeon caviars. It has a sturdier, almost cheesy texture that can stand up to garnishes of chopped scallions, sieved eggs, cream cheese, sour cream, and lemon juice. Salmon roe is a lovely garnish for fish mousses, smoked salmon, cocktail canapés and dips, and scrambled eggs and omelets.

AMERICAN STURGEON CAVIAR: A true sturgeon caviar with a Sevruga-like taste. The eggs have a brown to yellow-green tinge and are a most palatable substitute for Russian caviar.

WHITEFISH CAVIAR: Also known as golden caviar, it comes from the Great Lakes. It is a sweet, nonfishy caviar with a glistening golden color. It makes a pretty garnish, good hors d'oeuvres, or perfect cooking caviar.

BROILED OYSTERS WITH ARUGULA PUREE AND CHAMPAGNE SABAYON

Three elegant flavors with three favorite ingredients— oysters, arugula, and Champagne. When placed under the broiler with a sabayon, the oysters resemble miniature soufflés. They are absolutely elegant.

4 cups arugula leaves (2 bunches), well rinsed, dried
¾ cup Crème Fraîche (page 399) or heavy or whipping cream
1 tablespoon fresh lemon juice
Salt and freshly ground black pepper, to taste
4 shallots, finely chopped
1 cup plus 2 tablespoons Champagne
¾ cup (1 ½ sticks) unsalted butter, room temperature
2 egg yolks
24 fresh oysters on the half shell

1. To make the arugula purée, cook the arugula in a large pan of boiling salted water until tender, 5 to 7 minutes. Drain the leaves in a colander and refresh under cold running water. Squeeze as much water as possible from the leaves by wringing them with your hands or pressing them against the side of the colander with a rubber spatula. Place the arugula and ½ cup of the crème fraîche in a food processor fitted with a steel blade. Process until puréed. Add the lemon juice and salt and pepper to taste. Process until mixed.

2. To make the Champagne sabayon, heat the shallots and 1 cup Champagne in a small saucepan to boiling. Reduce heat and simmer until all but 1 tablespoon of the Champagne evaporates. Whisk in the butter, 1 tablespoon at a time, over the lowest possible heat. (You want the butter to emulsify with the mixture rather than to melt.) When all the butter has been added, whisk in the remaining ¼ cup crème fraîche. Season to taste with salt and pepper. Whisk the egg yolks and 2 tablespoons Champagne in the top of a double boiler until blended. Then whisk over simmering water until foamy and almost doubled in volume, 3 to 4 minutes. Gently fold into the butter mixture.

3. Preheat broiler.

4. Loosen the oysters from their shells, check for sand or grit, and return to the shells. Cover each oyster with 2 to 3 teaspoons of the arugula purée and then about 1 tablespoon of the Champagne sabayon.

5. Arrange the oysters in a shallow baking dish. Broil 6 inches from the heat until puffed and lightly browned, 4 to 5 minutes. Serve immediately with small cocktail forks. As a first course, arrange 3 to 4 oysters per person on a plate.

24 oysters

SPINACH AND BACON SALAD

An updated version of a standard spinach, mushroom, and bacon salad. We've added peppery arugula leaves, tender enoki mushrooms, and a shower of chopped eggs. Bacon and toasted sesame seeds provide lots of crunch, while a warm champagne vinegar dressing adds elegance.

1 ½ pounds spinach, stems trimmed, rinsed, and patted dry
4 ounces arugula, stems trimmed, rinsed, and patted dry
2 small red onions, thinly sliced
1 package (3.5 ounces) enoki mushrooms
4 ounces fresh cultivated mushrooms, thinly sliced
1 ½ cups Warm Champagne Vinegar Dressing (page 331)
8 ounces bacon, cooked crisp, drained, and crumbled
2 hard-cooked eggs, finely chopped
½ cup toasted sesame seeds

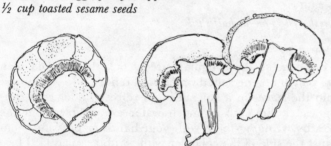

1. Tear the spinach and arugula leaves into bite-size pieces and place in a large salad bowl. Add the onion and enoki and cultivated mushrooms and toss to combine.
2. Make the hot dressing.
3. Pour 1 ½ cups of the dressing over the salad and toss to coat. Sprinkle with the bacon, eggs, and sesame seeds.
   6 main-course portions or 10 appetizer portions

CHICKEN BREASTS IN CHAMPAGNE

An extravagantly delicious combination of classics.

4 whole chicken breasts, halved
Salt and freshly ground black pepper, to taste
5 tablespoons unsalted butter
½ cup Cognac
3 tablespoons unbleached all-purpose flour
2 teaspoons dried tarragon
3 ½ cups nonvintage Champagne
½ cup heavy or whipping cream

HOLIDAY CHEESES

Winter holiday entertaining is often done on a more lavish scale than any other seasonal celebrations. We believe all of the world's most treasured foods belong on December's festive tables. These are our three top cheese choices:

VACHERIN MONT D'OR: a seasonal and irresistible mountain specialty from the Swiss and French Alps. Its creamy richness is the result of its being made from whole milk taken in only the final four months of the year, when the cows have eaten the last cuttings of Alpine grass before the winter snows. Vacherin's soft runny interior is complemented by a smooth, wine-washed white rind and by the hints of pine that come from its being wrapped in sprigs of spruce and balsam. We await its arrival in the late fall and winter with a fervor equal to that which accompanies the release of Beaujolais Nouveau in mid-November!

TETE DE MOINE: another seasonal specialty, made exclusively from the rich milk of summer when cows feed on the lush fresh grasses of the Swiss Jura. The cheese is made into 5-inch cylinders with brownish outer rinds. The interior is golden and firm, with a rich and spicy flavor. It is one of the most addictive cheeses we know, so overlook any adverse references to its unmistakable bouquet—this is one cheese that must be tried!

REBLOCHON: a mild monastery cheese from the Haute Savoie of France with an intriguing history. Reblochon's birth was the product of cow herders' hiding extra milk away from the watchful eyes of the dairy inspectors. To protect the secret, cheeses were made from the milk when it was still warm from the cow. The results were most serendipitous—a magnificent cheese of rich and buttery flavor, spreadable when ripe. It has taken a long time for the secret of Reblochon to be uncovered, and we are delighted to have discovered its exquisite savory flavor.

"I was enjoying myself now. I had taken two finger-bowls of Champagne, and the scene had changed before my eyes into something significant, elemental, and profound."
—F. Scott Fitzgerald

1. Sprinkle the chicken breasts with salt and pepper. Melt the butter in a medium-size Dutch oven over medium-high heat. Brown the chicken breasts, a few at a time, on all sides, about 10 minutes. Remove from the pan and set aside.

2. Pour the Cognac into the pan, warm it, and flame with a match. When the flames subside, stir in the flour and tarragon. Cook 2 minutes, stirring constantly. Gradually whisk in 3 cups of the Champagne. Return the chicken to the pan. Cover and simmer until the chicken is tender, about 45 minutes.

3. Remove the chicken to a warmed serving platter. Stir in the remaining ½ cup of Champagne and the cream. Cook the sauce over high heat until reduced and slightly thickened. Pour the sauce over the chicken and serve immediately.

6 portions

NUTTED WILD RICE

Golden raisins, dry sherry, and crunchy almonds complement the earthy flavor of wild rice. The perfect accompaniment to chicken or game.

1 cup golden raisins
½ cup dry sherry
1 cup wild rice
4 ⅔ cups Berta's Chicken Stock (page 396) or canned chicken broth, boiling
6 tablespoons (¾ stick) unsalted butter
1 cup brown rice
1 cup slivered almonds
½ cup chopped fresh parsley
Salt and freshly ground black pepper, to taste

1. Heat the raisins and sherry in a small saucepan to boiling. Reduce heat and simmer 5 minutes. Set aside.

2. Place the wild rice, 2 cups of the boiling stock, and 2 tablespoons of the butter in the top of a double boiler over simmering water. Cook covered for 1 hour.

3. Place the brown rice, remaining 2⅔ cups boiling stock, and 2 tablespoons of the butter in a medium-size saucepan. Heat to boiling. Reduce heat to low and cook until all the water is absorbed, about 50 minutes.

4. Sauté the almonds in the remaining 2 tablespoons butter in a small skillet over low heat until lightly toasted.

5. Combine the wild rice, brown rice, raisins with sherry, almonds, and parsley in a large mixing bowl. Season to taste with salt and pepper. Remove to a serving bowl and serve immediately.

8 to 10 portions

RUBY RADISHES

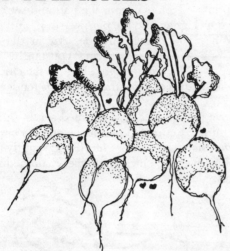

Radishes are delicious when cooked and add brilliant color to winter menus.

3 tablespoons unsalted butter
3 bunches red radishes (about 25), leaves and stems trimmed, rinsed
    and patted dry
2 teaspoons sugar
1 teaspoon red wine vinegar
1 ½ tablespoons snipped fresh dill
Fresh ground black pepper, to taste

1. Melt the butter in a medium-size skillet or sauté pan over medium heat. Add the radishes and toss to coat with the butter. Cover the pan and cook for 4 minutes, shaking occasionally.
2. Add the sugar and vinegar and toss over medium heat for 1 minute. Sprinkle with dill and season to taste with pepper. Serve immediately.
6 portions

KUMQUAT CITRUS TARTS

A glistening kumquat half nestles on top of a rich citrus filling to make these miniature tarts pastry-shop perfect.

PASTRY:

1 ½ cups unbleached all-purpose flour
⅓ cup confectioners' sugar
9 tablespoons unsalted butter, cold, cut into small pieces
1 egg
1 to 2 tablespoons ice water

CHAMPAGNE

From the high society days of eighteenth-century Versailles to the bubbly present, Champagne has exuded celebration and sparkled with romance. Although Champagne is made from the red and white grapes of the famed Burgundies, it seems to transcend wine and exist as a benevolent goddess whose powers uncork the secret ingredient for turning any simple celebration into a grand one. The effervescent, clean taste seduces like no other wine.

By law, the only sparkling wine that is permitted to be called Champagne must come from a specific area of the same name 75 miles east of Paris. Champagne is France's northernmost wine region, and the wine's unique character is the result of the interplay between soil, climate, grape variety, and the expertise of the maker.

The bubbles in Champagne result from a technique known as *la méthode champenoise*. The best sparkling wines in America and other countries are also made by this traditional method. Just before the Champagne base of fermented grape juice is bottled, a second fermentation is induced by adding in a mixture of cane sugar and special yeasts. The bottles are then capped, stored on their sides, and rotated over a period of time. The yeasts convert the added sugar into alcohol and carbon dioxide, which become trapped in the bottles and thereby create the natural sparkle of Champagne.

Champagne always means good news to us, but the best news is that French Champagne is now more affordable than ever, and many excellent sparkling wines are now being made in America and Spain by the time-honored *méthode champenoise*. All the more reason to indulge in Champagne and its sparkling cousins!

FAMOUS FRENCH CHAMPAGNE HOUSES

Bollinger
Deutz
Charles Heidsieck
Heidsieck Monopole
Krug
Lanson
Laurent-Perrier
Moët et Chandon
G. H. Mumm
Joseph Perrier
Perrier-Jouët
Philipponnat
Piper-Heidsieck
Pol Roger
Pommery
Louis Roederer
Ruinart
Tattinger
Veuve Cliquot

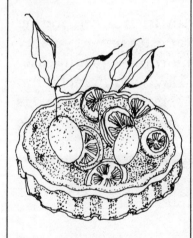

"No civilized person ever goes to bed the same day he gets up."
—Richard Harding Davis

FILLING:

1 egg
⅓ cup granulated sugar
1 teaspoon finely grated orange zest
1 teaspoon finely grated lemon zest
2 tablespoons fresh lemon juice
2 tablespoons fresh orange juice
2 tablespoons heavy or whipping cream

TOPPING:

24 kumquats
⅓ cup Cointreau or other orange liqueur

GLAZE:

⅓ cup apricot jam
2 tablespoons Cointreau or other orange liqueur

1. To make the pastry, process the flour, confectioners' sugar, and butter in a food processor fitted with a steel blade until the mixture resembles coarse meal. Add the egg. With the machine running, add enough of the water for the dough to gather into a ball. Do not overprocess. Wrap the dough in plastic wrap and refrigerate 2 hours.

2. Preheat oven to 400°F.

3. Divide the dough in half and roll out 1 half very thinly on a lightly floured surface. (Freeze the other half for another use.) Line sixteen 1-inch tart pans or small muffin cups with the dough. Trim the edges. Line each shell with waxed or parchment paper and weight with dried beans or pie weights. Bake on a baking sheet for 10 minutes. Remove the weights and let cool.

4. Reduce heat to 375°F.

5. To make the filling, process the egg, sugar, and orange and lemon zests in the food processor for 1 minute. Add the lemon and orange juices and the cream and process 30 seconds more.

6. Remove the paper from the shells and spoon 1 tablespoon of the citrus filling into each shell. Bake until the filling is set and lightly browned, about 15 minutes. Let cool to room temperature.

7. To make the topping, cut 8 of the kumquats in half and seed. Cut the remaining kumquats crosswise into thin slices and seed. Heat all the kumquats and the ⅓ cup Cointreau in a small enameled saucepan over medium heat to boiling. Cook, stirring constantly, until most of the liqueur has evaporated to form a syrupy coating over the kumquats. Remove from heat.

8. Remove the tarts from the pans. Make a circle of overlapping kumquat slices on top of each tart and place 1 kumquat half in the center.

9. To make the glaze, heat the apricot jam and 2 tablespoons Cointreau in a small saucepan until melted and smooth. Spoon the glaze over each tart.

Sixteen 1-inch tarts

NEW YEAR'S DAY

Last night's party was a roaring success, with friends celebrating the New Year in grand style. For overnight guests, provide plenty of hot coffee and lots of aspirin for New Year's morning—just in case. Follow it with plans for a leisurely New Year's Day with munchy fun foods to accompany the football games on TV. Have warm blankets available for curling up on the sofa, and set up board games to amuse the football-bored.

BLOODY MARY SOUP

The Bloody Mary seems to enjoy a universal popularity as a brunch eye-opener. For those chilly times when you still need the kick of a Bloody Mary but also crave something warming, we've created this soup.

4 tablespoons (½ stick) unsalted butter
4 ribs celery, minced
1 medium-size sweet red pepper, seeded, cored, and minced
1 jalapeño pepper, seeded and minced
2 cups drained canned tomatoes
4 cups tomato juice
Grated zest of 1 lime
3 tablespoons prepared horseradish
Salt and freshly ground black pepper, to taste
1 cup vodka
1½ teaspoons caraway seeds
Juice of 2 limes
1 tablespoon Worcestershire sauce
Dill sprigs (garnish)
Lime slices (garnish)

NEW YEAR'S DAY

On the first day of the new year, treat everyone gently—hangovers often prevail. Greet guests at the door with a Bloody Bull, dark glasses, or two aspirin.

In your preparation be precise and exciting—the first meal of the year sets the standard for those to follow. It's fun on this day to predict for one another the new year's future; put the "fortunes" in a pot, mix them up, and then guess whom each is for and who wrote it.

1. Melt the butter in a heavy large pan over low heat. Add the celery, red pepper, and jalapeño pepper. Cover the pot and sweat the vegetables over low heat until very soft, about 30 minutes.

2. Stir in the tomatoes, tomato juice, lime zest, horseradish, and salt and pepper to taste. Cook over medium heat 5 minutes.

3. Process the soup in a food processor fitted with a steel blade or a blender until smooth. Return to the pan and stir in the vodka, caraway seeds, lime juice, and Worcestershire. Heat until hot.

4. Ladle the soup into mugs and garnish with dill sprigs and lime slices.

6 portions

SMOKED SALMON AND CREAM CHEESE SOUP

The pastel colors of pale pink and green have a refreshing look on a winter day. Sprinkle some snipped chives over all.

6 tablespoons (¾ stick) unsalted butter
1 ½ cups finely chopped yellow onion
¾ cup chopped fresh dill
2 ripe medium-size tomatoes, seeded and chopped
8 ounces smoked salmon, finely chopped
2 tablespoons unbleached all-purpose flour
8 cups water
Freshly ground black pepper, to taste
2 cups fresh spinach (10-ounce package), stems removed and leaves finely chopped
2 packages (8 ounces each) cream cheese, preferably without vegetable gum
⅓ cup vodka
2 tablespoons fresh lemon juice
Snipped fresh chives (garnish)

1. Melt the butter in a medium-size stock pot over medium heat. Add the onion and sauté until soft, 10 to 15 minutes.

2. Stir in the dill, tomatoes, and smoked salmon. Cook 3 minutes; then add the flour and cook 1 minute more.

3. Gradually stir in the water. Heat to boiling. Reduce heat and simmer uncovered over medium-low heat 20 minutes. Season with pepper to taste. Stir in the spinach and simmer 5 more minutes.

4. Stir in the cream cheese, 1 ounce at a time, over low heat, allowing each bit to melt into the soup. When all the cream cheese has been added and the soup is smooth, stir in the vodka and lemon juice. Taste for seasonings. Serve immediately.

6 portions

NEW YEAR'S DAY

Bloody Mary Soup

Fig and Prosciutto Sandwich

Pastrami Melt

Smoked salmon and chèvre

Chocolate Amaretto Mousse

Rocky Mountain Oatmeal Cookies

Champagne or Beer

"I always wake up at the crack of ice."
—Joe E. Lewis

COMFORTING SHREDDED BEEF

This is a simple but wonderfully homey dish that is rich in meaty flavor. It is Julee's favorite, and easy to make. Keep it in the fridge and heat up a little when you want a very special treat. Nibble over a whole weekend! Also perfect on a cheese steak sandwich.

2 tablespoons unsalted butter
3 tablespoons olive oil
1 bottom round roast (4 pounds)
Salt and freshly ground black pepper, to taste
½ cup Cognac
2 cups Beef Stock (page 397)
3 cups (or as needed) Chianti or other full-bodied red wine

1. Heat the butter and oil in a Dutch oven over medium-high heat. Rub the roast all over with salt and pepper. Brown the beef on all sides in the hot butter and oil. It should take about 10 minutes.

2. Pour the Cognac into the pan, warm it, and flame with a match.

3. Pour in the stock and ½ cup of the wine. Cover the pan and simmer slowly over low heat for about 3 hours, adding more wine so that there is always about 1 cup liquid in the pan.

4. Remove from the heat and let cool to room temperature. Remove the beef and shred into small pieces, following the natural grain of the meat. It should fall apart very easily.

5. Return the shredded beef to the liquid in the pan. Heat until warmed through. Serve as is, sprinkled with parsley, on toast, or as a wonderful base for a cheese steak sandwich.

6 to 8 portions

SOFTLY SIMMERED ONIONS

Wonderful over a sliced steak sandwich.

1 cup (2 sticks) unsalted butter
10 cups sliced yellow onions (¼-inch-thick rings)
1 cup dry red wine
¾ cup red wine vinegar
½ cup sugar
1½ teaspoons freshly ground black pepper
½ teaspoon salt

COOKING WITH WINE

Many people have the misconception that poor wines are the best ones to cook with. You should no more cook with an inferior wine than you would assemble a dish from inferior ingredients. It is the alcohol in wine that evaporates in cooking, not the flavor. While it would be a waste to use noble growths and expensive wines in cooking, we recommend good solid wines. A cup of wine fortifies many a roast, stew, or soup and can add subtle nuances to a variety of sauces. In the case of long-cooking dishes in which wine is a principal ingredient, such as the French *coq au vin,* we do like to use a higher quality wine such as a non-vintage Burgundy or Bordeaux, or a good California Cabernet Sauvignon. Otherwise, we think that lighter red wines such as Beaujolais, Côtes du Rhone, and California Gamays are good cooking wines. For whites, we like Muscadet, Mâcon-Villages, and a variety of good California jug wines.

As a rule of thumb, never cook with something you wouldn't drink—half the fun in cooking with wine is sipping while you stir!

"The greatest dishes are very simple dishes."
—Escoffier

Melt the butter in a heavy large saucepan over low heat. Add the onions, wine, vinegar, sugar, pepper, and salt and stir well. Cover and cook slowly over low heat, stirring frequently, 1 hour. Remove the cover and cook 2 hours longer, stirring occasionally.

4 cups

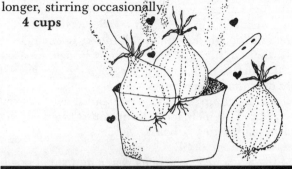

HERB BREAD WITH SWEET SAUSAGE

A spectacular looking and tasting loaf. The chunks of Italian sausage and smoked mozzarella make this practically a meal in itself.

2 teaspoons dried oregano
2 teaspoons dried basil
2 teaspoons dried thyme
2 teaspoons dried chervil
2 teaspoons dried rosemary
1 teaspoon fennel seeds
2 teaspoons freshly ground black pepper
3 tablespoons olive oil
2 packages active dry yeast
2 cups warm dry white wine (105° to 115°F)
2 tablespoons sugar
1 tablespoon salt
5 to 5½ cups unbleached all-purpose flour
1 pound sweet Italian sausages, removed from casings and crumbled
1 medium-size yellow onion, chopped
4 cloves garlic, minced
2 tablespoons finely chopped sun-dried tomatoes (packed in oil)
8 ounces smoked mozzarella, thinly sliced
1 egg
2 teaspoons water

1. Combine the oregano, basil, thyme, chervil, rosemary, fennel, pepper, and oil in a small bowl. Let stand at least 1 hour.

2. Stir the yeast into the warm wine in a large bowl and let stand 5 minutes. Stir in the sugar, salt, and herb mixture. Stir in enough of the flour, 1 cup at a time, to make a soft dough.

3. Knead the dough on a floured surface for 10 minutes, adding more flour if necessary.

4. Place the dough in a buttered large bowl and turn to

THYME

Thyme is an excellent addition to chowders and fish dishes, stews, salads, and eggs. Pungent when dried, there are a number of varieties available for the gardener. Bees love thyme, and thyme honey is especially good.

Legend has it that thyme was an essential ingredient in a magic brew that allowed the drinker to see the fairies. . . .

"No matter how big or soft or warm your bed is, you still have to get out of it."
—Grace Slick

coat with butter. Cover with plastic wrap and let rise in a warm place until doubled in bulk, 1 to 1½ hours.

5. While the dough is rising, combine the sausages, onion, and garlic in a skillet and cook over medium heat, breaking up the sausage with a wooden spoon, until the sausage is browned. Stir in the tomatoes. Set aside.

6. Punch the dough down and roll into a 12-inch circle on a lightly floured surface. Spread the sausage mixture evenly over the surface of the dough. Arrange the mozzarella slices evenly over the sausage mixture.

7. Roll the dough up like a jelly roll and shape it into a spiral in a buttered 10-inch springform pan. Cover and let rise in a warm place 1 to 1½ hours.

8. Preheat oven to 400°F.

9. Beat the egg and 2 teaspoons water in a small bowl. Brush the top of the loaf with the egg wash.

10. Bake in the center of the oven until the loaf is brown and sounds hollow when the bottom is lightly thumped, 45 to 50 minutes. Cool slightly and remove from the pan. Cool to room temperature and cut into wedges to serve.

1 round 10-inch loaf

FRESH FIG AND PROSCIUTTO SANDWICH

This bountiful sandwich is equally good cold—just eliminate the baking.

1 baguette, cut lengthwise in half
½ cup best-quality olive oil
½ cup coarsely chopped fresh basil leaves
4 ounces thinly sliced prosciutto
8 ounces sweet Gorgonzola or Saga blue cheese, room temperature
3 fresh ripe purple or green figs, cut lengthwise into thin slices
2 tablespoons fresh lemon juice
Freshly ground black pepper, to taste

1. Preheat oven to 350°F.

2. Scoop out a bit of bread from the centers of the bread halves.

3. Mix the oil and basil in a small bowl and drizzle evenly over both bread halves.

4. Arrange the prosciutto evenly over the bottom half of the bread. Gently spread the cheese over the prosciutto and top the cheese with sliced figs. Sprinkle with the lemon juice and black pepper.

5. Cover with the top half of the bread and wrap in aluminum foil, leaving the seam on top open slightly.

6. Bake until the cheese is melted and the sandwich is heated through, about 15 minutes. Cut into 8 equal pieces and serve immediately.

4 portions

WINE TASTING

There is no better way to learn about wine than to stage a party where four to five wines are tasted in a casual setting. While there are all sorts of rules governing formal wine tastings, we find most of our friends feel more comfortable not having to deal with a lot of pretense and tasting terminology. While we do provide pads of paper and pens to note down reactions, we turn the event into a competition, encouraging guests to come up with the most poetic, original, or outrageous description of the wine. A special bottle of Champagne is always stashed away as a prize to encourage guests to let their imaginations run wild.

Create a relaxed atmosphere for your wine tastings, keeping in mind that it is important to have plenty of clean glasses on hand for each type of wine being tasted and enough wine for everyone to taste. Plan on one bottle being adequate for 12 people. As tasting wine in small amounts seems to have a stronger cumulative alcoholic effect than drinking equal amounts of one type of wine, have plenty of simple and complementary bistro-style foods on hand.

Some wine tastings to try:

•Focus on Chardonnay varietals by comparing two California Chardonnays, an Italian Chardonnay, and two French Chardonnays. Make sure the wines are properly chilled and serve an assortment of goat's-milk cheeses, a crock of Rillettes of Smoked Trout, and thinly sliced French bread.

•Compare California Cabernet Sauvignons and Merlots with a sampling of French Bordeaux. Serve a platter of thinly sliced tenderloin with Béarnaise Mayonnaise, pumpernickel bread, Roquefort cheese, red grapes, and Comice pears.

• Celebrate rosés with a comparison between California Rosé of Cabernet and Rosé of Pinot Noir, Burgundy Marsennay-la-Côte, Côte du Rhone Tavel, and Provencal Bandol. Serve Fresh Salmon Beignets, a platter of smoked salmon, and Bucheron Tart with Fresh Herbs.

• Compare California champagne-style wines with French Champagne. Buy bottles in a wide price range and sample the bottles blindly to avoid preconceived notions about price and origin. Have plenty of flutes on hand and serve Crabmeat Mousse, a tray of triple crème cheeses, and a basket of crusty French bread.

• For a gala occasion, arrange a tray of different dessert wines— Sauternes, Muscat, Late Harvest Riesling, and Zinfandel. Complement with a lush buffet of irresistible desserts.

• Stage a vertical tasting of a favorite wine by purchasing bottles dating from four different years. Taste from youngest to oldest and accompany with a hearty selection of country pâtés and unusual cheeses.

''Too few people understand a really good sandwich.''
—James Beard

PASTRAMI MELT

A deli favorite made even better in a home skillet.

1 teaspoon Dijon-style mustard
2 slices caraway rye bread
3 tablespoons unsalted butter
4 slices lean pastrami
3 slices ripe tomato
2 thin slices red onion
2 slices Swiss cheese

1. Spread the mustard on 1 slice of the bread and 1 teaspoon of the butter on the other.

2. Layer the pastrami, tomato, onion, and cheese on 1 slice and cover with the second. Melt the remaining butter in a skillet over medium heat. Add the sandwich, weighting it down with a small plate. Cook on both sides until the cheese melts and bread browns.

1 sandwich

BROWN SUGAR–PECAN SHORTBREAD

Delicate cookies that will melt in your mouth! Lovely to give as a gift, packed in a decorative tin. They're slightly darker than regular shortbread because of the brown sugar.

2 cups unbleached all-purpose flour
1 cup pecan pieces
Pinch salt
1 cup (2 sticks) unsalted butter, room temperature
½ cup packed dark brown sugar

1. Grind the flour, pecans, and salt in a food processor fitted with a steel blade to a fine powder. Set aside.

2. Using an electric mixer or a wooden spoon, cream the butter and sugar. When the mixture is very smooth and creamy, mix in the pecan mixture.

3. Gather the dough into a ball, wrap in plastic wrap, and refrigerate at least 3 hours or overnight.

4. Preheat oven to 300°F. Line cookie sheets with parchment paper.

5. Roll out the dough ¼ inch thick on a lightly floured surface. Cut into shapes with 1-inch cookie cutters. Gather up the scraps, reroll, and cut into as many cookies as possible. Place on the prepared cookie sheets and bake until lightly colored, 20 to 25 minutes.

About 50 cookies

FIRESIDE FOODS

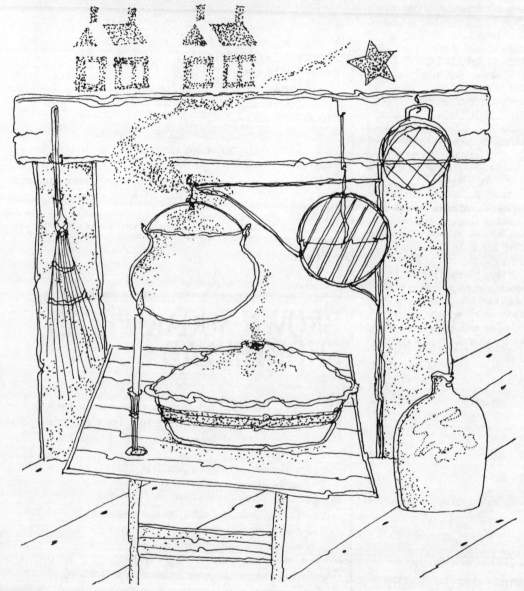

Winter's cold brings out the need in all of us to mother and be mothered. Food from the past soothes us, for we all hanker after tastes from our childhood. Sheila longs for her mother's chicken noodle soup, while even our most sophisticated customers react with delight to pot roast, meat pies, fried chicken, mashed potatoes, bread pudding, and apple pie. Comforting foods are certainly not confined to those with humble tastes. Long, hard workdays and convenience foods have made mother's cooking hard to come by. Enjoy these recipes when you're cosily at home on a blustery day.

''To make a good
soup, the pot must
only simmer or
''smile.''
—French Proverb

RATATOUILLE AND OATMEAL BRUNCH SOUP

A dark, rich, oaty soup speckled with jewellike colors. The soup is topped with golden garlic croutons and eggs sunny-side up. Serve in wide soup bowls with a rich red wine.

½ cup best-quality olive oil
1 large yellow onion, chopped
10 cloves garlic, chopped
1 medium eggplant, peeled and cut into ½-inch dice
2 sweet red peppers, cored, seeded, and cut into ½-inch squares
1 can (35 ounces) Italian plum tomatoes
1 tablespoon dried oregano
1 tablespoon dried basil
1 teaspoon fennel seeds
1 cup dry red wine
4 cups Berta's Chicken Stock (page 396) or canned chicken broth
Salt and freshly ground black pepper, to taste
2 cups old-fashioned rolled oats
2 cups (or as needed) water
8 eggs
4 teaspoons butter
Garlic Croutons to garnish (page 400)
Freshly grated Swiss or Parmesan cheese

1. Heat the oil in a large stock pot over low heat. Add the onion and garlic and sauté for 5 minutes. Add the eggplant and red peppers and sauté for 15 minutes.

2. Add the tomatoes with their juices and break up the tomatoes with a spoon. Stir in the oregano, basil, fennel seeds, wine, and stock. Season to taste with salt and pepper. Simmer covered for 25 minutes.

3. Toast the oats in a skillet over medium heat, stirring or shaking the pan constantly, until evenly golden brown. Stir the oats into the soup and simmer 10 more minutes. If the soup is too thick, thin it with up to 2 cups water. Taste and adjust the seasonings.

4. Fry the eggs, sunny-side up, in the butter in 2 skillets.

5. Ladle the soup into wide soup bowls and top each serving with a fried egg. Garnish with garlic croutons and pass the grated cheese.

8 portions

a bowl of plum tomatoes

WINTERGREEN SOUP

A hearty soup that earns its name from fresh spinach, dried and sweet peas, and the sparkle of garden herbs. Just add a bottle of red wine, crusty bread, and cheese for a soul-satisfying meal.

1 pound dried green split peas
5 cups Berta's Chicken Stock (page 396) or canned chicken broth
1 meaty ham bone or 2 ham hocks
2 ribs celery with leafy tops
2 parsley sprigs
1 bay leaf
¼ teaspoon dried thyme
Unsalted butter
½ cup finely chopped carrot
½ cup finely chopped yellow onion
2 large leeks (white only), well rinsed, dried, and thinly sliced
1 cup chopped fresh spinach leaves
½ cup frozen sweet peas
Dash cayenne pepper
Salt and freshly ground black pepper, to taste

1. Rinse the split peas under running water and pick through them, discarding any small pebbles. Combine the split peas and stock in a stock pot and heat to boiling. Add the ham bone, celery, parsley, bay leaf, and thyme. Reduce the heat and simmer, partially covered, for about 45 minutes.

2. Meanwhile, melt the butter in a Dutch oven over medium heat. Add the carrot, onion, and leeks and cook covered until the vegetables are tender and lightly colored,

"Almost every person has something secret he likes to eat."
—M.F.K. Fisher

> "Chowder breathes reassurance. It steams consolation."
> —Clementine Paddleford

about 25 minutes. Add the spinach and cook for another 5 minutes.

3. Transfer the cooked vegetables to the stock pot and add the frozen peas and cayenne. Simmer uncovered until the split peas and vegetables are very tender, about 30 minutes.

4. Remove the ham bone and cool slightly. Remove the meat from the bone, shred it, and set aside.

5. Process 1 cup of the soup in a blender or food processor fitted with a steel blade until smooth. Stir the purée and meat back into the remaining soup. Season to taste with salt and pepper.

6. Simmer over medium heat for 10 minutes. Serve immediately.

6 portions

HEARTY FISH SOUP

A full meal—with a broth that becomes thicker as it simmers. The herbs and spices of the Mediterranean and the East come into play. The pale colors are sparked with the fiery sunset color of the rouille.

½ cup olive oil
1 large yellow onion, chopped
2 leeks (white and green parts), well rinsed, dried, and sliced
1 fennel bulb, chopped
12 cloves garlic, chopped
1 pound boneless skinless salt cod, soaked overnight in several
    changes of water
1 pound smoked haddock
3 potatoes, peeled and cut into ½-inch dice
3 cups dry white wine
7 cups water
1 tablespoon dried basil
1 ½ teaspoons dried thyme
1 ½ teaspoons fennel seeds
1 ½ teaspoons curry powder
2 bay leaves
Large strip of lemon zest
2 cups half-and-half
2 cups heavy or whipping cream
¼ cup Chartreuse, Pernod, or brandy
Freshly ground black pepper, to taste
Rouille (page 178)

1. Heat the oil in a large stock pot over medium heat. Add the onion, leeks, fennel bulb, and garlic and sauté until the vegetables begin to soften.

2. Meanwhile, rinse the salt cod under cold water and flake it into small pieces, removing any bones. Cut the smoked haddock into 1-inch pieces.

3. Add the fish and potatoes to the soup and pour in the

WINTER CARNIVAL

Get together with friends to choose a theme and hold a neighborhood winter carnival. Each family decorates their front yard in keeping with the theme. On the Saturday of the carnival everyone brings a dish of their favorite food to the town hall or local school auditorium, where there is a big dinner after a parade of all the theme costumes. Awards are given for the most humorous, most unique, largest, prettiest, ugliest costumes. Everyone gets to judge—adults and children alike—and everyone goes home feeling like a winner.

wine and water. Add the basil, thyme, fennel seeds, curry powder, bay leaves, and lemon zest. Heat to boiling. Reduce heat and simmer uncovered until the potatoes are tender.

4. Stir in the half-and-half, cream, and liquor of your choice. Add pepper to taste. The soup will probably not need salt. Remove bay leaves and lemon zest.

5. Purée 4 cups of the soup in a food processor fitted with a steel blade or a blender and return it to the pot. Stir the mix and gently heat to blend flavors.

6. Ladle into large deep bowls and pass the rouille.

8 portions

CHICKEN NOODLE SOUP

When we think of comforting food, homemade chicken noodle soup is tops on any list. We add lots of vegetables to ours, and there is plenty left for the next day.

4 medium-size leeks (white part only)
8 cups water
2 tablespoons cider vinegar
1 cup (2 sticks) unsalted butter
2 medium-size carrots, peeled and finely chopped
3 ribs celery, finely chopped
2 teaspoons coarse (kosher) salt
1 teaspoon freshly ground black pepper
2½ quarts Berta's Chicken Stock (page 396)
1 cup dry white wine
2 whole chicken breasts, skinned and boned
8 medium-size mushrooms, wiped clean and thinly sliced
2 cups cooked thin egg noodles
4 ounces green beans, ends trimmed, diagonally sliced
3 tablespoons chopped fresh Italian parsley

1. Cut the leeks lengthwise in half and soak in the water mixed with the vinegar for 15 minutes. Drain and rinse the leeks. Cut into fine dice.

2. Melt the butter in a large heavy saucepan over medium-low heat. Add the leeks, carrots, celery, salt, and pepper. Cook gently for 5 minutes. Remove from heat.

3. Heat the chicken stock and wine in a second large saucepan to boiling. Add the chicken. Reduce heat and simmer uncovered for 15 minutes. Remove the chicken and let cool.

4. Add the stock and mushrooms to the vegetables. Simmer uncovered over low heat for 10 minutes.

5. Add the noodles and green beans and simmer for another 5 minutes. Remove from heat.

6. Shred the chicken breasts and add to the soup. Add the chopped parsley and stir well. Serve immediately.

14 portions

COOKING CHEESES

In the cold and gloomy depths of winter when the chills have settled permanently into our bones and our windows have become frosted with icy labyrinths, we crave warmth. While all the determined concentration in the world has never raised our body temperatures or defrosted our windows, we've discovered a vicarious pleasure and comforting satisfaction in soothing our woes with rich and warm melted cheese. We think of onion soup crocks with edges brimming and crusted with bubbling Gruyère, pizza oozing with runny mozzarella, the simple childhood delight of a grilled cheese sandwich, the rich satisfaction of creamy cheese-spiked pasta dishes, the rustic pleasures of raclette and fondue.

There is no better time to enjoy the delights of cooking with cheese than in the midst of winter. While there are many cheeses that have good melting properties, our thoughts turn most to those that come from the Alpine regions of Switzerland. The cold climate seems to have induced some of the most warming hot cheese treats we know. As a rule of thumb, dishes cooked with cheese should be cooked over a low flame and stirred frequently to prevent sticking and scorching. The cheese should be grated into small pieces to promote even melting.

VEGETABLE CHILI

We've made a vegetable chili that is just as lush and spicy as those with lots of beef and pork.

1 medium-size eggplant, unpeeled, cut into ½-inch cubes
1 tablespoon coarse (kosher) salt
¾ cup (or as needed) best-quality olive oil
2 medium-size yellow onions, cut into ¼-inch dice
4 cloves garlic, finely chopped
2 large green bell peppers, cored, seeded, and cut into ¼-inch dice
1 can (35 ounces) Italian plum tomatoes
1½ pounds fresh ripe Italian plum tomatoes, cut into 1-inch cubes
2 tablespoons chili powder
1 tablespoon ground cumin
1 tablespoon dried oregano
1 tablespoon dried basil
2 teaspoons freshly ground black pepper
1 teaspoon salt
1 teaspoon fennel seeds
½ cup chopped fresh Italian parsley
1 cup canned dark red kidney beans, drained
1 cup canned chick-peas (garbanzos), drained
½ cup chopped fresh dill
2 tablespoons fresh lemon juice

1. Place the eggplant in a colander and sprinkle with the coarse salt. Let stand for 1 hour. Pat dry with paper towels.

2. Heat ½ cup of the oil in a large skillet over medium heat. Add the eggplant and sauté until almost tender, adding a bit more oil if necessary. Remove the eggplant to a casserole or Dutch oven.

3. Heat the remaining ¼ cup oil in the same skillet over low heat. Add the onions, garlic, and green peppers and sauté just until softened, about 10 minutes. Add to the casserole with any oil.

4. Place the casserole over low heat and add the canned tomatoes with their liquid, fresh tomatoes, chili powder, cumin, oregano, basil, pepper, salt, fennel, and parsley. Cook uncovered, stirring frequently, for 30 minutes.

5. Stir in the kidney beans, chick-peas, dill, and lemon juice and cook for another 15 minutes. The eggplant peel should be tender. Stir well and taste and adjust seasonings.

6. Serve immediately with brown rice and lots of shredded Cheddar cheese.

8 portions

CHICKEN CHILI

A great new recipe for chili lovers everywhere—a colorful blend of bright red peppers, hot green jalapeños, and creamy white chicken meat. A spicy dash of cinnamon and a handful of grated chocolate make this dish reminiscent of Mexican mole. Lavish on the garnishes and make this meal into a fiesta.

6 tablespoons olive oil
1 very large yellow onion, chopped
5 cloves garlic, minced
2 sweet red peppers, seeded, cored, and diced
4 jalapeño peppers, seeded and minced
3 tablespoons chili powder
1½ teaspoons cumin seeds
1 teaspoon ground coriander
Pinch ground cinnamon
6 whole chicken breasts (12 halves), skinned, boned,
     and cut into 1-inch cubes
2 cans (16 ounces each) tomatoes in purée, chopped
8 ounces pitted ripe California olives, sliced
1 cup beer
¼ cup grated unsweetened chocolate
Salt, to taste
Sour cream (garnish)
Grated Cheddar cheese (garnish)
Sliced scallions (garnish)
Diced avocados (garnish)

1. Heat half the olive oil in a Dutch oven over high heat. Add the onion and garlic and sauté for 5 minutes.

2. Add the red and jalapeño peppers and sauté over medium heat for 10 minutes.

3. Stir in the chili powder, cumin, coriander, and cinnamon and cook for 5 minutes more. Remove from heat and set aside.

4. Brown the chicken in batches in the remaining 3 tablespoons oil in a large skillet just until cooked through.

5. Add the chicken, tomatoes with the purée, olives, and beer to the Dutch oven and stir to combine. Simmer over medium heat for 15 minutes.

6. Stir in the chocolate and season to taste with salt. Serve immediately. Pass the sour cream, Cheddar cheese, scallions, and avocado in separate small bowls.

6 portions

CHILI POWDER

Most chili powder on supermarket shelves is a blend of many different spices and herbs that produces a rather bland seasoning. In Mexico and areas in the Southwest, it is possible to buy individual powdered chiles such as *ancho, mulato,* and *pasilla* without the addition of any other ingredients. There is very little loss of flavor in these dried powders and they are an excellent substitute for the peppers themselves in cooked dishes. As the craze for spicy foods creeps north and eastward, we hope that these pure powdered chiles will become readily available.

Alleged dying words of Kit Carson: "Wish I had time for just one more bowl of chili."

NIGHTCAPS

EAUX-DE-VIE—or the "waters of life," are highly prized colorless alcohols that are dry and not to be confused with sweet liqueurs. Eaux-de-vie should be served chilled and straight up in small sipping glasses. They come in a variety of lush fruit flavors: *Kirschwasser* from small cherries, *framboise* from raspberries, *fraise* from strawberries, *mirabelle* from yellow plums, *quetsch* from purple plums, and *poire Williams* from pears of the same name. All have fragrant fruity aromas and pack a powerful wallop.

COGNAC—the potent result of grapes that yield bad wine but make great brandy. All French Cognac is aged in oak casks, which impart aroma and the distinctive amber color. Cognac should be sipped from small round glasses that can be cupped in the hand, thereby warming the liqueur. Breathe in the fragrant, complex bouquet, swirl it a bit, and let the flavor linger on into the wee hours.

ARMAGNAC—from Gascony, in the southwestern part of France, is enjoying a surge in popularity. At its best, properly aged Armagnac is dark, rich, and soul-tingling—one of the world's great brandies.

CALVADOS—a brandy distilled from apples in the French province of Normandy. The combination of a fruity bouquet and the warmth of brandy is a delight for many who find Cognac and Armagnac too strong. Look for "Pays d'Auge" on the label for the best quality.

BRANDY—almost every wine-making country distills some brandy. Some of it can be very good and some is raw and harsh. California brandy accounts for three out of four bottles drunk in the U.S. It tends to be lighter than the French counterparts.

DRAMBUIE—a popular after-dinner liqueur that combines the taste of honey and heather with highland Scotch whisky. It is predictably a favorite of Scotch lovers.

CHARTREUSE—one of the most famous liqueurs, Chartreuse is still produced by monks. Green Chartreuse has a potent, distinctly herbal flavor that has been described by its makers as a formula for an "Elixir to Long Life."

WINTER CLAMBAKE

Succulent seafood, robust sausages, and potatoes are combined in a rich broth flavored with vegetables and herbs. The idea is to gather around an indoor fire and grill the shellfish over the fire until they open. As they open, they should be removed from the shells and dropped into the soup base. The scallops should be added just before serving, for they will cook enough in the hot soup. Roll up your sleeves and enjoy with a Beaujolais.

SOUP BASE:

⅓ cup olive oil
2 large yellow onions, chopped
6 cloves garlic, minced
1 green bell pepper, cored, seeded, and diced
4 ribs celery, diced
3 carrots, peeled and minced
3 tablespoons Pernod
2 tablespoons unbleached all-purpose flour
1½ teaspoons dried thyme
1 teaspoon saffron threads
3 cans (28 ounces each) tomatoes
2 cups dry white wine
4 cups clam juice
4 cups water
Salt and freshly ground black pepper, to taste

CLAMBAKE INGREDIENTS:

8 baking potatoes, wrapped in foil
3 pounds smoked sausages, cut lengthwise in half
2 loaves best-quality French bread, cut into thick slices
Olive oil
Garlic cloves, cut in half
4 tablespoons (½ stick) unsalted butter, room temperature
3 dozen oysters, scrubbed
3 dozen littleneck or cherrystone clams, scrubbed
3 dozen mussels, scrubbed and bearded
1½ pounds bay scallops

1. To make the soup base, heat the oil in a large stock pot over high heat. Add the onions, garlic, green pepper, celery, and carrots and sauté for 10 minutes.

2. Add the Pernod, warm it, and flame with a match. When the flames subside, stir in the flour, thyme, and saffron. Cook, stirring constantly, for 2 minutes.

3. Stir in the tomatoes with their liquid, the wine, clam juice, and water. Season to taste with salt and pepper. Reduce the heat and simmer uncovered for 40 minutes.

4. While the soup base is simmering, prepare a fire.

Arrange a grate for grilling the sausages and shellfish over the fire, and set up an arrangement for simmering the soup base in the fireplace. A cauldron could be hung from a fireplace arm, or the pot can be placed on a high trivet, or bricks built up to keep the pot near but not in the fire.

5. Place the potatoes in the fire to bake.

6. Transfer the soup base to a cauldron or other large pot and place in the fireplace.

7. When the potatoes are soft, scoop the pulp into the simmering soup base. Place the sausages on the grate over the fire.

8. Butter the potato skins. Brush both sides of the bread slices with olive oil and then rub with garlic cloves.

9. When the sausages are nearly done, start grilling the shellfish. As each shell opens, remove the shellfish and drop it into the soup base.

10. Quickly grill the potato skins and bread on both sides.

11. Stir the scallops into the soup base and arrange the sausages, potato skins, and bread on serving platters. Ladle the soup and shellfish into wide bowls and serve immediately.

12 portions

WINTER TOMATOES

When buying fresh tomatoes in winter, let your eye be your judge. Stay away from any that look too pink. Once you have them, don't refrigerate—let them continue ripening. Much of summer's flavor can be recaptured by slicing or dicing the tomatoes a few hours before serving and marinating them with a dash of salt, pepper, sugar, and olive oil. Gently toss from time to time.

''The greatest pleasure in life is doing what people say you cannot do.''
—Walter Bagehot

TOMATO-SPINACH ROULADE

A wonderful combination of a rich, tomato-flavored dough, all spiced up with basil, oregano, and garlic, wrapped around a creamy spinach-Mascarpone filling. Great to have in front of a blazing fire after a brisk winter day of skiing.

14 ounces (half 28-ounce can) Italian plum tomatoes
2 packages active dry yeast
1 tablespoon sugar
1 small yellow onion, finely chopped
4 cloves garlic, finely chopped
1 tablespoon dried basil
1 tablespoon dried oregano
½ teaspoon celery seeds
2 teaspoons salt
1 cup grated Swiss, mozzarella, or Fontina cheese
5 to 6 cups unbleached all-purpose flour
1 tablespoon unsalted butter
1 small yellow onion, chopped
2 cups finely chopped fresh spinach
½ cup Mascarpone or ricotta cheese
1 tablespoon Marsala
2 teaspoons fresh lemon juice
Salt and freshly ground black pepper, to taste
1 egg
2 teaspoons water

1. Purée the tomatoes with their liquid in a blender. Pour into a medium-size saucepan and heat gently to about 115°F. Remove from heat and stir in the yeast and sugar. Let stand until foamy, about 10 minutes.

2. Transfer the tomato-yeast mixture to a large mixing bowl. Add the finely chopped onion, the garlic, basil, oregano, celery seeds, salt, and grated cheese and stir to mix. Stir in enough of the flour, 1 cup at a time, to make a firm dough.

3. Knead on a floured surface until smooth and elastic, about 10 minutes, adding more flour if necessary.

4. Place the dough in a buttered large bowl and turn to coat with butter. Cover with a damp towel and let rise in a warm place until doubled in bulk, 1 to 1½ hours.

5. While the dough is rising, melt the butter in a medium-size saucepan over medium-low heat. Add the chopped onion and sauté until translucent, 5 to 7 minutes. Stir in the spinach and cook 5 more minutes. Stir in the Mascarpone, Marsala, lemon juice, and salt and pepper to taste. Refrigerate covered until firm enough to spread.

6. Punch the dough down and divide it in half. Roll each half into a rectangle about ¾ inch thick and spread with the spinach filling. Roll up each rectangle like a jelly roll and place on greased baking sheets. Cover loosely with plastic wrap and let rise 1 hour.

7. Preheat oven to 375°F.

8. Beat the egg and 2 teaspoons water in a small bowl. Brush each loaf with the egg wash.

9. Bake until the loaves are lightly browned and sound hollow when lightly thumped, 40 to 50 minutes. Allow to cool on the baking sheets for 10 minutes. Turn out onto wire racks to cool completely.

2 loaves

BEEF POT PIE

For a hearty pot pie, a rich wintery beef stew with potatoes, carrots, and green beans is simmered in a slightly tart red wine sauce and baked under pâte brisée. All you need is a bottle of wine for a complete and comforting meal.

1 tablespoon unsalted butter
1 tablespoon olive oil
1½ pounds boneless beef chuck, cut into 2-inch pieces
1 medium-size yellow onion, coarsely chopped
2 cloves garlic, minced
2 tablespoons unbleached all-purpose flour
1 teaspoon salt
1 teaspoon freshly ground black pepper
2 cups sliced carrots (½ inch thick)
5 small new red potatoes, cut into 8 pieces each
½ cup chopped fresh Italian parsley
1 tablespoon Dijon-style mustard
1 cup dry red wine
1 cup canned beef broth
½ cup red wine vinegar
1 teaspoon dried thyme
2 tablespoons dark brown sugar
Pâte Brisée (page 399)
8 ounces green beans, ends
   trimmed, cut in half
1 egg
1 tablespoon water

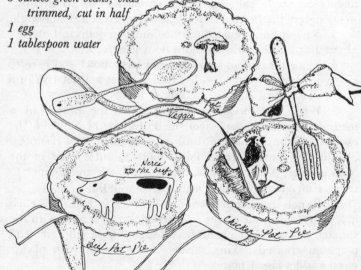

> "A meal without wine is like a day without sunshine."
> —Brillat-Savarin

WINE RACKS

Wine racks are designed to store wine properly on its side so the corks are kept moist. This protects the cork from harmful drying and shrinkage, which could let air seep into the bottle and spoil the wine. While you can stack bottles of wine on top of one another without a rack, the rack allows you to choose one bottle without having all the others come crashing down.

Racks should be made of durable material and positioned away from the light in a cool area (between 45° and 60°F.), as both light and temperature fluctuations can destroy wine. A cool basement or cellar is an ideal spot in many homes.

1. Preheat oven to 350°F.

2. Heat the butter and oil in a heavy skillet over medium heat. Add the beef, a few pieces at a time, and brown on all sides. Remove to a medium-size casserole.

3. Sauté the onion and garlic in the same skillet for 2 minutes. Add to the casserole.

4. Mix the flour, salt, and pepper and sprinkle over the beef. Toss to coat the beef and onion thoroughly.

5. Add the carrots, potatoes, parsley, mustard, wine, broth, vinegar, thyme, and brown sugar to the beef and stir to combine. Heat to boiling over medium heat. Cover and place in the oven. Bake for 1 hour. Remove the cover and bake for another 30 minutes.

6. While the beef is baking, make the pâte brisée.

7. Place the green beans and water to cover in a heavy medium-size saucepan. Heat to boiling. Reduce heat and simmer just until tender, about 5 minutes. Drain.

8. Remove the beef stew from oven. Increase the heat to 425°F. Stir the beans into the stew; taste and adjust seasonings.

9. Mix the egg and water in a small bowl. Pour the beef stew into a clean deep 2-quart casserole or soufflé dish. Roll out the pastry and place on the top of the dish. Trim the pastry, leaving a 1-inch border. Brush the edge of the dish with egg wash and press the overhanging dough onto the dish. Crimp the pastry decoratively and brush the top with egg wash. Cut a steam vent in the center.

10. Place the dish on a baking sheet and bake on the middle rack until the crust is golden, 20 to 25 minutes. Serve immediately.

6 portions

MORE WINTER CRAVINGS

... Warm take-out food held close to the body... homemade popcorn with butter... raspberries for Christmas breakfast... believing in Santa Claus ... a rare thick sirloin steak... lightly sautéed radishes... the smell of evergreen and eucalyptus... a laurel wreath... oysters at Brasserie Flo... chili and crusty bread... airplane tickets... persimmons... Dungeness crab in San Francisco... Key limes... calf's liver with sautéed onions... *coq au vin*... wearing our socks to bed... cassoulet... knickers and reindeer boots... roasted chestnuts... a fur coat with a hood ... pink grapefruit...

CHICKEN POT PIE

After a long day of work and late shopping, there is nothing more comforting than a chicken pot pie. Prepare it the night before and pop it in the oven to bake when you get home.

Pâte Brisée (page 399)
4 whole boneless skinless chicken breasts (2 pounds)
1 cup heavy or whipping cream
4 carrots, peeled and cut into ½-inch pieces
2 zucchini, unpeeled, cut into ½-inch pieces
5 tablespoons unsalted butter
2 small yellow onions (8 ounces), coarsely chopped
5 tablespoons unbleached all-purpose flour
1 cup canned chicken broth
¼ cup Cognac or dry white wine
1 tablespoon dried tarragon
1½ teaspoons salt
½ teaspoon freshly ground black pepper
1 egg
1 tablespoon water

1. Make the pâte brisée and refrigerate while preparing the filling.

2. Preheat oven to 350°F.

3. Place the chicken breasts in a single layer in a baking pan. Pour the cream over and bake 20 to 25 minutes. Remove the chicken from the cream; reserve the cream and cooking juices. Let the chicken cool and cut into 1-inch pieces.

4. Blanch the carrots in boiling salted water for 3 minutes. Add the zucchini and cook 1 minute more. Drain and cool under cold running water. Drain thoroughly.

5. Melt the butter in a large saucepan over medium heat. Add the onions and sauté until translucent, about 5 minutes. Add the flour and cook, stirring constantly, for 5 minutes. Do not let the flour brown.

6. Add the broth and cook, stirring constantly, until thickened. Stir in the reserved cream and cooking juices and the Cognac. Cook over low heat until thick, about 5 minutes.

7. Stir in the tarragon, salt, and pepper and simmer 1 minute. Add the chicken and vegetables and mix gently into the cream sauce. Remove from the heat.

8. Preheat oven to 425°F.

9. Mix the egg and water in a small bowl. Pour the chicken filling into a deep 2-quart casserole or soufflé dish. Roll out the pastry and place on the dish. Trim the pastry, leaving a 1-inch border. Brush the edge of the dish with egg wash and press the overhanging dough onto the dish. Crimp the pastry decoratively and brush the top with egg wash. Cut a steam vent in the center.

10. Place the dish on a baking sheet and bake on the middle rack until the crust is golden, 20 to 25 minutes. Serve immediately.

6 portions

VEGETABLE POT PIE

Pâte Brisée (page 399)
1 pound fresh spinach, well rinsed and dried, stems removed
2 tablespoons unsalted butter
12 ounces fresh mushrooms, wiped clean and thinly sliced
3 ripe large tomatoes (about 1 ½ pounds)
4 eggs
1 pound ricotta
6 tablespoons chopped fresh dill
1 tablespoon chopped fresh basil
1 tablespoon chopped fresh parsley
¼ teaspoon ground nutmeg
1 teaspoon salt
½ teaspoon freshly ground black pepper
2 tablespoons fresh lemon juice
1 teaspoon grated lemon zest
1 cup freshly grated Parmesan cheese
2 teaspoons water

WINTER FRUIT AND CHEESE COMBINATIONS

- ♥ Kumquats and Windsor Red
- ♥ Red Comice pears and Sage Derby
- ♥ Golden Delicious apples and farmhouse Cheddar
- ♥ Dried prunes, dates, figs, and St. Nectaire
- ♥ Seckel pears, lady apples, and Bleu de Bresse
- ♥ Clementines, Morbier, and Tomme served with a bowl of walnuts in the shell and a nutcracker
- ♥ Granny Smiths, Gruyère, Jarlsberg, and freshly shelled pecans
- ♥ Strawberries and fresh pineapple with Coulommiers
- ♥ Cream cheese mixed with chopped dried apricots, golden raisins, and toasted almonds served on wheatmeal biscuits or scones
- ♥ Rome apples, Havarti with mustard seeds, and sherry
- ♥ Navel oranges and black olives with Kasseri or feta
- ♥ A bowl of lingonberries with Munster and dark bread

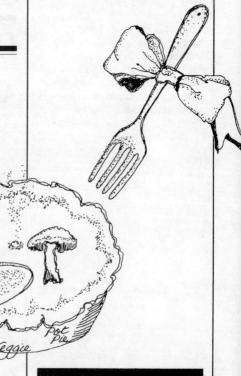

Over the past eight years at The Silver Palate, we have found that meat loaf is a constant best seller. It's comforting and reassuring, and no matter how we change it, update it, and add to it, we still call it meat loaf.

For a winter buffet, our new varieties are perfect fare. You can make them ahead of time for a large party. Chill them for a couple of hours so that it is easy to slice them fairly thin, and then arrange in a circular pattern on a pewter plate. Place earthenware crocks of mustard with little wooden spreaders around the meat loaves. Be sure to have at least three mustards—one grainy, one smooth, and one peppery.

Because of their fillings, the meat loaves are decorative when sliced and therefore need little garnish. They need no more than a large bunch of parsley on the side. Carefully place a few orange nasturtium or chrysanthemum blossoms on the platter for a dazzle of color. Arrange sliced breads in rustic baskets lined with large checked cotton or linen napkins. Use a few different types of bread, and leave a few whole loaves in the basket for display. It's nice to let your guests see the original loaf.

1. Make the pâte brisée and refrigerate 1 hour.

2. Finely chop the spinach. Melt 1 tablespoon of the butter in a large skillet over low heat. Add the spinach and cook uncovered until the liquid evaporates and the spinach is dry, about 10 minutes. Remove to a bowl.

3. Sauté the mushrooms in the remaining 1 tablespoon butter in the same skillet over low heat until the moisture evaporates, about 10 minutes. Remove to a separate bowl.

4. Blanch the tomatoes in boiling water for 1 minute. Plunge into cold water. Peel and seed the tomatoes. Finely chop the pulp and place in a sieve.

5. Combine 3 of the eggs, the ricotta, half the dill, the basil, parsley, nutmeg, salt, pepper, lemon juice and zest, and Parmesan in a large mixing bowl.

6. Preheat oven to 375°F.

7. Roll out half the pâte brisée on a lightly floured surface and line a deep 2-quart baking dish with the pastry. Spoon half the ricotta mixture into the dish. Place half the spinach over the ricotta and sprinkle with some of the remaining 3 tablespoons dill. Spread half the mushrooms over the spinach and sprinkle again with dill. Top with half the tomatoes. Repeat the vegetable layers and cover with the remaining ricotta mixture.

8. Mix the remaining egg and the water in a small bowl. Brush the edge of the pastry with egg wash. Roll out the remaining dough and place over the dish. Trim the pastry and crimp the edges together. Cut steam vents in the pastry and brush with egg wash.

9. Bake until golden brown, about 1 hour. Serve immediately.

6 portions

ITALIAN MEAT LOAF

A meat loaf is a wonderful palette for any of your favorite flavors. Hot or cold, this one is certain to be a crowd pleaser.

2 pounds ground beef chuck
1 pound sweet Italian sausage, casings removed
1 medium-size yellow onion, chopped
5 cloves garlic, minced
3 cups fresh bread crumbs
1 cup chopped fresh Italian parsley
2 tablespoons Italian seasonings
Salt and freshly ground black pepper, to taste
2 eggs, lightly beaten
½ cup tomato juice
½ cup dry red wine
2 cups fresh basil leaves
4 ounces sun-dried tomatoes (packed in oil), drained
1 pound smoked mozzarella, thinly sliced

1. Preheat oven to 375°F.

2. Combine the ground beef, sausage, onion, garlic,

bread crumbs, parsley, Italian seasonings, and salt and pepper to taste in a large bowl. Add the eggs, tomato juice, and wine and mix thoroughly.

3. Lay out 1 large sheet of waxed paper or parchment paper. Spread the meat loaf mixture out in a 15 x 12-inch rectangle on the waxed paper. Arrange the basil leaves over the surface. Scatter the sun-dried tomatoes over the basil and arrange three-fourths of the smoked mozzarella on top.

4. Using the waxed paper as an aid and starting from one short side, roll up the meat like a jelly roll. Peel back the paper as you roll. Place seam side down on a baking sheet lined with aluminum foil.

5. Bake 1 hour. Place the remaining smoked mozzarella over the top of the loaf and bake until the cheese is melted and bubbling, about 10 minutes more. Serve the meat loaf hot with Fresh Tomato Sauce (page 397), or refrigerate the meat loaf until cold and cut into thin slices like a pâté.

8 to 10 portions

ROQUEFORT MEAT LOAF

1 pound ground beef chuck
8 ounces ground pork
8 ounces ground veal
1 medium-size yellow onion, chopped
2 cups fresh bread crumbs
½ cup chopped fresh Italian parsley
¼ cup ketchup
1 tablespoon Dijon-style mustard
2 eggs, beaten
1 teaspoon dried thyme
Salt and freshly ground black pepper, to taste
½ cup light cream, scalded
8 slices firm white bread, crusts trimmed, diced
8 ounces Roquefort cheese, crumbled
1 egg, lightly beaten

1. Combine the ground meats, onion, bread crumbs, parsley, ketchup, mustard, 2 eggs, thyme, and salt and pepper to taste. Spread the mixture out on a large piece of waxed paper or parchment paper into a rectangle about 15 x 12 inches.

2. Preheat oven to 375°F.

3. Pour the scalded cream over the bread in a medium-size bowl and mix well. Add the cheese and lightly beaten egg and beat with a fork until smooth.

4. Spread the cheese mixture over the meat mixture, leaving a 1-inch border on all sides. Using the waxed paper as an aid and starting from one short side, roll up the meat like a jelly roll. Peel back the paper as you roll. Place seam side down on a foil-lined baking sheet.

5. Bake 1 hour. Cut into thick slices and serve immediately.

6 to 8 portions

VERSED IN VODKA

Vodka originated in Eastern Europe and it is consumed there throughout a meal in much the same way that wine is drunk in the West. We like our vodka Russian-style—straight from the freezer and straight up in small champagne flutes. We also love to infuse this potable with herbs, chile peppers, or citrus peel, and always add one of these flavorings to a fresh bottle. When it is poured, the effect of these additions floating in the crystal-clear liquid is beautiful, and the taste is sublime.

"Vodka is the aunt of wine."
—Russian Proverb

SKI WEEKENDS

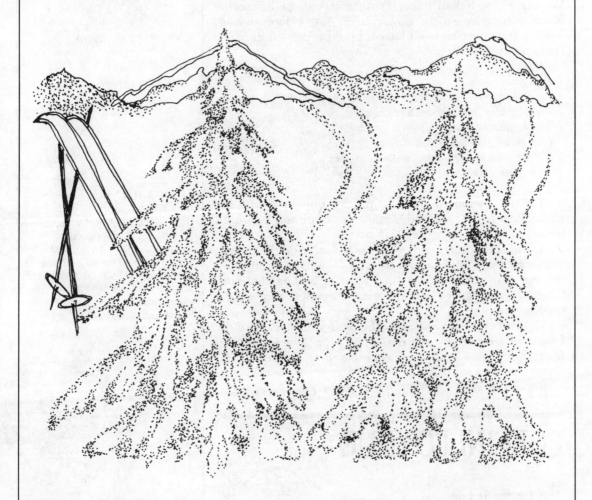

The romantic notion of a ski-weekend escape to a quiet little chalet in the Alps is all too often dispelled by the reality of a station wagon filled with kids, skis, boots, poles, and duffle bags bursting with winter paraphernalia. No sooner have all the kids been organized with lift tickets and ski school than it is time to feed the hungry lot.

Experience has taught us that it is best to plan these menus with foods that take little time to prepare, or with those that can be prepared in advance. Since large groups are often involved in these weekend excursions, it is also best to think economically. Fondues are great because they have an aura of romance and yet are easy to prepare at a moment's notice. The Polish Cabbage Tourte is stick-to-your-ribs fare that can be prepared in advance. Our aim is to get the cook out of the kitchen and onto the slopes, too.

PESTO FONDUE

An old favorite is made very special with an Italian twist. We use a dry Italian wine, Fontina cheese, and Pecorino Romano to spice up the Emmentaler. Just before serving, swirl in the pesto, and you have a bright green spiral in the center of the fondue.

1 clove garlic, halved
1 cup Italian dry white wine
1½ cups grated imported Fontina cheese
1½ cups grated Swiss or Emmentaler cheese
½ cup grated Pecorino Romano cheese
2 to 3 tablespoons unbleached all-purpose flour
½ cup Basic Pesto (page 398)

1. Rub a fondue pot or heat-proof ceramic pot with the garlic. Pour in the wine and heat over medium-low heat until hot.

2. Toss the cheeses with the flour to coat. Add the cheese, a handful at a time, to the wine, stirring constantly and waiting until each addition melts before adding the next. Check the consistency and add more cheese or more wine if needed.

3. Just before serving, swirl the pesto over the top of the fondue in a decorative pattern. Serve with 1-inch pieces of fried sweet Italian sausage, cubes of French bread, and cherry tomatoes for dipping.

6 to 8 portions

PORCINI FONDUE

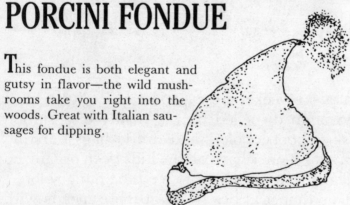

This fondue is both elegant and gutsy in flavor—the wild mushrooms take you right into the woods. Great with Italian sausages for dipping.

1 cup plus 2 tablespoons Marsala
¾ cup dried wild mushrooms, preferably Italian porcini
8 ounces imported Fontina cheese, grated
8 ounces Swiss or Emmentaler cheese, grated
2 to 3 tablespoons unbleached all-purpose flour
1 clove garlic, halved
2 cups dry white wine
½ cup grated Parmesan or Pecorino Romano cheese
Freshly ground black pepper, to taste

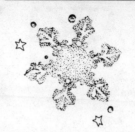

A NIGHT OF GAMES

Have a gaming night. Set up tables for cribbage, checkers, chess, backgammon, tarot, bridge, poker, and gin rummy. Print up the house rules and sell chips at the door, so the stakes are set for a night of fun. We suggest you ring a bell at night's end or your guests will be there 'til dawn!

1. Heat 1 cup Marsala just to boiling in a small saucepan and pour over the dried mushrooms in a small bowl. Let stand at least 1 hour.

2. Meanwhile, toss the Fontina and Swiss cheeses lightly with the flour.

3. Rub a heavy enameled pot or fondue pot with the garlic. Pour in the white wine and heat over medium-low heat until hot.

4. Add the cheese tossed with flour, a handful at a time, stirring constantly and waiting until each addition melts before adding the next. Then stir in the Parmesan.

5. Drain the mushrooms, squeezing out as much liquid as possible, and chop into fairly fine pieces. Stir the mushrooms, the remaining 2 tablespoons Marsala, and lots of freshly ground black pepper into the fondue. Serve with assorted breads and sausages for dipping.

6 main-course portions or 10 to 12 appetizer portions

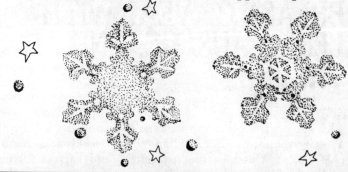

APRES SKI BUFFET

Porcini Fondue

Fried Rabbit with Sweet Mustard

Apple and Onion Tart

Pale Greens with Watercress Dressing

Crusty French bread cubes

Old-Fashioned Oatmeal Cookies

Cashew Butter Cookies

Barbera d'Alba

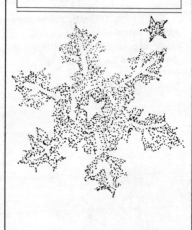

GREEK FONDUE

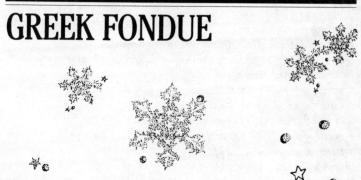

Eating fondue is a fun way to spend a cold winter evening. We've made several variations—in this one the Kasseri cheese is sharp and distinctive, and cinnamon and nutmeg add deep rich flavors.

1 tablespoon best-quality olive oil
2 cloves garlic, minced
1 tablespoon dried oregano
1½ cups (or as needed) dry white wine
1 pound Kasseri cheese, grated
2 to 3 tablespoons unbleached all-purpose flour
1 teaspoon finely grated lemon zest
Pinch ground cinnamon
Pinch ground nutmeg
Freshly ground black pepper, to taste
2 tablespoons brandy

1. Heat the oil in a heavy enameled pot or fondue pot over low heat. Add the garlic and oregano and sauté just until the garlic is soft but not brown.

2. Pour in 1½ cups wine and heat gently until hot.

3. Toss the Kasseri with the flour and add a handful at a time to the wine, stirring constantly and waiting until each addition melts before adding the next.

4. When all the cheese is melted and the mixture is smooth, stir in the lemon zest, cinnamon, nutmeg, and black pepper to taste. Stir in the brandy. If the fondue is too thick, thin it with a bit more wine.

5. Serve with sesame bread, pan-fried Greek sausage, pepper strips, cherry tomatoes, and Greek olives for dipping.

10 to 12 appetizer portions or 6 main-course portions

BREAST OF VEAL WITH LEEK, SAUSAGE, AND CHEVRE

This inexpensive cut of meat is made into a hearty meal with a luscious stuffing of spicy Italian sausage, leeks, and creamy goat cheese. Chopped onions, celery, and carrots further enrich the flavor of the meat. Serve with a hearty red wine.

1 tablespoon olive oil
1½ pounds sweet Italian sausage, casings removed
8 leeks (white part and two-thirds green), quartered lengthwise, well rinsed, dried, and sliced
6 ounces soft mild chèvre
1 teaspoon dried thyme
Salt and freshly ground black pepper, to taste
1 breast of veal (7 to 8 pounds), with pocket cut for stuffing
1 large onion, coarsely chopped
6 carrots, peeled and coarsely chopped
6 ribs celery, coarsely chopped
½ cup chopped fresh parsley
4 cloves garlic
Zest of 1 lemon
1½ to 2 cups dry white wine

1. Heat the oil in a large skillet over medium-low heat. Add the sausage and sauté, breaking up the meat with a fork, until the meat begins to lose its pink color. Add the leeks and cook until the leeks are tender and the meat begins to brown, 15 to 20 minutes.

2. Reduce heat to low and stir in the chèvre, breaking it into small pieces. Cook until the chèvre melts. Season with thyme and salt and pepper to taste.

3. Spoon the sausage mixture into the pocket of the veal. Secure with small skewers or tie with kitchen string.

4. Preheat oven to 375°F.

RACLETTE

On the chilliest of winter evenings, throw a raclette party. Much of the preparation can be done in advance.

Electric raclette machines are available, but we think it's more fun to place the cheese on an interesting trivet or ceramic platter close to a blazing fire. Don't despair if you can't find raclette cheese: Italian Fontina, Swiss Appenzeller, and Doux de Montagne make fine substitutes. You could even offer an assortment of different cheeses.

Serve accompaniments in rustic baskets lined with country-print napkins. Offer boiled new red potatoes, kept warm close to the fire. Make up a charcuterie board laden with assorted pâtés, sausages, cornichons, and sour cherries.

As the heat of the fire melts the cheese, each guest scrapes a little pool onto his plate and helps himself to potatoes and charcuterie. Glazed earthenware dinner plates add to the rustic atmosphere.

Serve the raclette with plenty of hearty red wine and enjoy a lovely evening, lingering by the fire.

To be really authentic, follow the Swiss tradition of hanging a large basket of pine cones by the fire. Keep the party and the fire going by tossing the cones onto the fire as kindling throughout the evening.

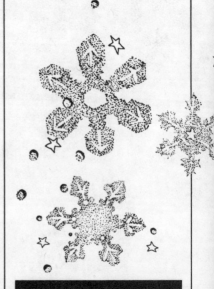

5. Line a roasting pan large enough to hold the veal with aluminum foil. Scatter the onion, carrots, and celery over the foil and place the stuffed breast of veal on the vegetables.

6. Mince the parsley, garlic, and lemon zest in a food processor fitted with a steel blade or by hand. Pat this mixture over the top of the veal.

7. Pour 1½ cups of the wine around the veal. Fold the edges of the foil around the veal and cover the top with more foil. Bake 1½ hours.

8. Remove the top foil and pour in the remaining ½ cup wine if the vegetables are too dry. Bake uncovered until the top is nicely browned, about 1 more hour.

9. Remove from the oven and let stand 10 to 15 minutes. Cut the veal into pieces between the rib bones and serve immediately.

6 to 8 portions

A KITCHEN SUPPER

Chicken Noodle Soup

Polish Cabbage Tourte

Green salad

Cranberry Currant Conserve Tart

Alsace or Washington State Riesling

Cozy kitchen food is great after a day of winter sports. Build healthy appetites by organizing some competition—skating relays, saucer races, cross-country-skiing scavenger hunts, or snowman-building contests. After dinner give warm toasts to the winners.

POLISH CABBAGE TOURTE

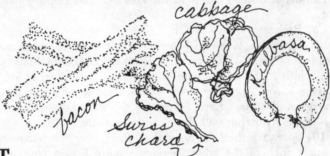

There is nothing more satisfying than good hearty peasant food. While this recipe may look intimidating, it is really just a wonderful mixture of earthy foods. The whole comes out a giant-stuffed cabbage—the best you've ever tasted.

1 large green cabbage, preferably Savoy
1½ cups chopped Swiss chard leaves, plus 5 or 6 perfect whole leaves
2 tablespoons unsalted butter
1 pound kielbasa, cut into ¼-inch dice
5 slices bacon, chopped
1 large Bermuda onion, chopped
¾ cup chopped leek (1 large leek)
1 bag (1 pound) sauerkraut, drained
1 bottle best-quality beer
⅓ cup dry sherry
3 juniper berries
2 tablespoons caraway seeds
1 teaspoon dried thyme
½ teaspoon ground nutmeg
½ teaspoon ground allspice
Salt and freshly ground black pepper, to taste
8 ounces cream cheese, cut into small pieces
3 tablespoons Crème Fraîche (page 399) or heavy or whipping cream
1 tablespoon grainy mustard
3 cups canned chicken broth

1. Using a small paring knife, make several cuts around the outside of the core of the cabbage. Drop the whole cabbage in a large pot of boiling salted water and boil for 10 minutes. Drain thoroughly and set aside.

2. Blanch the whole Swiss chard leaves for 5 minutes. Drain and set aside.

3. Heat the butter in a large cast-iron skillet over medium heat. Add the kielbasa and sauté until beginning to brown, about 10 minutes. Remove from pan and set aside.

4. Add the chopped bacon to the skillet and sauté over medium heat until the bacon starts to render its fat, about 2 minutes. Add the onion and leek and sauté for 10 minutes.

5. Add the sauerkraut, beer, sherry, juniper berries, caraway, thyme, nutmeg, allspice, and salt and pepper to taste. Heat to boiling. Reduce heat and simmer covered for 45 minutes.

6. Stir in the chopped Swiss chard and simmer 5 more minutes. Remove and discard the juniper berries.

7. Stir in the cream cheese, crème fraîche, and mustard over low heat. Simmer until the cream cheese melts. Taste and adjust seasonings. Stir in the kielbasa and remove from heat.

8. Preheat oven to 350°F.

9. Spread a 24-inch-square double thickness of cheesecloth in a large bowl. Cover with another double thickness of cheesecloth laid the opposite way. Separate the large outer cabbage leaves from the core. Form a circle of alternating cabbage and Swiss chard leaves on top of the cheesecloth. This is the layer that will show on the outside.

10. Spread a thick layer of the filling over the leaves to within 1 inch of the edge. Separate more leaves from the cabbage and make another layer of cabbage leaves over the filling. (The circles will get smaller as you go along because the leaves will be smaller.)

11. Spread another layer of filling over the leaves. Continue in the same manner, making increasingly smaller circles of leaves. You should be able to make 4 to 5 layers in all.

12. When all the filling has been used, gather the edges of the cheesecloth in the center to shape a rounded tourte. Twist the ends of the cheesecloth tightly and tie with a string. Cut off the excess cloth.

13. Place the bundle in an oven-proof casserole. Pour the chicken stock over the tourte. Cover and bake for 1½ hours.

14. Lift the bundle out of the broth and place in a colander to drain for a few minutes. Then untie the string and invert the tourte onto a platter. Remove the cheesecloth. Cut the tourte into wedges and serve immediately as is or with a tomato sauce.

12 appetizer portions or 6 main-course portions

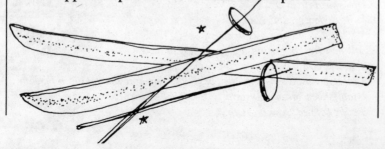

OF CABBAGES AND KINGS

To many Americans, cabbage has a bad reputation. Yet it is such a great favorite in Europe that the French use it as a term of endearment, calling loved ones *mon petit chou* ("my little cabbage"). Cooks around the world have developed many tricks for tempering cabbage in order to create dishes that are delicate and light. Salting and soaking in ice water is one method; another effective method for softening taste and texture is to blanch it. It can then be served as is, sautéed, or gently braised in order to absorb other flavors.

Cabbages may also be stuffed whole and then sliced, or each leaf can be used to encase a few tablespoons of a savory mixture containing a variety of meats and vegetables.

WINTER ESCAPES

There is a point in midwinter when even the groundhog hasn't dared to venture out, and you become convinced that spring will not only be a little late this year, but might not happen at all. A sense of desperation encroaches and thoughts turn to warm sand, mild ocean breezes, and tropical rum punches. There are those who hate winter so much that they fly now to exotic Morocco or secluded Caribbean islands and worry about facing the consequences later. And then there are those clever souls who know how to conjure up a change of scene in their own homes on the bleakest of winter days. You'd be surprised what a few tropical taste treats can do for your morale. After all, a tan lasts only a week . . .

BESTILLA PHYLLO TURNOVERS

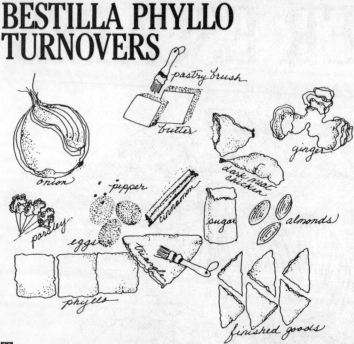

The wonderful sweet and exotic flavors of Moroccan spices are combined to make a miniature version of this classic dish. Serve on a beautiful brass tray and garnish with orange lilies.

2 tablespoons unsalted butter
1 medium-size yellow onion, chopped
2½ cups cooked diced dark chicken meat
1 teaspoon ground ginger
1 teaspoon turmeric
4 teaspoons ground cinnamon
Salt and freshly ground black pepper, to taste
½ cup chopped fresh parsley
1 cup lightly toasted sliced almonds
¼ cup canned chicken broth
3 eggs
1 pound phyllo dough, thawed if frozen
1 cup (2 sticks) unsalted butter, melted
3 tablespoons granulated sugar
Confectioners' sugar (garnish)

1. Melt 2 tablespoons butter in a large skillet over medium heat. Add the onion and sauté until soft and translucent, about 10 minutes. Add the chicken and sprinkle with the ginger, turmeric, 1 teaspoon of the cinnamon, and salt and pepper to taste. Stir in the parsley and almonds.

2. Beat the chicken broth and eggs until well blended and pour into a small saucepan. Cook, stirring constantly, until the consistency resembles soft scrambled eggs. Stir into the chicken mixture to bind. This is the bestilla mixture.

3. Preheat oven to 350°F.

4. Cut the sheets of phyllo dough crosswise into fifths. Lay 1 strip down and brush the top with melted butter. Cover the remaining dough with a slightly dampened kitchen towel

BON VOYAGE PARTY

Send friends off with a bang, whether it's for their holiday of a lifetime, to set up house in a new city, or to begin life at college. Set the scene of their forthcoming adventures when preparing the menu, when choosing the music, by posters, postcards, maps, newspapers, museum and restaurant guides. Complete the event with lots of confetti, balloons, and streamers. Let your other guests know whether or not to bring small farewell presents. You might want to pre-welcome the guests of honor to their destination with theater tickets or a restaurant reservation.

to keep it from drying out.

5. Combine the granulated sugar and remaining 3 teaspoons cinnamon and sprinkle a little evenly over the buttered strip. Top with another phyllo strip and brush it with butter. Place a heaping teaspoon of the bestilla mixture in the center of the strip about ½ inch from the base.

6. Fold a corner across the filling and continue to fold, as if you were folding a flag, until the strip is all folded into a neat triangle. Brush both sides with melted butter and place on a baking sheet. Repeat with the remaining phyllo, cinnamon sugar, and bestilla mixture (see Note, below).

7. Bake until golden, about 30 minutes.

8. Remove from the oven and let cool 5 minutes. Arrange on serving platters and dust the tops with sifted confectioners' sugar. Serve immediately.

60 turnovers

Note: The triangles can be prepared up to this point and then frozen. Do not thaw, but bake, brushing first with a little more melted butter, for about 45 minutes.

HEARTY WINTER SOUP WITH HINTS OF THE CARIBBEAN

Mix pork and sausages with fruits, add the surprise of lime juice, and you have cooked up a hearty Caribbean-style soup. Dazzle with a jigger of rum and garnish with the pale and dark greens of scallions.

2 pounds boneless lean pork, cut into ½-inch dice
1 or 2 pork bones, if possible
4 cloves garlic, chopped
1 tablespoon chopped fresh ginger root
2 bay leaves
10 cups (or as needed) water
1 cup dry red wine
2 sweet potatoes, peeled and cut into bite-size pieces
1 ½ cups diced jicama
1 large summer squash, cubed
6 tablespoons fresh lime juice (2 limes)
1 tablespoon curry powder
1 teaspoon ground coriander
½ teaspoon ground cloves
Pinch cayenne pepper
Salt and freshly ground black pepper, to taste
2 to 3 tablespoons sugar
1 ½ pounds sliced kielbasa or other smoked sausage
3 green (unripened) bananas, peeled and sliced
½ cup diced dried pineapple (optional)
1 to 2 ounces dark rum (optional)
8 scallions (green onions), sliced (garnish)

1. Place the pork, bones, garlic, ginger, bay leaves, 10 cups water, and wine in a large stock pot. Simmer covered 45 minutes to 1 hour.

2. Add the sweet potatoes, jicama, and squash. Add more water if the soup seems too thick. Stir in the lime juice, curry powder, coriander, cloves, cayenne, and salt, pepper, and sugar to taste. Heat to boiling. Reduce heat and simmer until the vegetables are tender, about 20 minutes.

3. Cut each of the kielbasa slices in half. Add them to the soup and simmer 5 more minutes. Add the bananas and pineapple, if desired. Simmer to blend the flavors, 7 to 10 minutes more.

4. Just before serving, remove the bones and bay leaves. If you like, fortify the soup with a jigger or two of rum. Serve steaming hot, garnished with scallions.

12 portions

LAMB TAGINE SOUP

A meal unto itself, this rich lamb, barley, and winter vegetable soup warms any palate with the flavors of Morocco.

2 to 2½ pounds lamb shanks or lamb stew meat with bones
1 medium-size yellow onion, chopped
1 tablespoon salt
2 teaspoons dried rosemary
¾ cup pearl barley
4 tablespoons (½ stick) unsalted butter
4 leeks (white and green parts), well rinsed, dried, and chopped
2 large parsnips, peeled and diced
4 carrots, peeled and cut into ¼-inch slices
1 sweet red pepper, cored, seeded, and diced
1 small head cauliflower, broken into small florets
2 white turnips, peeled and cut into coarse julienne
2 cups canned beef broth
1 cup dry red wine
Salt and freshly ground black pepper, to taste
1 can (16 ounces) chick-peas (garbanzos), drained
1 teaspoon ground cinnamon
Chopped fresh parsley (garnish)
Garlic Croutons to garnish (page 400)

1. One day before serving, place the lamb, onion, salt, and 1 teaspoon of the rosemary in a large stock pot and add water to cover. Heat to boiling. Reduce heat and simmer covered over medium heat 1 hour.

2. Stir in the barley and simmer uncovered until the barley is tender, about 45 minutes. Remove the soup from the heat, let it cool, then refrigerate overnight so the fat will solidify on the surface.

CALYPSO PARTY

Planter's punch

*Sweet Potato Vichyssoise
with Peanut Noshes*

*Chicken, Avocado, and
Papaya Salad*

Honey-Curry Bread

Lime and Macadamia Tart

By February it seems that it's been winter forever. Get a head start on spring with inspiration from the islands. Decorate with all the palms and island flowers you can find, give everyone a sarong or Hawaiian shirt, and serve plenty of fruity rum drinks. Let your guests calypso, hula, or laze away the evening.

3. The following day, melt the butter in a large stock pot over medium heat. Stir in the leeks and cook 8 minutes.

4. Stir in the parsnips, carrots, red pepper, cauliflower, turnips, stock, wine, and enough water to cover. Season with the remaining 1 teaspoon rosemary and salt and pepper to taste. Heat to boiling. Reduce heat and simmer uncovered until the vegetables are tender, about 20 minutes.

5. Meanwhile, remove and discard the fat from the lamb stock. Remove the lamb from the stock and cut the meat from the bones and into bite-size pieces. Return the meat to the stock.

6. When the vegetables are tender, add the lamb and stock. Stir in the chick-peas and cinnamon. Simmer the soup uncovered for 20 to 30 minutes.

7. Garnish the soup with lots of parsley and the garlic croutons.

8 to 10 portions

CHICKEN, AVOCADO, AND PAPAYA SALAD

A light chicken salad filled with the delicate and rich tastes of avocado and papaya. Coat this silky salad with a dressing of fresh lime juice and walnut oil and scatter crunchy chopped walnuts over the top.

3 whole boneless chicken breasts (6 halves), poached
2 ripe papayas, peeled and thinly sliced
2 ripe avocados, peeled, pitted, and thinly sliced
⅓ cup fresh lime juice
¾ cup walnut oil
Finely grated zest of 1 lime
Salt and freshly cracked black pepper, to taste
½ cup coarsely chopped walnuts
½ cup watercress leaves

1. Remove the skin and any fat from the chicken breasts and cut the meat diagonally into thin slices.

2. On 6 individual salad plates, alternate slices of papaya, chicken, and avocado.

3. Whisk the lime juice, oil, lime zest, and salt and pepper to taste together in a mixing bowl.

4. Spoon the dressing over each salad and then sprinkle with the walnuts and watercress leaves. Serve immediately.

6 portions

"I live on good soup, not on fine words."
—Molière

STUFFED CHICKEN LEGS WITH COUSCOUS

6 chicken legs (drumsticks and thighs), boned but bones reserved
3 cups water
1 cup dry white wine
½ cup celery tops with leaves
Salt and freshly ground black pepper, to taste
2 cups Berta's Chicken Stock (page 369) or canned broth
10 tablespoons unsalted butter
2 teaspoons ground cinnamon
1 teaspoon turmeric
1 teaspoon ground cardamom
½ teaspoon curry powder
1 cup couscous
¾ cup chopped dates
½ cup golden raisins
½ cup chopped carrots
1 small yellow onion, chopped
5 tablespoons fresh lemon juice
3 tablespoons ground almonds
½ cup minced fresh parsley
½ teaspoon orange-flower water (optional)
2 tablespoons pine nuts (pignoli)

1. Place the reserved chicken bones, the water, wine, celery tops, and salt and pepper to taste in a medium-size saucepan. Heat to boiling. Reduce heat and simmer uncovered for 2 hours. Strain the stock and return it to the saucepan. Heat to boiling and cook until reduced by half. You should have at least 1 cup of reduced stock.

2. Meanwhile, heat the 2 cups Berta's Chicken Stock, 2 tablespoons of the butter, the cinnamon, turmeric, cardamom, and curry powder to boiling in a medium-size saucepan. Gradually stir in the couscous and cook, stirring constantly, until the liquid is absorbed, about 1 minute. Remove from the heat and stir in the dates and raisins. Cover the pan; let stand 15 minutes.

3. Stir the carrots, onion, 3 tablespoons of the lemon juice, and 4 tablespoons of the remaining butter into the couscous. Season to taste with salt and pepper. Let cool slightly at room temperature.

4. Spread open 1 boned chicken leg, skin side down, on a work surface. Spoon ½ cup of the couscous mixture into the leg and roll it up to enclose the stuffing. Tie securely at both ends with kitchen string. Repeat with the remaining chicken legs and stuffing.

5. Melt the remaining 4 tablespoons butter in a large skillet over medium-high heat. Add the chicken legs and brown on all sides. Reduce the heat to low, cover the skillet, and cook until the chicken is done, about 45 minutes.

6. Remove the chicken to a serving platter and keep warm. Pour 1 cup of the reduced stock into the skillet and

"Wild oats will get sown some time and one of the arts of life is to sow them at the right time."
—Richard Le Gallienne

"They were glossed sticky dates, cold rich figs, cramped belly to belly in small boxes. . . ."
—Thomas Wolfe

ALMONDS

Almonds are one of our favorite nuts, and it seems they have universal appeal. They are frequently mentioned in the Bible, in Greek mythology, and by both Chaucer and Shakespeare. Although they come in two forms, sweet and bitter, it is the sweet almond that is most used in cooking and baking, while the bitter almond is usually confined to nonedible preparations such as cosmetics.

Almonds can be purchased unshelled, shelled, blanched, slivered, chopped, sliced, and ground. In our kitchen we prefer to go the extra distance and buy whole shelled unblanched almonds and prepare them ourselves. It really is worth the effort.

• To blanch almonds, drop them into boiling water for 30 seconds. Drain, and remove the skins by rubbing the slightly cooled nuts between your fingers.

• To toast almonds, spread them on a baking sheet and bake for 10 to 15 minutes in a preheated 350°F oven until they're fragrant and golden in color. Allow to cool before using. Store almonds in a covered container in your refrigerator or freezer.

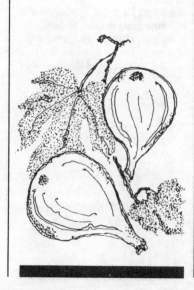

simmer 5 minutes, scraping up any browned bits stuck to the bottom of the pan.

7. Place the almonds, parsley, and orange-flower water in a food processor fitted with a steel blade and process to a paste. Stir the almond mixture into the skillet. Stir in the remaining 2 tablespoons lemon juice, pine nuts, and salt and pepper to taste. Spoon the sauce over the chicken legs and serve immediately.

6 portions

CHICKEN WITH FIGS

The flavor and appearance of this dish are equally spectacular. Marinated overnight, the fruit plumps and the chicken becomes tender and moist. Madeira, sugar, and pecans finish off this version of an old Silver Palate favorite.

2 chickens (2½ to 3 pounds each), cut into 8 pieces each
6 large cloves garlic, finely minced
2 tablespoons dried thyme
1 tablespoon ground cumin
1 teaspoon ground ginger
1 teaspoon salt
½ cup red wine vinegar
½ cup best-quality olive oil
4 teaspoons green peppercorns (packed in water), drained
1 cup imported black olives
1½ cups dried apricots
1 cup dried small figs or large fig pieces
¼ cup packed brown sugar
½ cup Madeira
1 cup large pecan pieces
Grated zest of 2 lemons

1. One day before serving, combine the chicken, garlic, thyme, cumin, ginger, salt, vinegar, oil, peppercorns, olives, apricots, and figs in a large bowl. Marinate covered in the refrigerator overnight. Remove the bowl from the refrigerator 1 hour before cooking.

2. Preheat oven to 350°F.

3. Arrange the chicken in a single layer in a large shallow baking pan. Spoon the marinade mixture evenly over the chicken. Sprinkle with the sugar and pour the Madeira between the pieces.

4. Cover the pan with aluminum foil and bake for 20 minutes. Remove the foil and bake, basting frequently with the pan juices, until the juices run clear when a thigh is pierced with a sharp skewer, 40 to 50 minutes.

5. Using a fork and slotted spoon, transfer the chicken, olives, and dried fruit to a large serving platter. Drizzle with a few large spoonfuls of the pan juices and sprinkle with the pecans. Sprinkle lemon zest over all. Pass the remaining pan juices in a sauceboat.

6 portions

LAMB STEW WITH LEMON AND OLIVES

An exotic blend of fruit and spices that conjures up images of palm trees, snake charmers, and Moroccan bazaars. Be sure to allow plenty of marinating time.

½ cup golden raisins
½ cup plus 3 tablespoons dry sherry
2 ½ to 3 pounds boneless lamb shoulder, cut into 2-inch pieces
1 cup fresh orange juice
4 cloves garlic, minced
4 tablespoons olive oil
1 medium-size yellow onion, chopped
1 teaspoon saffron threads
2 teaspoons ground coriander
2 teaspoons dried thyme
1 ½ teaspoons ground cumin
½ cup pine nuts (pignoli)
1 tablespoon unbleached all-purpose flour
½ cup dry red wine
Salt and freshly ground black pepper, to taste
3 tomatoes, seeded and cut into chunks
½ cup halved pitted Greek olives
1 lemon, cut into thin half slivers
2 tablespoons fresh lemon juice

1. Soak the raisins in ½ cup sherry for 3 hours.
2. Place the lamb, orange juice, and garlic in a large bowl. Marinate at room temperature at least 2 hours, turning the lamb occasionally. Drain, reserving the marinade.
3. Heat half the oil in a Dutch oven over medium-high heat. Brown the lamb, a few pieces at a time, in the oil, adding the remaining oil as needed. Remove the lamb with a slotted spoon to a bowl. Add the onion to the pan and sauté 5 minutes. Add the saffron, coriander, thyme, cumin, and pine nuts and cook 5 minutes more.
4. Stir in the flour and cook 1 minute. Add the raisins with the sherry, the reserved marinade, and the wine and stir to mix. Season to taste with salt and pepper.
5. Return the lamb to the Dutch oven and add the tomatoes and olives. Simmer covered 1 hour 15 minutes.
6. While the stew is simmering, place the lemon slices flat in a shallow bowl and sprinkle lightly with salt. Cover with boiling water and let stand for 10 minutes. Drain and set aside.
7. Remove the meat and solids from the pan and reduce the sauce over medium-high heat. When the sauce is the desired consistency, stir in the lemon juice and 3 tablespoons sherry.
8. Return the meat and solids to the pan. Reheat the stew. Serve immediately, topped with the lemon slices.

6 portions

MOROCCAN MYSTIQUE

Bestilla Phyllo Turnovers

Lamb Stew with Lemon and Olives

Honey-Curry Bread

Orange and red-onion salad

Persimmons, figs, dates Chocolate Orange Cookies

Cabernet or Bordeaux

Marrakesh . . . the ciy of intrigue . . . mystery . . . bazaars . . . the heat . . . the search for shade . . . olive trees . . . the aromas of mint, oranges, cinnamon, cloves . . . the perfume of flowers . . . Berber tribes . . . chants . . . the fantasy . . . and the Gardens of Allah . . .

WINTER FRUIT DESSERTS

- ♥ Sliced bananas with maple syrup, lightly broiled
- ♥ Fresh pineapple drizzled with kirsch
- ♥ Clementines, currants, and cooked cranberries tossed with brown sugar
- ♥ Prunes steeped in Zinfandel with cinnamon sticks and lemon and orange slices
- ♥ Pears poached in red Burgundy, whole cloves, and black pepper
- ♥ Prunes and apricots poached with a little sugar and served on top of a grapefruit half
- ♥ Grapefruit half with a scoop of grapefruit sorbet on top
- ♥ Poached oranges with candied zest and Grand Marnier syrup
- ♥ Candied citrus peels dipped in bitter chocolate
- ♥ Crushed raspberries, crumbled almond macaroons sprinkled with amaretto, and whipped cream
- ♥ Prunes plumped in Armagnac and dolloped with whipped cream
- ♥ A bowl of pomegranates and persimmons

LIME AND MACADAMIA TART

PASTRY:

1 ½ cups unbleached all-purpose flour
½ cup (1 stick) unsalted butter, cold, cut into small pieces
1 tablespoon sugar
Pinch salt
1 egg yolk
1 to 2 tablespoons ice water

FILLING:

2 large limes
½ cup sugar
2 eggs
½ cup ground unsalted macadamia nuts
6 tablespoons (¾ stick) unsalted butter, melted

GARNISH:

Whipped cream
6 to 8 toasted whole macadamia nuts

1. To make the pastry, process the flour, butter, sugar, and salt in a food processor fitted with a steel blade until the mixture resembles coarse meal. Add the egg yolk. With the machine running, add enough of the water for the dough to gather into a ball. Remove from the machine, dust with flour, and wrap with plastic wrap. Refrigerate the dough at least 1 hour.

2. Preheat oven to 400°F.

3. Roll out the dough into a 12-inch circle on a lightly floured surface. Line a 9-inch tart pan with the dough. Trim and crimp the edges. Prick the bottom of the dough all over with a fork. Line the shell with parchment paper and weight with dried beans or pie weights. Bake the shell for 15 minutes. Remove the weights and let cool.

4. To make the filling, remove the zest from the limes with a vegetable peeler and chop fine with a chef's knife. Place the zest, sugar, eggs, and ground nuts in a food processor fitted with a steel blade. Process for 30 seconds. Squeeze the juice from the limes and add the juice and butter to the egg mixture. Process until well combined, about 10 seconds.

5. Remove the paper from the shell and carefully pour in the filling.

6. Bake until the filling is firm and lightly browned on top, about 30 minutes. Let cool to room temperature.

7. Cut the tart into wedges and garnish each serving with whipped cream and whole macadamia nuts.

6 to 8 portions

VALENTINE'S DAY

Cupid's arrows send a wonderful frivolity to lighten the dark shadows of midwinter. Valentine's Day is the perfect excuse to let your imagination run wild with romantic notions. There can't be too many hearts or enough kisses.

Our Be Mine Menu is specially created to nourish the heart. A salad of velvety ruby radicchio and pale pink rose petals, a cozy Chicken Blanquette, and a creamy white Coeur à la Crème make for a guaranteed love potion.

BLANQUETTE OF CHICKEN

A delicious yet economical version of *blanquette de veau*, a Silver Palate favorite that appears in our first cookbook. We've added fresh carrots, zucchini, dill, and sweet tarragon and napped it all in a rich, creamy sauce.

8 cups water
2 cups white pearl onions
¾ cup (1½ sticks) unsalted butter
1 chicken (2½ to 3 pounds), cut into 8 pieces
4 tablespoons unbleached all-purpose flour
1 teaspoon ground nutmeg
1½ teaspoons salt
1½ teaspoons freshly ground black pepper
2 cups julienned carrots
½ cup chopped fresh Italian parsley
2 tablespoons dried tarragon
3 cups (or as needed) Berta's Chicken Stock (page 396)
2 cups julienned zucchini (about 1½ pounds)
½ cup heavy or whipping cream
¼ cup chopped fresh dill

"In spring a young man's fancy lightly turns to thoughts of love."
—Alfred, Lord Tennyson

1. Preheat oven to 350°F.

2. Heat the water to boiling in a large saucepan over high heat. Add the onions and boil for 3 minutes. Remove from heat and drain. Trim the ends and slip the skins off.

3. Melt ½ cup of the butter in a heavy casserole over medium heat. Brown the chicken, a few pieces at a time, on all sides. When all the pieces have been browned, return to the casserole.

4. Mix 3 tablespoons of the flour, the nutmeg, 1 teaspoon of the salt, and 1 teaspoon of the pepper in a small bowl. Sprinkle over the chicken, coat well, and cook over low heat for 3 minutes. Do not brown the flour.

5. Add the onions, carrots, parsley, tarragon, and enough of the stock to just cover the chicken and vegetables. Heat to boiling over medium heat. Cover the casserole and bake for 25 minutes.

6. Remove the cover, add the zucchini, and bake covered for another 10 minutes.

7. Remove the stew from the oven and pour it into a large strainer placed over a bowl. Reserve the solids and liquid separately.

8. Return the casserole to medium heat and melt the remaining ¼ cup butter. Sprinkle in the remaining 1 table-spoon flour and cook over low heat, whisking constantly, for 5 minutes.

9. Whisk 2 cups of the reserved cooking liquid slowly into the flour mixture and heat to simmering. Simmer, stirring constantly, for 5 minutes.

10. Add the cream, dill, remaining ½ teaspoon salt, and remaining ½ teaspoon pepper and stir until blended.

11. Return the chicken and vegetables to the casserole and simmer until heated through, about 5 minutes. Remove to a deep serving bowl or decorative casserole and serve immediately.

4 portions

VALENTINE'S SALAD

The romantic color of dark pink radicchio and the wonderful ecru colors of mushrooms and sprouts gently tossed with pink rose petals makes the most romantic of salads.

1 ½ cups radicchio leaves
1 package (3.5 ounces) enoki mushrooms
¾ cup radish or alfalfa sprouts
2 pink roses, fully bloomed
Valentine Dressing (recipe follows)

1. Divide the radicchio leaves between 2 salad plates.

BE MINE MENU

Salmon Spread

Black bread

Chicken Blanquette

Lemon Rice

Valentine's Salad

Poppy Coeur à la Creme and fruit

Pink Champagne or Cabernet Rosé

"Time is the least thing in love."
—Ernest Hemingway

Divide the enoki mushrooms and radish sprouts between the plates, placing them in the center of each salad. Add the rose petals from 1 flower to each plate and toss the petals, mushrooms, and sprouts gently together.

2. Make the dressing.

3. Gently spoon the dressing over each salad and serve.

2 portions

VALENTINE DRESSING

¾ cup walnut oil
¼ cup fresh lemon juice
3 tablespoons rose water
Salt and freshly cracked black pepper, to taste

Whisk the oil, lemon juice, and rose water together in a small bowl. Season to taste with salt and pepper.

About 1 cup

COEUR A LA CREME WITH FRESH FRUIT SALAD

Coeur à la crème—a delectable way to say I love you—but not too sweet because it is made with chèvre cheese and a bit of heavy cream. Serve with a raspberry–poppy-seed dressing.

8 ounces farmer's cheese
12 ounces cream cheese, preferably without vegetable gum
3 tablespoons crumbled Montrachet or other soft mild chèvre cheese
3 tablespoons confectioners' sugar
2 tablespoons poppy seeds
1 cup heavy or whipping cream
Assorted seasonal fruits (melon balls, whole strawberries, sliced
   bananas, orange segments, grapes, berries, sliced kiwis)
Poppy Seed–Framboise Dressing (recipe follows)

1. At least one day before serving, process the cheeses in a food processor fitted with a steel blade until smooth. Add the confectioners' sugar and poppy seeds and process until smooth. Add the cream and process until thoroughly incorporated.

2. Line a china coeur à la crème mold with a double thickness of slightly dampened cheesecloth. Fill the mold with the cheese mixture and place the mold on a plate or in a shallow bowl to catch the drippings. Refrigerate the mold until the cheese is firmly set, 24 to 48 hours.

3. Make the dressing.

4. Unmold the coeur à la creme on a large serving platter and arrange the fresh fruits around it. Pass the dressing.

One 8-inch heart

THE CHARM OF ROSE

We think rosé wines have been given an unfair lot in life. They have always been considered compromise wines. Wine experts claim that they do nothing to enhance the flavors in a meal or to elevate the spirit in any way. Furthermore, rosés suffer from an identity crisis since there is no such thing as a rosé grape. The color in the wine is obtained either by coloring a white wine with cochineal, mixing red and white wines, or by using ripe red grapes and leaving the skins in the freshly pressed juice just long enough to tint the wine. The latter method produces the best rosés.

While we like to drink rosé as a summertime aperitif or picnic wine, we also feel the color makes it perfect for Valentine's Day. Love can be so complex that the lightness of an uncomplicated wine can be a perfect antidote . . . or even an aphrodisiac!

''Nature never did betray
The heart that loved her.''
—William Wordsworth

POPPY SEED–FRAMBOISE DRESSING

3 tablespoons raspberry vinegar
2 tablespoons honey mustard
2 tablespoons dry white wine
2 tablespoons fresh lemon juice
3 tablespoons poppy seeds
1 tablespoon minced shallots
⅔ cup sugar
½ cup olive oil
½ cup vegetable oil
Salt and freshly ground black pepper, to taste
3 tablespoons framboise liqueur
3 tablespoons Crème Fraîche (page 399)

Whisk the vinegar, mustard, and wine together in a small mixing bowl. Add the lemon juice, poppy seeds, and shallots, and stir to mix. Stir in the sugar. Gradually whisk in the oils and season to taste with salt and pepper. Finally add the liqueur and crème fraîche and stir until smooth. Refrigerate covered until ready to serve.

2 cups

RASPBERRY SOUFFLE

What more luxurious dish than our raspberry soufflé? You can enjoy it all year round because it's made with frozen raspberries.

1 package (10 ounces) frozen raspberries (packed in light syrup), thawed
4 egg whites, room temperature
½ cup sugar
1 cup heavy or whipping cream, cold
2 tablespoons framboise liqueur or Grand Marnier

1. Preheat oven to 375°F. Butter 6 individual soufflé dishes and lightly coat with sugar.
2. Process the raspberries with syrup in a food processor fitted with a steel blade or a blender until smooth.
3. Beat the egg whites in a mixer bowl to soft peaks. Beat in the sugar, 1 tablespoon at a time, and continue beating until the peaks are stiff and glossy. Gently fold into the raspberry purée.
4. Pour the batter into the prepared dishes. Bake until puffed and light golden, 12 to 15 minutes.
5. While the soufflés are baking, whip the cream with the liqueur to soft peaks. Serve the soufflés hot from the oven, topped with whipped cream.

6 portions

"Flirtation, attention without intention."
—Max O'Rell

BASICS

SILVER PALATE COOKS

Most of us these days don't have the luxury of time to devote an entire day to the preparations necessary for a small dinner party let alone a large bash. And the joys of entertaining certainly dwindle if we're nervously scrambling to be ready on time. We would like to share some guidelines.

REREAD THE RECIPE: Assemble all ingredients, pots, pans, dishes, and equipment needed. Read through the recipe carefully and pay attention to the cooking times. Then allow extra time for preparing the ingredients and for cleanup.

CONSOLIDATE YOUR EFFORTS: If you're preparing a number of dishes, combine similar steps to save time. Wash all the vegetables and greens at one time; if several recipes require chopped onions, prepare them together, then measure out what you need for each dish. This is standard procedure in restaurants, and you'll be amazed at how much time you will save.

PREPARE INGREDIENTS IN ADVANCE: Most of the recipes in this book can be prepared in advance, in whole or in part. Sauces and vegetable purées can be made the morning of the party and reheated slowly in the top of a double boiler. Mousses, pâtés, dips, and fruit purées can be prepared a day or two ahead and kept well wrapped in the refrigerator. Take them out about half an hour before serving to let them come to room temperature.

FREEZING: Finished dishes (soups, casseroles, stews, and meats) freeze well. In fact, most soups and stews taste better when aged a little. Potatoes, however, tend to become mushy and waterlogged, so don't freeze a dish containing them.

Pastry dough freezes beautifully. Remember to double-wrap the dough to prevent moisture from seeping through. Finished cakes, breads, phyllo pastries, cookies, and muffins can be frozen, but we advise that you frost or glaze them after they've thawed. Sprinkle a little water on all types of breads before reheating.

Precooked vegetables can be frozen, but, because their crispness is lost when they are thawed and reheated, we recommend freezing leftovers only for future soups, stews, or any dish where crunchiness isn't essential.

Harder cheeses, such as Parmesan, Romano, and aged chèvres, can be grated and frozen in airtight containers; and certain soft cooking cheeses, such as mozzarella and ricotta, can be frozen because their altered state won't be detected in a cooked dish.

Freezing will diminish the flavor of certain spices, so don't forget to taste and adjust the seasonings before serving.

TIMESAVERS: Peel several heads of garlic, place the cloves in an airtight container, pour in oil to cover, and store in the refrigerator for 2 to 4 months. Use as needed.

• Make bread crumbs in batches using all stale breads and crackers. Freeze the unused portion in an airtight container.

• Roast extra peppers, remove the charred skin, and slice. Put them in a container with minced garlic, lemon juice, and olive oil, and store in the refrigerator. Great for antipasti, atop sandwiches, puréed for a dip for crudités, or with grilled meats and fish.

• Freeze extra or unused stock in ice-cube trays for delicious homemade bouillon cubes to flavor soups, stews, and pilafs.

• While you have the juicer out, squeeze extra lemons and store the juice in the refrigerator or freezer.

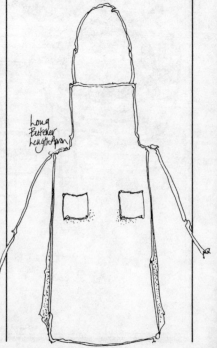

Long Butcher Length Apron

PARTY PLANNING

One of the first lessons we learned when we started catering was the need for organization and careful planning. Our kitchen at The Silver Palate isn't much bigger than a large home kitchen, so we have to plan our food deliveries and storage very carefully, as space is at a premium. We've never let our small confines limit us, however, although some have questioned our sanity when we accept catering jobs for a thousand!

Nothing is impossible once you learn how to be flexible and to adapt to certain variables such as kitchen capacity, the number of guests, budget, and time. We've outlined here some of the steps we follow in planning and catering a party. It can serve as a checklist for your future affairs.

CREATE A BUDGET: This is vital for us and also good discipline for home entertaining. Be sure to list everything, allocating money for food and liquor, invitations, candles, flowers, music, staffing, ice, cleaning supplies, and whatever else you may need.

PLAN THE MENU: Whenever we plan a menu, we always take three things into consideration—the theme of the party, the guest list, and the capacity of the kitchen where the party is being held.

Choose a menu with a balance of hot and cold foods so that your range top and oven aren't overloaded with last-minute cooking; your refrigerator and freezer aren't bursting; and your counter tops aren't crammed, leaving little workspace. Think of the food as traffic—as traffic manager, you surely don't want rush-hour jams and delays during the course of your party!

MAKE A SHOPPING LIST: List all the ingredients you will need. Include items you normally keep in the pantry, and check to make sure you have enough of each. If you just assume an ingredient is there, you may find yourself doing some last-minute, could-have-been-avoided scurrying to the market. As each item is located or purchased, check it off clearly.

PLAN A COOKING TIMETABLE: Post a list of all the items on your menu. Prepare as many of them as possible in advance, and check them off as they are completed. Include estimated preparation and cooking times.

PLAN A HOUSECLEANING TIMETABLE: As with the cooking timetable, make a list of all the jobs that need to be done, with estimated time requirements. Delegate as many of the responsibilities as possible, and don't forget to include polishing the silver, setting the table, setting up the bar, arranging the flowers, and selecting the serving pieces.

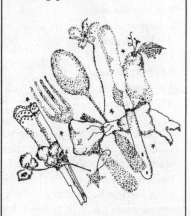

WRITE OUT INSTRUCTIONS: If you've hired a staff—of one or ten—to assist at your party, prepare a checklist for them that includes the menu, cocktail and dinner hours, and heating, serving, and cleaning-up instructions. Review the list with them before the party to avoid any misunderstanding. It's also wise to have extra plates, silverware, napkins, and glassware available any time you're entertaining; advise your staff where all of these are located.

CLEANING UP: Your party was a thoroughly organized, grand success, and you were able to enjoy it yourself because your planning was so well thought out. Don't ruin it by neglecting to plan the clean-up details. Make sure you have plenty of detergent, sponges, scouring pads, paper towels, and large garbage bags on hand.

BERTA'S CHICKEN STOCK

This delicious chicken soup is a recipe of Sheila's mother, who has dosed the family with it for years! Enjoy it as a cozy beginning, or strain it and use as chicken stock. For richer stock, begin with at least 1 cup more stock than is required for your recipe and reduce it to the amount you will need.

1 chicken (4 to 5 pounds), preferably a stewing hen
3 quarts water
1 tablespoon salt
1 large or 2 medium-size yellow onions
4 ribs celery with leafy tops
1 bunch fresh dill
4 carrots, peeled
3 parsnips, peeled
Salt and freshly ground black pepper, to taste

1. Rinse the chicken and trim off excess fat. Cut the chicken into quarters and place in a large stock pot. Add the water and 1 tablespoon salt. Cover the pot and heat to boiling. Uncover and skim off the scum from the top.

2. Add the onions, celery, and half the dill. Cover and simmer over low heat for 1 hour.

3. Cut the carrots and parsnips in half and add to the stock. Simmer until the chicken is fork tender, about 1 hour.

4. Remove the chicken from the pot and reserve for another use. Remove the carrots and parsnips and set aside.

5. Strain the stock through a fine-mesh sieve into a clean saucepan. Discard the solids. Let the stock cool. If you wish, this may be used whenever chicken stock is called for in a recipe.

6. Cut the reserved carrots and parsnips into julienne strips.

7. Ten minutes before serving, heat the stock. Season to taste with salt and pepper. Stir the julienned carrots and parsnips into the soup, or divide the julienne among individual soup bowls and ladle the broth into the bowls. Garnish with the remaining dill.

8 portions

ROOT CELLARS

In the good old days, many households relied upon cool, dark root cellars much as we rely upon our refrigerators and freezers today. Women would convert summer's harvest into preserves, relishes, chutneys, and bottled fruits and vegetables to last through the lean winter. Bins of onions, turnips, carrots, potatoes, garlic, and other root vegetables were laid down to be stored for use throughout the winter months.

If you're fortunate enough to have a root cellar or a cool basement, do store your root vegetables there. If not, keep them in a cool, dark cabinet in your kitchen or pantry and try to use them within two weeks. If kept too long, they begin to sprout and soften and lose their crisp vitality.

BEEF STOCK

3 pounds beef chuck, cut into 3 pieces
8 beef bones, preferably with marrow
7 quarts water
3 tablespoons salt
10 black peppercorns
1 bay leaf
1 large yellow onion, studded with 8 cloves
2 turnips, peeled and sliced
1 piece (1 inch) fresh ginger root, peeled
1 carrot, peeled and coarsely chopped
1 leek, well rinsed, dried, and coarsely chopped
3 ribs celery, coarsely chopped

1. Place the beef, bones, water, salt, pepper, and bay leaf in a large stock pot and heat to boiling. Skim off the scum from the top.

2. Add the remaining ingredients and simmer uncovered for 4 hours, skimming the top frequently.

3. Cool the stock slightly, strain, and reserve the beef for another use. Store the stock covered in the refrigerator up to 1 week or the freezer up to 2 months.

4 quarts

FRESH TOMATO SAUCE

2 tablespoons unsalted butter
2 tablespoons best-quality olive oil
2 cloves garlic, finely minced
½ cup thinly sliced yellow onion
4 ripe large tomatoes, seeded and sliced (4 cups)
2 teaspoons dried oregano
¾ teaspoon ground nutmeg
Salt and freshly ground black pepper, to taste
3 tablespoons freshly grated Parmesan cheese
3 tablespoons chopped fresh Italian parsley

CRUDITE UPDATE

Although crudités seem to have become common fare at every cocktail party from here to Kalamazoo, when done well they are always a visual feast and a healthful treat for diet-conscious guests. Summer, with its abundance of lush garden vegetables, is prime time for the creative crudité maker.

However, we suggest surprising fall and winter guests with the unexpected freshness of a seasonal crudité platter. Autumn crudités might consist of thinly sliced turnips, parboiled baby beets, whole baby carrots, Sweet-Potato Chips, and blanched Brussels sprouts arranged on a bed of leafy kale. Hollow out a red cabbage and use it as a vessel for our harvest-colored Oriental Mayonnaise. We guarantee a display as spectacular as the autumn foliage.

Winter crudités might consist of a simple and stunning holiday contrast of crisp green beans, tender white enoki mushrooms, and a luscious pink bowl of raspberry vinaigrette—a refreshing relief from rich celebration fare.

1. Heat the butter and oil in a heavy skillet over low heat. Add the garlic and onion and sauté gently for 5 minutes.

2. Add the tomatoes, oregano, nutmeg, and salt and pepper to taste and cook, stirring occasionally, for 5 minutes.

3. Stir in the Parmesan and parsley. Cook, stirring constantly, for 1 minute. Serve immediately.

3 cups; enough to sauce 1 pound pasta, 4 appetizer portions

BASIC PESTO

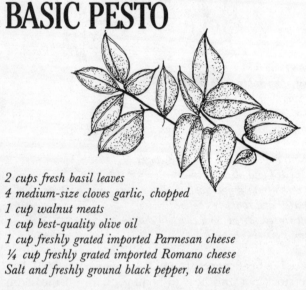

2 cups fresh basil leaves
4 medium-size cloves garlic, chopped
1 cup walnut meats
1 cup best-quality olive oil
1 cup freshly grated imported Parmesan cheese
¼ cup freshly grated imported Romano cheese
Salt and freshly ground black pepper, to taste

1. Process the basil, garlic, and walnuts in a food processor fitted with a steel blade—or in 2 batches in a blender—until finely chopped.

2. With the machine running, pour in the oil in a thin, steady stream.

3. Add the cheeses, a big pinch of salt, and a liberal grinding of pepper. Process briefly to combine. Remove to a bowl and cover until ready to use.

2 cups, enough to sauce 2 pounds of pasta

SAUCE HOLLANDAISE

3 egg yolks
1 to 2 tablespoons fresh lemon juice
Pinch salt
1 cup (2 sticks) unsalted butter, melted
White pepper, to taste

1. Whisk the egg yolks and 1 tablespoon lemon juice together in a heavy small saucepan or the top of a double boiler. Add the salt and whisk until thick and creamy.

2. Place the pan over very low heat or over simmering water in the double boiler and whisk until the egg mixture just begins to thicken (the wires of the whisk will begin to leave "tracks" in which you can see the bottom of the pan).

THE COOK'S HELPER

The computer is rapidly developing into a kitchen tool. It can file and retrieve recipes, analyze the nutritional and caloric content of menus to promote better health, and make swift calculations when we wish to alter recipes. In our kitchen a computer helps us estimate the cost of dishes and menus. It can also inventory the contents of our pantry and generate shopping lists for each week and month.

With the advancement of computer technology and the reduction in the cost of hardware and software, more and more households will turn to the computer for invaluable assistance in food preparation and kitchen management. What it can't do yet is come up with ideas.... That's still up to us.

3. Remove the pan from the heat and whisk in the butter in dribbles, leaving the milky sediment in the bottom of the pan.

4. Whisk in pepper and lemon juice to taste. The sauce will keep covered in a warm (not hot) place for at least 30 minutes.

About 1 ½ cups

CREME FRAICHE I

Packaged crème fraîche is becoming more widely available, but it is also easy to make. Here are two foolproof ways. It needs a couple of days to develop.

1 cup heavy or whipping cream (not ultra-pasteurized)
1 cup dairy sour cream

Whisk the 2 creams together in a small bowl until thoroughly blended. Pour into a jar, cover, and let stand in a warm place until thickened, about 12 hours. Stir well and refrigerate covered for 36 hours before using. Crème fraîche will keep 7 to 10 days.

2 cups

CREME FRAICHE II

2 cups heavy or whipping cream (not ultra-pasteurized)
2 teaspoons buttermilk

Pour the cream and buttermilk into a large glass jar. Cover and shake vigorously for 1 minute. Let stand in a warm place until thickened, at least 12 hours. Stir well and refrigerate at least 24 hours before using. Crème fraîche will keep 7 to 10 days.

2 cups

TRUST YOUR OWN GOOD TASTE IN THE KITCHEN

Learn to cook the no-shortcut way. Your goal should be to have cooking become a matter of instinct. It is great to experience cooking the way an infant learns about the world—through taste, feel, smell, sight. And where else to do it but in your own kitchen? The key is to taste new raw ingredients, spices, herbs, and flavors before you add them, and then afterward to see their effect. Taste, but don't eat when you cook. Nothing in excess—everything in moderation.

PATE BRISEE

1 ½ cups sifted unbleached all-purpose flour
½ teaspoon salt
½ cup (1 stick) unsalted butter, cold, cut into small pieces
¼ cup ice water

1. Mix the flour and salt in a large mixing bowl. Cut in the butter, using a pastry blender or 2 knives, until the mixture resembles coarse meal.

2. Add the ice water and blend into the flour mixture.

3. Turn the dough out onto a lightly floured surface and press large chunks of the dough away from you with the heel of your hand. Gather the dough into a ball and repeat.

4. Shape the dough into a thick circle, wrap in plastic wrap, and refrigerate at least 30 minutes before using.

IN A FOOD PROCESSOR

1. Process the flour and salt in a food processor fitted with a steel blade just to sift and mix.

2. Add the butter and process with repeated pulses until the mixture resembles coarse meal.

3. With the machine running, add the ice water through the feed tube and process until the dough leaves the side of the bowl.

4. Turn the dough out onto a lightly floured surface, shape into a thick circle, and wrap in plastic wrap. Refrigerate at least 30 minutes before using.

9-or 10-inch pie shell or 5 or 6 small tart shells

GARLIC CROUTONS

Slow cooking and lots of tossing is the secret to these crispy croutons.

3 tablespoons unsalted butter
3 tablespoons mild olive oil
3 cups stale bread cubes (about ½ inch)
2 large cloves garlic, minced
1 teaspoon mixed salad herbs (parsley, chives, tarragon, and chervil)
3 tablespoons grated Parmesan cheese

1. Heat the butter and oil in a large nonstick skillet over medium-high heat. Add the bread cubes and cook, tossing constantly with a wooden spoon, for 3 to 4 minutes. Reduce heat to medium-low.

2. Add the garlic and salad herbs. Continue to cook the croutons, tossing frequently, until golden brown, 20 to 25 minutes. Remove to a bowl and toss with the Parmesan. Store in an airtight container until ready to use.

3 cups

Variation: To make Pumpernickel Croutons, use stale pumpernickel bread.

"There is no love sincerer than the love of food."
—George Bernard Shaw

METRIC CONVERSION CHARTS

TABLESPOONS AND OUNCES
(U.S. Customary System)

GRAMS
(Metric System)

1 pinch = less than ⅛ teaspoon (dry) .... 0.5 gram

1 dash = 3 drops to ¼ teaspoon (liquid) .... 1.25 grams

1 teaspoon (liquid) .... 5.0 grams

3 teaspoons = 1 tablespoon = ½ ounce .... 14.3 grams

2 tablespoons = 1 ounce .... 28.35 grams

4 tablespoons = 2 ounces = ¼ cup .... 56.7 grams

8 tablespoons = 4 ounces = ½ cup (1 stick of butter) .... 113.4 grams

8 tablespoons (flour) = about 2 ounces .... 72.0 grams

16 tablespoons = 8 ounces = 1 cup = ½ pound .... 226.8 grams

32 tablespoons = 16 ounces = 2 cups = 1 pound .... 453.6 grams or 0.4536 kilogram

64 tablespoons = 32 ounces = 1 quart = 2 pounds .... 907.0 grams or 0.907 kilogram

1 quart = (roughly 1 liter)

TEMPERATURES: °FAHRENHEIT (F.) TO °CELSIUS (C.)

−10°F. = −23.3°C. (freezer storage)

0°F. = −17.7°C.

32°F. = 0°C. (water freezes)

50°F. = 10°C.

68°F. = 20°C. (room temperature)

100°F. = 37.7°C.

150°F. = 65.5°C.

205°F. = 96.1°C. (water simmers)

212°F. = 100°C. (water boils)

300°F. = 148.8°C.

325°F. = 162.8°C.

350°F. = 177°C. (baking)

375°F. = 190.5°C.

400°F. = 204.4°C. (hot oven)

425°F. = 218.3°C.

450°F. = 232°C. (very hot oven)

475°F. = 246.1°C.

500°F. = 260°C. (broiling)

CONVERSION FACTORS

ounces to grams: multiply ounce figure by 28.3 to get number of grams

grams to ounces: multiply gram figure by .0353 to get number of ounces

pounds to grams: multiply pound figure by 453.59 to get number of grams

pounds to kilograms: multiply pound figure by 0.45 to get number of kilograms

ounces to milliliters: multiply ounce figure by 30 to get number of milliliters

cups to liters: multiply cup figure by 0.24 to get number of liters

Fahrenheit to Celsius: subtract 32 from the Fahrenheit figure, multiply by 5, then divide by 9 to get Celsius figure

Celsius to Fahrenheit: multiply Celsius figure by 9, divide by 5, then add 32 to get Fahrenheit figure

inches to centimeters: multiply inch figure by 2.54 to get number of centimeters

centimeters to inches: multiply centimeter figure by .39 to get number of inches

INDEX